DIVIDED
SOVEREIGNTIES

DIVIDED SOVEREIGNTIES

★ ★ ★ ★

Race, Nationhood, and Citizenship in Nineteenth-Century America

ROCHELLE RAINERI ZUCK

The University of Georgia Press
ATHENS

Paperback edition, 2019
© 2016 by the University of Georgia Press
Athens, Georgia 30602
www.ugapress.org
All rights reserved
Designed by Kaelin Chappell Broaddus
Set in 10/13 Adobe Caslon Pro by Kaelin Chappell Broaddus

Most University of Georgia Press titles are
available from popular e-book vendors.

Printed digitally

The Library of Congress has cataloged the hardcover
edition of this book as follows:

Names: Zuck, Rochelle Raineri.
Title: Divided sovereignties : race, nationhood, and citizenship in
nineteenth-century America / Rochelle Raineri Zuck.
Description: Athens : The University of Georgia Press, 2016. |
Includes bibliographical references and index.
Identifiers: LCCN 2015043950 | ISBN 9780820345420 (hardcover :
alkaline paper) | ISBN 9780820349640 (ebook)
Subjects: LCSH: Minorities—United States—History—19th century. |
Sovereignty—Social aspects—United States—History—19th century. |
Nationalism—United States—History—19th century. |
Citizenship—United States—History—19th century. |
Political culture—United States—History—19th century. |
Sovereignty in literature. | American literature—Minority authors—
History and criticism. | United States—Race relations—
History—19th century. | United States—Ethnic relations—
History—19th century. | United States—
Politics and government—19th century.
Classification: LCC E184.A1 Z84 2016 | DDC 305.80097309/034—dc23

LC record available at http://lccn.loc.gov/2015043950

Paperback ISBN 978-0-8203-5680-8

For Joey, Sam, Abram, and Aurelia

CONTENTS

★ ★ ★ ★

ACKNOWLEDGMENTS ix

INTRODUCTION. Imperium in Imperio and the Division of Sovereignty in American Literature and Public Argument 1

ONE. "In the Heart of So Powerful a Nation"
Cherokee Sovereignty, Political Allegiance, and National Spaces 32

TWO. "And Ethiopia Shall Stretch Forth Her Hands"
African Colonization, Divided Sovereignty, and Rhetorics of an African American Imperium 69

THREE. "Space for Action"
Divided Sovereignty, Political Allegiance, and African American Nationhood in the 1850s 103

FOUR. "An Irish Republic (on Paper)"
The Fenian Brotherhood, Virtual Nationhood, and Contested Sovereignties 139

FIVE. "China in the United States"
Extraterritorial Sovereignty, the Six Companies, and Rhetorics of a Chinese Imperium 175

CONCLUSION. Becoming Minority Nations in Nineteenth-Century America 215

NOTES 221

BIBLIOGRAPHY 257

INDEX 283

ACKNOWLEDGMENTS

I OWE A TREMENDOUS DEBT of gratitude to the many people who provided help, encouragement, and friendship during this project.

First and foremost, I would like to thank Carla Mulford, without whose mentorship this project would have never come to fruition and whose example continues to inspire. I am truly grateful for her wisdom and generosity. Thank you also to Hester Blum, Robert Burkholder, and Stephen Browne for providing tremendous guidance and feedback at formative stages and to Cheryl Glenn, Lovalerie King, Christopher Castiglia, Sean Goudie, Deborah Clarke, and Kathryn Hume for their help and advice.

I would also like to acknowledge my wonderful colleagues (current and former) at the University of Minnesota, Duluth. Thanks to the members of the English Department, most especially Paul Cannan, Evan Brier, Krista Twu, Carol Bock, Marty Bock, Carolyn Sigler, and Hilary Kowino. I would also like to thank Jill Doerfler, Heidi Kiiwetinepinesiik Stark, Kristen Hylenski, and Joseph Bauerkemper. I am grateful to Linda Krug, Olaf Kuhlke, Susan Maher, and the generous support of the College of Liberal Arts and the University of Minnesota, which was of tremendous help as I reshaped and revised this project. Special thanks to Michele Larson and Tom Ambrosi for all of their assistance over the years. I am grateful to be a part of such a collegial community of faculty, students, and staff.

In 2005, I was fortunate to attend the Committee on Institutional Cooperation seminar at the Newberry Library in Chicago. Led by Phillip Round, this seminar, "Authors and Indians: Performance, Manuscript, and Print in Nineteenth-Century Native America," was a transformative experience for me in terms of both content and approach. I have benefited from the wisdom of all involved, especially Phillip Round, Katy Chiles, and Jill Doerfler.

My sincerest thanks to the libraries and archives where I have worked over the course of this project, including the Library Company of Philadelphia, the Newberry Library, the Library of Congress, the Philadelphia Archdiocesan

Historical Research Center (PAHRC), and the American Catholic History Research Center and University Archives. I am grateful for the assistance of the librarians and staff at these institutions, especially James N. Green and Connie King at the Library Company of Philadelphia, Shawn Weldon at the PAHRC, and William J. Shepherd at the American Catholic History Research Center.

I thank the mentors and friends far and near who have supported me throughout this journey and contributed to the project directly and indirectly. I am particularly grateful to Christopher MacGowan at the College of William and Mary for getting me started on the right foot and for his continued encouragement. My thanks to Lindsey Simon-Jones for her intelligence, humor, and good sense. I am also grateful to Jill Treftz, Rosalyn Collings Eves, Stacey Sheriff, and Pia Deas for reading early drafts of this book and offering invaluable feedback. I also appreciate the friendship and support of Heather Murray, Rob Bleil, Steve Thomas, Kristin Shimmin, and Greg Pierrot.

My sincerest thanks to everyone at the University of Georgia Press who has made this such an enjoyable experience, most especially Walter Biggins, Nancy Grayson, Jon Davies, Bethany Snead, and the rest of the editorial and production staff. Merryl Sloane provided excellent copyediting, and Ina Gravitz did a wonderful job on the index. I am most appreciative of their invaluable contributions. My thanks also to the anonymous readers of the manuscript for their thoughtful feedback, which has enhanced this book in many ways.

Last but certainly not least, words cannot express fully the depth of my gratitude to my wonderful family. My parents, Josephine and Samuel, have given me unfailing love and support from the beginning. Their love of learning and generosity of spirit is a model that I aspire to follow. Abram Anders, my life partner and best reader, makes this and all projects worth doing. I look forward to the next chapter.

INTRODUCTION

Imperium in Imperio and the Division of Sovereignty in American Literature and Public Argument

WITH ITS LATINATE TITLE and sustained account of the formation of an African American nation in Texas dubbed "the Imperium," Rev. Sutton E. Griggs's 1899 self-published novel, *Imperium in Imperio: A Study of the Negro Race Problem*, tells an engaging and complicated story that explores the points of intersection between race, nationhood, sovereignty, and collective allegiance in the post–Civil War era. The novel opens in the year 1867 and introduces readers to two young African American men who live in Winchester, Virginia: Belton Piedmont and Bernard Belgrave. In its depiction of their early years and educational experiences in a one-room school and later in universities, the novel draws distinctions between the two boys based on race and class status. Belton, the fourth of five children, is raised in impoverished conditions by his mother, Hannah, after his father abandons the family. Bernard, described as having lighter skin than Belton, is the son of a biracial woman and a white senator and grows up in more privileged circumstances. Bernard attends Harvard University, while Belton graduates from the fictional Stowe University, an all-black institution in Nashville, Tennessee. At Stowe he is introduced to black secret societies that will shape his involvement in the Imperium, an African American nation with its capital in Waco, Texas.

Belton offers the following description of the Imperium to Bernard shortly before informing Bernard that he (Bernard) has been elected president: "Another government, complete in every detail, exercising the sovereign right of life and death over its subjects, has been organized and maintained within the United States for many years. This government has a population of seven million two hundred and fifty thousand."¹ Belton asserts that because the U.S. federal government has not protected the civil rights of African Americans, they have formed their own government, which performs "all the functions of a nation" (194). In addition to a standing army, the Imperium features an "organized judiciary," a "Congress," "[b]ranch legislatures . . . in each state," and a "constitution . . . modeled after that of the United States" (195). The Imperium has purchased land in the South, and its treasury now holds $500 million, in addition to the $350 million possessed by the citizenry (196). What Griggs's novel depicts is a radical division of sovereignty, a nation formed within the territorial limits of the U.S. nation whose purpose is to protect the rights of African Americans from a "defect in the [U.S.] Constitution" that has prevented the U.S. government from protecting black Americans from abuses at the hands of the states (194).

Through its depiction of the Imperium and its territorial and political relationship to the United States, Griggs's novel imagines African Americans creating a shadow government within the putative borders of the United States in order to address a specific political problem related to the division of sovereignty between state and federal authorities. The Imperium's constitution resembles the U.S. Constitution, but its strategic revisions make the original document speak differently on questions of black citizenship. I read Griggs's novel as representative of a larger effort on the part of various nineteenth-century peoples to reconfigure their collective relationship to the United States. By positioning themselves as a *nation*, members of the fictional Imperium did not work to articulate a coherent sense of racial identity but instead strove to engage the United States on a nation-to-nation basis rather than as a racial minority. Griggs's decision to name this nation "the Imperium" connects his work with a much larger literary and political tradition. Moreover, the novel's title page features the 1866 state seal of Ohio with its motto of "Imperium in Imperio," a visual example of how this rhetoric was adopted and adapted during the nineteenth century to speak to issues of race, nationhood, and citizenship.

Intellectual historian Forrest McDonald translates imperium in imperio as "supreme power within supreme power, sovereignty within sovereignty, the division of sovereignty within a single jurisdiction" and emphasizes its importance to the political culture of the Revolutionary period and through Reconstruction.² During the eighteenth and nineteenth centuries, this term was used to refer to politically divided sovereignty—either in the form of two sovereign powers vying for control of the same territory or in the kind of divisions involved in the federal system created by America's founders. This phrase was also interpreted in geographic terms as in the case of distinct sovereign bodies/nations with contiguous but not necessarily overlapping jurisdictions (such as Monaco and France). The translation of "nation within a nation" in which *na-*

tion referred to a cultural construction rather than a political one also was used to denote a form of racial and cultural separatism. As I discuss in more detail below, this racial interpretation of imperium in imperio reanimated old anxieties about internal division and strife in nineteenth-century American public discourse; conceptual arguments about political solecism and geographic overlap circulated alongside anxieties about embodied racialized threat. Yet, the concept of imperium in imperio also offered writers and speakers such as Griggs an entrée into broader political debates. The centrality of this phrase to Griggs's novel suggests that in the 1890s imperium in imperio was more than just a political figure of speech or a marker of classical learning; it had some broader literary and cultural currency on which Griggs hoped to capitalize. Throughout the nineteenth century, writers and speakers occupying different political positions used the phrases *imperium in imperio*, *nation within a nation*, and *divided sovereignty* fluidly and, at times, interchangeably to fit the shifting exigencies of America at that time.[3] With its vision of the strategic possibilities of the rhetorics of imperium in imperio, Griggs's novel provides a point of entry into a much larger story in nineteenth-century American literature and public argument, a story that constitutes my focus here.

The title of this book, *Divided Sovereignties*, reflects my broad argument that by crafting a federal system, America's founders created a form of government that was uniquely characterized by the division of sovereignty between state and federal powers and, as ongoing fears of imperium in imperio suggest, was also uniquely vulnerable to unexpected divisions. The U.S. Constitution both enshrined imperium in imperio and sought to manage its applications; yet, in ways likely unanticipated by its creators, it provided a model for various groups that in the nineteenth century sought to renegotiate the terms of their relationship with the United States from racialized population to nation. I contend that the rhetorics of imperium in imperio were central to engagements between the United States and Cherokees, African Americans, and particular immigrant groups, specifically the Irish and Chinese, engagements that informed the development of American ideas of sovereignty, nationhood, and collective allegiance. As I show in this book, during the nineteenth century, fractures in the U.S. nation were projected onto "other" populations, which were depicted as nations emerging from within the United States and threatening its sovereignty. This rhetoric functioned as a means of representing the perceived unassimilability of various populations into the U.S. body politic and often drew distinctions between the imperium and imperio, framing them as fundamentally different kinds of nations. But what began as an attempt to create a more coherent American "national narrative" (to borrow Jonathan Arac's term) actually led to a proliferation of perspectives on nationhood itself, which challenged America's territorial and political boundaries.[4]

Cherokees, African Americans, Irish Americans, and Chinese immigrants took up this rhetoric to assert their national status so as to engage the United States on political rather than racial terms and to challenge notions of territorial sovereignty and the kind of legal and administrative techniques utilized before, during, and after the Civil War.[5] They employed a number of genres, including written constitutions, to articulate alternative visions of individual and collective political allegiance and to shift the meanings of America's own founding documents. Ultimately, I suggest that while contemporary scholarship has linked the phrase imperium in imperio (or nation within a nation) with racial separatism along black-white lines, such a reading does not capture fully the political and territorial valences of this phrase nor the multiple groups that turned to this rhetoric in their attempts to gain political advantage during the nineteenth century.

In *Divided Sovereignties* I examine four populations—Cherokees, African Americans, Irish Americans, and Chinese immigrants—that were represented as racialized "other" nations within the putative borders of the United States and that worked to engage the United States on political terms during the nineteenth century. That these groups were framed as internal nations testifies to their perceived significance and to conceptions of them as, by virtue of their alien status and racial affiliations, unassimilable into the American body politic. Racialized depictions of these purportedly internal nations distinguished them from the Confederate States of America (CSA), perhaps the consummate example of a nation that emerged from within the United States in the nineteenth century. Coleman Hutchison has ably argued in *Apples and Ashes: Literature, Nationalism, and the Confederate States of America* that the literature of the CSA was invested in the project of representing the Confederacy as what Étienne Balibar deems a "fictive ethnicity" (one of Anglo-Saxon or Caucasian origin).[6] Yet, while the CSA attempted to frame its nation as a distinct racial population of Anglo-Saxons, this argument was not taken up in American public argument writ large. What makes groups such as African Americans, American Indian nations, Irish Americans, and Chinese distinct from the CSA is that at key moments of conflict between state and federal authorities, they were identified as "nations" within the United States (with the term *nation* carrying various meanings—including political, territorial, and racial/cultural elements—that are explored in the following chapters) whose removal, containment, or management was held up as a possible solution to internal problems. Focusing on what David Kazanjian calls "flashpoints," moments of "emergence or transformation," in *Divided Sovereignties* I am concerned with a specific set of strategic engagements between the United States and the populations mentioned above.[7] I chart the ways in which such engagements shaped conceptions of nationhood, sovereignty, and political affiliations (including constructions of state and national citizenship) in ways that we have yet to fully understand.

This book is positioned at the intersection of ongoing, dynamic scholarship about nationalism and transnationalism, and I draw from both approaches by exploring how transnationalism—understood as engagement with nations imagined both outside and inside of U.S. borders—informed American literature, politics, and culture throughout the nineteenth century. Proof of the centrality of national approaches to the study of literature and culture can be found not only on library shelves but also through a survey of secondary and postsecondary syllabi and curricula.[8] Despite the "transnational turn," which intensified calls to "move beyond the nation as the primary unit of analysis" and instead focus on contact zones, networks, and flows, studies of nations and nationalism have remained important, particularly in African American studies, American Indian studies, and ethnic studies.[9] Such work has recovered various and, at times, competing visions of nationhood, sovereignty, and political affiliation that shaped and were shaped by those that circulated in American literature and public argument writ large. Yet, transnationalism and related avenues of inquiry have had a profound effect on the study of American literature and culture. Numerous scholars have attended to the transatlantic, transpacific, transnational, transamerican, and hemispheric circulations of individuals, goods, and ideas.[10] A significant portion of transnational scholarship has focused on exchanges with England and other nations of Western Europe and has demonstrated that even as Americans sought to distinguish themselves politically and culturally from those nations, they looked across the Atlantic for inspiration. Scholars in American Indian studies have offered a different approach to transnationalism, modeling a focus on relations between the United States and Native nations, which Vine Deloria Jr. and Clifford M. Lytle refer to as "the nations within," rather than merely focusing on transatlantic or hemispheric interactions.[11]

One work of transnational scholarship that is of particular relevance to this book is Christopher Hanlon's *America's England*, which reads the sectionalism of nineteenth-century America in the larger context of a transatlantic political vocabulary derived, in part, from England. He argues that nineteenth-century American writers and orators "engaged in forms of transatlanticism that reconfigured the political tensions threatening the federal Union, positioning these forms of national friction as if continuous with much older antagonisms endemic to the political and cultural history of England."[12] He thus reads the American Civil War and the fierce debates that preceded it as "almost continuously embedded in a series of struggles over Englishness," expressed "through terms that bound the United States to a larger and more complex North Atlantic entity."[13] In reading the Civil War as informed by transatlantic (as opposed to merely domestic) forces, Hanlon addresses a criticism that Paul Giles has levied against scholars of the nineteenth century who, he argues, have focused on the Civil War to the exclusion of international conflicts, such as the Mexican-American War.[14] Extending the work of Hanlon's *America's England*, in this book I examine the ways in which a particular rhetorical thread, imperium in imperio, understood in part through readings of English common law, was adopted and adapted to suit particular exigencies in nineteenth-century America. Yet, while sectional tensions are addressed throughout *Divided Sovereignties*, and the Civil War is discussed in particular in chapters 3 and 4, in this book I read the Civil War and the CSA alongside a variety of what were framed as *international* disputes between groups that sought to function as nations within the United States and to exercise various forms of sovereignty vis-à-vis the United States.

While it has been central to political science, law, history, and Native studies for some time, the issue of sovereignty has generated additional scholarly attention among American literature scholars in the wake of the transnational turn and the growth of law and literature as a field of study. Efforts to define and advance tribal sovereignty have raised a question that is germane to this project: is sovereignty merely a "political-legal concept," or is there a cultural element as well?[15] Paul Downes, Jennifer Greiman, Jeannine Marie DeLombard, and Jonathan Elmer have made significant contributions to our understanding of the operation of sovereignty in a democracy and how American notions of sovereignty were shaped by both transatlantic political discourses and encounters with racialized populations. They have explored the nature of sovereignty in eighteenth- and nineteenth-century America; how it was enacted in literature, public argument, and, in some cases, violence; and its effects on individuals and communities, concerns that to various extents also inform my project. Both Downes and Greiman assert that earlier modes of sovereign power, those associated with monarchy and the figure of the absolute sovereign, persisted in various forms in the popular sovereignty of the post-Revolutionary and antebellum eras. Greiman uses Alexis de Tocqueville's discussion of sovereignty in *Democracy in America* to explore issues that Tocqueville himself takes up, namely, as Greiman puts it, "the coexistence in the U.S. of unfreedom and popular sovereignty."[16] Greiman's opening example of "democracy's spectacle" is Frederick Douglass's arrest and subsequent "punitive, impromptu parade" (26) along Easton Road, during which he observed that he was subject not only to the law but to "the power of public opinion" (2–3). Greiman's concern with literary expressions of the nexus of sovereignty, violence, and the individual links her work with DeLombard's *In the Shadow of the Gallows*, which notes that from the seventeenth through the nineteenth centuries, "when enslaved people (especially men) of African descent spoke in print as individuals, their first person narratives were often occasioned by or responsive to their encounters with the law."[17] For DeLombard, these narratives reveal an important aspect of how African Americans were constituted by the law as different from women and other noncitizens: "slaves alone were credited with a legal agency that was legible only as criminality" (10). Although the law recognized African American personhood for the purposes of meting out punishment, DeLombard notes that those seeking to parlay this legal recognition into political opportunity faced a difficult task: "They had to detach black personhood from the criminality in which it had become firmly rooted and graft it onto a civil personality that might, then, flower into full-blown citizenship" (11). In an engagement with the "political imagination of Atlantic modernity," Elmer's *On Lingering and Being Last* contends that sovereignty was (and is) a racialized concept that can be explored through two literary representations of the "racialized sovereign individual"—the "royal slave" (African) and the "last chief" (American Indian).[18] America, for Elmer, is the site where the racial logics of sovereignty are uniquely visible, most explicitly in representations of enslaved Africans and of American Indians.

In *Divided Sovereignties* I start from a similar premise—that racial logics informed the development of conceptions of sovereignty—but I differ from both Elmer and Greiman in terms of my shift away from questions of identity. In exploring the operations of sovereignty in early America, both Greiman and Elmer are, at a basic level, concerned with the relationship between the few and the many. Greiman contends that in a democracy, sovereign power creates the conditions in which "disparate groups ... act metonymically as a public," and it "produces a series of homologous subjects of exception, from the slave to the prisoner to that abstract exile whom Tocqueville calls simply the 'stranger'" (26). The interplay between the "public," which is separate from but complicit with the state, and the "subjects of exception" creates the drama she dubs "democracy's spectacle." Elmer seeks to "help us see how the modern problem of sovereignty, as that unfolds in the new world, exemplifies a racialized logic of personification that conjoins individual and collective identities" (7). The figure of the "racialized sovereign individual" represents both an individual and collective identity. The four groups explored in this study are best understood not as *publics* or as individuated subjects produced by a sovereignty that depends on representational logics (i.e., those that define the contours of their collective or individual identity) but as *networks* engaged in a series of strategic engagements with the state through written texts, oratory, and collective action.

In each chapter I attend to the genre of the written constitution, which I argue was important to the efforts of various groups to relate to the United States on political rather than racial terms. By virtue of its necessarily corporate authorship, lack of an individual speaking subject, explicitly political focus, and engagement with legal discourses, the constitution in particular pressures understandings of the literary, but it was a key component of the kind of engagements I discuss here. Scholarly works by Eric Slauter and Elizabeth Beaumont offer comprehensive treatments of the history of the U.S. Constitution, moving beyond the efforts of the founding fathers to show the influence of a range of contexts, ideas, individuals, and groups on the nation's founding document.[19] Beaumont's concept of "civic founders," a group that includes "revolutionaries, antifederalists, abolitionists, and suffragists," highlights the political contributions of a "broad[er] swath of Americans" who sought to gain political advantage by working within the "constitutional system."[20] In *America's Forgotten Constitutions*, Robert L. Tsai looks at the ways in which the constitutional process and the concept of popular sovereignty encouraged various groups to write their own constitutions when they became dissatisfied with American political culture. Tsai looks at a series of constitutions, two of which are also treated here (John Brown's Provisional Constitution and that of the csa), and develops a taxonomy of the different modes of sovereignty expressed by each. *Divided Sovereignties* builds on the work of Slauter, Beaumont, and Tsai by looking at a range of civic founders who were framed as threats to American political culture and sought to use written constitutions as a means of gaining situated political advantage and reimagining their collective relationship to the United States.

Like the constitutions examined in each chapter, many of the texts discussed here are not canonical works of American literature. To chronicle the myriad functions of imperium in imperio and its role in the unfolding of conceptions of nationhood, sovereignty, and individual and collective political allegiance, I draw on a variety of fictional and nonfictional sources in addition to written constitutions: novels, poems, sermons, petitions, newspaper articles, pamphlets, speeches, legal documents, and personal correspondence. This kind of recovery work contributes to long-standing efforts to expand the literary canon and can be seen as a critical practice that resonates with Foucault's conception of genealogy. In his 1977 essay, "Nietzsche, Genealogy, and History," Foucault offers the following explanation, which provides insight into the scope and methods of this book:

> Genealogy does not pretend to go back in time to restore an unbroken continuity that operates beyond the dispersion of forgotten things; its duty is not to demonstrate that the past actively exists in the present, that it continues secretly to ani-

mate the present, having imposed a predetermined form to all its vicissitudes. Genealogy does not resemble the evolution of a species and does not map the destiny of a people. On the contrary, to follow the complex course of descent is to maintain passing events in their proper dispersion; it is to identify the accidents, the minute deviations—or conversely, the complete reversals—the errors, the false appraisals, and the faulty calculations that gave birth to those things that continue to exist and have value for us; it is to discover that truth or being do not lie at the root of what we know and what we are, but the exteriority of accidents.[21]

Informed by Foucault's and Nietzsche's methods of genealogical criticism, in *Divided Sovereignties* I concentrate on the small rhetorical moments and on the strategic practices on which literary, political, and cultural histories can turn. Following this genealogical approach, the discussions of sovereignty and imperium in imperio that follow are narratives of emergences, accidents, deviations, and unintended outcomes rather than seamless stories of literary and political development. I proceed from the belief that the texts examined in this book were influential not because they functioned to solidify definitions of sovereignty, nationhood, and citizenship, but because they challenged, fractured, and proliferated such definitions as part of situated attempts to gain political advantage. Rhetorics of imperium in imperio were central to the initial creation of U.S. federalism in varied and often unexpected ways and, I suggest, were vital to the ongoing process of making the U.S. Constitution, a process that Beaumont argues did not end in 1789.[22] The centrality of constitutions to this study is suggested by the term itself, the verb form of which is defined by the *Oxford English Dictionary* as the "action of constituting, making, establishing," while the noun form refers to the documents that are engaged in the process of making. They are active texts that are continually creating order and deconstructing and producing new orders. The various constitutions and other texts examined here contributed to national narratives. They resonated with one another thematically and not only sought to establish the national status of a particular group but also were engaged in the process of producing America's founding documents, making them speak differently on issues related to nationhood, sovereignty, citizenship, and political allegiance.

My focus on engagements rather than just representation departs from the critical assumptions and hermeneutics associated with identity politics, which has made significant contributions to the study of nineteenth-century American literature and culture but does not fully account for the significance of the rhetorical encounters outlined here. In American literary studies, identity-based criticism, with its focus on racial *representation*, is often contrasted with aesthetics and formal analysis. The 1990s and 2000s were a particularly fertile period for scholarship on the ways in which various groups throughout American history used literature to produce coherent identities as a means of resisting oppression. Such projects were intimately connected with the important work of recovery and canon expansion, and provided scholars with a much broader view of American literature and the literary writ large. They also attuned us to the distinctive features of the literary and cultural productions of women, African Americans, Native people, immigrant populations, people of different sexual orientations, and so forth.[23]

A focus on identity production, however, can limit our ability to see the ways in which particular rhetorical strategies and literary techniques were taken up by multiple populations, and can thus forestall comparative approaches. Making sense of the myriad functions of imperium in imperio requires a mode of analysis that allows for readings of this trope across the literary and cultural landscape of the nineteenth century. Such a project also requires attending to political practices rather than focusing on expressions of racial identity. My readings of rhetorics of imperium in imperio bear out Gilles Deleuze and Félix Guattari's equation of representational logics with the tools of "the State," a method of fixing populations and trying to make them conform to a particular set of expectations and practices that they refer to as "territorial representation."[24] Texts produced by Cherokees, African Americans, Irish Americans, and Chinese immigrants reveal a focus on strategic engagements for particular political purposes rather than on articulating a coherent sense of racial identity. Moreover, their varied and sometimes competing constructions of nationhood, sovereignty, and political allegiance functioned to deconstruct static representations, to restructure their position relative to the United States rather than telling a coherent story about individual or collective identity. Through a comparative approach and with a broad temporal focus, I examine how nineteenth-century literary and cultural productions reflect the impact of engagements between the United States and various populations on conceptions of nationhood, sovereignty, and political affiliation. That is to say, I question how U.S. ideas of nationhood developed in dialogue with those of other "nations" imagined as existing within America's putative borders, a dialogue in which written constitutions played a central role.

Race, Nation, and Sovereignty in Early America

Before considering the emergence of rhetorics of imperium in imperio in American literature and public argument, I want to first briefly survey eighteenth- and early nineteenth-century conceptions of *race* and *nation* (terms that resonated with and at times overlapped with one another) and understandings of sovereignty, all of which inform the analytical work in the chapters that follow. I begin by highlighting the historical connections between conceptions of race and nation before tracing important shifts that occurred in the late eighteenth century, as race began to be increasingly linked with biology and nation became increasingly understood in terms of territorial possession in American thought. It is important to note, however, that such terms refer to social constructions that are always in flux, and other visions of race and nation did not disappear with the rise of scientific racism and rhetorics of Manifest Destiny. A similar argument could be made about *sovereignty*, the third term taken up in this section, which, like ideas of nationhood, became increasingly linked with space in nineteenth-century America, yet remained the subject of intense debate.

There was a significant amount of overlap between the terms *race* and *nation* in Western thought prior to the eighteenth century, and some of that persisted through the early nineteenth century. As Nicholas Hudson observes, some of the earliest English and European dictionary definitions of *race* and *nation* associated both terms with genealogy, as Samuel Johnson's dictionary and the French *Dictionnaire de l'Académie Française* (1687) suggest. Johnson's *Dictionary of the English Language* (1755) draws on a definition by Sir William Temple and posits: "A nation properly signifies a great number of families, derived from the same blood, born in the same country, and living under the same government and civil constitution."[25] Although literary and scientific discourses were, by the eighteenth century, using "race" to invoke physical and mental differences between people, the distinctions between race and nation were not clearly drawn. Thomas Jefferson proposed a close but hierarchical relationship between the two categories: *race* referred to physiology and culture, while *nation* constituted a political construct. For Jefferson and for succeeding generations of racial theorists, this meant that a race could be composed of various nations.[26]

The fluidity of the discourses of race and nation led to classifications that differ greatly from those that historians and anthropologists would use today. For example, in 1832 natural historian Constantine Samuel Rafinesque received an award from the Society of Geography for his study of the origins of "Asiatic Negroes." In an article that appeared in the *Atlantic Journal and Friend of Knowledge*, Rafinesque wrote of the "Black Nations of America" as well as the "primitive White Nations," blending discussions of country of origin, political affiliation, and physiological features.[27] Samuel Morton, who founded the "American School" of ethnology, often associated with the beginning of "scientific racism," also drew on understandings of nations as subdivisions of a race. In *Crania Americana* and *Crania Aegyptiaca*, he published the results of his studies of the skulls of various racial groups, which drew on Johann Blumenbach's five racial categories: Caucasian, Mongolian, Malay, American, and Ethiopian. In Morton's work, each race could be further broken down into "families" or nations.[28] Yet, constructions of race and nation also began to diverge from one another in the late eighteenth century, roughly coincidental with the formation of the United States.

In seeking to define the term *race* and its significance to American literature and culture, scholars point to the fluidity of the term and generally acknowledge a shift that occurred between eighteenth-century theories of "human variety" and the kind of scientific racism that crystallized in the nineteenth century.[29] With the rise of natural history in the 1770s, environmentalism joined Christian accounts of creation and other theories as a way to understand and predict differences in people. Winthrop Jordan's landmark work *White over Black* contends that conceptions of racial difference did not begin to supplant understandings of religious difference until the late eighteenth century. It was during this period, according to Roxann Wheeler, that race began to be linked with physical features, particularly skin color. Yet, there remained a widespread belief that such features were subject to change. In her book *Transformable Race*, Katy L. Chiles analyzes accounts of racial transformations, and she details three eighteenth-century individuals who were thought to have changed their race: Henry Moss, John Bobey, and Maria Sabine. Americans were particularly concerned about the effects of the New World's climate and environment on English and European peoples and expressed a great deal of anxiety about the possibility of creole degeneracy, which testified to their understanding of race as a malleable rather than a fixed construct. Chiles sums up changes in racial theory between the eighteenth and nineteenth centuries thusly: conceptions of the term *race* itself transformed from one denoting external, changeable physical characteristics to one communicating internal, fixed biological traits in the nineteenth century.[30] Yet, even with the rise of so-called scientific racism in the 1830s and 1840s, race remained a fluid and unstable construct, and the presence of diverse peoples on the American continent pressured existing definitions of race and the modes of distinguishing between peoples.

The eighteenth and early nineteenth centuries also witnessed shifting and sometimes competing constructions of nationhood, constructions that sometimes challenged current understandings of the distinction between states (legal, political, territorial) and nations (cultural, historical, ideological).[31] In defining the term *nation*, literary scholars often turn to the work of Benedict

Anderson, who conceives of the nation as an "imagined political community," produced in part through the development of print media. Writing specifically of the American nation, David Waldstreicher emphasizes the literary aspects of a nation, which is "an encompassing narrative or set of competing narratives."[32] Anthony D. Smith, one of the major figures in the study of nation formation, differentiates between two types of nations and provides a vocabulary that will be invoked in later chapters: "civic-territorial" and "ethnic" nations. Civic-territorial nations, as defined by Smith, resonate with the Western vision of the territorial nation-state that exercises exclusive jurisdiction over a particular territory. This type of nation is characterized by the following features: "[h]istoric territory, legal-political community, legal-political equality of members, and common civic culture and ideology."[33] Smith's description of civic-territorial nations echoes Anderson's vision of the nation as an "imagined political community" but dwells more on the connection between this polity and a particular space that may or may not be currently occupied. Civic-territorial nations, for Smith, differ from ethnic nations, which "stress descent . . . rather than territory" and imagine the nation as a kind of "fictive 'super-family.'"[34] These models of nationhood circulated alongside one another in early American literature and culture.

Popular imagery of the nation in late eighteenth- and early nineteenth-century America tended to emphasize the human element. Newspapers, broadsides, and novels discussed the people as the essence of the nation. Early novels such as William Hill Brown's *The Power of Sympathy* (1789) and Hannah Webster Foster's *The Coquette* (1797) evidence great concern for women's sexual behavior and reading habits, linking these with the overall health of the body politic. During public festivals and national celebrations, Americans were surrounded by music, visual art, and rhetorical performances, but most of all by other *people*; the rhetorical spaces of national holiday were constructed in such as way as to offer visual reinforcement that as a group, the American people comprised the nation.[35] Yet, territorial visions of the nation also captured the public imagination and became increasingly prominent in the nineteenth century as America extended its territorial reach across the continent. From the paintings of Emanuel Leutze to the lush landscape descriptions and contested frontier spaces of James Fenimore Cooper, Americans were also encouraged to conceive of their nation as a discrete, yet expanding portion of the continent. As I suggest below, the political and territorial claims of Cherokees, African Americans, Irish Americans, and Chinese immigrants pressured existing definitions of state and nation and were represented as challenges to American sovereignty.

Often cited as a key feature of Western understandings of nationhood, *sovereignty* is now and has historically been a rather protean concept that is difficult to define. Lorraine Elliott suggests that "[a]lmost all discussions of sovereignty point to the fact that it is difficult to define in any kind of comprehensive way, that it is a contested concept, and that in any case the practice of sovereignty has never matched the theory."[36] Some of the earliest uses of the term *sovereignty* demonstrate no appreciable link with the political meanings that the term would later acquire, but merely denoted "supremacy." There is some disagreement among scholars as to the precise etymology of this word, but many trace its emergence to the thirteenth-century Old French term *souveraineté*. The *Oxford English Dictionary* contains numerous definitions for *sovereignty*, the oldest of which suggests "[s]upremacy or pre-eminence in respect of excellence or efficacy."[37] Over time, usage shifted from the term denoting the supreme and indivisible authority of God over his Christian subjects to suggesting the secular rule of a single monarch over his subjects and, eventually, the political will of "the people" as exercised across a bounded national space. Medieval and early modern conceptions of sovereignty focused on a single entity who exercised authority over those people born into a particular community of allegiance. The Peace of Westphalia in 1648, which marked the end of the Thirty Years' War, was a watershed moment in the development of conceptions of sovereignty, signaling a "shift in Europe from the medieval world to the modern international system" and the growing importance of territory to constructions of sovereignty.[38] Rather than being linked to a particular individual (the sovereign), sovereignty began to be linked to a bounded territorial space. From the sixteenth century on, European and American constructions of sovereignty developed as a result of domestic debates, the interaction of European nations with one another, and the interaction of English people and other Europeans with African and Native peoples whom they encountered as a result of their imperialist efforts. In the seventeenth century, as civil wars raged across Europe and challenges were raised in the colonies, various nations grappled with competing constructions of the absolute sovereignty of the monarch, parliamentary sovereignty, mixed government, popular sovereignty, and the exigencies of empire. Emmerich de Vattel, the author of *The Law of Nations*, which David J. Bederman classifies as the "single most influential international law treatise for the Framing generation," was instrumental in theorizing external sovereignty, understood as authority exercised outside of the putative borders of a state, and the relations between nations.[39] Constructions of sovereignty changed to meet new political, economic, and cultural needs and became more focused on the relationships between people and space rather than on the relationship between individual subjects and the body of the king. Throughout the movement from spiritual to secular authority and from the rule over people to the control of space, traces of earlier constructions of sovereignty remained even as popular and territorial sovereignty became ascendant.[40]

During the Revolutionary and early national periods Americans drew their ideas of sovereignty from a wide range of sources, including classical writers and European thinkers of the eighteenth century. In his discussion of the sources of American political thought, Bernard Bailyn notes that American political thinkers frequently referenced classical writers such as Aristotle, Polybius, Cicero, and others, but argues that "this elaborate display of classical authors is deceptive" because "[o]ften the learning behind it was superficial."[41] According to Bailyn, eighteenth-century Americans engaged on a deeper level with the writings of Enlightenment thinkers such as Thomas Hobbes, John Locke, Jean-Jacques Rousseau, Montesquieu, Samuel von Pufendorf, Hugo Grotius, Vattel, and Jean Bodin. Bailyn's assessment of early American understandings of classical sources has been challenged by Bederman, who concedes that while Americans did not always encounter classical sources in their original form, they were well versed in the political thought of Greek and Roman antiquity. He notes that American thinkers often turned to secondary sources, such as Montesquieu's *The Spirit of the Laws* (1748), to familiarize themselves with the political thought of the Greek and Roman republics.[42] Despite or perhaps because of their engagement with this vast archive of material, questions remained about the nature of sovereignty, where it resided, and whether it could be limited or divided without compromising the stability of the political community. Ultimately, the concept of popular sovereignty, in which the sovereignty of the monarch was transferred to "the people," came to the forefront of American conceptions of sovereignty. In his 1835 work, *Democracy in America*, Tocqueville reflects on the emergence of popular sovereignty: "Then came the American Revolution. The dogma of popular sovereignty emerged from the towns and took possession of the government. All classes enlisted in its cause. People fought and triumphed in its name. It became the law of laws."[43] Tocqueville's comments presume a kind of shared vision of popular sovereignty and a movement from local to national that is somewhat complicated by the historical record. Yet his narrative does capture with particular clarity the ways in which popular sovereignty was imagined to permeate all aspects of American political life.

While sovereignty in early America was and remains to this day a contested term, there are some key features that, while not necessarily representative of early American visions of sovereignty writ large, nonetheless provide a set of terms that can provide a starting point for discussions of nation-state sovereignty. Wendy Brown distills some of these features of sovereignty in her *Walled States, Waning Sovereignty*:

> Here we may simply note that a composite figure of sovereignty drawn from classical theorists of modern sovereignty, including Thomas Hobbes, Jean Bodin, and Carl Schmitt, suggests that sovereignty's indispensible features include supremacy (no higher power), perpetuity over time (no term limits), decisionism (no boundedness by or submission to law), absoluteness and completeness (sovereignty cannot be probable or partial), nontransferability (sovereignty cannot be conferred without cancelling itself), and specified jurisdiction (territoriality). If nation-state sovereignty has always been something of a fiction in its aspiration and claims to these qualities, the fiction is a potent one and has suffused the internal and external relations of nation-states since its consecration by the 1648 Peace of Westphalia.[44]

The power of the sovereign in this formulation is at once boundless and bounded; it is not limited by other, potentially stronger authorities or by the passage of time; it is incapable of being shared or divided; yet it can only operate within a particular territorial space. Such features began to crystallize after the Peace of Westphalia and were tested by the extension of empire in the New World and in the crucible of the revolutionary movements of the eighteenth century. As I show in the next section, questions regarding supremacy and absoluteness—that is, whether decision-making political power could be shared and what form that sharing would take—and territoriality informed debates about divided sovereignty both during and after the Revolutionary period. Conceptions of divided sovereignty, framed in British common law as a political impossibility, became both a cornerstone of American political thought and a source of anxiety in white Americans' engagements with Indigenous peoples, African Americans, and various immigrant groups. What made the rhetorics of imperium in imperio so powerful and potentially transformative was that they disrupted and deconstructed the boundedness and absoluteness of sovereignty—both political and territorial—and gave voice to the political possibilities and attendant dangers of divisible sovereignty.

America's Two-Headed Monster: Imperium in Imperio and the Division of Sovereignty

Rhetorics of imperium in imperio and divided sovereignty informed American political debates beginning in the eighteenth century, first as an intellectual obstacle to American resistance to the British Parliament, then as a defining feature of American political culture, and finally as a vehicle for articulating racialized threats to the body politic. The term *imperium*, derived from Roman law, can be defined as "independent and absolute sovereignty."[45] Generally speaking, it refers to the kind of power that states exert over individuals. Imperium in imperio has been translated variously as "a nation within a nation," "an empire within an empire," and "a sovereign power within another sovereign power"; from the latter proceeds one particular interpretation of imperium in imperio as a form of divided sovereignty in which two sovereign powers attempt to operate in the same political community and/or geographic space. As American constructions of nationhood became increasingly territorial and concerned with racial homogeneity during the nineteenth century, white Americans returned to the argument from sovereignty used by British supporters of parliamentary sovereignty and to earlier European formulations of indivisible sovereignty in order to represent various populations as political anomalies and racial threats to the U.S. body politic.

The vision of sovereignty that dominated English political thought in the decades preceding the American Revolution was one in which Parliament constituted the supreme, indivisible, but not arbitrary power. In his *Commentaries on the Laws of England*, English jurist Sir William Blackstone crystallized what was a widely held belief in eighteenth-century England: "[T]here is and must be in all of them [forms of government] a supreme, irresistible, absolute, uncontrolled authority, in which the *jura summi imperii*, or the rights of sovereignty, reside."[46] For Blackstone, that sovereign power resided in Parliament. Blackstone warned of the influence of a "foreign power" in England and asserted that Roman Catholics would create an imperium by "by paying that obedience to papal process, which constitutionally belonged to the king alone."[47] Catholics, in other words, could not be good subjects because their loyalty would always be divided between the king and the pope. The supreme and indivisible sovereignty of Parliament was seen to operate both in Britain and in the colonies, even though in practice colonial legislatures exerted a great deal of authority. As James Kettner asserts, this was stated quite clearly in the Declaratory Act of 18 March 1766, which claimed for Parliament the "full power and authority to make laws and statutes of sufficient force and validity to bind the colonies and people of *America*, subjects of the crown of *Great Britain*, in all cases whatsoever."[48] English theorists based their claims that Americans were subject to parliamentary sovereignty on two key arguments, which have been ably summarized by Kettner. The first was that "Americans were subjects, that all subjects were under Parliament, and that therefore Americans were under Parliament" (Kettner, *Development*, 133). The second argument appealed to constructions of sovereignty as indivisible and "presupposed a certain fusion of the ideas of the empire and the community of allegiance" (133).

The British Empire was framed as a single state, albeit one spread over a vast geographic area: "Building on the premise that two sovereign powers could not exist within the same state, British spokesmen argued that the empire was a state, that Parliament was its sovereign power, and that as members of the empire the colonies were of necessity under Parliament's sovereign authority" (133). Thus, to admit the sovereignty of colonial legislatures was to create a division of sovereignty between Parliament and local authorities, an imperium in imperio that supporters of Parliament were not prepared to tolerate.

American colonists initially found the charge of imperium in imperio a kind of intellectual stumbling block to their resistance of parliamentary authority. James Otis Jr., a Massachusetts lawyer and provincial assembly member, conceded the basic premise of indivisible sovereignty in his 1764 *Rights of the British Colonies Asserted and Proved*. In words that echo Blackstone, he writes, "A supreme legislative and a supreme executive power, must be placed *somewhere* in every commonwealth."[49] In a later pamphlet entitled *A Vindication of the British Colonies* (1765), he characterizes imperium in imperio as "the greatest of all political solecisms."[50] As for the location of sovereignty, Bailyn explains that Otis agreed with the current thinking on popular sovereignty, that "[w]here there is no other positive provision or compact to the contrary, those powers remain in the *whole body of the people*."[51] For English people and British colonists, that power was located in Parliament, a belief that, as Bailyn points out, led Otis to make some inconsistent arguments. Parliament was the supreme authority, Otis suggested, and all British subjects were obliged to obey that body. Yet, he insisted that while Parliament was invested with ultimate and indivisible power, that power should not be arbitrary, and Parliament should not conclude "that 'tis always expedient and in all circumstances equitable for the supreme and sovereign legislative" to exert its authority over its subjects.[52] Here Otis mixed the argument from sovereignty with an appeal to expedience in the administration of a transatlantic empire. That Parliament had the power to compel the obedience of its colonial subjects did not, for Otis, mean that it should always use that power.

In working toward a rhetorical position that would allow them to contest parliamentary acts such as the Declaratory Act and the Stamp Act, colonial writers and orators considered alternative views of sovereignty that would allow for the division of sovereignty without the dissolution of government. Some, like Richard Bland, Stephen Hopkins, and Benjamin Franklin, drew a distinction between the colonial legislatures' ability to regulate internal matters, such as taxation, and Parliament's exclusive authority over the "EXTERNAL government" and its right to legislate on matters such as trade.[53] John Dickinson's *Letters from a Farmer in Pennsylvania, to the Inhabitants of the Brit-*

ish Colonies makes this distinction explicit. Of parliamentary sovereignty, he writes: "We are but parts of *a whole*; and therefore there must exist a power somewhere, to preside, and preserve the connection in due order. This power is lodged in the parliament; and we are as much dependent on *Great-Britain*, as a perfectly free people can be on another."[54] He denies, however, the right of Parliament to "*raise money upon us*, WITHOUT OUR CONSENT" by taxing items that it has forbidden the colonies to produce themselves.[55] This distinction of internal and external sovereignty constitutes one of the first attempts to theorize a separation of sovereignty in a way that preserved the colonies' relationship to Great Britain.

Another argument for divisible sovereignty arose in relation to the concept of empire. According to Kettner, colonial Americans conceived of the British Empire as "a 'body politic' composed of separate and independent sovereignties linked together by a common king" (*Development*, 163). In this construction of empire, "the empire was not a true 'state,' as the term was commonly used, [and thus] the accepted theory of sovereignty could not be used to sustain Parliament's authority over the colonies" (162). Given the geographic distance that separated the colonies from the metropole, the king's sovereignty was embodied in the local legislatures and assemblies. Therefore, the colonists claimed that their local authorities did not constitute an example of divided sovereignty, but rather enacted the exercise of the king's sovereignty over his colonial subjects. In *The Creation of the American Republic*, Gordon S. Wood explains that the colonists saw themselves as subject to the king, not to Parliament: "The colonial legislatures had thus become miniature parliaments, each headed by the same royal authority of the King, together forming a loosely federated empire of independent states which did no violence to the principle of sovereignty."[56] They rejected the notion of the king-in-Parliament and framed their relationship with the king himself as he was represented in the various colonial legislatures. The colonists' belief in the body-politic model spurred their calls for greater representation and their belief that King George III could and should exercise restraint over parliamentary actions that threatened the rights of his subjects. Calls for restrictions on Parliament suggested, according to Bailyn, an assumption on the part of the colonists that sovereignty "was in some sense divisible."[57]

Throughout the late 1760s and early 1770s, representatives of the Crown, Loyalists, and those who hoped to avoid war repeated their argument that parliamentary sovereignty over the colonies could not be limited or divided. Notable expressions of this position include the 1773 letters of Lieutenant Governor Thomas Hutchinson of Massachusetts to the two Houses of Assembly, in which he claimed that "it is impossible there should be two independent Legislatures in one and the same state" because "two Legislative bodies will make two governments as distinct as the Kingdoms of England and Scotland before the Union" (qtd. in Wood, *Creation of the American Republic*, 344). In "A View of the Controversy between Great Britain and Her Colonies," Samuel Seabury, a Tory from New York, argued that if the authority of colonial legislatures is not "subordinate to the supreme sovereign authority of the nation . . . there is *imperium in imperio*: two sovereign authorities in the same state; which is a contradiction."[58] In what would become a familiar conflation of internal division and monstrosity, a Pennsylvania delegate to the First Continental Congress, Joseph Galloway, described imperium in imperio as "a *monster*, a thing *out of nature*."[59] White Americans would echo this rhetoric in their representations of the various populations attempting to form nations within the U.S. nation in the nineteenth century.

Colonists answered the British charges of imperium in imperio by either dismissing it out of hand or by suggesting that the current situation did not constitute a political solecism because Parliament did not have supreme authority over the colonies. In his 1774 pamphlet *To the Inhabitants of Great Britain*, lawyer and future Supreme Court justice James Iredell characterized the perceived "necessity of *one* supreme power residing *somewhere* in every state" as "narrow and pedantic."[60] He suggested that the "great solecism of an *imperium in imperio*," which was used to support arguments based on "the necessity of an absolute power residing *somewhere* in every state," did not relate to an arrangement of "several *distinct and independent legislatures*, each engaged within a *separate* scale, and employed about *different* objects."[61] Anyone supporting the theory that "two independent legislatures cannot exist in the same community," argued a British naval officer and one-time governor of West Florida, George Johnstone, revealed "a perfect ignorance of the history of civil society."[62] Writing as "Novanglus," John Adams responded to the claims of Daniel Leonard, a Tory author who wrote under the name of "Massachusettensis," by asserting that two sovereign authorities cannot exist in the same state, since that "would be what is called *imperium in imperio*, the height of political absurdity" (qtd. in Wood, *Creation of the American Republic*, 351). Yet, from this, Adams drew the conclusion that it was the colonial legislatures, not Parliament, which constituted the sovereign authority. Alexander Hamilton likewise concluded that two legislatures operating within the same state "cannot be supposed, without falling into that solecism, in politics, of *imperium in imperio*" (352). In his reading of these debates, Wood asserts that the "legislative authority of Parliament was disavowed, but the concept of legislative sovereignty was not; it was only transplanted" (352).

Yet, imperium in imperio and questions of sovereignty persisted as intellectual challenges to the creation of a new American government, as suggested by the conflicting perspectives articulated in the Articles of Confederation. Robert Clinton describes the post-Revolution situation thusly: "The locus of sovereignty after independence was and is a subject of serious dispute."[63] Some imagined a sovereign national government, others maintained an allegiance to the states, and still others remained committed to the sovereign figure of the king and the colonial legislatures. The relationship of the states under the Articles of Confederation was, as the document's title asserts, one of "Perpetual Union," and, as Bederman notes, Article XIII articulated a "form of supremacy clause."[64] Yet, Article II suggests that "[e]ach state retains its sovereignty, freedom, and independence, and every Power, Jurisdiction, and right, which is not by this confederation expressly delegated to the United States, in Congress assembled." Thus, the Articles of Confederation simultaneously declared the supremacy of the Confederation and the absolute sovereignty of the states. However, it also demonstrated explicit concern about imperium in imperio and the possibility of emergent states. Article XI envisioned a future in which Canada might become part of the United States but declared that no other colony could be added without the agreement of all the states. New states simply could not emerge from within the existing states nor be added without permission; both of these possibilities threatened the sovereignty and territorial integrity of the existing states. Reaction to the Articles of Confederation was mixed, with some arguing for strengthening the Confederation and increasing the powers of Congress, while others declared that each state must possess "*Complete Sovereignty*" (qtd. in Wood, *Creation of the American Republic*, 360). Wood contends that the "obvious weaknesses of the Articles of Confederation" prompted calls for the Philadelphia Convention (467).[65]

In their consideration of a national constitution, the founders were concerned with issues of sovereignty and its division. Citing historical examples, James Madison and Alexander Hamilton suggested in *The Federalist Papers* that divided sovereignty was problematic: "a sovereignty over sovereigns, a government over governments, a legislation for communities, as contradistinguished from individuals," is "subversive of order and [the] ends of civil policy."[66] In 1787, Madison further acknowledged that "an individual independence of the States is utterly irreconcilable with the idea of an aggregate sovereignty" and that "consolidation of the whole into one simple republic would be as inexpedient as it is unattainable"; yet Madison hoped a "middle ground" could be achieved.[67] Indeed, such a middle ground is suggested by the U.S. Constitution, which in the branches of the government aims to separate power without creating a dangerous dividing sovereignty. As the Tenth Amendment states: "The powers not delegated to the United States by the Constitution, nor prohibited by it to the States, are reserved to the States respectively, or to the people." Instead of forestalling the division of sovereignty, the founders sought to incorporate it into their system of government and, in so doing, manage its revolutionary potential. Despite attempts in Article I and Article IV to distinguish between state and federal roles, the distinctions between the separation of powers and the division of sovereignty between state and federal authorities remained contested, opening the door for new interpretations of divided sovereignty.

Like the Articles of Confederation, the Constitution attempts to prevent certain forms of divided sovereignty by offering similar prohibitions on new states. Article IV, section 3, reads: "New States may be admitted by the Congress into this Union; but no new State shall be formed or erected within the Jurisdiction of any other State; nor any State be formed by the Junction of two or more States, or Parts of States, without the Consent of the Legislatures of the States concerned as well as of the Congress." Congress here is given the exclusive power to admit new states into the Union and to prohibit the formation of a new state within an existing one, which would constitute an imperium in imperio. This kind of division of sovereignty, suggests the Constitution, is politically undesirable, if not impossible. Such a situation had, in fact, arisen in 1784 when the state of Franklin (otherwise known as the Free Republic of Franklin) was formed on land that had been ceded to Congress by North Carolina. The leaders of Franklin launched a failed petition for statehood before declaring themselves an independent republic, a status that they maintained for only a brief period before internal collapse and external pressures led to Franklin's downfall.[68] Like Franklin, which emerged before the ratification of the U.S. Constitution, the unauthorized formation of "new" states within existing states could cause jurisdictional conflicts. Congress asserted its authority to regulate the management of state borders and new territories and did so as states such as North Carolina and Georgia ceded their western territories to the federal government. The distinctions between state and federal powers in the Constitution generated controversy for decades and are still contested today. From its natal moments, the United States has been an example of divided sovereignty, yet the Constitution also guards against divisions that could prove politically problematic.

The process of ratifying the Constitution revived discussions of imperium in imperio and debates about the nature of sovereignty. During the ratifying convention in New York, delegate Thomas Tredwell offered the following warning: "The idea of two distinct sovereigns in the same country, separately possessed of sovereign and supreme power, in the same matters at the same time, is as supreme an absurdity, as that two distinct separate circles can be bounded exactly by the same circumference."[69] Here Tredwell echoes British arguments about sovereignty and also uses a spatial metaphor of bounded circles that foreshadows the territorial dimensions that such debates would take on during the nineteenth century. As part of his argument for a strong federal government in *The Federalist Papers*, Hamilton wrote that those who argued for states' rights "seem to cherish with blind devotion the political monster of an *imperium in imperio*."[70] Similarly, Madison, dubbed one of the "staunchest champions of the theory of divided sovereignty," wrote to Jefferson in 1787 that the Constitution, with its division of powers between state and federal authorities, "involves the evil of imperia in imperio."[71] John Adams viewed the Constitution as a "fresh essay at *imperium in imperio*," which would prevent conflict for a time but ultimately would need to be reworked.[72] Constructions of popular sovereignty ultimately provided colonial theorists with a way to think beyond imperium in imperio. Their fears were mediated, at least for a time, by the argument that sovereignty resided not in the various branches or levels of government, but in the people. Advocates of the federal system argued that authority could be divided between state and federal governments without truly dividing sovereignty, which ultimately resided in the people as a unitary body. Regardless of their position on the Constitution and the political culture of the new republic, political figures at the time continued to draw on rhetorics of imperium in imperio as they considered the nature and location of sovereignty.

As time went on, imperium in imperio lost many of its negative associations and was embraced by Americans and visitors alike as a defining feature of American political culture. Supreme Court justice James Wilson argued that the sovereignty of "the people" could be dispersed without consequence, unlike that vested in the figure of a monarch or in other institutions.[73] In 1793 the Supreme Court decision in the case of *Chisholm v. Georgia* articulated the division of sovereignty between the state and federal powers: "The United States are sovereign as to all the powers of government actually surrendered," while "[e]ach state in the Union is sovereign as to all the powers reserved."[74] Reflecting on the American political system, Madison declared that "[i]t is so difficult to argue intelligently concerning the compound system of government in the United States, without admitting the divisibility of sovereignty, that the idea of sovereignty, as divided between the Union and the members composing the Union, forces itself into the view, and even into the language of those most strenuously contending for the unity and indivisibility of the *moral being* created by the social compact."[75] Supporting the federal (or compact) system of government, argued Madison, made it almost linguistically impossible to deny the divisibility of sovereignty. Many, like Madison, eventually rejected the doctrine of indivisible sovereignty, finding virtue in the fact that sovereignty was not concentrated in the hands of a single individual or entity.

Popular literature also cited divided sovereignty as a key feature of American government and public life. A letter published in the *Atlantic Magazine* in 1825 characterizes the relationship between the state and federal governments of the United States as a "qualified *imperium in imperio*."[76] The author, writing to his father of his impressions of American politics, observes that "[a]bstractly, this plan [divided sovereignty] is extremely difficult to comprehend," but the American example of imperium in imperio has been "stripped indeed of all of the fancied terrors it once possessed for the rational lovers of freedom."[77] Divided sovereignty could now be imagined without recourse to the language of impossibility and monstrosity.

Tocqueville similarly describes divided sovereignty as a key component of American federalism in *Democracy in America*, praising its ability to "combine the various advantages" associated with large nations with those of smaller ones.[78] However, he concedes that there are problems with the transmission of this system to other states and cites Mexico as a prime example. Although the Mexicans copied the American system, they are frequently "ensnaring themselves in the machinery of their divided government" because "a fragmented sovereignty will always be weaker than one that is complete" (187–188). Thus, for Tocqueville, it is worth noting "how artfully the Americans managed to circumscribe the power of the Union within the narrow ambit of a federal government yet at the same time give it the appearance and, to a certain extent, the power of a national government" (188). In this way, they "diminished the danger inherent in the nature of confederations but were unable to eliminate it entirely" (188). But despite the optimism that attended the American political project and the celebratory narrative of American federalism, the "fancied terrors" of divided sovereignty did not simply disappear. It was still seen by some Americans as a political impossibility. As John C. Calhoun, an ardent supporter of state sovereignty, proclaimed, "Sovereignty is an entire thing;—to divide, is,—to destroy it."[79] Moreover, even those who agreed that America was a successful model of divided sovereignty doubted if sovereignty could or should be divided further or in new ways. Questions remained about what kinds of division were appropriate, how such divisions would work in practice, and who constituted the sovereign entity known as "the people."[80] In the midst of contentious debates regarding state and federal sovereignty, fears of imperium in imperio were transferred to various "other" nations, which were imagined as threats to American sovereignty and to fictions of national unity.

But how did a phrase that frequently was associated with state formation come to be used in discussions of populations such as African Americans and American Indians, and immigrant groups such as the Irish and Chinese? The answer relates to constructions of nationhood as having political, territorial, and ethnic dimensions and the investment of sovereignty in the people. The political claims made by the Cherokees and other Native nations, African Americans, and Irish and Chinese immigrants troubled the fiction of a unified and homogenous American "people," and arguments about these groups' political status amplified existing rifts between state and federal authorities. Such struggles required the story of American sovereignty to be continually retold, and part of this retelling involved narratives that downplayed friction between state and federal powers and located the source of tension instead in other nations that were identified within the putative borders of the United States. Dealing with these nations reinforced the internal unity of the majority population and demonstrated the role of the United States in *international* debate. Sovereignty could be divided, it was argued, but only in certain ways and among certain kinds of people. The attendant dangers of divided sovereignty had not disappeared completely but had been put to new uses.

Constituting Nations in the Nineteenth Century

While the U.S. Constitution and, to an extent, the various state constitutions have garnered a great deal of critical attention, they are by no means the only written constitutions produced in America. In addition to the various nations examined in this book and the CSA, many different kinds of nineteenth-century groups published written constitutions, some of which were modeled on U.S. federal and state documents while others were invented whole cloth.[81] To date, there are no comprehensive studies of constitution making in America nor of the interplay between constitutions and other literary and cultural productions, but the written constitution is an important genre that is deserving of sustained critical inquiry. The U.S. Constitution, dubbed a "political bible" by Thomas Paine,[82] spawned a whole host of imitations that both appropriated portions of the original and rearticulated key claims to meet their writers' political and social exigencies, which, in turn, changed the original in subtle ways.

The genre of the written constitution is largely a product of the eighteenth century.[83] Initially, American legal theorists such as James Wilson claimed that their rebellion against Britain adhered to "both the letter and the spirit of the British Constitution" (Wilson qtd. in Wood, *Creation of the American Republic*, 12). Yet, the British constitution was not a written document but rather "an unwritten hodgepodge of statutory law, legal precedent, and custom."[84] As English theologian William Paley observes, the British constitution "is one principal division, head, series, or title of the code of public laws, distinguished from the rest only by the superior importance of the subject, of which it treats."[85] It was, to borrow the language of Fredric Jameson, a "shared code," but one that was not written down.[86] While they initially framed their efforts as sanctioned by the British constitution, Americans began to shift their rhetoric as the Revolution progressed and to develop a different conception of constitutions. They sought to create, as John Adams asserts, a republic that would be "an Empire of Laws, and not of Men," one that could not be easily altered to suit the whims of particular leaders.[87] In the words of Gordon Wood, they understood a constitution to be "a written superior law set above the entire government against which all other law is to be measured" (260). Paine's understanding of a constitution as a "*written* Charter" (emphasis added) that outlines how a government would be formed came to inform the drafting not only of national and state constitutions, but also those of various other groups, which used constitutions as means of formally outlining their purpose and organizational structure.[88]

The generic features of constitutions differentiate these texts from many other kinds of fictional and nonfictional works. First, they are distinguished by their corporate authorship and multiple audiences. Whether they speak for "We the People of the United States" or for the members of the Hebrew Ladies Sewing Circle of Louisville, Kentucky, written constitutions are a collective enunciation produced, ostensibly, by a group of individuals. In terms of audience, they speak to both members and nonmembers, writing an organization into existence and communicating its status to a larger public. The opening articles of the Constitution of the American Anti-Slavery Society, ratified in 1833, establish the group's name and its purpose, which, according to Article 2, was "the entire abolition of slavery in the United States."[89] As Adams and the other American founders suggested, constitutions are designed to be self-perpetuating, outliving particular individuals and historical moments. They are designed to continually reproduce the conditions of their creation, establishing rules of belonging, organizational structures, elections, officers, and so forth.[90] Yet, as Fredric Jameson argues, constitutions function not to curtail individual acts but rather to "forestall certain kinds of political and historical events and catastrophes: most notably revolutions, but also more limited types of power seizure and power imbalance."[91] Put another way, written constitutions create the conditions for both continuity and revolution through the distinctions that they draw between the conditions of their production/replication and violations of those conditions.

The U.S. Constitution empowered various groups to produce their own constitutions, which both articulated their own political claims and rearticulated those of their model.[92] Perhaps the most well known of these is the Confederate Constitution, modeled on the U.S. Constitution with the addition of a stronger statement on state sovereignty and stronger protections for the institution of slavery.[93] This constitution communicated the Confederacy leaders' belief that they, not the Northern states, were the true heirs of the American Revolution. Like the Cherokee Constitution of 1827 (discussed in chapter 1), the constitution produced by the Negro Convention movement in 1834 (chapter 2), John Brown's Provisional Constitution (chapter 3), the constitution of the Irish Republic of the United States (chapter 4), and the constitutions produced by the Chinese Six Companies (chapter 5), the Confederate Constitution communicated the group's political status and rearticulated elements of the U.S. Constitution. Nations were not the only groups to turn to written constitutions. Nineteenth-century temperance societies, antislavery societies, the Chautauqua movement, and sewing circles all produced written constitutions. There were even published templates such as that produced by Isaac Knapp in 1838, entitled *Constitution of the ... Anti-Slavery Society* (with the ellipses indicating where a group could add its own name), which new groups could use in lieu of producing their own document. In reading the various constitutions, I focus not on issues of originality or authorial identity (individual or collective), but rather on the strategic engagements between these texts and America's founding documents.

Overview of This Book

The Civil War era marked a shift in American concerns about sovereignty from largely "domestic" territorial concerns about the extension and maintenance of U.S. geopolitical borders and jurisdiction across the American continent to debates about the implications of the extension of U.S. extraterritorial sovereignty abroad for nationhood, citizenship, and political allegiance.[94] Chapters 1 through 3 of this book focus on the Cherokees and on African Americans, whose relationship to the North American continent predated the American Revolution and the creation of the United States. These three chapters detail how imperium in imperio functioned as part of a process of territorializing these populations, both in the Deleuzian sense of fixing the other within a particular set of categories and trying to make them conform to a set of norms and in the literal sense of organizing their relationship to space. In her reading of Deleuzian notions of "style and stutter," Christa Albrecht-Crane suggests that territorialization "functions through processes that organize and systematize social space and language production" and notes that "[i]n most Western societies, territorializations manifest themselves in how culture reads and categorizes individuals in terms of 'their' race, class, gender, nationality, religion, physical ability, and so on."[95] I suggest that rhetorics of imperium in imperio constitute such a manifestation, revealing the ways in which the United States sought to "organize" and "read" various populations as part of arguments for their collective removal or continued enslavement.[96]

After the Civil War, the process of organizing such populations became more administrative in nature. This is not to say that the regulation of domestic space was no longer important, but the extension of extraterritorial sovereignty (i.e., the extension of U.S. jurisdiction beyond its territorial borders) created new exigencies for the management of internal populations. As I suggest in chapters 4 and 5, in an increasingly mobile world in which U.S. citizens carried U.S. sovereignty into other nations, Irish Americans and Chinese immigrants were seen as introducing other sovereign powers into the United States. They were met with administrative and legal techniques meant to capitalize on their potential as labor while containing their political capabilities, and groups such as the Fenian Brotherhood and the Chinese Six Companies worked to engage in international diplomacy among multiple nations. Throughout *Divided Sovereignties*, I examine the ways in which various forms of "virtual" nationhood were set in dialogue with Westphalian constructions of the territorial nation.[97] All of the chapters are linked by my attention to the ways in which rhetorics of imperium in imperio worked to contain and manage threats to U.S. sovereignty and to open up new avenues of political engagement for Cherokee, African American, Irish American, and Chinese people, who participated in situated attempts to gain political advantage in their dealings with the state.

In chapter 1, I examine the textual productions surrounding the legal battles between the Cherokees, the state of Georgia, and the U.S. federal government during the height of the debate over Indian Removal in the late 1820s and 1830s. The ratification of the 1827 Cherokee Constitution, which emphasized maintaining the territorial integrity of the nation and exercising sole political jurisdiction within those borders, elicited charges of an imperium in imperio from Georgia's political leaders and other supporters of Removal. Such discussions of a Cherokee imperium conflated visions of territorial usurpation, political threat, and racial anomaly that point to the myriad ways imperium in imperio functioned in American public argument of the nineteenth century. The competing visions of divided sovereignty that emerged from these debates informed engagements between the United States and various groups throughout the rest of the century, and the Cherokee Constitution stands at the beginning of a vibrant period of constitution making, in which various groups turned to written constitutions as means of articulating their political claims. Cherokee leaders, including Principal Chief John Ross and Elias Boudinot, the editor of the *Cherokee Phoenix*, echoed the territorial concerns of the 1827 constitution and sought to engage the United States on national rather than racial terms. However, because of the exigencies of Removal, both Ross and Boudinot were forced to rethink the relationship between nationhood, sovereignty, and territorial possession. While their perspectives have often been framed as diametrically opposed, my analysis of the rhetorics of imperium in imperio offers new insight on the differences and points of intersection in their political thought. The chapter concludes with an examination of the ways in which rhetorics of imperium in imperio continued to play a role in Cherokee political culture as the Cherokee Nation was reconfigured after Removal.

In chapters 2 and 3, I attend to the ways in which supporters of African colonization framed African Americans, particularly free black people, as a virtual nation within the United States that could and should be removed to meliorate fractures in the United States. "Virtual" in this context was linked to the fact that unlike Indigenous peoples, African Americans did not claim to hold land collectively. They were framed as a kind of nation-to-be that colonizationists claimed could be actualized in Africa. Chapter 2 focuses on another "flashpoint" (to borrow Kazanjian's term), the turbulent decades surrounding the Missouri crisis in which rhetorics of a free black imperium began to emerge, largely through the efforts of the African Colonization Society (ACS). Focusing on the literary and political efforts of the Negro Convention movement, including its 1834 constitution and "Declaration of Sentiment," and the work of writers and orators such as Robert Alexander Young, David Walker, Maria W. Stewart, and Hosea Easton, I trace the ways in which African Americans reworked conceptions of imperium in imperio in an attempt to engage white Americans on political rather than racial terms. They recovered earlier conceptions of divine sovereignty and argued for the potential of multiple national affiliations in order to counter racial representations and rethink the connections between nationhood and space.

Chapter 3 extends this argument into the 1850s, a period marked by fierce debates regarding state and federal sovereignty and by deepening divides in the United States. As in the 1820s and 1830s, fractures in the U.S. nation were projected onto the presence of a threatening black imperium, a move used by supporters of colonization to argue for the removal of free black people. Supporters of chattel slavery also repurposed the rhetorics of imperium in imperio to defend slavery as a form of government uniquely suited to African Americans. Against this fraught backdrop, John Brown and the members of the Chatham Convention enacted their own vision of imperium in imperio by creating the Provisional Constitution in 1858, which established a temporary antislavery government and rearticulated the U.S. Constitution by writing slavery out of the national landscape. Martin Delany and Frederick Douglass, who were both acquainted with Brown and the Provisional Constitution, recognized the strategic importance of engaging the United States on national terms and explored the political possibilities of imperium in imperio as part of their quest for abolition and black enfranchisement. Their writings, like Brown's, suggest that "America" could be a multinational space and engage in a reconsideration of the relationship between nations, sovereignty, and territory. This chapter concludes with a brief reading of the Confederate Constitution and its revision of the U.S. Constitution's treatment of slavery, territoriality, and imperium in imperio.

In chapter 4, I discuss the Fenian Brotherhood, an organization that was founded in 1858 as the American wing of the Irish Republican Brotherhood, which grew in size and influence during and immediately after the Civil War. I argue that in the wake of large numbers of Irish immigrants during the Great Famine years, rhetorics of imperium in imperio were repurposed as part of a process through which Irish Catholics were territorialized as a distinct racial other whose political and economic activities must be managed, even as they were eligible for naturalized citizenship. In the 1860s, this rhetoric functioned to frame the Fenians as a threat to U.S. sovereignty. This organization, made up of both naturalized and native-born American citizens, created an Irish Republic in America, held yearly conventions, ratified a written constitution, and made several unsuccessful attempts to invade Canada. Its members also produced a significant amount of literary works along the way. Through its political, military, and literary practices, the Fenian Brotherhood pressured widely accepted dichotomies between domestic and foreign, and alien and citizen, and questioned the relationship of territory to definitions of sovereignty and nationhood. It synthesized radical tactics honed in Ireland with a commitment to multiple political allegiances in an attempt to craft a "virtual" Irish state within the putative borders of the United States, which the members hoped would improve the political position of Irish people both in the United States and in Ireland.

In chapter 5, I examine representations of the Chinese Six Companies as an imperium in imperio, a charge that circulated in California and in broader public argument amid concerns about the implications of extraterritorial sovereignty during the Reconstruction era. If U.S. sovereignty followed its citizens abroad, could immigrant populations such as the Chinese introduce foreign sovereignties into the United States? Such questions informed debates about the legal position and political allegiances of Chinese immigrants, who were not eligible for U.S. citizenship and remained subjects of the Chinese emperor even while residing in the United States for years. Discussions of a Chinese imperium were closely linked with anxieties about the "yellow peril" and, as with the other groups studied here, operated as part of a larger process through which Chinese were coded as unassimilable and in need of management. I demonstrate the myriad ways that the Six Companies and their American allies positioned their organization as a kind of virtual extension of Chinese sovereignty, which functioned to support (not challenge) that of the United States. Their vision of divided sovereignty and multiple allegiances, articulated in part through written constitutions, represented attempts to improve the lived experiences of Chinese workers in California in a period marked by legal restrictions and to engage both the United States and China on political terms.

Finally, in the conclusion, "Becoming Minority Nations in Nineteenth-Century America," I turn to Deleuze's understanding of minorities and their creative processes. I return to Griggs and his Imperium and reflect on the rhetorics of divided sovereignty as the nineteenth century came to a close. I argue that Griggs's novel can serve as a kind of transitional piece that reveals the shifting articulations of U.S. sovereignty.

CHAPTER ONE

★ ★ ★ ★

"In the Heart of So Powerful a Nation"

Cherokee Sovereignty, Political Allegiance, and National Spaces

ALTHOUGH THE AMERICAN REVOLUTION was formally concluded with the Treaty of Paris in 1783, historians and literary scholars have argued that the establishment of the American nation and the "securing [of] the Revolution" took far longer than the conflict itself.[1] From the contentious constitutional debates to the fraught political wranglings of the 1790s, "U.S. nationalism remained," in the words of Robert S. Levine, "highly conflicted and contingent."[2] The United States was not universally described in *national* terms in its early years. Indeed, the U.S. Constitution avoids the word "nation" altogether, instead referring to America as a "Union" or the "several States," terms that emphasize confederacy over national unity. Conflicts threatened to boil over at various points during the early nineteenth century: some New England Federalists warned of secession during the War of 1812, slavery threatened the tenuous unity of the states, and South Carolina's efforts at nullification challenged the sovereignty of the federal government in the early 1830s. These conflicts reanimated Revolutionary-era debates about the location and nature of sovereignty and revealed competing notions of state and federal jurisdiction that had not been resolved by the U.S. Constitution. During this period, there was, according to Jonathan Arac, no "fully operative national culture."[3] The United States was, he suggests, writing itself into existence and looking backward to earlier moments in its history as part of the creation of a "national narrative."[4]

Representations of and engagements with American Indian peoples played a key role in the crafting of the national narrative, as Joshua Bellin and others have noted.[5] Authors such as James Fenimore Cooper, Catharine Maria Sedgwick, and Lydia Maria Child produced frontier romances populated by Anglo-American, European, and Native people that depicted the competing territorial and political claims to the lands claimed by the United States. In his reading of these frontier romances, Ezra Tawil argues that they "helped to redefine 'race' for an emerging national culture" and constituted "narratives about racial conflict."[6] At the same time, I would suggest, they helped to redefine nationhood by dramatizing frontier spaces as decidedly *multinational* sites characterized not just by "racial conflict," but by contests over sovereignty and jurisdiction. While some scholars have portrayed Cooper in particular as an apologist for the spread of the American empire and the forced dispossession of Native peoples, the original three *Leather-Stocking Tales*—*The Pioneers* (1823), *The Last of the Mohicans* (1826), and *The Prairie* (1827)—look back to earlier moments in America's history to offer a critical assessment of the nation's past and possible future.[7] From the violent imperialist aims of the European combatants in *The Last of the Mohicans* to the wasteful and destructive practices of settlers in *The Pioneers* and *The Prairie*, Cooper exposes the human and environmental costs of territorial expansion.

The final novel in what Cooper originally conceived as a trilogy, *The Prairie* dramatizes the western frontier as a site marked by porous borders and contested jurisdictions in which multiple nations operate within the putative borders of the newly expanded United States. When Ishmael Bush and his family leave the East for the newly acquired lands of the Louisiana Territory, they enter a space that has yet to be brought under the control of American law. The murder of Ishmael's son Asa brings the complicated legal landscape into sharp relief and highlights the question of who can claim jurisdiction over the prairie and its inhabitants even though the land technically belongs to the United States. Rather than the neat binaries of domestic/foreign or Indian/American, Cooper's novel features the interactions of a multinational cast: Anglo-American migrants, a Spanish captive, and Teton Dakota and Pawnee peoples inhabit this shifting and complicated web of political and social affiliation. Cooper's vision of this contested, multinational American landscape resonated with the complicated political geographies of the 1820s and 1830s, in which the political and territorial claims of Indigenous polities challenged the uneasy balance of state and federal authority and pressured existing definitions of sovereignty, nationhood, and citizenship.

Perhaps nowhere were such issues more hotly debated in the antebellum period than in the arguments between the state of Georgia, the Cherokee Nation, and the U.S. federal government.[8] Fractures in the U.S. nation between state and federal authorities that had not been fully mediated by federalism were projected onto the presence of this "other" nation, whose removal, it was implied, could help to heal internal divisions. As Priscilla Wald observes, "A Cherokee Nation posed an important symbolic threat to the Union" by "recapitulat[ing] the prerevolutionary colonies' relationship to England: '"imperium in imperio" (a state within a state),' conceptually complicating American exceptionalism, absorptiveness, and republicanism."[9] While the Cherokees were not the only Native group to be faced with forced dispossession, their legal and political struggles, which went all the way to the U.S. Supreme Court, were among the most widely publicized. Arguments produced by and about the Cherokees are the most fully documented and representative example of how rhetorics of imperium in imperio, which had been central to Revolutionary-era debates about the nature of sovereignty and the challenges of federalism, came to inform discussions of Native nationhood and Indian Removal in nineteenth-century America.

Through my reading of these debates, in this chapter I chart the ways in which rhetorics of imperium in imperio were adopted and adapted by proponents of Removal in response to the ratification of the Cherokee Constitution of 1827 and by Cherokee leaders and their white American supporters. I uncover two competing visions of imperium in imperio that circulated in this context: (1) a binary opposition of two sovereign powers occupying and vying for supremacy in the same geopolitical space, as argued by proponents of Removal, and (2) the multiple, contiguous, and sometimes overlapping sovereignties and political allegiances proposed by Principal Chief John Ross, Elias Boudinot, John Ridge, and other Cherokee spokespeople. The first interpretation reveals a growing emphasis on territoriality in American conceptions of U.S. nationhood and sovereignty, driven in part by Indigenous land claims, but also by a desire to code Indigenous nations as nonterritorial or moveable polities whose political status was not dependent on territorial possession. The interpretation of imperium in imperio offered by Cherokee leaders focused not on issues of identity, but on supporting their political and territorial claims while acknowledging the multiple individual and collective political allegiances of Native nations. The debates over Removal constituted a flashpoint in which Ross, Boudinot, and others were forced to reconsider the relationship between land, nationhood, and sovereignty. After it was forcibly dispossessed of its lands in the East, the Cherokee Nation continued to grapple with rhetorics of imperium in imperio as its leaders negotiated their political future with the Old Settlers in what would later be called Indian Territory.

In each of these instances, imperium in imperio proved a flexible rhetorical device, capable of sustaining varied and sometimes contradictory arguments about sovereignty, political allegiance, and national space. During the debates surrounding the Cherokee cases, rhetorics of imperium in imperio engaged established legal discourses and tapped into widely held cultural fears that federalism had not addressed fully. The arguments were legal in nature, yet were not wholly *about* the law. Rather they brought a legal trope, which had proven useful in the conceptualization and management of the diverse and widespread British Empire, to bear on the multinational nature of the North American continent. The two formulations of divided sovereignty examined in this chapter helped to set the terms for various engagements between the United States and other groups that claimed national status. The Cherokee Constitution of 1827 is of particular importance to this study because it stands at the beginning of a century-long struggle in which Native nations, African Americans, and certain immigrant groups reworked America's founding documents in their attempts to force the United States to deal with them on political rather than racial terms.

Constituting the Cherokee Nation

The Cherokee Nation of the early nineteenth century faced unique political challenges and opportunities, engaging in broad debates about the definition of nationhood and the nature of sovereignty and political allegiance. The territorial and political claims of Indigenous peoples predated those of the individual states and the U.S. federal government, yet Native and U.S. conceptions of nationhood were produced in dialogue with one another. The recognition of Native political and territorial sovereignty, while certainly far from universal, was of strategic value for the fledgling United States and helped to solidify its own position as a sovereign nation that engaged with and was recognized by other nations. The Cherokee Nation, with which the United States negotiated numerous treaties, outlined its status as a sovereign state in its 1827 Constitution.[10] This document, which was modeled in part on the U.S. Constitution, offered a clear statement of territorial sovereignty that reaffirmed Cherokee landholdings and pressured the silences of the U.S. document on issues of citizenship, Native sovereignty, and territoriality. In addition to establishing the boundaries of the nation, the 1827 Constitution worked to articulate the relationship of the Cherokee Nation to the United States, a vision of imperium in imperio in which the two polities were imagined as having contiguous borders and close political ties while maintaining their geographic and political distinctness. This document is the first written constitution ratified by a Native nation and the first of a number of constitutions and foundational documents drafted by various populations in the nineteenth century that sought to gain political traction vis-à-vis the United States.

American Indian polities were unique from African American and immigrant populations because of their status as Indigenous peoples who occupied the lands over which they claimed jurisdiction and because they asserted nation-to-nation relationships with the United States. Following British precedent, the emergent U.S. federal government's recognition of the sovereignty of American Indians and the validity of their land claims through treaties was a matter of expediency and necessity. Treaty making was governed by the material and political realities facing the United States, which was limited in its ability to engage in sustained military efforts. According to President George Washington's secretary of war, Henry Knox, treaty negotiations and the recognition of American Indians' sovereignty functioned to appease Indian peoples and avoid costly wars.[11] Vine Deloria Jr. and David E. Wilkins assert that at the time the U.S. Constitution was ratified, "Indian tribes, as independent sovereigns, were wholly free to align themselves with any sovereign they wished to or to remain nonaligned if they so chose."[12] They note that England and Spain were seeking to align themselves with powerful American Indian confederacies and that the United States did not occupy a "position of primacy among the sovereigns competing for midcontinent Indian allegiance."[13] Creating and honoring treaties represented an attempt to prevent other nations from involving themselves in relations between the United States and Native peoples. Deloria and Wilkins contend that the "opinions of foreign nations at the abrogation of Indian treaties would have provided the European nations with the excuse they needed to meddle in American affairs."[14] American Indian sovereignty and U.S. federal sovereignty were arguably mutually reinforcing during the late eighteenth century and into the nineteenth. For the fledgling United States, treaty negotiations with Native polities functioned as proof of mutual recognition and, as Mark Rifkin suggests, an endorsement of the primacy of federal power.[15] Seen in this light, the recognition of Native nationhood through treaty negotiations lent support to U.S. internal sovereignty and its external sovereignty vis-à-vis European nations. As part of establishing the external sovereignty of the U.S. federal government, Native polities were referenced by the United States as existing nations with which they could treat, not as "new" states emerging from within the United States. Yet, as Fay Yarbrough has suggested, nineteenth-century American racial hierarchies began to group American Indian peoples with African Americans as "one group united by their nonwhiteness."[16] Because of the slippage between the terms *race* and *nation*, this rhetoric circulated alongside and inflected representations of Native nationhood, leading to the conclusion that there was a qualitative difference between the U.S. nation and the "savage" Indian nations in terms of their behavior and political capacity.[17]

Before moving on, I want to examine the nuances of terms such as *sovereignty* and *nationhood* when discussing American Indian political life in the eighteenth and nineteenth centuries. Scholars such as Eric Cheyfitz and Mark Rifkin read Native nationhood as produced by interactions with the U.S. state, emerging through processes of "translation" and "imperial interpellation," wherein Native political culture was subsumed as part of a process that ultimately reinforced U.S. land claims. Rifkin writes, "Native peoples' categorization as 'nations' seems at worst to be merely a conceit to manage jurisdictional conflict by enabling sale and at best legally to recognize the right to sell as opposed to the right to stay."[18] Such a reading dovetails with historical studies of the Cherokees that emphasize a binary opposition between traditionalists (aligned with prenational political practices) and assimilationists (linked with nationalism).[19] The work of Cheyfitz, Rifkin, and Theda Perdue suggests that it is important to recognize discourses of sovereignty and nationhood as historically and culturally contingent and deeply bound up with the forces of imperialist power and with various forces in nineteenth-century Cherokee culture. Daniel Heath Justice and Joshua B. Nelson offer an alternative perspective, challenging the assumption that nationalism was diametrically opposed to traditional Cherokee political structures. They emphasize the strategic value of the rhetorics of Native nationhood that were employed by Cherokee leaders John Ross, Elias Boudinot, and others as part of their arguments for Cherokee sovereignty. In *Progressive Traditions*, Nelson classifies nationalism as a "necessary adaptation to historical circumstances attended by both successes and failures as it drew from, improved on, and betrayed traditions" (138). To this I would add that in a period characterized by imperialist expansion and the dominance of Westphalian constructions of nation-state sovereignty, rhetorics of nationhood provided a point of entrance into an international conversation about political culture and territoriality rather than a "domestic" one about race. Engaging rhetorics of nationhood allowed Cherokee leaders to assert their sovereignty and land claims and to force representatives of the United States to deal with them as a legitimate (if, in the eyes of some, inferior) political institution rather than as a racial group.

In addition to complicating the binary of traditionalists and assimilationists, works such as those by Justice and Nelson question familiar readings of nineteenth-century Cherokee politics that linked nationalism with a "mixed-blood" elite and traditional Cherokee political culture with "full-bloods." They challenge the utility of terms such as "mixed-blood" and "full-blood" to describe the political perspectives of nineteenth-century Cherokee people and, on a broader level, ask us to reconsider commonly held assumptions about the connection between blood quantum and political perspective among the nineteenth-century Cherokees.[20] Nelson reminds us that while not all Cherokees supported the move to a centralized national authority, "[a]s a widespread effort to retain independent control over society and land, it required input and consent from many quarters of the Cherokee social and political spectrums."[21] As Justice and Nelson assert, bicultural or mixed-blood Cherokees such as Ross, who was principal chief from 1828 to 1866, were a driving force in shaping Cherokee political culture during the first half of the nineteenth century, but they were not, as Georgia governor Wilson Lumpkin and others argued, demagogues who sought to deceive Cherokee traditionalists and "full-bloods." The race-based arguments of Georgia's leaders reveal efforts to territorialize Native peoples by reading them in racial rather than political terms. Although nineteenth-century critics seized on the fact that Ross was "only one-eighth Cherokee by the racist blood quantum standards of the day" and was actively engaged in many Anglo-American cultural practices, Justice writes that Ross enjoyed the support of a majority of the Cherokee Nation during his years as principal chief, support that included "the mass of fullbloods and ceremonial traditionalists" (*Our Fire Survives*, 69). Thus, while the political thought of Ross and other bicultural Cherokees was shaped by a variety of influences and may not reflect the full spectrum of perspectives held by Cherokees in the early nineteenth century, it did, particularly in Ross's case, reflect a view that had widespread support, and Ross had a mandate to govern. Justice also highlights what he calls the "Chickamauga rhetoric" (56) of Chief Ross as part of his larger argument that Cherokee literature, including works produced on behalf of the Cherokee Nation in the context of Removal, is "deeply rooted in Indigenousness" (13).[22]

While Georgia's authorities warned of the emergence of a new state in the 1820s, the Cherokee Nation had a much longer history and went through a number of profound political changes in the first few decades of the nineteenth century. The Cherokee Nation that Principal Chief John Ross led was a diverse group of people who had historically lived in what would become Tennessee, North and South Carolina, Georgia, and Alabama. When Europeans first arrived in North America, the Cherokees inhabited a space that encompassed more than 124,000 square miles. Over time, the Cherokees ceded significant portions of their land to the United States, and by 1819, the Cherokees claimed only about 17,000 square miles of land. It is difficult to pinpoint the precise political beginnings of the Cherokee Nation, in part because of various (and sometimes conflicting) definitions of nationhood. The Cherokees were discussed as a nation in eighteenth-century treaties made with the United States, including the 1785 Treaty of Hopewell, a point that Cherokee leaders cited in their dealings with federal and state authorities. However, historian

William McLoughlin argues that the Cherokees "did not think of themselves as a nation in 1776 or in 1789," a point that presumes a political and territorial conception of the nation-state. Rather, he claims that they saw themselves as a community, a "people united by language, customs, and kinship."[23] McLoughlin traces the beginnings of Cherokee nationhood to the 1794 reunification of the tribe and its political reorganization during the first Removal crisis of 1806–1809. It was in 1794 that the Cherokees formed their National Council and created the positions of principal and second principal chief. McLoughlin highlights the redefinition of Cherokee citizenship in 1809 as a key moment in the development of the Cherokee Nation. Membership in the Cherokee Nation had been linked initially to cultural affiliation and involvement in treaty negotiations. After the year 1809, Cherokee citizenship was defined more territorially and linked to place of residence. To be members of the Cherokee Nation, individuals had to reside within the established limits of the Cherokees' traditional homelands.[24] This shift coincided with territorial discourses of American nationhood, which were increasingly emphasizing geographic concerns and the nation as a bounded space. In 1817, the Cherokees established a republic with a bicameral legislature that included the National Council and a newly formed National Committee, a move that made their nation more closely resemble U.S. political culture. The Cherokee Constitution of 1827 outlined Cherokee constructions of nationhood, sovereignty, and citizenship for its members and communicated their national status to others.

The Cherokee Constitution drew inspiration from the U.S. Constitution and those of individual states, such as Georgia, but offered a strong statement of territorial sovereignty that challenged Georgia's assertion of its own territorial boundaries in its 1798 constitution.[25] Unlike the U.S. Constitution, which opens with a discussion of the three branches of government, the Cherokee Constitution immediately defined the nation's territory. In Article 1, the Cherokee Constitution established the physical boundaries of the Cherokee Nation in relation to the United States: "The boundaries of this nation embracing the lands solemnly guaranteed and reserved forever to the Cherokee Nation by the treaties concluded with the United States is as follows, and which shall forever hereafter remain unalterably the same."[26] This article foregrounded the importance of land rights and responded to the first article of Georgia's most recent constitution. Article 1, section 23, of the 1798 Georgia State Constitution, which delineated Georgia's territorial boundaries, also looked forward to "an extension of settlement and extinguishment of Indian claims in and to the vacant territory of this State to the east and north of the said river Chatahoochee" and envisioned a future in which Georgia would possess all the land within its putative borders (including that claimed by the Cherokees).[27]

The Cherokee Constitution rewrote that imagined future, contending that the Cherokee Nation would not relinquish its territorial claims and trying to forestall further encroachments. In a historical moment in which the Cherokees were experiencing pressure to cede additional lands, the opening of the Cherokee Constitution was an attempt to maintain the territorial integrity of the nation and speak back to key U.S. federal and state documents.

In addition to stressing the Cherokee Nation's territorial sovereignty, the Cherokee Constitution also challenged the representations of Native polities in both the U.S. Constitution and the 1798 Georgia constitution, adopting and adapting their form and language to make them speak differently on the subject of Native nationhood. Through its reference to the history of treaty making, Article 1 of the 1827 Constitution not only articulated the physical boundaries of the nation, but also insisted on the nation-to-nation relationship between the United States and the Cherokee Nation. It recast the U.S. Constitution's commerce clause, which offered an oft-debated reference to "foreign nations," "several states," and "Indian tribes" that was interpreted by supporters of Indian Removal to distinguish Native peoples from both foreign nations and domestic states and represent them as an internal racial group.[28] Through its assertion of sovereign nationhood, the Cherokee Constitution clarified the position of Native nations vis-à-vis the United States and individual states as that of foreign nation-states that are closely related to the United States by virtue of the treaty relationship. Likewise, the 1827 Constitution reworked the references to "Indian claims" in the opening of Georgia's constitution. The Cherokee Constitution's framers refigured generic references to "Indian tribes" and "Indian claims" and replaced them with a vision of a tribally specific and sovereign *nation* in order to relate to federal and state authorities on political terms rather than as a racialized other.

The Cherokee Constitution also delineated the conditions for membership in that nation, a subject on which the U.S. Constitution was relatively silent. The Cherokee Constitution fused constructions of citizenship based on place of birth and residence with those that focused on lineal descent. While membership in the nation was limited to "descendants of Cherokee men by all free women, except the African race" and "the posterity of Cherokee women by all free men," citizenship was explicitly linked with residence within the borders of the nation.[29] Fay A. Yarbrough argues that the "Cherokee regulation of citizenship and intermarriage . . . reveals Cherokee prejudices toward people of African descent."[30] She claims that in the nineteenth century, Cherokees employed racial ideologies to distinguish themselves from other groups in order to maintain their national sovereignty. The focus on territory in the constitution was part of this effort to challenge representations of Cherokees, and Native peoples writ large, as members of an inferior race. The 1827 Constitution states that "whenever any such citizen or citizens shall remove with their effects out of the limits of this Nation, and become citizens of any other government, all their rights and privileges as citizens of this nation shall cease; Provided nevertheless, That the Legislature shall have power to re-admit by law to all the rights of citizenship any such person or persons, who may at any time desire to return to the Nation on their memorializing the General Council for such readmission."[31] Here citizens are imagined as part of a volitional agreement wherein they can relinquish their Cherokee citizenship and become members of another polity (presumably the United States). Yet, this passage also raises the possibility that such individuals may return to the geopolitical space of the Cherokee Nation and to its community of allegiance. It suggests that Cherokee sovereignty is envisioned as bounded by the territorial limits of the nation. Citizenship is connected to residence, and leaving the Cherokee Nation physically with one's "effects" is rhetorically linked with exiting the political community and the nation's jurisdiction. This formulation of external sovereignty mirrors that of the United States during this period, which did not assume that its jurisdiction followed its citizens when they traveled beyond its territorial borders. It also echoes Vattel's conception of "states bound by unequal alliance," the idea that nations may enter into agreements with stronger states for the purposes of obtaining protection without relinquishing their internal sovereignty.[32] In this way, the Cherokee Constitution emphasized that the nature of the relationship between the Cherokee Nation and the U.S. government was characterized by mutual obligation and was one in which the sovereignty of both states was acknowledged.

As Cherokee leaders refashioned their nation in the early nineteenth century, they crafted a particular vision of divided sovereignty that echoed the theories of Vattel in *The Law of Nations*. The 1827 Constitution represented the Cherokee Nation and the United States as contiguous polities that, while unequal in strength, nevertheless recognized one another's sovereign status. According to this formulation, the Cherokee Nation exercised internal sovereignty over the land and people within its borders, yet imagined those borders to be somewhat porous, with Cherokee citizens able to leave and, in some cases, to return to the political community. The suggestion of limited extraterritorial sovereignty aligned the Cherokee Nation with the United States by mirroring the U.S. definition of sovereignty and by framing the two nations as bound together in a relationship in which the United States traded its protection for the honor and friendship of the Cherokees. The state of Georgia, however, was effectively written out of this relationship. In her reading of the Cherokee Constitution of 1827, Cheryl Walker claims that this document was "[d]esigned to give the Cherokees a legal basis upon which to remain independent" and "situated the nation as an 'imperium in imperio'—a state within a state—much like the status of the American colonies before the Revolution."[33] The Cherokees' vision of imperium in imperio, however, differed greatly from those that would emerge from Georgia's leaders and other supporters of Indian Removal policies. Outraged by the ratification of the Cherokee Constitution, many supporters of Indian Removal began to talk about the Cherokees in *national* terms—as a threatening, racialized polity—and appealed to arguments about the indivisibility of sovereignty that had informed British support of Parliament in the pre-Revolutionary debates.

Imperium in Imperio and the Shifting Nature of Sovereignty

During what Maureen Konkle calls "the most heated years of their struggle against removal," the period from 1826 to 1837, Cherokee spokespeople, along with Georgia's political leaders and the U.S. federal government, engaged in vigorous debates about sovereignty, nationhood, and Indigenous land claims.[34] Some interpreters of the commerce clause granted the federal government the exclusive right to treat with Native tribes, while Southern supporters of Indian Removal framed the management of tribes that existed "within" their borders as a facet of state sovereignty.

The ratification of the Cherokee Constitution in 1827 brought these issues to the forefront of American public argument. Georgia's leaders framed the Cherokee Nation as a new and anomalous state that threatened the American body politic from within. Their arguments regarding the *newness* of the Cherokee state were of particular importance, as this allowed them to argue that the existence of the Cherokee Nation violated Article IV of the U.S. Constitution and warranted a federal response. Representations of the Cherokees as a threatening imperium circulated in regional and national publications and exposed rifts between state and federal authorities on issues of sovereignty and jurisdiction. Pro-Removal arguments worked to attenuate the territorial and political claims of the Cherokees and rewrite their relationship with the United States from affiliation to opposition. The Cherokees' lawyers and advocates seized on rhetorics of imperium in imperio as a means of exposing the sectional and class-based dimensions of these pro-Removal arguments, seeking to reveal the ways in which such arguments attempted to manipulate political and geographic space to recode the Cherokee Nation as *within* the state of Georgia. Throughout these debates, the various parties offered radically different interpretations of imperium in imperio that served to further complicate, rather than clarify, existing definitions of sovereignty.

Debates between state and federal authorities over land issues, treaties, and other dealings with American Indian tribes had flared up periodically in the years following the ratification of the U.S. Constitution. The framers of the U.S. Constitution had recognized that it would be politically problematic to have individual states making their own treaties with Native nations, and so they drafted the commerce clause as a means of classifying treaty making and diplomacy with Native peoples as the sole prerogative of the federal government. Moreover, creating and honoring treaties was an attempt to prevent other nations from involving themselves in relations between the United States and Native peoples. In the wake of the War of 1812, in which the United States claimed victory over Britain and its American Indian allies, and the political ascension of states' rights supporters such as John C. Calhoun and Andrew Jackson, several states, particularly those in the Southeast, began to challenge the sovereign status afforded to Native communities and the exclusive right of the federal government to negotiate with them. Southern advocates of Removal, such as Alabama Supreme Court judge John M. Taylor, defined "commerce" narrowly, as a relationship "which consists in trade or traffic," and challenged the equation of the phrase "Indian tribes" with foreign states. In Taylor's reading of the U.S. Constitution, the fact that the president had never appointed ambassadors to Native communities challenged the arguments that framed them as federally recognized nations.[35] Thus, while one reading of the commerce clause reinforced a hierarchical relationship between the federal government and the governments of its subordinate states, Southern supporters of states' rights emphasized a reading in which the federal government had been granted certain limited powers (such as regulating trade with Native peoples) to protect the interests of the sovereign states.

Of the struggles between individual states and the federal government over issues related to Native peoples, those involving the state of Georgia and the Cherokee Nation gained the most attention during the early nineteenth century. Conflicts over land escalated during and after a series of land deals made between Georgia and the federal government, which resulted in the sale of Georgia's western lands. In the years after the Revolution, Georgia's territory had extended to the Mississippi River, but like other states, such as North Carolina, Georgia was unable to settle and defend the western part of its landholdings. Following several attempts to promote the formation of counties there, Georgia governor George Mathews signed the Yazoo Act in 1795. This land transfer, often referred to as the Yazoo land fraud or Yazoo land scandal, included the sale of 35 million acres to four companies for $500,000 (which, according to Stuart Banner, works out to less than "a penny and a half per acre"). There were protests and petitions circulated against the sale because of the corruption involved, but it went through despite the controversy. The sale was revoked in 1796, but as Banner has noted, by that time much of the land had been sold to other parties, who continued to claim the rights to the land despite the repeal of the original sale.[36] In 1802, Yazoo lands were ceded to the federal government for $1.25 million. As part of what became known as the Compact of 1802, the federal government also promised the state of Georgia that it would remove the Creeks and Cherokees—thus opening up new lands for settlement—and extinguish their land titles "as soon as it could be done peacefully and upon favorable terms."[37] As the state's population increased, Georgia became impatient for the extinguishment of Native land titles and argued that the federal government had not fulfilled its promises to promote and protect the rights of Georgia and its citizens. Issues surrounding Georgia's land claims surfaced in the Yazoo case, *Fletcher v. Peck* (1810), and in later debates about the forced dispossession of the Cherokees as Georgia pressured the U.S. government to honor its 1802 agreement. Supporters of Removal in Georgia asserted their claim to Cherokee lands by right of compact, discovery, and conquest, framing the Cherokees as mere "occupants" of the land.[38]

While Georgians used various legal justifications to support their claims, after the ratification of the Cherokee Constitution in 1827, they turned to rhetorics of imperium in imperio with increasing frequency in order to generate fears of conflict and division and to subvert Cherokee political and territorial claims. Wilson Lumpkin, who served both as Georgia's governor and as a congressman during his long political career, seemingly acknowledged the sovereignty of the Cherokee Nation in an 1828 speech before Congress, but framed that sovereignty as at war with the sovereignty of both the United States and Georgia. In the wake of Georgia's decision to extend its jurisdiction over the Cherokee Nation, he described the situation within the borders of the Cherokee Nation as an "anomaly," in which "three separate and distinct governments, exercis[e] sovereignty of jurisdiction under conflicting laws, enacted by three separate and distinct legislatures, over the same people, and at the same time, [and] in some cases these three distinct sovereign legislatures have enacted laws upon the same identical subjects, which laws do not harmonize in their provisions."[39] Here Lumpkin offered a Hydra-like image of three competing governments trying to operate within a single space, while eliding issues of jurisdiction and the separation of powers between state, federal, and Cherokee authorities. He cited as an example the conflicting laws about the sale of alcohol in the Cherokee Nation.

For Lumpkin it was enough to say that three polities claimed the right to pass laws over a particular space; he did not interrogate the question of which polity had the right to make laws for the space in question. Rather, in a move that connected the Cherokee Nation with the ancient Israelites, he argued that "these unfortunate people" should be told that Removal is inevitable so "[t]hat they may send their Calebs and Joshuas to search out and view the promised land, for situated *as they now are, and where they are*, there is no rest for the sole [of] an Indian foot."[40] Linking the Cherokees' current situation with the Egyptian bondage of the Israelites and with nomadism, Lumpkin ignored Cherokee links to lands in the East and proposed Removal as the mutually beneficial solution to the "anomaly" of the Cherokee Nation. In her reading of the rhetoric surrounding Indian Removal, Maureen Konkle has argued that the Cherokees had to constantly combat the historicizing tendencies of Removal supporters, who characterized them as occupying a "timeless prepolitical state of nature."[41]

However, discussions of a Cherokee imperium depended for their rhetorical force on the newness of the Cherokee Nation, which was depicted as an unconstitutional state that arose from within the state of Georgia and, as such, had no claims to the territory that it currently occupied. In an address to the Georgia legislature in 1828, Governor John Forsyth characterized the Cherokee Nation as "a government professing to be independent" that had recently emerged "in defiance of the authority of Georgia, Tennessee, Alabama, and North Carolina."[42] He presented the Cherokee Nation as a threatening and subversive imperium, imitating an independent nation while lacking valid claims of sovereignty. In later recollections on the Removal debates, Lumpkin remarked of the Cherokee Nation, "Their very first attempt at sovereignty and independence, as a state, nation, and people brought them into direct conflict and collision with not only the several State governments in whose limits they sojourned, but irreconcilable conflict and collision with the intercourse laws of the United States which so long had shielded and protected them from the operations of the laws of the States in which they dwelt."[43] In a kind of rhetorical sleight of hand, temporality informed arguments about geopolitical relationships. Lumpkin and other pro-Removal politicians used the charge that the Cherokees constituted a *new* nation, one that had developed after the formation of the state of Georgia, to support the assertion that the Cherokee Nation arose from within Georgia's territorial limits. Georgia was imagined to predate the Cherokee Nation—as a nation—which then made the emergence of a Cherokee republic a dangerous and unconstitutional division of sovereignty. As Francis Paul Prucha writes, after Congress did not respond to the ratification of the Cherokee Constitution, "Georgia finally began to move against the Cherokees, contending that it could not abide an *imperium in imperio* within the state."[44]

Charges of a Cherokee imperium were echoed in Southern periodicals, which drummed up fears of internal division and framed the issue as a conflict between a legitimate state and a pretender. An article from the *Petersburg Intelligencer* that was reprinted in the Milledgeville *Southern Recorder* declared: "Common sense can never tolerate a savage *imperium* in a civilized Commonwealth—and it is absurd to urge in argument the *natural rights* of the Indians."⁴⁵ Similar sentiments were published in the *Richmond Enquirer* and republished in the *Southern Recorder*. An article entitled "The Georgia Question" referred to the Cherokees as a "pretended *imperium in imperio*," a community within the territorial borders of the state of Georgia that was trying to pass as a government.⁴⁶ The article suggested that such a move could not be allowed and required the state of Georgia to exercise its jurisdiction over this "pretended" nation. The *Federal Union*, also published in Milledgeville, Georgia, included a discussion of a Cherokee imperium that was originally published in the 31 March 1832 issue of the *Washington Globe*. The excerpt ended with a series of questions that were crucial to the conflict between the Cherokee Nation, the state of Georgia, and the federal government: "Can they [the Cherokees] expect to maintain their present position? To establish an independent government, having undefined and undefinable relations with the State of Georgia? To add another *imperium in imperio* to our complicated system?"⁴⁷ The anonymous author suggested that while the relation of state and federal governments constitutes an imperium in imperio, sovereignty could not be further divided to include Native nations arising from "within" the states, whose relationship to the states that surround them is essentially unknowable. For this author, it was the ambiguity posed by Native nations such as the Cherokees that threatened to destabilize an already tenuous system.

Rhetorics of a Cherokee imperium also appeared in periodicals with Northern readers and, in some cases, national circulations. These accounts, in publications such as the *North American Review* and the *Western Recorder*, described how opponents of the Cherokee Nation drew on the perception of an imperium as a political monstrosity and a threat to national sovereignty.⁴⁸ An article published in the *Columbian Star* entitled "Indian Colonization" on 12 September 1829 expanded on fears of political "solecism" and offered a grim vision of what would happen if the Cherokees retained their current geographic and political status:

> Removal to some distant point, and concentration, as far as possible, into one body, appears to be the only means which can guard the Indian name and interest against total extinction. Experience has demonstrated, that for them to remain under the jurisdiction, and within the limits of any of the States, is inevitable annihilation of their name and specific character. At the same time, their location within

the States, as a distinct, independent nation, would form a solecism in politics. What would result from the existence of two or more separate, sovereign bodies, contiguous to each other, and resident upon the same soil? The destruction of one or the other, would be the ultimate consequence.[49]

In a paradoxical move, the author represented the Cherokee Nation and the state of Georgia as both "contiguous" (neighboring) and "resident upon the same soil." The Cherokees were thus framed as both separate from and competing with the state of Georgia for land and resources. While this anonymous author claimed to be concerned with preventing the "annihilation" of the Cherokees, his statements also suggest an interest in making the Cherokees more easily governable. In order to better regulate the behavior of the Cherokees, he argued that they should be removed somewhere beyond the jurisdiction of any U.S. state and "concentrate[d] . . . into one body." In language that resonated with that of the African colonization movement, this writer argued that Native peoples needed to be consolidated so that they could be saved from "extinction" and brought more fully under federal control.[50] Many Indians in this case would become one Indian, a body whose behavior could be managed and regulated more fully. This was not an argument for the destruction of the Cherokees, the author claimed, but an argument for the creation and maintenance of a particular kind of Indian subject, who would no longer be a threat to Georgia's sovereignty.

Echoing the charges made by Georgia politicians and their supporters in the press, members of Andrew Jackson's administration also drew on the rhetoric of imperium in imperio to challenge the Cherokees' political actions as the creation of a new state and to subvert their land claims as Indigenous people. Federal authorities were quick to blame the Cherokees for drafting a written constitution and forming a republican government, acts which, according to Secretary of War John Eaton and other members of the Jackson administration, revealed their intent to create an imperium in imperio. In a June 1829 letter to the Cherokee delegation to Washington, which consisted of Chief John Ross, Richard Taylor, Edward Gunter, and William S. Coody, Eaton criticized the Cherokees for threatening the sovereign rights of the state of Georgia: "The course you have pursued of establishing an independent, substantive, government, within the territorial limits of the state of Georgia, adverse to her will, and contrary to her consent, has been the immediate cause, which has induced her, to depart from the forbearance she has so long practiced; and in virtue of her authority, as a sovereign, independent, state, to extend over your country, her legislative enactments."[51] Glossing over Georgia's long history of attempts to effect the removal of the Cherokees, Eaton characterized the extension of state jurisdiction as a response to the Cherokees' formation of an "independent, substantive, government, within the territorial limits of the state." The Cherokee Nation, he argued, was formed without the "consent" of the state and had caused Georgia to act to maintain its sovereign authority. Eaton went on to say that the federal government could not intervene on behalf of any group that attempted to form a "separate government within the limits of a state."[52] He reduced a complicated historical relationship between the Cherokees, the U.S. federal government, and several states into a binary opposition between the Cherokees and the state of Georgia.

Like Eaton, President Jackson alluded to a Cherokee imperium in his annual message to Congress, delivered in December 1829, as part of a larger discussion of the conflict between the Cherokees and the state of Georgia. Jackson devoted significant attention at the beginning of his message to "foreign relations" with countries such as Great Britain and France, while he discussed Native peoples in the context of domestic issues, such as the status of the army. He acknowledged that the "condition and ulterior destiny of the Indian tribes within the limits of some of our States have become objects of much interest and importance," particularly in the cases of tribes located in close proximity to Alabama and Georgia.[53] He noted that these two states claim a form of indivisible sovereignty: "These States, claiming to be the only sovereigns within their territories, extended their laws over the Indians, which induced the latter to call upon the United States for protection" ("President Jackson on Indian Removal," 47). Such protection cannot be offered, he contended, because it would be unconstitutional: "The Constitution declares that 'no new State shall be formed or erected within the jurisdiction of any other State' without the consent of its legislature. If the General Government is not permitted to tolerate the erection of a confederate State within the territory of one of the members of this Union against her consent, much less could it allow a foreign and independent government to establish itself there" (47). Like Georgia's leaders, Jackson drew on rhetorics of imperium in imperio as part of an argument for the *newness* of the Cherokee Nation, a key component of the argument against their territorial claims to the lands that they occupied. The dispossession of Indigenous peoples with a history of occupancy and treaties with the U.S. federal government required such a logical sleight of hand. Moreover, while Jackson sometimes discussed Native peoples in the context of domestic rather than international issues, here he classified them as a "foreign and independent government," which suggests the dual position that American Indian peoples were seen to occupy in relation to the United States: they were both domestic and foreign.

Jackson's characterization of the Cherokee Nation as a new and threatening imperium also revealed internal divisions between Northern and Southern states. In Jackson's version of American political history, Georgia entered the Union as a sovereign state with complete control of the land within its chartered limits and should not be made to tolerate any "new" polities. He then suggested what might happen in Northern states if the Cherokees were allowed to maintain their own government. Georgia, he claimed, should not be forced to tolerate a situation that Maine or New York would resist:

> There is no constitutional, conventional, or legal provision which allows them [Georgia] less power over the Indians within their borders than is possessed by Maine or New York. Would the people of Maine permit the Penobscot tribe to erect an independent government within their State? And unless they did would it not be the duty of the General Government to support them in resisting such a measure? Would the people of New York permit each remnant of the Six Nations within her borders to declare itself an independent people under the protection of the United States? Could the Indians establish a separate republic on each of their reservations in Ohio? And if they were so disposed would it be the duty of this Government to protect them in the attempt? If the principle involved in the obvious answer to these questions be abandoned, it will follow that the objects of this Government are reversed, and that it has become a part of its duty to aid in destroying the States which it was established to protect. ("President Jackson on Indian Removal," 47–48)

Jackson argued that Northern states would not tolerate Native nations within their own borders and implied that they were now defending the Cherokees because of sectional prejudices rather than because of a belief in Native sovereignty. The only solution, for Jackson, was the removal of American Indians east of the Mississippi so that they could form a nation in the West, outside of what he imagined to be the combined jurisdictions of the sovereign states. Such a move would help to allay some of the sectional tensions that were threatening to divide the U.S. nation. While Jackson did not explicitly use the phrase imperium in imperio, his arguments depended on its logic for their rhetorical force.

Appeals based on imperium in imperio informed the congressional debates over the Indian Removal Act the following year, as advocates of Removal reiterated their claims that the Cherokees were attempting to create a new and unconstitutional state within the boundaries of the state of Georgia. According to Theda Perdue and Michael D. Green, Jackson made Indian Removal a priority for Congress, and the issue was taken up first by the Senate. Senator Theodore Frelinghuysen of New Jersey was one of the leading voices opposing the Removal bill, and his arguments were echoed by other Northern senators, such as Peleg Sprague from Maine and Asher Robbins from Rhode Island. Not surprisingly, John Forsyth from Georgia was one of the staunchest supporters of the bill. After a debate that spanned several weeks, the Senate approved the bill by a margin of twenty-eight to nineteen with most senators voting along party lines. Debates in the House drew on many of the same arguments, but as Perdue and Green suggest, supporters of Removal "followed Forsyth's lead but with added emphasis on the unconstitutionality of *imperium in imperio*, the erection of a Cherokee state in Georgia."[54] While the vote was closer than it had been in the Senate, the ultimate outcome was the same: the bill passed the House.

The William Penn essays, written by Jeremiah Evarts, an editor and a member of the American Board of Commissioners for Foreign Missions, under the pseudonym "William Penn," played a key role in the congressional debates and challenged the characterization of the Cherokee Nation as a threatening imperium. Perdue and Green note that during the Senate debates, a bound volume of Evarts's essays was given to every senator and particularly informed the statements of Frelinghuysen.[55] The twenty-four essays—originally published in the *National Intelligencer* from 5 August through 19 December 1829, and reprinted in a variety of other venues and in pamphlet form—expressed Evarts's opposition to Removal and to the Jackson administration's treatment of the Cherokees. He also tried to convince the general public that arguments about a Cherokee imperium were merely a ploy to cheat the Cherokees out of their lands. In No. XXIII, Evarts dubbed the charges of imperium in imperio "altogether chimerical":

> It has been alleged, that great inconveniences will be experienced, by having an *imperium in imperio*;—a separate, independent community surrounded by our own citizens. But in what do these frightful inconveniences consist? A little pacific community of Indians, living among the mountains, attending to their own concerns, and treating all who pass through their borders with kindness and hospitality, is surely no very great cause of alarm. If there were a territory in possession of a powerful and hostile nation, and in the immediate vicinity of our white settlements, where our rivals and enemies might shelter themselves, while plotting against our peace, and where fugitives from justice could find a refuge, there might be some reason for apprehension; though even these circumstances would never excuse a violation of treaties. But the Cherokees can never have any interest adverse to our national prosperity. They have solemnly agreed to live under our protection, and to deliver up fugitives from justice. We have by treaty a free navi-

gation of their waters, and a free passage through their country. What more can we reasonably desire?⁵⁶

Evarts did not dispute the argument that the Cherokee Nation constituted an imperium (defined here as a "separate, independent community"), but rather asserted that this situation did not present "inconveniences" for the state of Georgia.⁵⁷ Evarts emphasized that the Cherokees were not taking up valuable land in the center of Georgia, but live "among the mountains" and keep to themselves. Evarts further asserted that while the Cherokees did not interfere in the affairs of Georgia, they also did not limit travel within their borders and assisted the state in capturing fugitives. All of this supported his claim that the Cherokees "can never have any interest adverse to our national prosperity" and, in fact, historically had worked to promote it. Evarts framed the Cherokees as maintaining a kind of collective allegiance to and reciprocity with the United States, arguing that they "live under our protection."

In these essays, Evarts attempted to speak to Southern concerns about territoriality and to resituate the Cherokee Nation as outside of the state of Georgia. He represented the Cherokee Nation as occupying a "remote" corner of Georgia that was not, as Lumpkin had asserted, among the "best land" in the state. Evarts noted that the land in this portion of Georgia was far less valuable and fertile than the territories claimed by white settlers. He emphasized that the Cherokee lands were made up of "mountains and barren tracts" and would be considered "worthless" by all who were familiar with Georgia geography. Thus, although he acknowledged that this land was a "healthful" and desirable place of residence for the Cherokees, it would not be an ideal place for Georgia farmers.⁵⁸ While Governor Lumpkin and other proponents of Removal figured the Cherokees as living in the veritable center of the state of Georgia, blocking Georgians' access to the coast and taking up valuable farmland, Evarts presented the Cherokees' national space as wholly outside of the state. In No. XV, he wrote, "It is not admitted that the Cherokee are now, or ever were, in the State of Georgia."⁵⁹ Evarts's attempts to locate the Cherokees on the margins (rather than in the center) of the state of Georgia and his efforts to question Georgia's valuation of Cherokee land worked to present the Cherokee Nation as outside of, and thus not a threat to, Georgia's sovereignty.

To support the arguments of the William Penn essays, Evarts published other texts that challenged the charge of imperium in imperio and defended Cherokee national sovereignty. One key example, to which a number of prominent white activists attached their signatures, was the 1829 pamphlet *A Brief View of the Present Relations between the Government and People of the United States and the Indians within Our National Limits*. Evarts summarized his earlier arguments and emphasized Georgia's attachment to the rhetoric of imperium in imperio: "Again, it is supposed, that the existence of a little separate community of Indians, living under their own laws, and surrounded by a community of whites, will be fraught with some great and undefined mischief. It is called *an anomaly*, an *imperium in imperio*, and by various other pedantic epithets."[60] He suggested that while the Cherokees are "surrounded by a community of whites," they are not part of it and are subject to laws of their own making. Moreover, Evarts contended that arguments about a Cherokee imperium ignored the realities of Western politics in an attempt to delude the public. He wrote, "And as to the learned chimera of *imperium in imperio*, it is, and always has been, one of the most common things in the world. The whole of modern Germany is nothing else but one specimen after another of *imperium in imperio*. Italy has an abundance of specimens also. As to our own country, we have governments within governments of all sizes, and for all purposes, from a school district to our great federal union."[61] As in the William Penn essays, Evarts did not argue that the Cherokees were not an imperium, but rather that this concept was being willfully manipulated by those who wished for the dispossession of the Cherokees. Imperium in imperio is "one of the most common things in the world," Evarts argued, not an anomaly unique to Native nations. Moreover, he explicitly linked the Cherokees to European nations—and to the United States itself—rather than with other Native peoples or racial groups in order to emphasize their political capacity.

Others suggested that the Cherokee Nation was an extension of, not a threat to, the political culture of the United States. In his memorial to the Georgia Senate in support of the Cherokees, Robert Campbell, a citizen of Georgia, reported hearing from Georgia politicians that "it is contrary to all principle, and cannot be permitted, to allow a government to exist within the territory, and be independent of another government, an *imperium in imperio* as it is termed."[62] Campbell countered this charge with appeals to U.S. political culture and to other historical examples: "What are these United States but an example of *imperium in imperio*? or if they are not, what becomes of all the arguments we have lately heard in support of *states rights* and *state sovereignty*, in support of which they seem willing to jeopardize the safety of this glorious and happy union? How shall we dispose of the historical example of the Republic of St. Marino, which has continued sovereign and independent within the limits of another sovereignty for upwards of one thousand three hundred years?"[63] Campbell deftly deflected any fear of imperium in imperio by suggesting that the United States, particularly as it was imagined by supporters of states' rights (such as Georgia), was itself an example of imperium in imperio. If the Cherokee Nation constituted an imperium, he suggested, it was part of the larger system of divided sovereignty on which U.S. political culture was based. Such a suggestion may have only served to amplify Georgia's concerns about Cherokee nationhood.

The phrase imperium in imperio offered opponents of Removal a rhetorical toehold, a place from which to launch their arguments. An article from *The Spirit of the Pilgrims* in 1830 that was written in response to Lewis Cass's piece in the *North American Review* offered a pointed discussion of the ways in which the Jackson administration had adopted the language of imperium in imperio in its discussions of the Cherokee Nation:

> It appears from the President's message and from a communication of the Secretary of War, that the Cherokees have given special umbrage to the Executive, in consequence of an alleged encroachment upon the constitution of the United States. They are said to have established an independent government within the limits of a sovereign State—an *imperium in imperio*—thus infringing upon that article, which provides that no new State shall be formed within another State. The Cherokee government, therefore, must be abolished.—None but a bad cause would ever have resorted to such a pitiful sophism. *Have not the Cherokees always had an independent government?* If not, who *have* governed them? Have the people of Georgia, or the people of the United States? Surely not. They have been governed by their own laws and their own chiefs. Within a few years, they have *changed the form* of their government; but to pretend that they have now been establishing a government in Georgia—an *imperium in imperio*—when they have merely *changed the form* of a government which they have had and exercised from time immemorial, is preposterous.
>
> But in regard to this *imperium in imperio*—this Gorgon which has of late so marvelously troubled the imaginations of some of our public men, what evils has it hitherto occasioned? For more than forty years, the Cherokees have been at peace with the United States, and are likely to remain so from age to age, unless they are wantonly molested. And if great and distressing evils existed in consequence of their situation in the midst of the whites, *who should remove?* The Georgians, or the Cherokees? The Georgians settled around them, not they in the midst of the Georgians. Hence the Indians are the last that should suffer. There is, however, not the least necessity of collision from the geographical positions of the two parties.[64]

The author summarized the centrality of imperium in imperio to the Removal debate and dismissed such claims as a "pitiful sophism" that ignores the historical presence of the Cherokees and misrepresents a change in governmental form as the emergence of a new state in order to undercut the Cherokee Nation's political and territorial claims. His likening of imperium in imperio to the Gorgon of Greek mythology reveals the ways in which white Georgians conflated divided sovereignty and monstrosity as part of their arguments for Removal. Ultimately, the author concluded that if anyone had formed an imperium, it was the state of Georgia, and thus Georgia, not the Cherokees, should remove. This bold claim suggests the rhetorical flexibility of imperium in imperio and the ways in which it can be employed to serve various political purposes.

Many defenders of the Cherokees concurred that the label of imperium was merely a manipulation of language, a use of what Evarts called "learned and hard names" to subvert the political and territorial claims of the Cherokee Nation. In *Brief View*, Evarts highlighted the "pedantic epithets" used to describe the Cherokees.[65] These recurring references to academic learning and its extreme form, pedantry, suggest that the Cherokees' advocates sought to persuade the general American population by distinguishing their own beliefs, informed by both common sense and benevolent feelings, from the harsh and often manipulative intellectualism of Removal advocates. Debates about the use of Latin reveal that the Cherokees' supporters framed the conflict not merely in political terms—the Cherokee Nation versus the state of Georgia—but also in class-based terms as ordinary people versus the classically educated elite. The cause of the Cherokees was thus suggested to be the cause of the common people who were being threatened by the Southern aristocracy. This characterization also was informed by sectional conflicts over issues of slavery and economics. Discourses of a Cherokee imperium were used by Southern (primarily Georgian) politicians and journalists, and these were presented by white Northern supporters of the Cherokees as another way in which the Southern elites sought to exert their will on a national level.

The legal team hired by the Cherokees to represent their interests in front of the U.S. Supreme Court also engaged rhetorics of imperium in imperio as part of their arguments in favor of the Cherokees' sovereignty, their status as a foreign nation, and their territorial jurisdiction. The arguments made by John Sergeant and William Wirt in the injunction filed against the state of Georgia disputed the notion of a Cherokee imperium by renegotiating the placement of the Cherokee Nation and comparing it to foreign nations like Mexico and Canada. They claimed that, according to the terms of the U.S. Constitution, the Cherokees constituted a "foreign state, not owing allegiance to the United States, nor to any state in this union, nor to any other prince, potentate, or state, other than their own."[66] They cited the eleventh article of the Treaty of Hopewell (1785) as proof that *"the territory of the Cherokee nation is not within the jurisdiction of either of the states or territorial districts of the United States."*[67] Furthermore, Sergeant claimed that since the Cherokees were located within the geographic borders of the United States, but were not a state in the Union, "what then can they be but a foreign state."⁶⁸ Arguments as to the "foreign" nature of the Cherokees were predicated on their political autonomy and spatial understandings of their position vis-à-vis the United States: they were not one of the twenty-four states that comprised the Union, but were a separate nation existing within America's borders. Sergeant located the Cherokee Nation within the borders of the United States, but not within the borders of the state of Georgia. Such a move suggested that the Cherokees were equal to, rather than subordinate to or enclosed by, the state of Georgia.

Echoing some of the dismissals that circulated in the press, Wirt contended that charges of a Cherokee imperium were nothing more than an attempt to manipulate popular opinion through the use of high-flown rhetoric. Rather than using more familiar English phrases, such as "nation within a nation" or "divided sovereignty," supporters of Removal employed Latin, the language traditionally associated with institutional powers—law, medicine, religion—in order to impress on the general population the gravity of the situation in Georgia and to represent the Cherokees as unassimilable. Wirt argued that the use of Latin was intended to dupe the public and obscure the real facts of the case: "Half enlightened persons, who see men only as trees walking, seem to consider this [imperium in imperio] as an unanswerable objection: for no other reason that I can imagine, than that it is expressed in a foreign and learned language which they do not understand; and that men always fancy that there is something unfathomably deep in what lies beyond the reach of their own land. Those, who understand the objection in its true meaning, see that it has no manner of application to the case."⁶⁹ The unenlightened, Wirt claimed, could not answer this charge because they do not readily understand it and are merely impressed by the "foreign and learned" quality of the phrase. The use of Latin and the allusions to British common law and the Imperium Romanum had allowed the state of Georgia, Wirt asserted, to "bewilder twilight intellects" and convince the people that the Cherokees have no legal right to their lands.⁷⁰ Reversing the charges of demagoguery levied against the Cherokees' lawyers and Northern missionaries, Wirt claimed that it was state officials who were trying to manipulate popular opinion. Wirt's statements about the "half enlightened" and the "twilight intellects" served to belittle his political and legal opposition and assert his own, ostensibly more intellectually informed, position. Moreover, as Tim Alan Garrison explains, "The only *imperium in imperio* that would exist in this situation, Wirt charged, would be if the Court allowed Georgia to extend its jurisdiction over the Cherokee Nation."⁷¹

In one of the key moments in this debate, Wirt offered his own definition of an imperium before the U.S. Supreme Court in the case of *Cherokee Nation v. Georgia* (1831). Wirt argued that the charge of imperium in imperio did not apply to the Cherokees and distinguished between divided sovereignty and a smaller nation whose territory was surrounded by that of a larger state:

> *A government* within *a government* does not mean *a state* surrounded *by the territories of another state*, and *yet retaining its separate political character*: for in this there is nothing more incongruous than in the every day's occurrence of a small landholder having his estate surrounded by the lands of his more wealthy neighbour, and yet retaining his separate independence and sovereign right of property.... The *imperium in imperio* has no application to two distinct governments operating at the same time *on separate territories*; for the one *government* is not *within the other government* although the *territory* over which one acts, may be *encircled by the larger territories* of the other. It is the conflict of *two sovereignties on the same territory at the same time*, which is meant by the *imperium in imperio*. Even in this sense, it is no longer a paradox in the United States, for every state exhibits an example of it. But *in this sense*, it has no application to the state of Georgia and the Cherokee nation, for they are *separate sovereignties exerted over separate territories*; and there is therefore no *imperium in imperio* in the case.[72]

In this passage, Wirt worked to correct the perception that two governments existing in geographic proximity—specifically a situation where one government existed within the chartered territory of the other—constituted an imperium in imperio. Such a condition occurs, he claimed, only when there is a contest between sovereignties that occupy the same political space (such as a military coup), not merely when one independent government exists in close proximity to another. Such national spaces could still be considered separate, Wirt asserted, even if one space were contained within the borders of another. He reminded his audience that the United States itself was an example of smaller, weaker powers (states) encircled by a larger national government, a point echoed by many pro-Cherokee journalists.

Despite all of the attempts by the Cherokees' advocates to rhetorically locate the Cherokee Nation outside of the state of Georgia and the United States and to deflect charges of imperium in imperio, Chief Justice John Marshall's decision in *Cherokee Nation v. Georgia* placed the Cherokees (and all American Indian nations) firmly under U.S. jurisdiction. His opinion on the case shares the kind of spatial logic advanced by those who characterized the Cherokee Nation as a threatening imperium:

> The Indian Territory is admitted to compose part of the United States. In all our maps, geographical treatises, histories, and laws, it is so considered. In all our intercourse with foreign nations, in our commercial regulations, in any attempt at intercourse between Indians and foreign nations, they are considered as within the

jurisdictional limits of the United States, subject to many of those restraints which are imposed upon our own citizens. They acknowledge themselves in their treaties to be under the protection of the United States; they admit that the United States shall have the sole and exclusive right of regulating the trade with them, and managing all their affairs as they think proper; and the Cherokees in particular were allowed by the Treaty of Hopewell, which preceded the constitution, "to send a deputy of their choice, whenever they think fit, to Congress." Treaties were made with some tribes by the state of New York under a then unsettled construction of the confederation, by which they ceded all their lands to that state, taking back a limited grant to themselves, in which they admit their dependence.[73]

Here Marshall articulated a particular kind of imperium in imperio specific to Native peoples—the "domestic dependent nation." To support his argument that the Cherokees were a "domestic dependent nation" rather than a foreign state, Marshall explicitly defined *nationhood* in territorial terms. He contended that the Cherokees' territory existed within the boundaries of the United States and "is admitted to compose part of the United States." Marshall alluded to a variety of documentary evidence—maps, treatises, histories, and legal writings—to evoke visual images of the containment of the Cherokees. And, as Priscilla Wald has noted, Marshall used "passive construction" ("is admitted" and "they are considered") to imply an already-formed "consensus" on the status of American Indian peoples.[74] In contrast with the distinctions made by Wirt, Marshall concluded that any territories enclosed by the borders of the United States were within its political jurisdiction.

Marshall's argument that the Cherokee Nation existed within the jurisdiction of the United States and/or the state of Georgia because there were maps that represented it as such was contested in both legal and popular venues. The dissenting opinion by Justices Smith Thompson and Joseph Story challenged Marshall's definition of territorial nationhood and argued for the Cherokees' *foreignness* on the basis of their separate political structure.[75] Thompson argued:

[I]t is their [the Cherokees'] political condition that constitutes their *foreign* character, and in that sense must the term *foreign*, be understood as used in the constitution. It can have no relation to local, geographical, or territorial position. It cannot mean a country beyond the sea. Mexico or Canada is certainly to be considered a foreign country, in reference to the United States. It is the political relation in which one government or country stands to another, which constitutes it foreign to the other. The Cherokee territory being within the chartered limits of Georgia, does not affect the question. When Georgia is spoken of as a state, reference is had to its political character, and not to boundary; and it is not perceived that any absurdity or inconsistency grows out of the circumstance, that the jurisdiction and territory of the state of Georgia surround or extend on every side of the Cherokee territory.[76]

Here foreign versus domestic is not presented as a set of spatial relationships, but rather is predicated on political status. Nations with contiguous borders, as in the case of the United States and Mexico, still constitute foreign sovereignties despite their close proximity because they represent distinct communities of allegiance. Thompson draws a clear distinction between the state of Georgia as a political entity, which is separate from the polity of the Cherokees, and Georgia's geographic boundaries, which surround those of the Cherokee Nation.

In his arguments before the Supreme Court, Wirt observed that the rhetoric of imperium in imperio was presented by supporters of Removal as "unanswerable," as the last word on Cherokee nationhood. Its Latin origins carried the weight of legal authority, and its associations with political turmoil suggested that such a condition was not to be endured. Indeed, this phrase circulated widely in the debates over Indian Removal policy and the status of the Cherokee Nation and provided rhetorical opportunities for all sides. These rhetorics not only informed the Marshall Court's thinking on the status of the Cherokee Nation but also played a role in how the issue was talked about in the popular press. Proponents of Removal, who included many in Georgia and in Jackson's administration, drew on what was by the late 1820s an established language for identifying political threats. In applying this language to the Cherokees, Removal advocates conflated political solecism, racialized threat, and intolerable monstrosity. Their opponents seized on the flexibility of this discourse, reworking it to suggest its implications for appeals to states' rights and what they believed to be its fundamental misrepresentation of Cherokee sovereignty and national development. They also highlighted issues of class, asserting that Southern aristocrats and pedants were using phrases such as imperium in imperio to dupe the general public, relying on the Latin term's authoritative sound more than its actual meaning. For Cherokee leaders, the concept of divided sovereignty, in the form of a nation within a nation, would provide a rhetorical theme for their political appeals and conceptions of sovereignty.

Narrating Cherokee Nationhood and Sovereignty in the Removal Era

The ratification of the Cherokee Constitution of 1827 served as a rallying point for Georgia's leaders and for supporters of Removal, who framed the Cherokee Nation as a threatening imperium. In that sense, the Cherokee Constitution succeeded in shifting the terms of public debate from issues of race to political questions about nationhood. The increasing calls for Removal pressured the internal divisions in the Cherokee Nation and highlighted distinctions between territorial conceptions of nationhood and sovereignty and conceptions of the nation in more ethnic terms as a *people*. It was a precarious rhetorical situation: to assert territorial sovereignty was to risk inflaming charges of imperium in imperio and galvanizing support for Removal, while to argue for the nation as a group of people might result in the attenuation of territorial claims altogether.

Two of the leading voices in this conversation were Principal Chief John Ross and Elias Boudinot, the editor of the *Cherokee Phoenix*, who agreed on a number of points regarding the nation and its relationship to neighboring polities.[77] In their published works and private correspondence, they questioned whether nations could maintain their sovereignty if they did not exercise exclusive jurisdiction over a national space and whether nations could be reconstituted in spaces other than the ones in which they developed. Echoing the territorial concerns of the Cherokee Constitution, Ross articulated a territorial definition of the nation, while Boudinot came to define the nation as its people rather than its land after initial arguments in favor of a more territorial perspective. When responding to the new political situation in Indian Territory, however, Ross countered the Old Settlers' claims of exclusive territorial jurisdiction, couched in the language of imperium in imperio, with the kind of nation-as-people arguments that Boudinot had advanced earlier. This change in position reveals the ways in which Ross, Boudinot, and others were engaged in strategic efforts to gain political traction and not in a representational project to narrate their identity. In the face of incredible pressures from state and U.S. federal authorities, they were less concerned with articulating a coherent position on Cherokee nationhood than they were about making arguments to gain specific political advantage.

To deflect charges that the Cherokee Nation was a dangerous division of sovereignty, Cherokee leaders drew on ideas gleaned from American political culture and international law to describe the relationship between the Cherokee Nation and the United States as a mutually beneficial alliance between contiguous states. They maintained that they were a foreign state, but one with close ties with the U.S. federal government. In his annual message to the Cherokee people on 24 October 1831, Chief Ross described the political condition of the Cherokee Nation as resembling those of individual states and the United States. Knowing that this message would be reprinted and circulated among white readers, Ross played to ideas of the Cherokee Nation as subordinate to, but also closely aligned with, the United States: "A weak defenseless community as we are, forming an alliance with, and placed in the heart of so powerful a Nation as the United States, and having surrendered a portion of our sovereignty, as a security for our protection, and our intercourse being confined exclusively with our protector, must necessarily produce that identity of interest and bond of friendship so natural to the ties of such an alliance."[78] Here Ross echoed Vattel's conception of states bound together in unequal alliance, but added a sentimental element to his description. According to Ross, the Cherokees "surrendered a portion of our sovereignty, as a security for our protection," a move that placed the Cherokees in a subordinate but politically significant position, linked to the United States. He stressed affiliation rather than opposition and reminded the United States of its end of the bargain, which was to protect the Cherokees against outside threats, implied here to be the state of Georgia. This bargain was suggested to be beneficial for the United States, which received the friendship and honor of the Cherokee Nation.

In this same passage Ross drew on sentimental language to link the Cherokee Nation to a particular space and to transform the notion of a Cherokee imperium from a threatening element to a cherished part of the United States. Using a passive construction—"placed in the heart of so powerful a Nation"—Ross worked to naturalize the presence of the Cherokee Nation within the borders of the United States (but outside the state of Georgia). Here he reworked the language of imperium in imperio used by Georgia politicians, who characterized the Cherokees as a nation lurking in the bosom of an unwilling state, to create a vision of the Cherokees as peacefully residing in the "heart" of the United States, a sentimental as well as a geographic relationship. To be in someone's heart means to have ties to their affections, while the phrase "in the heart of" has been used, according to the *Oxford English Dictionary*, since the fourteenth century to describe a geographic location: the middle. Ross thus reworked the concept of imperium in imperio to have a positive, sentimental component. Through his allusion to the social contract and his location of the Cherokee nation in the heart of the United States, Ross asserted that the Cherokees occupied a political position similar to that of Georgia, emphasizing relationality rather than opposition.

While arguing that the Cherokee Nation existed in the metaphorical heart of the United States, throughout his writings and speeches, Ross also drew on treaties to emphasize that the Cherokee Nation existed outside of the chartered political limits of the state of Georgia. In an 1830 letter to Hugh Montgomery, Ross lamented President Jackson's statement that he could not interfere on behalf of the Cherokees because to do so would infringe on Georgia's rights as a sovereign state. Ross concluded that Jackson "considers our territory to be within the ordinary jurisdiction of individual States, and that the

Cherokees must consequently submit to the State laws."[79] Ross countered this conclusion by citing treaties in which the United States promised protection to the Cherokee Nation so long as it did not enter into treaty relations with any other sovereign powers. Specifically, he mentioned that in "the preamble of the same Treaty (of Holston) [1791] the inhabitants of this nation are called citizens of the Cherokee Nation, and in the 11th article thereof it is irresistibly implied that the Cherokee country is not 'within the jurisdiction of any state,' nor 'within the jurisdiction of any of the Territorial Districts of the United States.'"[80] Ross claimed that, according to these documents, the Cherokee Nation had historically been understood to be separate from both the United States and individual states and not under the jurisdiction of either. This letter suggested that while imperium in imperio may function as a figurative construction describing the close relationship between the United States and the Cherokee Nation, it could not be used to support the notion that the Cherokee Nation falls under Georgia's jurisdiction.

Both Ross and Boudinot refuted the temporal aspects of arguments regarding a Cherokee imperium, which represented the Cherokee Nation as a new state that recently formed within Georgia's territorial limits. As Maureen Konkle argues, Ross and other Cherokee spokespeople "claimed to form a modern Indian nation, one that could not be characterized as representing a timeless prepolitical state of nature."[81] Ross's and Boudinot's efforts suggest, however, that while they worked to show the nation as "modern," they actively subverted claims that it was *new* in response to pro-Removal arguments about an emergent imperium. In his 1828 annual message, Ross explicitly denied the charge that the Cherokees were a new nation and linked their history with that of the United States:

> The circumstances of our Government assuming a new character under a constitutional form, and on the principles of republicanism, has, in some degree, excited the sensations of the public characters of Georgia, and it is sincerely to be regretted that this excitement should have been manifested by such glaring expressions of hostility to our true interests. By the adoption of the Constitution, our relation to the United States, as recognized by existing Treaties, is not in the least degree affected, but on the contrary, this improvement in our government, is strictly in accordance with the recommendations, views and wishes of the Great [George] Washington under whose auspicious administration our Treaties of peace, Friendship and protection, were made, and whose policy in regard to Indian civilization has been strictly pursued by the subsequent administration.[82]

Ross was careful to clarify that the Cherokee government had assumed a "new character," but was not a new state that might run afoul of the U.S. Constitution. Appealing to the American public's veneration of the founders, he contended that the Cherokee Nation was acting in accordance with the "recommendations, views and wishes" of George Washington. Nothing had changed, Ross asserted, except the form of the Cherokee government. It was not a new nation threatening the sovereignty of Georgia, but an improved version of a preexisting state affiliated with the United States. Boudinot echoed similar thoughts in 1829, claiming, "The pretext for Georgia to extend her jurisdiction over the Cherokees has always existed. The Cherokees have always had a government of their own."[83] The Cherokees were neither new nor timeless, but could trace their political nativity to a point that preceded that of Georgia.

Both Ross and Boudinot traced the origins of Cherokee sovereignty, understood as the right to regulate their own political affairs within the territorial boundaries set by the 1827 Constitution, and of the nation itself to a divine source, stressing their nation's relationship with God. They echoed the Cherokee Constitution's emphasis on the nation's allegiance to and dependence on the "sovereign ruler of the Universe."[84] In a message to both houses of Congress dated 27 February 1829, Ross offered the following description of the source of the Cherokees' sovereignty: "The right of regulating our own internal affairs is a right which we have inherited from the Author of our existence, which we have always exercised, and have never surrendered. Our nation had no voice in the formation of the Federal compact between the States; and if the United States have involved themselves by an agreement with Georgia relative to the purchase of our lands, and have failed to comply with it in the strictest letter of their compact, it is a matter to be adjusted between themselves."[85] Here Ross refuted arguments that the Cherokees had lost their sovereignty by virtue of conquest or had "surrendered" it in treaty documents. God granted them their sovereign existence, he contended, and secular leaders could not withdraw that sovereignty. Furthermore, the Cherokee Nation was not involved in the creation of the United States nor in the Compact of 1802, and neither political event had any impact on the ability of the Cherokees to see to their "internal affairs."

Boudinot also appealed to divine agency in his defense of the Cherokee Nation and stressed its allegiance to a divine sovereign. As part of a larger argument that the fate of the Union depended on America's conduct toward the Cherokees, Boudinot invoked Providence in his discussion of the location of the Cherokee Nation. He wrote of the Cherokees, "They reside on the land which God gave them—they are surrounded with guarantees which this Republic has voluntarily made for their protection and which once formed a sufficient security against oppression. If those guarantees must now be violated with impunity for purposes altogether selfish, the sin will not be at our door, but at the door of our *oppressor* and our faithless *Guardian*."[86] Here Boudinot also offered an implicit challenge to pro-Removal formulations of imperium in imperio by suggesting that the location of the Cherokees was the result of divine agency, which predated federal and state governments. What they are "surrounded with" here is not Georgia, but rather the "guarantees" that the United States made in various treaties. If the United States honors these treaties, he implied, as a nation it will receive divine blessings, while failing to honor the treaties risks divine retribution. In this single paragraph, Boudinot shifted the terms of the debate from physical space, to spiritual geography, to legislative terrain. He dramatized the unstable and fluid landscape that the Cherokees occupied while also subtly refuting the notion that they constituted a division of either Georgia's sovereignty or that of the United States.

Ross and Boudinot agreed on points related to the geopolitical location and origins of the Cherokee Nation, reframing conceptions of imperium in imperio to emphasize the nation's affiliation with the United States and to refute accounts of its recent development. They emphasized the positive and mutually beneficial nature of the relationship between the Cherokee Nation and the United States in order to mitigate claims of a threatening and subversive imperium. Yet they would come to disagree over the Cherokee Nation's future, a debate deeply rooted in definitional arguments about whether nations are primarily ethnic (that is, defined as a people) or territorial in nature. In a split that eventually led to the creation of two rival factions, one made up of Ross and his allies and the other made up of Major Ridge, his nephew John Ridge, Elias Boudinot, and others, both sides claimed to be working to preserve the Cherokee Nation (according to their own definitions of nationhood), and each accused its rival of selfish motivations.[87] As calls for Removal intensified, the Cherokee Nation was forced to take up questions that many other groups during the nineteenth century would consider, such as whether nations could be grown in once place and moved to another location and whether land was a precondition and an ongoing requirement for nationhood.

Ross framed territory as central to nationhood. He was, in Justice's estimation, a "passionate Chickamaugan defender of Cherokee land tenure" (*Our Fire Survives*, 69). In a letter to Indian agent Hugh Montgomery, dated 16 April 1828, Ross asserted that the Cherokee Nation was a polity that "claims for its self & always maintained sovereign jurisdiction over its Territorial limits."[88] His use of words such as "jurisdiction" and "Territorial limits" mirrored the language found in U.S. federal and state discourses of sovereignty. The Cherokee Nation, Ross emphasized, exists in space, and not just any space, but the particular bounded space over which it claims jurisdiction. In his resistance to Removal, he gave voice to the will of the majority of Cherokees, who, as Perdue and Green suggest, "opposed removal and wanted to resist the United States at any cost."[89] Maintaining the Cherokee Nation meant keeping the lands that they currently held. When, in the wake of the Supreme Court cases, it became clear to Ross that the Cherokees would not be able to maintain their landholdings in Georgia, he wrote to Jackson questioning whether the Cherokees could gradually be incorporated into the United States as citizens in exchange for ceding their lands. He envisioned this as allowing time for a transition, rather than an immediate cession. For Ross, the loss of the land seemed tantamount to denationalization.

Ross's territorial conception of the nation was not without its critics. In a letter to Major Ridge and others, John Ridge offered a different reading of Ross's views on land and claimed that Ross was planning to "act falsely to his people & sell the Nation either by getting Reservations of land or taking the whole in money on pretense of going out of the limits of the U. States."[90] Boudinot also criticized Ross's emphasis on land and claimed that the Removal crisis might have unfolded differently, aside from the "mere loss of soil," had Ross taken a different approach: "The whole of that catastrophe, I mean aside from the mere loss of soil ... might have been averted, if Mr. Ross, instead of identifying himself with the contemptible prejudice founded upon the *love of the land*, had met the crisis manfully ... and unfolded to his confiding people the sure termination of all these things."[91] Boudinot claimed that Ross's "love of the land" blinded him to other issues facing the Cherokees and prevented him from negotiating a favorable treaty with the United States.

Boudinot had come to equate the nation not with the land, but with the Cherokee people. Boudinot emphasized the centrality of nationhood to the future of Indian peoples, which suggests the value of rhetorics of nationhood to articulating political claims. When he wrote of the nation in an 1829 article for the *Cherokee Phoenix*, he highlighted the political community and governmental structure: "While he possesses a national character, there is hope for the Indian. But take his rights away, divest him of the last spark of national pride, and introduce him to a new order of things, invest him with oppressive laws, grevious [sic] to be borne, he droops like the fading flower before the noon day sun."[92] Here Boudinot linked the fate of the nation as a political community to the future of American Indian peoples. He asserted that most tribes in the Northeast had already been denationalized in this way, as had the Catawbas of South Carolina. Even in his early writings, when he opposed Removal, Boudinot had drawn some philosophical distinctions between a nation and the land it occupies. Land, in Boudinot's formulation, was important because it facilitated the kind of political community that he associated with the nation by bringing the people together in a consolidated space. Removal then was not just about the loss of physical space; it was an attempt to "disorganize" the Cherokees and to "cut a vital string in their national existence."[93]

In Boudinot's reading, a love of the land did not constitute patriotism. Writing to Elijah Hicks, then editor of the *Cherokee Phoenix*, Boudinot responded to claims that he was unpatriotic and offered an alternative vision of Cherokee patriotism: "In one word, I may say that my patriotism consists in the *love of the country*, and *the love of the People*. These are intimately connected, yet they are not altogether inseparable. They are inseparable if the people are made the first victim, for in that case the country must go also, and there must be an end of the objects of our patriotism. But if the country is lost, or is likely to be lost to all human appearance, and the people still exist, may I not, with a patriotism true and commendable, make a *question* for the safety of the remaining object of my affection?"[94] Boudinot argued that if given a choice between saving the land and saving the people, one must choose the people. For him, the nation could survive a loss of land, because land alone does not make the nation. Furthermore, he wrote, "I will only say that I am not *detached from*, but *attached to*, the nation, and that there are those connected with the Judicial, Executive, and Legislative departments of our little Government, men of intelligence and patriotism, who cordially approve of the remarks and suggestions contained in the article upon which you have commented."[95] Boudinot's argument that Removal was necessary to preserve the Cherokee Nation was informed by his separation of the "nation" from the Cherokees' landholdings in the East.

The forced dispossession of the Cherokees and the outcome of the Ross–Ridge dispute are well documented, but less well known are the ways in which rhetorics of imperium in imperio continued to inform the political position of the Cherokee Nation led by Ross as it worked out its future with the Old Settlers in Indian Territory. To accomplish their goal, these two groups needed a shared political vocabulary. Both sides drew on rhetorics of imperium in imperio and appeals to indivisible sovereignty, very much like those that were voiced by Georgia in the Removal debates, to advance their own arguments. That they returned to these arguments suggests both the rhetorical currency and flexibility of imperium in imperio, but also the ways in which it emerged in times of crisis as a way to subvert challenges to political and territorial claims.

The Old Settlers (or Western Cherokees), who had moved to parts of Arkansas Territory, East Texas, and Indian Territory, had already established their own government and were living under their own laws by the time that the Cherokees who were forcibly dispossessed by the Indian Removal Act arrived. As explained by Ross in an 1839 "Address to a General Council of the Cherokees," the "great body of the people who have recently been removed into this Country, emigrated in their National Character, with all the attributes, from time immemorial, which belonged to them as a distinct Community, and of which they have never surrendered." Ross in particular hoped for reunification, which he understood to mean that the Old Settlers would be absorbed into the nation governed by the 1827 Constitution: "Let us never forget this self evident truth—that a House divided against itself cannot stand—or, 'united we stand and divided we fall.'"[96] Ross also resorted to the nation-as-people argument that Boudinot had offered and conceptions of indivisible sovereignty. The Cherokees were one people, he claimed, which should be reflected in their political and legal culture. The division of the Old Settlers and the eastern migrants, he suggested, weakened their political position relative to the United States.

The Old Settlers concurred with this final point and suggested further that it would be a political impossibility for the two nations to operate within the same space, a rhetorical move that appealed to threatening visions of divided sovereignty as two competing claims to the same jurisdiction. Old Settlers John Brown (first chief of the Old Settlers), John Looney, and John Rogers expressed their position in an 1839 letter to John Ross and George Lowry: "As it respects your wishes for your original laws, created beyond the Mississippi, to be brought here, brought to life, and to have full force in this nation, it is believed by the National Council that such an admission is, and would be, entirely repugnant to the government and laws of the Cherokee Nation, which would thereby create great dissatisfaction among the people. To admit two distinct laws or governments in the same country, and for the government of the same people, is something never known to be admitted in any country, or even asked for by any people."[97] The representatives of the Old Settlers denied that the recent migrants could bring their laws into the West because it would create the political solecism of two nations occupying the same space, a situation they claimed had never been known nor desired. Here the Old Settlers employed the concept of imperium in imperio in an attempt to maintain their own national position and to prevent Ross and the recent migrants from asserting their own vision of the Cherokee Nation. Linking laws with concepts of jurisdiction and territoriality, the writers suggested that the laws created east of the Mississippi could not simply be carried west and "brought to life" within the space of an already established nation without creating a dangerous division of sovereignty.

The disagreements between the two groups were lessened with the ratification of the Constitution of the Cherokee Nation in 1839. This document largely reproduced the 1827 Constitution with the exception of the territorial boundaries of the nation, which were redrawn to reflect their new geographic location. In the debates between the Old Settlers and the Cherokees led by Ross, imperium in imperio at least provided a starting point from which to begin complicated political negotiations, a point of entry into a larger conversation about Cherokee nationhood and sovereignty.

Conclusion

Charges of imperium in imperio continued to inform the relationships between the U.S. government and various Native nations, relationships that became increasingly complicated as corporations sought to exert their influence in Indian Territory. An 1882 article for the *Cherokee Advocate*, edited by Daniel Hicks Ross, a descendant of Chief John Ross, discussed a bill that was being debated in Congress, one of several pieces of legislation that involved awarding rights-of-way to railroad companies so that they could build on American Indian lands.[98] In this particular case, the Chickasaw Nation sought to prevent the Choctaw Nation from granting a right-of-way to the St. Louis and San Francisco Railroad, and Senator Samuel Maxey, a Texas Democrat, raised the question of whether American Indians possessed the legal right to prevent railroads from building on their lands: "We have got to meet the question of whether there is an *imperium in imperio* in this country; whether there is a portion of the United States around which a Chinese Wall may be erected to which the right of eminent domain does not apply."[99] Maxey's statement is problematic on a number of levels, from its framing of Chickasaw and Choctaw lands as "a portion of the United States" to its representation of their expressions of sovereignty as a "Chinese Wall" or barrier to industrial progress. The *Cherokee Advocate*, however, seized on the phrase imperium in imperio, which, as Ross noted, had played a significant role in the political arguments surrounding *Cherokee Nation v. Georgia* (1831) and *Worcester v. Georgia* (1832). Ross reminded his readers that Cherokee people had heard this phrase before.[100] This "insane cry" may have helped Georgia justify the forced Removal of the Cherokee Nation from its lands, but Ross hoped that Georgia had since paid a price for the greed of its citizens. Moreover, while the charge of imperium in imperio may have proved rhetorically useful to Georgia in the 1820s and 1830s, because of a shift in the overall rhetorical situation, he implied, this argument would not benefit Texas, Missouri, Kansas, or Arkansas in 1882. Despite the profound social and political changes that had occurred in the more than fifty years since *Cherokee Nation v. Georgia*, arguments about an American Indian imperium did have some effect. The bill under discussion was signed into law on 2 August 1882, just a few months after the publication of the article in the *Advocate*, and it allowed the U.S. government to extend eminent domain over lands held by American Indian nations.

Beginning with the debates over the Removal of the Cherokees, rhetorics of imperium in imperio, conceptualized as a dangerous division of sovereignty within a single territory, had proven effective in generating anxiety and subverting the land claims of Indigenous peoples. The historical presence of Native peoples and their occupation of the territories that they claimed required advocates of Removal (and, later, proponents of eminent domain) to return to Revolutionary-era arguments about the indivisibility of sovereignty in order to frame the Cherokees and other Native nations as both politically foreign and geographically within territory claimed by the United States. The exigencies of Removal prompted Cherokee leaders to reconsider the relationship between land, nationhood, and people and to think through a particular kind of virtuality in which political and social potential was not linked to any particular territory but could survive the trauma of forced dispossession. Through their written constitutions and other documents, Cherokee leaders attempted to shift the terms of the debate to one of multiple affiliations rather than internal divisions in order to assert their political and territorial sovereignty and remind the United States of its treaty obligations. As I show in the next two chapters, the terms of this debate were reimagined as part of discussions of a threatening black imperium and African Americans' assertions that they were a nation affiliated with the United States in a web of individual and collective allegiance.

CHAPTER TWO

★ ★ ★ ★

"And Ethiopia Shall Stretch Forth Her Hands"
African Colonization, Divided Sovereignty, and Rhetorics of an African American Imperium

SHORTLY AFTER THE TRIALS of Denmark Vesey and his coconspirators, who had allegedly plotted a violent uprising in Charleston, South Carolina, for 14 July 1822, the magistrates who presided over the trials published an account entitled *An Official Report of the Trials of Sundry Negroes, Charged with an Attempt to Raise an Insurrection in the State of South-Carolina*. This document describes fractures in the United States and fears that African Americans could exploit such divisions through collective acts of violence against their masters and the slaveholding society writ large.

In the preface to the account of the trial itself, Kennedy and Parker suggest that the congressional debates about Missouri's entrance into the Union "furnished him [Vesey] with ample means for inflaming the minds of the colored population of this state."[1] By providing a partial account of the debates and "distorting certain parts of those speeches ... he persuaded but too many that Congress had actually declared them free, and that they were held in bondage contrary to the laws of the land."[2] This account represents disagreements in Congress, which reflected deep-seated sectional tensions, as informing the rhetoric of black leaders like Vesey and inciting black rebellion. Douglas Egerton, who wrote a biography of Vesey, lends support to Kennedy and Parker's perspective on the situation: "Reading the debates [about Missouri] in Charleston—and they were widely covered in both newspaper[s] and pamphlet[s]—Vesey came to understand that America was two countries, and that the North, if not hospitable to African Americans, might prove a bit tardy in riding to the defense of the Southern planter class."[3] Statements in the *Offi-*

cial Report assert that Vesey hoped to capitalize on the divisions between these "two countries" with the help of troops from Haiti and Africa, and then travel to Haiti to form a black "American" nation. The *Official Report* imagines three nations existing within America's putative borders in the wake of the Missouri crisis—the North, the South, and a virtual black American nation threatening to rise up. By making the connection between congressional debates and slave uprisings, this document dramatizes the process through which fears of internal divisions were transferred onto African Americans, particularly free black people, as fears over slave rebellions increased and tensions rose between state and federal authorities, Northern and Southern states, and various other interests.

While African Americans had been discussing themselves as a nation since the eighteenth century, in the wake of the Missouri crisis, rhetorics of an African American nation within the United States began to circulate more widely, a point that has been overlooked by studies that focus on competing representations of racial identity. The African colonization movement played a key role in promoting rhetorics of African American nationhood because its entire project rested on championing the *national* potential of African Americans. Among their various rhetorical strategies, white American colonizationists turned to the concept of imperium in imperio to emphasize this national potential and hint at the consequences that would arise from allowing this nation to remain in the United States. The early uses of this rhetoric were somewhat fragmentary but suggest the ongoing process through which marginalized groups were figured as nations, the removal of which might ameliorate the already uneasy divisions of sovereignty within the United States. For African American writers and orators of the era, rhetorics of African American nationhood provided a means of galvanizing collective action in the black community and demanding that white Americans relate to them on political rather than racial terms.

One significant actor in this period was the National Negro Convention movement, which positioned itself as the representative body of free people of color within the United States and held conventions from 1830 until 1864. This organization produced founding documents that echoed the Declaration of Independence and the U.S. Constitution and engaged America's founding documents in ways that made them speak differently on the topics of slavery and African American citizenship. The movement traced the source of African American sovereignty to God and attempted to use its national status as leverage in arguments for citizenship and greater political freedom within the United States. In a similar fashion, African American writers and orators such as Robert Alexander Young, David Walker, Maria W. Stewart, and Hosea Easton found in national rhetorics a powerful tool for articulating individual and collective political allegiance both to a virtual black nation and to the United States, rearticulating the idea of divided sovereignty or a nation within a nation. Like the members of the Negro Convention movement, they articulated varied and sometimes contradictory visions of nationhood to complicate the territorial and racial logics of colonization and to gain political rights for African Americans. I suggest that what has sometimes been seen as tension between what Robert Levine calls a "United States–based black nationalism" (*Dislocating*, 73) and a pan-African or transnational perspective can be read as part of a larger attempt to complicate and challenge territorial constructions of nationhood and national sovereignty informed by racial prejudice.

I argue that there were some key rhetorical themes that circulated in discussions of African American and Native nations—and some points of departure—all of which shed light on how U.S. sovereignty was conceived in American public argument. White Americans used rhetorics of imperium in imperio to represent both African Americans and Native peoples as "alien but not foreign" (to borrow a phrase from Mark Rifkin), outside of the American community of allegiance but within its geopolitical boundaries.[4] Proponents of African colonization characterized free black people as a *virtual* nation—one that did not yet possess a national space—an argument predicated on the assumption that African Americans could not be assimilated into the U.S. body politic because of their racial and national affiliation to Africa. As in the case of the Cherokee Nation, discussions of a black imperium constituted a strategy of containment rather than marginalization. This strategy spoke to both the significance of the free black population in antebellum America and the ways in which colonization operated as part of a process of territorialization, both in the Deleuzian sense of "fixing" the other so as to manage them effectively and in the literal sense of managing the relationship of African Americans to space. Yet, even as Indian Removal and African colonization worked to create coherence in the United States through their opposition to and relocation of "other" nations, these efforts depended on figurative language that undercut constructions of unified nationhood, indivisible sovereignty, and birthright citizenship in the United States. The Cherokee Constitution of 1827 and the documents produced by the Negro Convention movement both mirrored and challenged the foundational documents of the United States, asserting the national status of their framers and making the original documents speak differently on issues related to sovereignty, citizenship, and nationhood. Texts produced by African American writers and orators reveal the ways in which they sought to relate to the United States on a nation-to-nation basis, countering oppositional rhetorics with those that emphasized multiple political affiliations.

*Sovereignty, Citizenship,
and an African American Imperium*

Weaknesses in the fiction of a unified American people, a people who possessed common characteristics of culture, religion, traditions, descent, and attitudes, emerged during and after the Missouri crisis. As Levine argues, "The Missouri crisis made clear that there was no single 'American ideology' at this time but instead fiercely contested notions of what such an ideology might be" (*Dislocating*, 67). He notes that the complicated political landscape included "expansionists and antiexpansionists, regionalists and sectionalists, unionists and nullifiers, and a host of other groups who laid claim to the mantle of nationalist" (67). The congressional debates over the Missouri statehood bill of 1819 reenergized sectional rivalries, tensions between state and federal powers, and concerns about slavery and territorial expansion.

In an attempt to mediate such divisions, congressmen led by Henry Clay and Jesse B. Thomas created the Missouri Compromise wherein Maine would join the Union as a free state and Missouri as a slave state, and slavery would be prohibited "in all that territory ceded by France to the United States, under the name of Louisiana, which lies north of thirty-six degrees and thirty minutes north latitude," which was not part of Missouri.[5] Yet, when Missouri's proposed state constitution included a ban on the entry of free black people into the state, arguments resumed anew.[6] Following the Missouri crisis and the debates over race and citizenship that it generated, which coincided with the most intense struggles between the Cherokee Nation and the state of Georgia, internal sectional divisions began to be linked with an African American imperium in American public argument. This nation of African Americans was represented by supporters of African colonization to be a virtual one in the sense that it was a nation in the making, unable to fully achieve its national status until it could exercise political jurisdiction within a distinct national territory. Such claims were an attempt to intervene in increasingly vitriolic debates about state and federal sovereignty and the nature of nationhood and citizenship in America.

Competing interpretations of the U.S. Constitution and understandings of sovereignty and nationhood emerged throughout discussions of African American citizenship and mobility in Missouri. While other states, such as Virginia, Georgia, South Carolina, and Ohio, had passed discriminatory laws restricting the rights of free black people, according to Rogers Smith the "most direct federal confrontation with the question of black citizenship came . . . in the debates over the admission of Missouri to statehood, which led to the Compromise of 1820."[7] Levine summarizes Missouri's argument thusly: "Missouri's constitutional convention concluded that blacks never were and never could become citizens, and that the 'free negro' therefore had no place in the new slave state because, by the very logic of the Constitution itself, the free black simply did not exist as a legal entity" (*Dislocating*, 75). Regardless of their place of birth, black people were ineligible for American citizenship because of their race, argued supporters of Missouri's constitution. Critics of Missouri's laws contended that many free black people *were* citizens of some Northern states and therefore had the fundamental right to travel from one state to another. They offered dire predictions of what would happen to the Union if Missouri's constitution was allowed to stand. Representative Joseph Hemphill argued during the Missouri debates: "[I]f being a native, and free born, and of parents belonging to no other nation or tribe, does not constitute a citizen of this country, I am at a loss to know in what manner citizenship is acquired by birth."[8] Senator Justin Morrill of New Hampshire decried Missouri's proposed constitution and claimed that if states were able to make their own laws regarding citizens and ignore the U.S. Constitution, "[y]our national existence is lost; the Union is destroyed; the objects of confederation annihilated, and your political fabric demolished."[9] Missouri's proposed constitution revealed the wide gulf between states' rights supporters, who located sovereignty in the state governments except when expressly delegated to the federal government, and those who argued for the primacy of federal authorities and the overarching power of the U.S. Constitution. Appeals to popular sovereignty did little to quell the controversy, since the definition of "the people" was at the very heart of the arguments in Missouri. Complicating matters even further was the fact that, as Levine points out, a "'national' position on the question of black citizenship simply did not exist" in the early nineteenth century" (*Dislocating*, 75).

Representations of enslaved and free black people as essentially mobile rather than rooted to a particular place also were used to justify the denial of citizenship to black people. In *Notes on the State of Virginia*, Thomas Jefferson referenced the classification of enslaved Africans as "moveables," which differentiated them from real estate as property that was not tied to a particular location.[10] This classification had broad cultural impacts as well as legal ones. Rhetorically separating African people from the American land justified their exclusion from the American body politic because owning property, particularly one's own body and labor, was closely linked with ideas of citizenship and political capability. Free black people were also linked with mobility in discusions of their potentially destabilizing ability to cross borders and foment rebellion. Attempts by free and enslaved people to rise up against slaveholders—most notably the Gabriel plot of 1800, Denmark Vesey's 1822 uprising, and the Nat Turner rebellion in 1831—highlighted for many white Americans the dangers of sharing their country with African Americans and heightened the fear of unregulated black movement. Supporters of slavery worried about the extent to which enslaved people were susceptible to the influence of a free black population that could circulate freely across state borders. Depictions of African Americans as moveable property or as dangerous circulating threats contrasted sharply with idealized images of the rootedness and emplacement of the white American citizen-farmer, and a fundamental belief in the racial inferiority of Africans and African Americans was an organizing principle that shaped American political culture at all levels. Thus, it must be noted that rhetorics of an emergent African American nation existed alongside other representations of black people that expressly denied their political potential and even their humanity.[11]

In the years surrounding the Missouri crisis, when the United States was divided on a number of fronts, rhetorics that discussed African Americans as a nation began to emerge. One such argument suggested that increasing numbers of enslaved people in the United States might form their own nation and threaten American sovereignty. An 1826 article published in the *Boston Recorder and Religious Telegraph* claimed that the number of enslaved people in the South was rapidly increasing, and slaves thus were "concentrating" in the Deep South. Projecting a time in the not-so-distant future when African Americans would outnumber white people in the South, the author warned of the possible consequences of further increases in the African American population: "Will not that part of the country come under the complete control of the blacks? They are fast gaining upon the whites, and unless some powerful means are speedily taken to prevent it, we shall have a nation of blacks nearer than St. Domingo."[12] The author predicted that the United States would soon split into two nations, one in the North and one in the South, but envisioned the break happening along racial rather than political lines. He imagined not that the Southern states would secede, but that African Americans might overtake whites in the South and form their own nation within the geopolitical borders of the United States. The reference to "St. Domingo," the site of a violent revolution led by Toussaint Louverture and Jean-Jacques Dessalines, implies that the emergence of this other nation would not be a peaceful process.

Haiti provided an example of a "nation of blacks" that many white Americans were terrified would be replicated on American shores. Echoing Jefferson's predictions of racial warfare, advocates of colonization highlighted the threat of violent uprisings, predicting that unless something was done, African Americans would resort to "[n]oyades, fusillades, the gallows or the guillotine."[13] They pointed to the Haitian Revolution as proof that emancipation and enfranchisement would lead to violence. The declaration of Haiti as "the second independent republic of the Americas" in 1804 only heightened the anxiety of many white Americans.[14] They feared the presence of this "black nation" so close to their borders and the effect that it would have on free and enslaved people in the United States. One writer for the *Literary Magazine* categorized the efforts of Toussaint Louverture as "a specimen of that miserable and childish spirit of imitation" rather than as the self-directed acts of a political leader. Yet, the idea that black people could imitate whites' military and political efforts caused significant concern.[15] The author in the *Literary Magazine* predicted that descendants of Africans in North and South America would never organize politically, but he forecasted the emergence of several sovereign black nations in the Caribbean.[16] Some in the South claimed that ending slavery and removing free black people was the only way to avoid the emergence of "a Toussaint [sic], or a Spartacus, or an African Tecumseh" within the borders of the United States.[17] As P. J. Staudenraus notes, "Santo Domingo became a shibboleth of colonization."[18]

References to free black people as a virtual nation within the larger U.S. nation, a potential nation that was not yet actualized because it did not possess its own space, gained new currency with the rise of the African colonization movement in the early nineteenth century. While the removal of African Americans had been proposed as early as the eighteenth century and various colonization plans had been discussed over the years, the American Colonization Society (ACS) was the first formal organization created to promote the emigration of African Americans.[19] To persuade government officials and the American public to fund the project of sending free black people to Africa to found a nation, colonizationists needed a way to show that such a plan would yield desirable results. One strand of colonization rhetoric focused on the removal of a threatening presence and cast free black people as a potential nation that was trapped within the United States. Charles Carroll Harper told the voters of Baltimore in 1826 that African Americans are "[s]hut out from the privileges of citizens, separated from us by the insurmountable barrier of colour, they can never amalgamate with us, but must remain forever a distinct and inferior race, repugnant to our republican feelings, and dangerous to our republican institutions."[20] The Reverend Stephen Foster from Knoxville, Tennessee, echoed this sentiment in an 1828 Fourth of July address, describing the free black person as "insulated from the world; without a home of his own, without a community of his own, without a country of his own, without a government of his own, without any system, intellectual or moral, in which his own individual existence forms a part of the machinery."[21] Through the use of terms like "shut out" and "insulated," Harper and Foster created a visual image of African Americans as trapped within an American nation that did not recognize their political subjectivity. If the current situation were allowed to continue, colonizationists argued, the result would be an African American imperium. Describing the creation of the American Colonization Society in an 1827 speech, a Mr. Knapp of Boston declared that "[w]e wanted no nation of blacks here."[22]

A writer for the *Christian Watchman* highlighted the threat of an African American imperium with the suggestion that African Americans would never abandon their allegiance to Africa even after prolonged residence in America. The anonymous author warned in an 1833 article that without colonization "we shall have an *imperium in imperio*, a nation within a nation, in the worst sense of the term."[23] In such a scenario, the writer suggested, there would be "more than half a million citizens, not only distinguished by their complexion, but bound together by a feeling of nationality among themselves" ("Colonization and Anti-Slavery Societies," 132). African Americans should never be American citizens because they will always act "as Africans in America" (132). The "African nation," the author claimed, "will feel that it has a cause of its own to guard and to promote, and a policy of its own, by which it is to be promoted" (132). Here political allegiance is framed in explicitly ethnic/racial rather than territorial terms and imagined to be unchanging, at least in the case of African and African American people. In an argument that was also used against the Irish and other immigrant groups, such statements claimed that Africans in America were a nation that was fundamentally unassimilable because physical differences and sentimental attachments would prevent African Americans from being seen as and seeing themselves as Americans. Colonization emerged as a way to rid the American landscape of a potentially threatening racialized population that possessed the potential to incite large-scale slave revolts and could never be assimilated into American political and social life.

Another strand of colonization rhetoric described African Americans in more positive terms as a "nation-to-be" that only lacked the proper space to become a nation in the civic and territorial senses. Although related to discourses of racial difference, this argument relied more heavily on the link between nationhood, sovereignty, and territorial possession. What was necessary for African Americans to found an actual nation, argued many colonizationists, was merely the right place and land they could possess. Knapp offered the following description of the ACS founders at the 1827 annual meeting of the organization: "They looked around them with the humane endeavor to find a place where the liberty of the African might be real—where it might be no longer the emptiest of mockeries: for what is freedom without the emancipation of intellect? What land should give freedom to this degraded race? They could not hope to fix a colony in America."²⁴ He recalled that colonizationists mused about where the "holy spot" for an African American nation might be, returning always to Africa.²⁵ References to the search for a "holy spot" for African American nationhood resonated with the sacralization of territory and the centrality of space to constructions of U.S. sovereignty. The distinction between a virtual African American nation and an actualized one was framed in territorial terms; writers could imagine the possibility of a nation of free black people, but to become an actuality that nation would have to exercise sovereignty over a national space. Proponents of colonization saw two options: either free black people would take land in the United States by force, or they could be removed to an alternative location. Within the space of the American nation, an African American imperium was threatening; it was in direct competition for the very land that comprised the U.S. national space, and it disrupted the fiction of an ethnically and racially homogenous American nation. African colonization was framed as a way to prevent free black people from claiming space within the United States and challenging American territorial sovereignty; the United States had expansionist aspirations of its own to pursue.

In the rhetoric of African nation building, the imperialist aims of replicating American nationhood abroad and reinforcing it at home were made quite explicit. The report of the 1825 annual meeting of the American Colonization Society included the following statement: "Who knows but what this Society may yet behold a great and flourishing republic rise on the shores of Africa? Who knows but what the Society may hear that Republic saying to the world, 'it was America that founded me?—In me, the New World taught the old.—The chains that once bound my children are now broken in sunder, and from a feeble colony, behold I have become a great empire!'"²⁶ In a reversal of Bishop Berkeley's famous statement in "Verses on the Prospect of Planting Arts and Learning in America" (1752) about the "[w]estward . . . course" of empire, the New World now had the opportunity to extend its influence eastward. Institutional power, operating through organizations like the ACS and missionary groups that supported colonization, worked to inculcate potential colonists with the American liberal values that underscored ideas of the nation as both political institution and territorial space: the benefits of the social contract, private property, and free enterprise. As David Kazanjian argues in *The Colonizing Trick*, supporters of colonization imagined their efforts as long-term "resettlement projects meant to establish a Christian nation-state of free-black Americans in the image of, closely allied with, and even controlled by the United States" (91). They saw colonization as a confirmation of American values and, as Kazanjian puts it, "the completion of . . . the American Revolution's emancipatory promise of universal equality" (31). African Americans' efforts at self-government were said to be educational opportunities, managed and mediated by what one colonizationist deemed the "instrumentality" of their white benefactors.[27]

The "instrumentality" of white colonizationists also worked to promote particular ideas of nationhood and citizenship at home. Drawing on Toni Morrison's concept of "American Africanism," Christopher Castiglia argues that the ACS shaped white Americans' notions of citizenship and "helped establish citizenship in the image of whiteness, which it also shaped and defined."[28] He further asserts that contemplating the "expulsion" of free black people allowed whites to imagine "the apparent coherence of white national hegemony."[29] That rhetorics of black nationhood and colonization began during a time of sectional divide between Northern and Southern states and persisted through debates over American Indian nationhood and the nullification crisis suggests that the emergence of rhetorics of African nationhood served an important function in American culture. Such rhetorics territorialized free black people as a collective entity that was alien to the United States and could be managed by the same kind of large-scale action as Indian Removal. The circulation of colonizationist rhetorics reveals that ideas of nationhood among the white population were increasingly tied to the idea of the nation as a bounded geographic space and to ideas of racial homogeneity. The fiction of a unified American nationhood that was presented in these arguments, and that would be reinforced by the creation of an African American "sister republic," worked to resolve sectional divisions and mediate threats of secession. If the threatening black nation in their midst could be transported somewhere else, perhaps the North and South would be able to put aside their differences.

During the 1820s and 1830s there were intense struggles over sovereignty, nationhood, and citizenship, particularly as they related to the government of the western territories and the regulation of slavery.[30] The entrance of states, such as Missouri, into the Union functioned as flashpoints that raised difficult questions and challenged representations of national unity. What John Adams had called America's "fresh essay at *imperium in imperio*" was in serious danger of breaking apart.[31] In the contentious political landscape that surrounded the Missouri crisis, rhetorics of a threatening black imperium grew out of the colonization movement and circulated alongside rhetorics that denied the national capacity of African Americans by virtue of their race or enslaved status. These emergent discourses signaled the ways in which imperium in imperio would be used in American public argument over the course of the nineteenth century and beyond. Earlier discussions of imperium in imperio in the Revolutionary era had focused largely on institutions—particularly state and federal governments—but during discussions of Indian Removal and African colonization in the 1820s, this rhetoric began to be used as a way to talk about people. Rather than a means of discussing "political solecisms," rhetorics of imperium in imperio began to be used to identify racial populations that were seen as threats to American sovereignty. Writing to a public that was conditioned to associate imperium in imperio with a political threat, colonizationists employed this language as part of their arguments for the removal of free black people to Africa. Yet, this rhetorical construction provided African Americans with a point of entry into broader debates about sovereignty, citizenship, and their political status within the United States.

African Americans and Virtual Nationhood

By the time the United States was formed, African people and their descendants had been living on the North American continent for close to three hundred years. Unlike Indigenous nations, such as the Cherokees, African Americans as a group did not possess a separate national space, and thus they did not stake their claims to nationhood on territoriality but rather on biblical and historical accounts of a national past that could be revived with divine aid. Yet they faced myriad challenges while trying to generate collective action.

In *Dislocating Race and Nation*, Levine argues that "[o]ne of the specific challenges facing African American literary nationalists, however, was that their community (unlike, say, communities based on sectional, regional, or tribal allegiances) was itself hard to define, given its scattered and fragmented nature" (69). As many scholars have noted, early African American writers and orators addressed themselves to an audience that was not yet fully constituted, an audience they were, in a sense, writing into existence.[32] Beginning in the eighteenth century, African Americans wrote and spoke to this audience in *national* terms informed by geopolitical understandings of nationhood and by biblical representations of Ethiopia and of the ancient Israelites as a diasporic nation. They disputed the colonizationists' emphasis on territoriality, instead linking the actualization of this nation to the achievement of political rights rather than to the acquisition of space. To this end, they began to build institutions and organizations to support broader networks among African American people, including the National Negro Convention movement, which began in Philadelphia in 1830. The founders of the Negro Convention movement selectively engaged and reworked America's founding documents so as to make them offer a more inclusive vision of the American body politic. They produced documents that communicated their conception of African Americans as a nation existing within the borders of the United States but subject to divine rather than earthly jurisdiction.

Historically, scholars of black nationalism have paid relatively little attention to the work of eighteenth- and early nineteenth-century African American writers, characterizing them as "protonationalist" and focusing more on figures from the second half of the nineteenth century forward.[33] The timeline changes based on how one chooses to define *black nationalism*, which has itself been the subject of considerable scholarly debate. One point of contention focuses on whether black nationalist thinking is by definition territorial and concerned with the establishment of separate nation-states, or whether black nationalism is more broadly concerned with what Dexter B. Gordon calls "black autonomy in culture, economics, and politics."[34] Can writers and speakers who do not advocate leaving the United States be considered black nationalists? Michael C. Dawson reminds us that there have been many instantiations of black nationalism, not all of which have been territorial in nature: "Black nationalist conceptions of a 'black nation' ranged from . . . a people with no defined territory, but whom were constituted as a nation and had the right to self-determination; formulations that attached nationhood and self-determination to a specific territory whether in the southern United States (the most common formulation); or . . . versions that associated nationhood to territories outside of the borders of the United States."[35] Territorial visions of black nationalism are often contrasted with Paul Gilroy's transnational vision of transatlantic routes and the kind of cosmopolitanism that informs the works of critics such as Ifeoma Kiddoe Nwankwo and Srinivas Aravamudan.[36] Yet, early African American materials often challenge neat categorization as nationalist or transnationalist. Works produced by African Americans in the eighteenth and early nineteenth centuries suggest myriad and capacious understandings of nationhood, few of which emphasized territorial possession as a *precondition* of nationhood. Rather, they focused on shared origins, spiritual geographies, or multiple and overlapping national affiliations. In ways that reflected the diasporic experiences of African people throughout the Atlantic world, many formulations suggested that nations were mobile rather than static entities, a framework that challenged increasingly territorial constructions of U.S. nationhood.

African Americans began to refer to themselves collectively as a nation or a people in the late eighteenth century. Scholars have pointed to the nation-building efforts of eighteenth-century African American writers and activists, such as Phillis Wheatley, Lemuel Haynes, Cyrus Bustill, Prince Hall, John Marrant, George Liele, Andrew Bryan, Absalom Jones, and Richard Allen.[37] In "A Winter Piece" Jupiter Hammon classified the institution of slavery as an example of God's mercy in that it introduced Africans as a nation to Christianity. Such a statement resonated with Calvinist theologies that emphasized the sovereignty of God, whose ways might seem arbitrary but were ultimately for the good of humanity. Hammon wrote of Africans in America: "[W]e are a poor despised nation, whom God in his wise providence has permitted to be brought from their native place to a christian land, and many thousands born in what are called christian families, and brought up to years of understanding."[38] Here he echoed sentiments written by poet Phillis Wheatley in "On Being Brought from Africa to America," which also emphasized the spiritual salvation that was possible in America:

> 'Twas mercy brought me from my *Pagan* land,
> Taught my benighted soul to understand
> That there's a God, that there's a *Saviour* too:
> Once I redemption neither sought nor knew.
> Some view our sable race with scornful eye,
> "Their colour is a diabolic die."
> Remember, *Christians*, *Negros*, black as *Cain*,
> May be refin'd, and join th' angelic train.[39]

Like Wheatley, Hammon located African Americans both geographically and spiritually as farther from their "native land" but closer to God. Later in the same piece, he referred to his audience as "Africans by nation."[40] By using the term *nation*, Hammon addressed not a political institution nor a specific geographic space but a group of people who could trace their descent from common ancestry and who shared common cultural features.

Constructions of African Americans as members of a larger African nation continued throughout the early nineteenth century, and these presentations, like Hammon's, often asserted the difficulties facing this nation and the promise of future redemption. In 1817, Jacob Oson, "a descendant of Africa," published an address entitled *A Search for Truth; or, An Inquiry for the Origin of the African Nation*, which was addressed to his "people and nation." Oson took up the claims that the African nation was descended from Cain or Noah's son Ham, working to exonerate the African people and to create what Van Wyck Brooks terms a "usable past" by presenting historical examples of African greatness.[41] Oson referred specifically to African Americans as a "nation ... enslaved" within the United States and predicted that the African people would be "raised to their former dignity" without having to leave Egypt "borrowing gold" like the Israelites.[42] Throughout this address, Oson considered questions of origins and genealogical descent rather than territorial possession. To determine the nature of the African nation and argue for its significance, he felt it was important not to describe its geographic location or political culture but rather to trace its genealogy and national history. Departing from the Exodus story, Oson implied that African Americans as a nation would not have to leave to find their Promised Land. Unlike the Israelites, the African nation could find freedom in the nation that had previously held them in bondage. Oson foreshadowed the arguments of later opponents of the colonization movement, such as David Walker and Maria W. Stewart, and offered an important alternative to U.S. discourses of nationhood, which were increasingly linked to territorial possession. He asserted the validity of a conception of ethnic nationhood with membership based on descent rather than territorial ideas of the nation that based membership on land ownership. That is not to say that the possession of territory, both national and individual, was not important, but it was not, for Oson, a precondition for being a *nation*. Within this definitional framework, African nationhood could be realized within the space of America, or anywhere else that African people formed communities. America emerged from his writings not as the sole province of the U.S. nation, but as the site of multiple nations, defined by different criteria.

Like the Cherokees, African Americans began to create institutions that mirrored those of the United States, but that were designed to ameliorate the increasingly fraught conditions of free black people. Their efforts included the formation of independent societies, churches, and educational institutions, including the African Masonic Lodge, formed in Boston by Prince Hall in the late eighteenth century. The lodge did not receive its official charter until 1787, but Hall and others had begun meeting as early as 1775. The Reverends Richard Allen and Absalom Jones created the Free African Society in 1787. In 1816, the same year that saw the formation of the American Colonization Society, the first African American church was formed in America: the African Methodist Episcopal (AME) Church. Created in Philadelphia by Rev. Allen and a group Richard Newman has dubbed the "Black Founding Fathers," the AME Church was a leading voice against slavery and oppression.[43] Other churches, such as the New Bedford AME Zion Church, at which Frederick Douglass preached, and various African Baptist churches, soon followed. Secular associations, such as the Massachusetts General Colored Association (founded 1826), whose members included free black men and women, were formed to protest slavery and other forms of oppression. There were also a number of benevolent associations, including the African Society for Mutual Relief, the Phoenix Society, and the Philomathians. While the opportunities for formal education available to African Americans were limited, some institutions, such as the Abiel Smith School in Boston, Massachusetts, were created to educate African American children. *Freedom's Journal*, edited by John Russwurm and Samuel Cornish, was founded in 1827, and other publications, such as the *Rights of All* and the *North Star*, followed. While the fraternal organizations, aid societies, churches, schools, and newspapers established by African Americans were prompted by the realities of segregation and exclusion, they contributed to the formation of networks and communities that would prove important to later political movements and supported the virtual black nation that was being hailed in written and spoken arguments.[44]

On a broader level, print media were central to the formation of African American communities and the crafting of narratives that allowed African Americans to see themselves as members of what Anderson terms "imagined communities," both the United States, within whose geopolitical borders they resided, and an African nation to which they were linked by genealogy, history, culture, and so forth. Richard Newman, Patrick Rael, and Philip Lapsansky, the editors of *Pamphlets of Protest*, suggest that "[b]etween the 1790s and the 1860s, African American writing became a prominent part of both black protest culture and American public life."[45] They detail the variety of literature produced by black authors and contend that the pamphlet played a particularly important role in African American communities and in American public argument more broadly. The 1820s saw a marked rise in the volume of African American publications. Levine writes, "[David] Walker and other black activists regarded print, rather than oratory, as promising to link together the disparate and scattered African American communities of the early Republic" (*Dislocating*, 71). Walker and others were, according to Levine, concerned with "efforts to put bodies and texts in motion" (96). The circulation of African American people and printed materials challenged repressive state laws and also resonated with a vision of nationhood predicated not on the static occupation of space, but on the ability to move across space and to speak with a collective voice.

David Walker played a key role in the development of this collective voice. While he is best known for his 1829 *Appeal*, he had addressed the Massachusetts General Colored Association (MGCA) a year earlier and called for the formation of a national body of African Americans that could gain political traction in the United States. In this address, which was printed in *Freedom's Journal*, Walker characterized the current state of African Americans as "unorganized" and called on them to work on creating a stronger network that would adhere to the dictates of federal rather than state laws: "*First* then, Mr. President, it is necessary to remark here, at once, that the primary object of this institution, is, to unite the colored population, so far, through the United States of America, as may be practicable and expedient; forming societies, opening, extending, and keeping up correspondences, and not withholding any thing which may have the least tendency to meliorate *our* miserable condition—with the restrictions, however, of not infringing on the articles of its constitution, or that of the United States of America."[46] Walker here presented an organized and politicized network of African Americans as permissible under U.S. law, so long as they abided by the dictates of the U.S. Constitution. Positioning this national body within the federal system, Walker implied that a national body of African Americans would be subject to federal laws but did not suggest that they would be bound to abide by the laws of any particular state. Linking the constitution of the MGCA and that of the United States, Walker offered a particular vision of imperium in imperio by suggesting that in their current condition, African Americans were subject to two sets of secular laws—those they created for themselves and those of the United States.

Walker exhorted his listeners to take an active role in creating a politicized national community and, with God's help, relating to the United States on political terms rather than racial ones. He questioned: "Ought we not to form ourselves into a general body, to protect, aid, and assist each other to the utmost of our power, with the beforementioned restrictions?"[47] By way of an answer, Walker asserted that African Americans have a spiritual as well as an earthly motivation to act on their own behalf. "Yes, Mr. President," Walker contended, "it is indispensably our duty to try every scheme that we think will have a tendency to facilitate our salvation, and leave the final result to that God, who holds the destinies of people in the hollow of his hand, and who ever has, and will, repay every nation according to its works."[48] Walker imagined a dynamic and mutually reinforcing relationship between human beings and God, with the ultimate authority residing in God. However, if African Americans would not work for their own betterment, he warned, God would not reward them as a nation. Throughout his calls for racial uplift, Walker wove in suggestions of national potential, which stemmed, in part, from the sheer numbers of African American people living in the United States. In a rhetorical move aimed at both his immediate audience and the broader community, Walker emphasized the size and strength of the potential black nation: "Two millions and a half of colored people in these United States, more than five hundred thousand of whom are about two-thirds of the way free. Now, I ask, if no more than these last were united (which they must be, or always live as enemies) and resolved to aid and assist each other to the utmost of their power, what mighty deeds could be done by them of the good of our cause?"[49] References to the half a million people who were "two-thirds of the way free" and the "mighty deeds" they might do doubtlessly inspired his African American audience even as his numerical qualifications highlighted the limitations placed on the "free" black population (who were, he argued, only "two-thirds of the way free"). Indeed, just two years after Walker gave this address, the kind of national organization he called for began to coalesce.

The National Negro Convention movement was founded in 1830 by Hezekiah Grice and marked an important moment in the development of African American collective agency.⁵⁰ The group first met in 1830, and in 1831 the First Annual Convention of the People of Colour was held in Philadephia. The location was significant for both symbolic and practical reasons; it was the birthplace of both the AME Church and the U.S. nation and home to a sizeable free black population. As the Fenian Brotherhood would in the 1860s, the convention movement held meetings in Philadelphia to link their national narrative with that of the United States. African American conventions were held annually from 1830 to 1835, with Philadelphia hosting all but one of those years (New York hosted in 1831), and a total of eleven conventions took place between 1830 and 1861. During the same period, there were also numerous conventions held at the state and local levels, which encouraged collective action and supported the national movement. The attendees at these conventions were elected delegates who were positioned as representatives of the free black people in the United States. They took up a number of issues of interest, including slavery, emigration, temperance, moral reform, and education, addressing themselves to both African American and white audiences. Along with other African American secular and spiritual organizations, the National Negro Convention movement and the formation of "quasi-political bodies" were central to the foundation of networks of individuals and communities that were addressed as a nation within the United States.[51]

The documents produced by the conventions of the 1830s responded to colonizationists' representations of an African American imperium as justification for their removal from the United States in various ways. Leaders of the first convention proposed an alternative plan of establishing a "refuge" in Canada for those free black people whose lives had become intolerable in the United States (although the wisdom of leaving the United States would be debated in later meetings). Proponents of this plan acknowledged that Canada was under British law but framed it as American in a geographic sense (i.e., North American). In so doing, they troubled the alignment of political and geographic borders and pressured the definition of *America* in ways that anticipated the emigrationist thought of Martin Delany. They also pressured the language used by white Americans to refer to people of African descent by multiplying and reimagining the terms of the debate and using terms such as "coloured persons," "people of colour," "descendants of Africa," "Americans," "Fellow Citizens," and "descendants of the ancient Egyptians."[52] That the early conventions referred to free black people at times as "persons of colour" dovetailed with a broader trend in African American public argument during the 1830s and other projects of nation formation.

Charlton W. Yingling has argued that "from 1827 to 1841 the free black press of New York City undertook a racial formation project that centered the racially redemptive power of Haiti as its incontrovertible evidence, countering hegemonic aspersions against blacks' intelligence, solvency, social responsibility, and ethics."[53] He suggests that as part of this effort, African American writers employed the term "colored" and moved away from representations of pan-Africanism. The *Colored American*, one of the earliest African American newspapers in New York City, explained its title as an attempt to account for the "peculiarity of our circumstances [which] require special instrumentalities and action" while also challenging those "who would rob us of our nationality and reproach us as exoticks [sic]."[54] The article went on to say, "We are written about, preached to, and prayed for, as *Negroes*, *Africans*, and *blacks*, all of which have been stereotyped, as names of reproach, and on that account, if no other, are unacceptable."[55] Such statements reveal an attempt to claim the political power of self-definition, while abandoning terms that had become associated with racial stereotypes. Thus, while the move from *African* to *colored* might be read as an attempt to distance themselves from certain kinds of national affiliation, it was part of a larger political strategy to elide the racial representations imposed on them by whites. On a national level, the members of the convention movement sought to combat racist representations and exclusionary practices and to articulate their sense of their multiple affiliations by proliferating the terms by which free black people were addressed, reappropriating America's founding documents, and exercising their own legislative capacity.

The leaders of the Negro Convention movement engaged the Declaration of Independence and the U.S. Constitution in ways that made those documents communicate the equality of African American people and challenge the institution of slavery. At the 1831 convention, the Committee on the Condition of the Free People of Colour of the United States recommended that "the Declaration of Independence and Constitution of the United States, be read in our Conventions; believing, that the truths contained in the former are incontrovertible, and that the latter guarantees in letter and spirit to every freeman born in this country, all the rights and immunities of citizenship."[56] In their reading of the U.S. Constitution as providing for black citizenship, the authors anticipated Frederick Douglass's 1849 analysis of this document: Douglass argued that "if 'strictly construed according to its reading' . . . [the U.S. Constitution] is not a pro-slavery instrument."[57] In his discussion of this interpretation, Hoang Gia Phan contends that Douglass distinguished between "a law's 'original intent and meaning' based on the historical context of its framing and its *legislative intent based on the 'strict construction' of its language*."[58] For those attending the conventions, reading America's founding documents aloud served as a kind of performance of political capacity, a way for the conventions' leaders to insert themselves into America's national narrative and insist on their own, more emancipatory interpretation of the language. They did not comment on nor criticize these documents so much as make them speak differently on issues related to the rights of African Americans through engagement with them. The minutes of the conventions in the 1830s quoted the Declaration of Independence in support of African American citizenship and political rights, reappropriating it for their cause. For example, in the 1834 "Declaration of Sentiment," the authors declared, "Let no man remove from his native country, for our principles are drawn from the book of divine revelation, and are incorporated in the Declaration of Independence, 'that all men are born equal, and endowed by their Creator with certain inalienable rights, that among these are life, liberty and the pursuit of happiness.'"[59] Here they slightly reworked the Declaration of Independence's famous phrase and included it in their own "Declaration" as a repudiation of colonization. While some white Americans took the phrase "all men" to refer only to whites, the authors of the "Declaration of Sentiment" made this phrase more capacious through their use of it.

By drafting their own constitutions and "Declaration of Sentiment," the leaders of the convention movement asserted their legislative capacity and took on the rights spoken of in the Declaration of Independence. Just as the Declaration of Independence pronounced the American colonists free of British tyranny, the authors of the "Declaration of Sentiment" challenged the sovereignty of the United States directly by declaring slavery to be unlawful: "Therefore, under whatever pretext or authority laws have been promulgated or executed, whether under parliamentary, colonial, or American legislation, *we declare* them in the sight of Heaven wholly *null* and *void*, and should be *immediately abrogated*" ("Declaration of Sentiment," 28). Bolstered by the sovereignty of God and their sense of their own "patriotism," the authors took for themselves the decision-making power to nullify laws that reinforced slavery, thereby enacting a form of popular sovereignty. In a statement that echoed Wheatley's "On Being Brought from Africa to America," the declaration asserted that African Americans' victory and the spread of Christianity might, in some way, make up for "the downfal [*sic*] of Africa from her ancient pride and splendour" ("Declaration of Sentiment," 29). The declaration further argued that such efforts would be best achieved on American soil, but outside of the body politic: "Let us not lament, that under the present constituted powers of this government, we are disfranchised; better far than to be partakers of its guilt. Let us refuse to be allured by the glittering endowments of official stations, or enchanted with the robe of American citizenship" (29). Although they were not formally considered to be U.S. citizens, the authors of the declaration claimed, they were "patriots," a position not incompatible with their status as members of the African nation and their arguments for multiple political affiliations (29). They raised a "moral flag" rather than a material one with the motto "do unto others, as you would have them do unto you" (31).

The minutes of the 1834 convention demonstrate the ways in which attendees maintained a sense of dual affiliation to both Africa and America, which contrasted with the vision of a threatening black imperium proposed by colonizationists. The authors of the "Declaration of Sentiment" cited the glorious national past that African Americans claimed, but also the injuries they had suffered. They described their current condition thusly: "[W]e find ourselves, after the lapse of three centuries, on the American continent, the remnants of a nation amounting to three millions of people, whose country has been pillaged, parents stolen, nine generations of which have been wasted by the oppressive cruelty of this nation, standing in the presence of the Supreme Ruler of the Universe, and the civilized world, appealing to the God of nations for deliverance" (28). Here African Americans were described as the "remnants of a nation," a group that was nonetheless connected both to a glorious past and to the promise of national regeneration. This regeneration, the authors asserted, would be achieved with the help of God, who was described as the "Supreme Ruler of the Universe" and positioned above earthly authorities. The declaration sought to create a usable national past that located the African nation in time and space. By not focusing on the physical borders of the nation, this document departed from the kind of territoriality expressed by the Cherokee Nation in its 1827 Constitution and instead focused on spiritual geographies. In fact, the declaration positioned the struggle as decidedly political rather than territorial in an effort to combat colonizationist rhetoric and to distance African Americans from the logics of Indian Removal. The authors "rejoice that we are thrown into a revolution where the contest is not for landed territory, but for freedom; the weapons not carnal, but spiritual; where struggle is not for blood, but for right; and where the bow is the power of God, and the arrow the instrument of divine justice; while the victims are the devices of *reason*, and the prejudices of the human heart" (28). African Americans were, this text asserted, fighting a spiritual battle on spiritual terrain and were not part of a struggle over land and resources. This functioned to undercut the territorial arguments of colonizationists who asserted that territorial possession was a precondition for political capacity, and it allowed the convention's leaders to link themselves with both African and American nations.

The 1835 convention emphasized the multiple political affiliations of African Americans and took up the concept of birthright citizenship. Attendees at this convention produced an address titled "To the American People," which hailed white Americans as "Fellow Citizens" and argued strenuously for birthright citizenship.[60] The authors of this address explained that they refer to themselves as "American citizens" who "will not waste our time by holding converse with those who deny us this privilege, unless they first prove that a man is not a citizen of that country in which he was born and reared" (30). This statement stressed the pervasiveness of the doctrine of birthright citizenship in American political thought and put the onus on white Americans to justify why African American people would *not* qualify for citizenship. It also revealed something about the distinction that they drew between the African nation from which they descended and the American one with which they aligned themselves currently. Their link with Africa was historical and genealogical, while their association with America was political and legal (given their own interpretation of U.S. laws). According to this line of argument, people can and do maintain multiple national affiliations with different types of nations and are all ultimately subject to the sovereignty of God even as they must adhere to various civil laws.

Nations under God: Literary Expressions of Divided Sovereignty and African Nationhood in America

African American writers and orators of the late 1820s and 1830s echoed the points made by the Negro Convention movement's documents and earlier African American figures. Their literary productions offered not a consolidated ideological position but rather a proliferation of perspectives that mirrored broader challenges to U.S. national unity and deconstructed formulations of territorial sovereignty. Like the documents produced by the convention movement, the literary productions of Robert Alexander Young, David Walker, Maria W. Stewart, and Hosea Easton (who was involved with the conventions) worked to unyoke definitions of nationhood from territorial possession. They blended legal and religious language to suggest the presence of an African nation that was subject to the sovereignty of God and bounded by spiritual rather than geopolitical borders.[61] Such an argument constituted a challenge to the discourses of territorial nationhood and divided sovereignty that circulated in American public argument and a recovery of overlapping notions of secular and divine authority. One of the central points to emerge from these writings was the sense that one could be a member of the African nation created by God *and* argue for political inclusion within the United States. In the context of the Missouri crisis and the African colonization movement, the proliferation of perspectives on an African nation in America challenged with particular rhetorical force the ideological links between sovereignty, citizenship, and the exclusive possession of national space.

One of the most important vehicles for literary arguments about an African nation in America was the jeremiad, defined by Sacvan Bercovitch as a "political sermon" or "state-of-the-covenant address," which functioned as a religious analogue to the constitution.[62] This genre has a long history in American public argument. As Perry Miller, Bercovitch, and others note, these sermons, often delivered on holidays or other public occasions, reminded listeners of their covenant with God, enumerated the ways in which the community had fallen away from the covenant, and exhorted the people to change their behavior and maintain their faith. These sermons reflected a key point of Puritan theology—the emphasis on the *sovereignty* of God. As Miller suggests, of all the characteristics that Puritans attributed to God, they emphasized sovereignty the most. God was represented as the supreme authority who set the terms of the covenant with his chosen people.[63] Yet, even though the covenant was, in some ways, predetermined, human beings still had a role to play. Bercovitch explains it thusly: Keeping the covenant "was a process of 'living to God,' involving a mutual obligation" and "entailing struggle and temptation at every stage."[64] As in the relationship between earthly sovereigns and their subjects, the relationship between God and Christian people was framed to be reciprocal. In exchange for protection and care, subjects were expected to adhere to the laws of their earthly or heavenly ruler.

As Wilson Moses and others argue, African American writers and orators adopted the genre of the jeremiad to craft forceful arguments against slavery and oppression. Moses defines the "black jeremiad" as "the constant warnings issued by blacks to whites, concerning the judgment that was to come from the sin of slavery."[65] African American writers of jeremiads presented themselves as a "chosen people" in the larger context of America as a "chosen nation with a covenantal duty to deal justly with the blacks" (Moses, *Black Messiahs*, 31). David Howard-Pitney has expanded on this argument, claiming that "the dominant black American jeremiad tradition conceives of blacks as a chosen people *within* a chosen people. The African American jeremiad tradition, then, characteristically addresses *two* American chosen peoples—black and white—whose millennial destinies, while distinct, are also inextricably entwined."[66] Not only was the jeremiad intended to circulate among "*two* American chosen peoples" whose futures were "inextricably entwined," but it was also uniquely positioned to address both enslaved and free African Americans, speaking to what Dexter B. Gordon has dubbed a "collective subject."[67] The works of David Walker, Robert Alexander Young, Frederick Douglass, Booker T. Washington, Ida B. Wells-Barnett, and others have all been discussed in the context of the jeremiad, as attempts to exhort white Americans and African Americans to keep the terms of their covenants with God.

African American writers' and orators' use of the jeremiad form to communicate the sovereignty of God and the national status of African people in America can be traced to the eighteenth century. One early example comes from Prince Hall, who used the language of Freemasonry in his 1797 "Charge" to the African Masonic Lodge and referred to Christ as the "head and grand master" of "the kingdoms of the whole earth," of which the Ethiopian nation was one example.[68] Hall's "Charge" suggests a vision of sovereignty in which divine authority supersedes that of secular rulers and is spiritually rather than territorially bounded. Prince Saunders, one of the leading voices in Philadelphia's African American community, addressed the Pennsylvania Augustine Society, an African American benevolent association, in 1818 and blended political and spiritual language to argue for the value of Christian education. He too emphasized that African American Christians were subject to the sovereignty of God:

> Under the influence of this spirit, this benevolent spirit, practical Christians, of every denomination, have elevated their views far beyond the circumscribed boundaries of selfishness, sectarianism, and party zeal; and, being bound together by the indissoluble links of that golden chain of charity and kind affection, with which Christianity invariably connects its sincere votaries, and standing upon the common ground of Christian equality, they encircle the great community of those who profess the religion of our divine Master, in the arms of their charity and love, and become co-workers and fellow labourers in the illumination, the improvement, and the ultimate felicity of those who will, undoubtedly, eventually belong to the commonwealth of the Israel of our God.[69]

Here the "boundaries" of self-interest were contrasted with the "golden chain of charity and kind affection" that surrounds the Christian community. His references to golden chains and the "divine Master" evoked images of the physical chains and secular masters to whom enslaved African Americans were subject in the American South and juxtaposed spiritual and earthly mastery. Saunders framed God as presiding over the "commonwealth of . . . Israel," a community to which African Americans could belong even as they were marginalized in the commonwealth of Pennsylvania and in the United States. Citing Acts 17:26, Saunders contended that God "made of one blood all nations of men who dwell upon the face of the whole earth," a claim that challenged racist arguments for polygenesis and framed God as the creator of nations and the source of sovereignty.[70] Saunders reworked territorial visions of imperium in imperio to suggest that, like members of all the other nations of the world, Africans in America were members of a nation with a covenantal role within the larger commonwealth of God. The work of Hall and Saunders constituted more than just statements of Christian orthodoxy; they fused religious rhetoric and rhetorics of nationhood to frame African Americans as part of a nation whose existence was not limited to any one geopolitical space.

Drawing on the work of earlier figures like Hall and Saunders, African American writers and orators of the 1820s and 1830s challenged calls to remove the African American imperium beyond the borders of the United States with their own visions of nationhood and divided sovereignty that were grounded in their readings of the Bible. One of the cornerstones of such arguments was the so-called Ethiopian prophecy, which was used by Robert Alexander Young, David Walker, Maria W. Stewart, and others to position African Americans within an Ethiopian nation whose existence spanned the geopolitical borders of the United States. As Albert Raboteau has suggested, Psalm 68:31 is "the most quoted verse in black religious history."[71] This psalm was the cornerstone of Ethiopianism, defined by Theophus Smith as a "[b]lack literary expression" that "depends for its rhetorical and prophetic force on Psalm 68:31 (King James Version): 'Princes shall come out of Egypt; Ethiopia shall soon stretch out her hands to God.'"[72] Scholars such as Susan Gillman, Eric Sundquist, and Wilson Moses note that the nature of "Ethiopianism" is difficult to define. Gillman's definition closely resembles that of Smith: "the religious, literary, and political philosophy derived from the biblical passage picturing Ethiopia stretching forth her hands to God (i.e., Psalm 68:31)."[73] Disagreement arises, however, as to whether Ethiopianism was linked to black nationalism, as Moses argues, or to pan-Africanism, as Gillman and others suggest. When one considers this verse in the broader context of debates surrounding divided sovereignty—a nation within a nation—and competing constructions of nationhood, these positions do not seem to be diametrically opposed, as my readings of Young, Walker, and Stewart suggest. Ethiopianism revealed a different conception of nationhood than the Westphalian model of the territorial state but can be seen as concerned with nation formation. According to proponents of Ethiopianism, this African nation could not be plotted on a map because it was defined first and foremost in relation to spiritual geographies rather than geopolitical borders; moreover, it could exist within and alongside other nations.

Young's work, which draws heavily on the jeremiad form, constitutes one of the most sustained uses of the Ethiopian prophecy to think through the possibilities of divided sovereignty—in the form of an African nation within a nation—and to challenge territorial visions of nationhood. Young published *The Ethiopian Manifesto* in New York in February 1829, the same year that Walker's *Appeal* appeared, and it addressed African Americans as the Ethiopian nation mentioned in the Bible and suggested that they occupied the position of a nation within a nation, even in Africa. Young exhorted his audience: "Know, then, in your present state or standing, in your sphere of government in any nation within which you reside, we hold and contend you enjoy but a few of your rights of government within them. We here speak of the whole of the Ethiopian people, as we admit not even those in their state of native simplicity, to be in an enjoyment of their rights, as bestowed to them of the great bequest of God to man."[74] Here Young asserted that the Ethiopian people resided in a separate "sphere of government" within the nations that they inhabited and that they were in fact a nation, although not a territorial nation in the Westphalian sense. They "reside" in particular nations but have been denied access to civic culture and the right to self-government, as individuals or as a people, by secular leaders. Yet their national existence is predicated on their relationship to God, not on the possession of space or involvement in particular governments.

While David Walker called for a national organization of African Americans in his address to the MGCA, Young called for his audience to form themselves into a "body politic," which reveals his sense that acting as a *nation* might help African people gain political traction in the political communities in which they currently resided. Such an organization, he suggested, would improve the conditions of the Ethiopian people:

> The impositions practiced to their state, not being known to them from the heavy and darksome clouds of ignorance which so woefully obscures their reason, we do, therefore, for the recovering of them, as well as establishing to you your rights, proclaim, that duty—imperious duty, exacts the convocation of ourselves in a body politic; that we do, for the promotion and welfare of our order, establish to ourselves a people framed unto the likeness of that order, which from our mind's eye we do evidently discern governs the universal creation. Beholding but one sole power, supremacy, or head, we do of that head, but hope and look forward for succour in the accomplishment of the great design which he hath, in his wisdom, promoted us to its undertaking. (Young, *Ethiopian Manifesto*, 86)

The "body politic" that Young sought was one that recognized "one sole power, supremacy, or head": God. The Ethiopian people were subject to the ultimate sovereignty of God, and it was from this divine source that the Ethiopians believed their rights proceeded. Young paraphrased Psalm 68 to give voice to God's response to Ethiopia's pleas: "surely hath the cries of the black[s], a most persecuted people, ascended to my throne and craved my mercy; now, behold! I will stretch forth mine hand and gather them to the palm, that they become unto me a people, and I unto them their God" (87). This reworking of Psalm 68 emphasized not only God's sovereignty but also the reciprocal relationship between that sovereign power and those in the community of allegiance, a move that highlighted the ideal relationship between sovereigns and their subjects. Ethiopia extends a hand to God, and God in turn responds with assistance. In the meantime, Young exhorted his audience to attempt "such government of yourselves as should be responsible but to God, your maker, for the duty exacted of you to your fellow-men" (88). As David Walker would do later that year, Young forecasted divine retribution for those who held the Africans in bondage, the "vain bloated upstart worldling of a slaveholder" (87). As lawgiver and sovereign, God would punish those who had oppressed the African nation in their midst.

David Walker's *Appeal in Four Articles* (1829), which also drew on the jeremiad form and America's founding documents, resonated with Young's *Manifesto* in his use of the Ethiopian prophecy in his formulation of an African nation, which contrasted sharply with the conceptions of territorial nationhood and indivisible sovereignty advanced by colonizationists.[75] In the third edition, published in 1830, Walker alluded to an Ethiopian nation as part of his exhortation to potential readers:

> It is expected that all coloured men, women and children, of every nation, language and tongue under heaven, will try to procure a copy of this Appeal and read it, or get some one to read it to them, for it is designed more particularly for them. Let them remember, that though our cruel oppressors and murderers, may (if possible) treat us more cruel, as Pharaoh did the children of Israel, yet the God of the Ethiopeans [*sic*], has been pleased to hear our moans in consequence of oppression; and the day of our redemption from abject wretchedness draweth near, when we shall be enabled, in the most extended sense of the word, to stretch forth our hands to the LORD our GOD, but there must be a willingness on our part, for GOD to do these things for us, for we may be assured that he will not take us by the hairs of our head against our will and desire, and drag us from our very, mean, low and abject condition.[76]

Here Walker referred to the "God of the Ethiopeans" as the figure who would ameliorate the suffering of African people in America and elsewhere, and he echoed Young's contention that the relationship between African Americans and their sovereign God was one of reciprocity. He, like Young, rephrased Psalm 68 to make it communicate a more urgent sense of the action African Americans would need to take in order to advance their political and social position. His reference to the "coloured men, women and children, of every nation, language and tongue under heaven" along with his overall address to the "coloured citizens of the world" challenged constructions of indivisible political sovereignty by highlighting the multiple affiliations that all people have to both divine and secular authorities.

Religion forms a conceptual link between Walker's use of a black nationalism centered in the United States and what might be called a kind of transnational or diasporic perspective, both of which functioned to reimagine the visions of territorial nationhood and indivisible sovereignty championed by supporters of colonization. Walker's *Appeal* has been described by scholars as both a foundational text of U.S. black nationalism and, in the words of Peter Linebaugh and Marcus Rediker, a "manifesto of pan-African freedom."[77] Levine highlights the "tensions in his [Walker's] writing between a black nationalism conceived in relation to a conflicted U.S. nationalism and a black nationalism conceived diasporically" (*Dislocating*, 71). He concludes that "[t]here is no easy way to 'locate' Walker's black nationalism" (71). Walker addressed multiple audiences in his *Appeal*, including the "coloured citizens of the world," who were subject to the sovereignty of God. He also directed his remarks "particularly and very expressly to those of the United States of America" and the "coloured citizens of this country."[78] While here "citizen" could merely mean "resident," it seems unlikely that Walker would ignore the political meaning of this term. These populations are not necessarily to be read as two different audiences, but rather as evidence of Walker's conception of nationhood as allowing for multiple affiliations. He suggested that one could be both a "coloured citizen of the world" and a "coloured citizen of this country." Walker's understanding of nationhood was capacious and multiple, including imagined political communities forged by racial, cultural, and religious ties and territorially based states governed by political institutions. Individuals can and do have multiple national allegiances and are subject to multiple laws; while divine sovereignty is indivisible, earthly sovereignty is and can be divided. From this perspective, Walker imagined a future in which the United States could be a site of regeneration for the nation he envisioned.

Like Young and Walker, Maria W. Stewart, the first African American woman to deliver public orations, used Ethiopia as a metaphor for an African nation that she believed would be regenerated within and extend beyond U.S. borders in her versions of the jeremiad. In an 1833 "Address at the African Masonic Hall," she offered the following survey of African history and forecasted a national regeneration:

> History informs us that we sprung from one of the most learned nations of the whole earth; from the seat, if not the parent, of science; yes, poor despised Africa was once the resort of sages and legislators of other nations, was esteemed the school for learning, and the most illustrious men in Greece flocked thither for instruction. But it was our gross sins and abomination that provoked the Almighty to frown thus heavily upon us, and give our glory unto others. Sin and prodigal-

ity have caused the downfall of nations, kings and emperors; and were it not that God in wrath remembers mercy, we might indeed despair; but a promise is left us; "Ethiopia shall again stretch forth her hands unto God."[79]

While Moses argues that Stewart's address can be considered nationalistic "only in the sense that it contains a biblically inspired perception of African Americans as a people with a special God-given mission and destiny,"[80] Stewart's argument for a national past and her use of scripture offered a subtle yet powerful message about the remaking of African nationhood. By the time Stewart delivered her address at the Masonic Hall in 1833, Psalm 68 was a well-known component of discussions of the current status and possible future of Africans and African Americans. Note that in her reworking of this psalm, Stewart replaced the word *soon* with the word *again* so that it reads: "Ethiopia shall *again* stretch forth her hands unto God" (emphasis added). Rephrasing the psalm in this way highlighted the regenerative power of God, who will reforge Ethiopia and free its people from bondage in the nation in which they currently reside.

Like Psalm 68, the Exodus story played a key role in discussions of colonization. In addition to likening African Americans to the Ethiopian nation mentioned in the Bible, Walker drew on Exodus to challenge colonizationist rhetorics of a black imperium that had to be removed from within the borders of the United States. As Moses argues, "It is clear that Walker believed that African Americans were a national entity in the same sense that the Old Testament Hebrews had been a nation."[81] The Israelites of the Old Testament were compelling for Walker—and key to his conception of nationalism—precisely because they were not geographically separate from the Egyptians. Indeed, Walker often used the word *people* interchangeably with *nation* to complicate understandings of nationhood predicated on territorial possession. When Walker spoke of the "coloured people of the United States" in his 1829 *Appeal*, he referred to not just an audience of human beings, but to a political community of "coloured citizens." He addressed African Americans as a "people," or a nation that existed within the United States but also transcended its geopolitical borders.[82] The term *people* for Walker not only suggested the basic humanity of Africans and their descendants, but also the sense that they, like the Israelites, were an ethnic nation with a shared origin, history, and destiny. He declared in article 3, "We are a people, notwithstanding many of you doubt it" (42). For Walker, a people could be culturally, racially, and religiously unified even if they were not geographically located in the same political and physical space. The "coloured citizens of the world," separated as they were by geographic, political, and economic obstacles, could thus be considered a nation in the sense that the Israelites were. That is to say, they could be a diasporic nation that either did not or had yet to occupy a territorial space. Through his construction of African Americans as a "people," Walker reworked dominant discourses of nationhood that predicated a nation's existence on its possession of a national territory and addressed African Americans as members of a divinely authored *nation*.

Walker admired the capacity of the Israelites to endure as a *nation* within the space of Egypt even when they could not be said to possess their own national space. Subject as they were to the authority of the Egyptians, they were also bound by their covenant to God. Walker cited a passage from Genesis 47, before the death of Joseph and the enslavement of the Jewish people. In this passage, Pharaoh tells Joseph the following after learning that his father and brothers had come to Egypt: "The land of Egypt is before thee: in the best of the land make thy father and brethren to dwell; in the land of Goshen let them dwell: and if thou knowest any men of activity among them, then make them rulers over my cattle" (qtd. in Walker, *Appeal*, 9). Thus, Jacob and his sons, the progenitors of the nation of Israel, lived for a time on what Walker called "the most fertile land in Egypt" (9). Moses raises the possibility that Walker used this story to suggest that Americans should grant African Americans territory of their own but concludes that Walker's thoughts on the matter cannot be fully discerned.[83] As a metonym for the nation of Israel, Jacob and his sons live in the nation of Egypt, yet they remain subject to the authority of God. They are geographically within, but spiritually separate from, the nation in which they reside. By comparing his audience to the ancient Israelites, Walker shifted the terms of the discussion from geopolitical borders to spiritual geographies and again contended that African Americans (like the Israelites) constitute a nation within a nation. As in the case of the Israelites, he predicted that this division of sovereignty would be temporary until they eventually, with the help of God, escaped from bondage.

Yet Walker also held up the Israelites as a point of contrast and was strategic in his invocation of the Exodus story, given the broader conversation about removing free black people to Africa. Walker was hardly original in turning to Exodus. Many nineteenth-century African American writers drew on the biblical story of Exodus to tell a compelling tale of the movement from slavery to freedom, a journey they hoped Africans in America would soon take.[84] Yet, Walker departed from this established tradition in significant ways in order to resist the colonizationist position that the virtual black nation must be removed to Africa so that it could claim the territory necessary to achieve its national potential. In the *Appeal*, he mentioned as an aside that the Egyptians were Africans, thus complicating the identification between African Americans and the Israelites and suggesting perhaps the cyclical nature of history: "For the information of such, I would only mention that the Egyptians, were Africans or coloured people, such as we are—some of them yellow and others dark—a mixture of Ethiopians and the natives of Egypt—about the same as you see the coloured people of the United States at the present day" (8). While African people were currently slaves, they were once masters and, it was implied, might be again. Contrasting Walker with Richard Allen and other African Americans who drew on Exodus, Chris Apap argues that Walker "upends the narrative logic of the Exodus story" and "turns the spatial logic of Exodus—that of a literal movement out of the land of slavery—on its head, and in so doing develops a forceful reinterpretation of both the sacred and secular histories of Christianity."[85] Apap notes that in the context of colonization, narratives of a nation "fleeing the land of slavery en masse" were problematic because they dovetailed with the ACS rhetorics of the removal of free black people to a space where they could create their own nation.[86] He further suggests that Walker reversed the Exodus story by emphasizing human rather than divine agency; while God led the people out of Egypt, African Americans must take a more active role in achieving their freedom. Ultimately, Walker can be seen to draw parallels between the African nation in America and the ancient Israelites, while framing the exodus of the former as a political and spiritual journey rather than a physical one.

For Walker, Stewart, and others, the link between an African nation in America and national and biblical models of Ethiopia and Israel did not justify emigration to present-day Africa. The links with Africa were historical and genealogical, they asserted, not *territorial*. With this argument, they worked to deconstruct the links that colonizationists sought to forge between African American people and the physical space of Africa and to align themselves with the American landscape. Stewart warned in her 1833 Masonic address: "They would drive us to a strange land. But before I go, the bayonet shall pierce me through. African rights and liberty is a subject that ought to fire the breast of every free man of color in these United States, and excite in his bosom a lively, deep, decided, and heartfelt interest."[87] Stewart explicitly distanced African American people from Africa itself, referring to it as a "strange land." Like Richard Allen and Phillis Wheatley, Stewart challenged the notion of Africa as the home of African Americans. Its strangeness suggests Stewart's awareness of the linguistic and cultural differences (and perhaps the problematic imperialism) that would hinder African colonization. But more important for Stewart and for other opponents of colonization, the Africa of the nineteenth century was "strange" because it was not a Christian society. They did not conceive of historical and metaphorical connections with "Ethiopia" as precluding membership in the American nation nor did these historical connections require political or geographic links with Africa. Railing against what he called "the colonizing trick" (67), Walker troubled representations of Africa as the "home" of free black people in his *Appeal*: "What our brethren could have been thinking about, who have left their native land and home and gone away to Africa, I am unable to say. This country is as much ours as it is the whites, whether they will admit it now or not, they will see and believe it by and by" (55). Here and elsewhere, Walker challenged representations of colonization as the return of black people to their homeland. The United States, for all of its problems, was the "native land" and "home" of African Americans, to whom he referred in communal terms. Alluding to the territorial logic of American nationhood, Walker argued that black people have a strong claim on the American landscape. He questioned the argument that African Americans were stateless because they did not possess a national territory and sought to revise the ways in which the relationships between nations and space were understood.

Claiming a place for an African nation within the United States required opponents of colonization to elide languages of possession by virtue of conquest, discovery, and legal title, and argue instead for affective and labor-based relationships with the land. Writers such as Walker and Stewart worked to articulate a relationship to land that was not based on individual ownership but rather on communal claims. For Walker, it was because of their labor that African Americans had as much claim on the U.S. landscape as did whites. He contended: "America is more our country, than it is the whites—we have enriched it with our *blood and tears*. The greatest riches in all America have arisen from our blood and tears:—and will they drive us from our property and homes, which we have earned with our *blood?*" (65). He also quoted a letter from Richard Allen, originally published in *Freedom's Journal*: "This land which we have watered with our *tears* and *our blood*, is now our *mother country*, and we are well satisfied to stay where wisdom abounds and the gospel is free" (qtd. in Walker, *Appeal*, 58). Three years later, Maria W. Stewart, a friend of David Walker, used almost the same wording to discuss the "benighted sons and daughters of Africa, who have enriched the soils of America with their tears and blood."[88] Walker, Allen, and Stewart refuted the depiction of African Americans as trapped in a strange land where they could not flourish. In her "Address Delivered at the African Masonic Hall" (1833), after enumerating the cruelties that white Americans had committed toward Native Americans and African Americans, Stewart declared that "now that we have enriched their soil, and filled their coffers, they say that we are not capable of becoming like white men, and that we can never rise to respectability in this country."[89] It was

African American labor, these writers and speakers argued, that gave U.S. land economic value. The blood and tears of enslaved African Americans fertilized the land and formed an inseparable bond between the worker and the land. As a result, they argued, African Americans should maintain their relationship to the American landscape and should resist all inducements to leave.

Hosea Easton, an African American minister, activist, and opponent of colonization who was involved with the Negro Convention movement, placed more emphasis on land than some of his contemporaries but also implied that the African nation could and should be renationalized within the borders of the United States. In *A Treatise on the Intellectual Character and Civil and Political Condition of the Colored People of the United States*, published in 1837, Easton argued that "the injury sustained by the colored people, is both national and personal; indeed, it is national in a twofold sense." Because Africans were stolen from their countries of origin and forced into slavery, all "legal or natural relations" between Africa and African Americans had been severed. He wrote:

> They are no longer her children; therefore, they sustain the great injury of losing their country, their birthright, and are made aliens and illegitimates. Again, they sustain a national injury by being adopted subjects and citizens, and then being denied their citizenship, and the benefits derivable therefrom—accounted as aliens and outcasts, hence, are identifiable as belonging to no country, denied birthright in one and had it stolen in another—and, I had liked to have said, they have lost title to both worlds, for certainly they are denied all title in this, and almost all advantages to prepare for the next. In this light of the subject, they belong to no people, race, or nation; subjects of no government—citizens of no country—scattered surplus remnants of two races, and of different nations—severed into individuality—rendered a mass of broken fragments, thrown to and fro, by the boisterous passions of this and other ungodly nations. Such, in part, are the national injuries suffered by this miserable people.[90]

Easton framed slavery and the discrimination faced by free black people in America as grievous "national injuries" and linked these injuries specifically to a loss of land. African Americans had been doubly displaced by being separated from the land of their birth and forced to live as "illegitimates" in the United States. Unlike earlier writers, Easton drew on legal rhetorics of property ownership, but reworked them in order to discuss both spiritual and earthly territories. He claimed that African Americans were "denied all title" in this world and were unable to "prepare for the next" world. Easton's *Treatise*, which also argued for monogenesis, blended discourses of law and religion in framing its discussion of slavery in terms of national loss. Despite his claims that descendants of Africans "belong to no people, race, or nation," were "subjects of no government ... [and] citizens of no country," Easton's implied argument was that because this situation was the result of man-made circumstances, that nation could be remade if slavery and racial oppression ceased.

In his *Treatise*, he shifted the terms of the discussion from issues of race to issues of nationhood and property, forcing readers to consider the descendants of Africans as political beings. Like Prince Saunders in "An Address before the Pennsylvania Augustine Society" (1818), Easton referenced Acts 17:26 as an argument for monogenesis, which he asserted was now accepted "by all Christendom."[91] Citing biblical authority that "God hath made of one blood all nations of men for to dwell on all the face of the earth," Easton countered the notion that Africans and their descendants were racially inferior or physiologically different from white people (67). Variations in physical features such as hair and skin, he argued, were a result of the same natural processes that create variation throughout the natural world. Later in the *Treatise*, he transposed political rhetoric onto a discussion of physiognomy and asserted that "their [African Americans'] complexion is as truly American as the complexion of the whites" (113). Easton interjected the political into discussions of race and identity, equating skin color with nationality rather than with race. He also infused the label "American" with a sense of multiplicity, in this case of complexion. His use of religious and political rhetoric allowed him to shift the terms of the debate away from racial identity and toward a discussion of political status.

Conclusion

During the tumultuous decades of the 1820s and 1830s, the projects of Indian Removal and African colonization were predicated on the idea that American Indians and free black people constituted internal nations that could and should be moved beyond the putative borders of the United States. Representing these groups as nations rendered them more easily knowable and governable than masses of individuals. Because African Americans did not claim their own discrete territory, colonizationists framed them as a kind of virtual nation, a nation in the making that required land to achieve its full potential. Within America's borders, a "nation of blacks," to use Knapp's phrase, represented a dangerous division of sovereignty and a competing claim on American national space. Supporters of the African Colonization Society hoped for the kind of federal support that Andrew Jackson had provided for the Removal of the Cherokees and other Southeastern tribes. Such support never materialized, yet colonization continued to circulate in American public argument as a means of dealing with the free black population well into the nineteenth century. The ongoing interest in colonization and rhetorics of an African American imperium reveal the ways in which nationhood and sovereignty were increasingly linked with territorial possession in American thought and that the removal of populations was increasingly seen as a prerogative of federal sovereignty.

While African Americans had been discussing themselves in national terms for some time, such conversations gained new urgency in the context of the Missouri crisis, the passing of increasingly repressive state laws on both sides of the Mason-Dixon Line, and the growing interest in African colonization. While scholars have contrasted black nationalism with transnationalism (and related concepts, such as cosmopolitanism and a hemispheric perspective), I argue that during the period in question both U.S.-oriented black nationalism and more transnational perspectives, such as Ethiopianism and pan-Africanism, were part of a larger response to the increasing hegemony of territorial nationalism, which was being deployed in the service of arguments to remove free black people from the United States and arguments that Africans could never become part of the American community of allegiance because of their connections to Africa. Organizations such as the National Negro Conventions and public figures such as Robert Alexander Young, David Walker, Maria W. Stewart, and Hosea Easton offered varied and sometimes competing visions of the national affiliations of African Americans. They reappropriated America's founding documents to make them offer a more inclusive vision of American nationhood and drafted their own national documents in order to speak to white Americans on political terms. They recovered earlier rhetorics of divine sovereignty (understood as political and spiritual power) as part of their argument that territorial possession was not a precondition for sovereignty and nationhood. Moreover, this emphasis on divine sovereignty allowed them to suggest that individuals could be considered members of multiple nations, some based on history, culture, and shared experience and others based on political and territorial factors. The idea of an African nation in America was framed as an ongoing reality, not a political impossibility nor a racially inferior community that could be removed en masse.

CHAPTER THREE

"Space for Action"

Divided Sovereignty, Political Allegiance, and African American Nationhood in the 1850s

AT THE CONCLUSION of Harriet Beecher Stowe's bestselling novel *Uncle Tom's Cabin* (1852), several of the central characters emigrate to Africa, including George and Eliza Harris; their children; George's sister Emily; Eliza's mother, Cassy; and Topsy. George explains his decision in a letter to a friend by suggesting that his "sympathies are not for my father's race, but for my mother's" (*UTC*, 393). For George, extending his "sympathies" to his mother's race means leaving Canada, where he had been living with his family, and going to Liberia to assist in the nation-building project. He writes, "On the shores of Africa I see a republic,—a republic formed of picked men, who, by energy and self-educating force, have, in many cases, individually, raised themselves above a condition of slavery.... There it is my wish to go, and find myself a people" (393–394). He wants to join this political community and "find a people" because he feels that there is nothing he can do for the enslaved population of the United States: "Can I break their chains? No, not as an individual; but, let me go and form part of a nation, which shall have a voice in the councils of nations, and then we can speak. A nation has a right to argue, remonstrate, implore, and present the cause of its race,—which an individual has not" (394). Here the novel emphasizes the importance of *national* status as a point of entry into a larger political community. Individuals and racial groups have very little political leverage in the international community, but nations can exert pressure on this community and improve the conditions of all of its members. Despite the novel's tremendous popularity, readers have struggled with the ending since its initial publication, with Martin Delany concluding in an 1853 letter to Frederick Douglass, "Mrs. Stowe knows nothing about us [free black people]."[1] African colonization remained a controversial topic in the 1850s, but George Harris's statements about the strategic value of national status resonated with other discussions of black nation formation at the time and connected with the larger rhetorical tradition of framing collective identity in national terms.

As I explored in the previous chapter, characterizations of an African American nation that emerged from colonization rhetorics had largely focused on free black people as a virtual nation. As Stowe's novel suggests, that strand of colonization rhetoric did not disappear, but by the 1850s the conversation had changed considerably. The United States was wracked by fierce debates over issues of sovereignty regarding the treatment of escaped slaves and the extension of slavery in the western territories, and multiple narratives emerged about American nationhood and its political future. In this fraught context, prominent defenders of slavery turned to rhetorics of imperium in imperio to frame chattel slavery in political terms, as a form of government, in an attempt to defend themselves against growing antislavery sentiment in the North. In fact, they claimed that slavery was the best form of government for African Americans and provided them with a productive relationship to the American landscape. In this chapter, I argue that during the 1850s, conceptions of imperium in imperio were reimagined both as a defense of slavery and as a form of radical popular sovereignty, enacted by John Brown and the members of the Chatham Convention.

The Provisional Constitution and the "Declaration of Liberty" produced by Brown were, according to Martin Delany, inspired by the Constitution of the Cherokee Nation, suggesting the influence that the Cherokees had on the political projects of other nineteenth-century nations. Brown and his followers strove to create a "provisional" or virtual antislavery nation within the larger United States but outside of any particular state jurisdiction. Their documents highlighted their belief that multiple nations could share the same space, and they rearticulated key political and legal documents, granting membership regardless of race and nullifying the *Dred Scott* decision's denial of African American rights. Following my reading of Brown's documents, I turn to the work of Martin Delany and Frederick Douglass, both of whom were involved with the National Negro Convention movement and with Brown and his provisional government but later distanced themselves from his attack on Harpers Ferry. While they disagreed on many points, both Delany and Douglass recognized the strategic value of claiming national status, strategically engaged rhetorics of imperium in imperio to deconstruct the political and territorial contours of the American nation, and thought through the possibility of multiple political affiliations.² I conclude this chapter with a brief discussion of the constitution of what is perhaps the most famous nation to emerge from within the United States—the Confederate States of America (CSA). Ratified just a few years after Brown's trial, which drew widespread attention to his Provisional Constitution, the Confederate Constitution also engaged the U.S. Constitution's treatment of slavery, territoriality, and imperium in imperio. While Brown's provisional government differed radically from the CSA, both drew on the power of written constitutions to articulate their national status vis-à-vis the United States.

A House Divided: Imperium in Imperio and Competing Visions of Nationhood and Sovereignty in the 1850s

For many white Americans, mid-nineteenth-century arguments about the extension of slavery in the West had little to do with African American rights but had everything to do with the political character of the U.S. nation and with questions of sovereignty. Levine's observation that there was no single "American ideology" in the years surrounding the Missouri crisis is even more true of the 1850s, when fictions of a single, unified American nation and national ideology became even more tenuous. In this fraught context, debates about what the presence of these other nations might mean for the United States began to circulate with increasing frequency. At the same time, discussions continued to address questions about the nature of sovereignty and where it resided—in the people, the state governments, or the federal government. As a writer from the *South Side Democrat*, a newspaper published in Petersburg, Virginia, pointed out: "To introduce or abolish slavery is an attribute of sovereignty."³ With this statement, the author summed up the political zeitgeist of the 1850s and 1860s, which culminated in the creation of two national constitutions with diametrically opposed positions on slavery—John Brown's Provisional Constitution and that of the CSA. Departing from the vague language of the U.S. Constitution, both documents framed decision-making power with regard to slavery as a fundamental element of state and federal sovereignty as well as a key component of whites' individual liberty.

In the midst of this contentious political landscape, the removal of free black people, a plan predicated on their national potential, was still held up as a way to overcome political difference and maintain the Union. Drawing on the new rhetorical links between sovereignty and slavery, some slavery apologists also repackaged the language of imperium in imperio as a defense of slavery. From such a perspective, slavery was represented not as perpetual servitude, but as an appropriate form of government for an African American imperium.

The passage of the Compromise of 1850 brought competing visions of sovereignty, slavery, and territory to the forefront of American politics and public argument. Issues surrounding the treatment of fugitive slaves had already prompted a number of showdowns between state and federal authorities, but reactions to the Fugitive Slave Act of 1850 revealed the Union to be in a state of crisis. Those who supported the compromise felt that it was a necessary measure to prevent the dissolution of the Union by providing for the capture of escaped slaves and by establishing popular sovereignty as a guiding principle in the government of the western territories.[4] The term *popular sovereignty* had a lot of currency in the 1850s, but the meaning of the term differed greatly from the kind of sovereignty that the Revolutionary generation would have associated with "the people." As Gordon Wood explains in *The Creation of the American Republic*, the founding generations believed that the people expressed their sovereignty through representative government, which was divided so as to prevent any one faction or individual from assuming too much power and abrogating the rights of the people. Ronald Formisano argues that this formulation of popular sovereignty persisted through the administration of James Madison in the nineteenth century.[5]

The version of popular sovereignty that dominated the debates of the 1850s had its roots in the kind of populism that emerged during the administrations of Andrew Jackson and Martin Van Buren, both of whom advocated strenuously for states' rights. During an 1830 debate in the Senate over nullification, Massachusetts senator Daniel Webster expressed this populist sentiment: "It is, sir, the people's constitution, the people's Government, made for the people; made by the people; and answerable to the people.... The States are, unquestionably, sovereign, so far as their sovereignty is not affected by this supreme law [the Constitution]. But the State legislatures, as political bodies, however sovereign, are not yet sovereign over the people."[6] When it came to deciding how territories in the West were to be governed, questions of sovereignty took on new urgency. Lewis Cass, then a senator from Missouri, made the case to Congress in 1847 that popular sovereignty might offer a solution to arguments over the government of the territories. In the earlier part of the century, Congress had claimed the right to govern the territories until such time as they were organized into states.[7] In the wake of the Treaty of Guadalupe Hidalgo (1848) and the acquisition of vast lands from Mexico, calls increased for the people of the territories to decide their own political futures. First and foremost among the issues to be considered was the question of whether a particular territory would allow slavery within its borders.

One of the main voices in the discussion was Senator Stephen A. Douglas from Illinois, who drew on the new version of popular sovereignty in creating the Kansas-Nebraska Act (1854), which in effect repealed the Missouri Compromise and the geographic division between slave states and free states. In the context of intense disagreements over the fate of slavery in the West, which threatened to dissolve the Union, popular sovereignty was imagined by Douglas and others to refer not to the general political will of the people, but rather to the idea that regional variations would necessarily lead to variations in state and territorial laws and policies. David Zarefsky explains: "Douglas had based his theory of popular sovereignty on the belief that the decision for or against slavery could be made by the actual inhabitants of a territory, acting through their representatives in the territorial legislature."[8] A number of scholars have debated Douglas's motivations in writing popular sovereignty into the Kansas-Nebraska Act, with some arguing for his "sincere belief" in the territories' ability to govern themselves and others citing his political ambitions and desire for a transcontinental railroad. James L. Huston has noted that while Stephen Douglas played only a "minor" role in the creation of ideologies of popular sovereignty, he nonetheless became a lifelong proponent of its doctrines.[9]

The congressional debates over what was then called the Nebraska Bill were contentious and revealed divergent views of popular sovereignty.[10] While Northern Whigs emphasized the sovereignty of the federal government, Southern Democrats argued for the indivisible sovereignty of the people of the sovereign states. Both sides were skeptical of popular sovereignty when understood as territorial self-government by "the people," an idea that was maligned throughout the debates as "squatter sovereignty." Joseph R. Chandler, a Whig from Pennsylvania, defined sovereignty as political independence and contended that the "sovereignty of every State is limited by the sovereignty of the United States."[11] For Chandler, the Supreme Court should function as the enforcer of federal sovereignty and could declare state laws to be unconstitutional. However, he suggested that this was beside the point in the case of territorial governments, which were not fully sovereign states but existed in a state of "pupilage" that made them dependent on the federal government.[12] Senator Thomas Hart Benton of Missouri echoed Chandler's conception of the territories, framing them as the "children" of the states, "minors" who need the guidance of their elders.[13] Sovereignty could be both divided and limited, and territories, while in the process of becoming sovereign, were not yet sovereign states. Their opponents, such as William O. Goode from Virginia, were wary of popular sovereignty because it might allow the territories to prohibit slavery and prevent Southern slaveholders from bringing their slaves into the newly organized territories. Goode declared, "The Government of the United States is not sovereign. In this country no government is sovereign; sovereignty *abides* only with the *people of the several States*."[14] The federal government, he argued, "exercises only a few of the attributes of sovereignty" and should not "discriminate against the South" by trying to restrict slaveholders' rights with regard to what they have deemed their property.[15] Southerners have the right, he claimed, to carry their property (including the enslaved people they considered property) into the territories, and neither the federal government nor the people of the territories should be able to interfere.

Dred Scott v. Sandford (1857), in which Dred Scott sued for his freedom based on his residency in a free state, involved a test of that very right. This case, which is infamous for its denial of black citizenship and Chief Justice Roger Taney's assertion that black people possess "no rights which the white man was bound to respect" (407) also declared that the federal government could not limit slavery in the western territories. In his opinion, Taney reinforced the Southern position that the federal government could not limit what were considered the internal affairs of the territories. One of the other issues addressed by the case was the interpretation of the privileges and immunities clause of the U.S. Constitution and its relationship to African Americans. If an African American were recognized as a citizen of one state, would that person then be considered a citizen of all the states? According to Rogers Smith, Taney advanced a somewhat tortured argument that there were "two types of state citizens: those who were only state citizens and not U.S. citizens, and those who held both citizenships."[16] Since some states did grant citizenship to African Americans—Frederick Douglass was a citizen of New York, for example—Taney was forced to acknowledge that black people could be state citizens, but he declared that they could never possess federal citizenship because they did not merit birthright citizenship and could not be naturalized. They could not qualify for birthright citizenship, he claimed, because they were not recognized as citizens by the founding generation and at the time of the creation of the Constitution were "excluded from civilized Governments and the family of nations, and doomed to slavery" (410). While American Indians could be naturalized as "free and independent people" (403), Taney claimed that African Americans did not qualify for naturalization and thus had no path to federal citizenship. His endorsement of the foreign status of Native people constituted, according to Priscilla Wald, "a deliberative shift of emphasis that elucidates an important difference" between American Indians and African Americans.[17] That is, American Indians could, for Taney, be seen as foreign and outside of American political culture, while African Americans were viewed as an internal threat. As I discuss below, John Brown and his colleagues strove to align their nation with the model provided by the Cherokees, a move that emphasized African Americans' political potential and capacity for multiple political affiliations.

In the midst of these political and legal debates, colonizationist rhetoric of the 1850s continued to highlight the position of African Americans as a nation-to-be that existed outside of the American body politic. As in previous decades, colonizationists attempted to resolve sectional tensions between the North and South through the removal of free black people from the United States. As Claude Andrew Clegg III argues, even on the eve of the Civil War, "Abraham Lincoln still envisioned a great black exodus."[18] Colonizationists declared Liberia a "transplanted republic" and communicated their belief that in their nascent form, nations could be moved. An article published in the Boston *Traveler* and reprinted in the *African Repository* in 1852 was an example of this perspective: "To inoculate a nation like France with republicanism is a hazardous experiment. But to transplant an organized republic, in its germ, to expend itself on a foreign shore is no impossibility."[19] The author suggested that the "germ" of an African American nation, grown and developed in the United States, could and should be transplanted to Liberia. The French Revolution was held up as a point of contrast, a change in government marked by violent upheaval, while the formation of Liberia was framed in agricultural terms as a transplantation to more conducive national soil. The project of colonization had changed drastically since the 1830s, however, and the United States faced new issues about how to relate to a black nation. Liberia had declared itself a republic in 1847, but was still struggling to achieve the formal recognition of other nations, including the United States. For U.S. politicians, the recognition of Liberian and Haitian nationhood raised troubling issues about racial equality, international relations, and the possible fallout from Southern states if the sovereignty of a black nation were acknowledged. If these polities were recognized as foreign states, the United States would have to send diplomats to them and receive Liberian and Haitian representatives as well; black diplomats would be walking the halls of government alongside those dispatched from European nations. Moreover, these nations would serve as an example for free and enslaved people of blacks' political potential. It would not be until 1862 that the United States negotiated a treaty recognizing the sovereignty of Liberia, which established commercial policies and structured the relationship between the two nations "on the footing of the most favored nation."[20]

The subject of colonization and a virtual African American nation in Africa was taken up not just by politicians but also by writers of popular literature in the 1850s. Published shortly after *Uncle Tom's Cabin*, Sarah Josepha Hale's *Liberia; or, Mr. Peyton's Experiments* (1853) reveals colonization's deft blending of civic-territorial and ethnic conceptions of nationhood. As a novelist and the editor of popular periodicals such as the *Ladies' Magazine* and *Godey's Lady's Book*, Hale exerted significant cultural influence, and her fiction articulated some of the key debates of her time. As Susan M. Ryan suggests, Hale "promotes African colonization as a way of not only preserving the Union as she conceives of it (that is, as Protestant and Anglo-Saxon) but also of replicating, among ex-slaves in a 'new' country, American-style nation building, national identity, and citizenship, as she defines them."[21] The "experiments" alluded to in Hale's novel's title are the various places Mr. Peyton, a Southern slaveholder, tries to relocate his slaves. He wants to see what location would be most suitable for their emancipation and sends them to a nearby farm, the city of Philadelphia, and Canada. In each of these locations, he determines that his slaves could not be productive members of society and would remain unassimilable. The novel suggests that, when surrounded by white society but not governed by it, African American people will not work. Peyton finally decides to send them to Liberia, and once Junius, Keziah, and the others arrive in Africa, a dramatic transformation takes place. In Ryan's reading, "Hale also implies, though, that it is the very experience of superiority that effects the emigrants' transformation. By the end of the novel it becomes clear that the absence of whites is a necessary, but not sufficient, condition for black actualization; the emigrants must also have a group of people whom *they* can dominate. The African natives, of course, serve that purpose."[22]

Throughout *Liberia*, Hale used the word *nation*, which she equated with the exclusive possession of national and individual property, and presented Africa as the space in which the dormant African American nation could be actualized.[23] This vision of *civic-territorial* nationhood echoed those circulating more broadly in American literature and public argument and dovetailed with the rhetorics of Manifest Destiny. Moreover, the apparent ethnic homogeneity of this Liberian nation mirrored back to the United States what *it* should be: one ethnically and racially unified nation.[24] In this way, Hale's novel reflected efforts to *territorialize* and rhetorically manage the African American population and to inculcate particular ideas of ethnic nationhood among the white American population. For white Americans, such a fiction of ethnic unity was only intelligible as part of discussions of the removal of nonwhite people and the suppression of any other forms of alternative nationalism. Such discussions were particularly important at a historical moment when the Mormons were asserting their own version of American nationalism, fears were circulating of Irish and Chinese nations emerging from within the United States, and calls for secession raised the specter of separate American nations divided along regional lines.

The idea that America was a nation of white people and Africa should contain a parallel nation of black people continued to be expressed by prominent literary figures throughout the 1850s. For example, while he later claimed to have been "anti-slavery, always," Walt Whitman had, in the words of biographer David S. Reynolds, "a divided history on the issues of race and slavery."[25] Scholars have pointed out that Whitman's views on race and slavery varied between his poetry and his prose and also note changes over time.[26] In 1858, Whitman asserted that African Americans and white Americans could never "amalgamate," but that "we believe there is enough material in the colored race, if they were in some secure and ample part of the earth, where they would have a chance to develop themselves, to gradually form a race, a nation that would take no mean rank among the peoples of the world."[27] Here Whitman tapped into the common parlance of describing African Americans as a nation-to-be, a virtual nation that had enough "material" to advance but that could not flourish in the American national space. Reynolds links Whitman's early views on colonization and abolition with those commonly held in Brooklyn, New York, where he lived and worked for significant portions of his early life. According to Reynolds, "colonization took hold strongly in Brooklyn, and abolitionism was generally opposed as divisive and disruptive."[28] Whitman's statement in 1858 echoed some of the themes of colonization rhetorics; he coded African Americans as incapable of assimilating into American society and related races and nations on a temporal scale of development, with races having the potential to develop into nations. This national development was linked with the exclusive possession of national space and could not occur in America. For the American continent was, Whitman claimed, "for the whites."[29] Like Hale, Whitman created an image of America and Africa as two ethnically and racially pure nations, each with its own distinct territory.

While supporters of colonization continued to draw on rhetorics of the national possibility of free black people, some slavery apologists reworked rhetorics of imperium in imperio to frame chattel slavery as a form of government, one that contained the potential threat posed by African Americans and distinguished their position from that of Native peoples (as Taney did in *Dred Scott*). The enslavement of black people, they argued, was not oppression, but rather a variation on the social contract that brought African American people into the American political structure (although they occupied the lowest level of the political hierarchy). In an 1838 speech, Senator John C. Calhoun of South Carolina had described the political organization of the South thusly: "The Southern States are an aggregate, in fact, of communities, not individuals. Every plantation is a little community, with the master at its head.... These small communities aggregated make the State in all, whose action, labor, and capital is equally represented and perfectly harmonized."[30] In *America's Forgotten Constitutions*, Tsai describes Calhoun as "grounding political authority in the plantation" (121–122), and, I would add, Calhoun framed those plantations as miniature governments within the larger state. Offering a similar vision in the context of the Kansas-Nebraska Act debates, William Andrew Smith, the president of Randolph-Macon College and a professor of philosophy, likened the condition of American slaves to that of an imperium in order to counter discussions of a threatening Southern presence in Kansas. In a series entitled "Lectures on the Philosophy and Practice of Slavery, as Exhibited in the Institution of Domestic Slavery in the United States, with the Duties of Masters to Slaves" (1856), Smith argued, "Domestic slavery is one of the subordinate forms of civil government. It may be defined [as] an *imperium in imperio*—a government within a government: one in which the subject of the inferior government is under the control of a master, up to a certain limit defined by the superior government, and beyond which both the master and the slave are alike subject to control by the superior government."[31] Here imperium in imperio was represented as an administrative technique, contributing to the process of ordering a multiracial society by territorializing African American people within the American body politic. Smith described slavery as a "government within a government" in which the government of the slaves is subject to the government of their master, who in turn is subject to the superior state and federal powers. For Smith, this functioned as a defense of slavery, a counter to those who argued that the system was antithetical to the democratic principles of the United States. He represented slavery as an extension of, not a threat to, American federalism.

Just a few years later, a Methodist minister and editor, Holland Nimmons McTyeire, who was involved with the establishment of Vanderbilt University, made similar arguments in his *Duties of Christian Masters* (1859). He proclaimed that "[e]very Southern planation is *imperium in imperio*" and likened slave owners to "the mayor of a city or the governor of a State."[32] In McTyeire's formulation, slavery empowered "those whose nature qualifies them to govern" with the responsibility of regulating "that class of population whose government elsewhere gives society the most trouble."[33] McTyeire suggested that this division of sovereignty supported rather than subverted American sovereignty by adding another—ostensibly necessary—layer of governance for African Americans. It also provided a kind of training ground for those with natural political abilities. For him, Southern plantations were miniature governments that relieved the "trouble" that society might otherwise encounter from African Americans. Thus, McTyeire's vision did not represent one African American imperium, but many smaller states made up of African Americans but led by whites. Like Smith's work, McTyeire's *Duties of Christian Masters* suggested the flexibility of rhetorics of imperium in imperio as part of a larger effort to fix African Americans in the existing political and social categories, justifying slavery in the name of social order.

Yet another facet of this territorializing move defended slavery on the grounds that it connected African Americans to the U.S. landscape and protected the body politic by offering a form of governance that limited black mobility. In his vitriolic writings on the subject, George Fitzhugh, a staunch supporter of slavery, argued that Africans required the governance of white masters and that allegiance to a master connected black people to a particular space. In *Sociology for the South*, Fitzhugh presented slavery as a model of socialism that "Fourier might envy."[34] He argued that free labor divorced individuals from one another and from the land itself, whereas in a feudal society or a slave state, laborers occupied the home of their masters.[35] Capitalism, like that found in the Northern states and in England, Fitzhugh contended in *Cannibals All!*, created a situation in which only a few could flourish economically and created classes of people who were totally disconnected from the land because they could not own property: "nomads," "beggars," "Gypsies," and "bandits." These "nomadic races" were threats to the security and sovereignty of the nation because they were not under the governance of any one community. By linking people with a particular space and bringing them under the governance of a master, slavery would provide a solution to Europe's "nomadic" peoples, Fitzhugh suggested, just as it provided a way of managing African Americans in the American South.[36] The implication of Fitzhugh's argument is that because African Americans could not own property, there needed to be some other way to yoke them to a particular place and to prevent them from being profligate and dangerous wanderers. Like Smith and McTyeire, Fitzhugh conceived of an African American imperium as part of a larger strategy of containment in which slaves would be "governed" by white masters, an attempt to justify slavery as a political strategy, not as a form of racial oppression. But John Brown and the members of the Chatham Convention challenged both territorial justifications of slavery and understandings of exclusive territorial possession as a precondition for nationhood in their expression of an antislavery imperium, which hinged on radical definitions of popular sovereignty and politicized discussions of African Americans' national potential.

John Brown, the Chatham Convention, and the Provisional Government of the United States

In the wake of the *Dred Scott* decision, with its complete denial of African Americans' rights, John Brown wrote in an April 1858 letter of a "quiet convention" that would take place in Chatham, Ontario, that May.[37] At the Chatham Convention, notable for its location in a Canadian community of former slaves, a group of thirty-four African Americans and twelve white people (including Brown) ratified the Provisional Constitution. It was based loosely on the U.S. Constitution and created a provisional government in which slavery was abolished and a radical form of popular sovereignty would be the order of the day. The following year, shortly before his ill-fated raid on Harpers Ferry, Brown produced a companion document, "A Declaration of Liberty by the Representatives of the Slave Population of the United States of America," which declared the rights of the "circumscribed citizens" to self-government and personal liberty.[38] Taken together, these documents outlined a temporary government that would help the United States transition from a slaveholding nation to one characterized by universal liberty. Along with earlier documents produced by Brown and his supporters in Kansas, the Provisional Constitution and the "Declaration" demonstrated an emphasis on mobility as a national trait rather than on the occupation of territory.[39] Brown and his fellow framers engaged in critiques of U.S. territorial sovereignty, which by the 1850s seemed inextricably linked with the institution of slavery. Their vision of a provisional government resonated with conceptions of national mobility expressed by Martin Delany and the leaders of the Fenian Brotherhood, a group that was coalescing during the height of Brown's efforts, and contrasted sharply with the territoriality of both the U.S. Constitution and the soon-to-be-formed Confederate States of America. Rhetorics of imperium in imperio proved central in Brown's eventual trial as part of larger arguments as to whether he had in fact founded a nation.

The Provisional Constitution was not Brown's first foray into written documents as a strategy of self-government. Tsai recounts the "covenant" created by Brown and thirty-five of his supporters in Kansas during the summer of 1856: "Bylaws were added to the covenant, providing for the election of officers, the handling and disposal of booty, the prosecution of the laws, and the barring of profane, uncivil, drunken, or disorderly conduct, as well as theft and waste" (*America's Forgotten Constitutions*, 87). As Tsai notes, the focus was not on staking out a particular territory nor on creating institutions since "these nascent rules were made for a small group on the move" and were largely concerned with military-style discipline (87). As the Fenian Brotherhood would do in the 1860s, Brown and his "Kansas regulars" engaged in practices that were both disruptive and constitutive, which were predicated on their ability to move across space rather than to possess it. According to John Stauffer and Zoe Trodd, Brown had "read histories of guerrilla warfare, notably of the Haitian Revolution and its leader, Toussaint-Louverture, which he treated as a sort of personal guidebook" (*The Tribunal*, xxvi). Like the writings of Martin Delany, who assisted in the organization of the Chatham Convention, Brown highlighted mobility as a strategic advantage for individuals and nations rather than static territorial occupation.

Brown's attempt to create a more formal political institution that, like the Cherokee Nation, could deal directly with the U.S. federal government came in 1858. In his account of the Chatham Convention, Delany described to biographer Frances Rollin how the group settled on creating a nation within the larger U.S. nation and specifically likened it to the Cherokee Nation. He recalled that the initial plan was to create a separate state government, but this idea was abandoned because "according to American jurisprudence, negroes, having no rights respected by white men, consequently could have no right to petition, and none to sovereignty."[40] Delany then explained how the convention members sought to overcome this obstacle: "To obviate this, and avoid the charge against them as lawless and unorganized, existing without government, it was proposed that an independent community be established within and under the United States, but without the state sovereignty of the compact, similar to the Cherokee Nation of Indians, or the Mormons. To these last named, references were made, as parallel cases, at the time."[41] The concept of the provisional nation that Delany described is one that, like the other nations examined in this book, would exist "within and under the United States" as a form of imperium in imperio.[42] In Delany's account, the formation of an imperium in imperio demonstrated the national potential of African Americans and attempted to forestall criticism that would frame their actions as "lawless." Like the model of the Cherokee Nation, which he noted was a point of discussion among those in attendance, the provisional nation also sought to deal directly with the federal government as a nation without having to obtain a "state sovereignty... compact." Thus, this nation would neither be answerable to any state nor held accountable as a state in the Union. Brown's Provisional Constitution, notes his biographer David S. Reynolds, "was meant to reform, not supplant, the American system."[43] Reynolds cites Article 46, which reads: "The foregoing articles shall not be construed so as in any way to encourage the overthrow of any State government, or of the general government of the United States, and look to no dissolution of the Union, but simply to amend and repeal."[44]

Although it was signed by the attendees of the Chatham Convention, the Provisional Constitution was largely Brown's creation, but Frederick Douglass may have made some contributions.[45] Accounts name Douglass's Rochester, New York, home as the birthplace of the Provisional Constitution. Brown visited Douglass for a month in early 1858, and Douglass recalled the visit and the creation of the constitution in his account of his relationship with Brown in *The Life and Times of Frederick Douglass*: "When he [Brown] was not writing letters, he was writing and revising a constitution which he meant to put in operation by the men who should go with him into the mountains. He said that to avoid anarchy and confusion, there should be a regularly constituted government, to which each man who came with him should be sworn to honour and support. I have a copy of this constitution in Captain Brown's own handwriting, as prepared by himself at my house."[46] In Douglass's version of the story, Brown recognized the power of constitutions as "social code[s]" (to borrow Jameson's phrase) and the ways in which they functioned to prevent internal chaos. Like the leaders of the Cherokee Nation and the members of the National Negro Convention movement, Brown acted on the belief that it was not enough to have a shared sense of purpose; the group needed a written constitution to provide stability and to communicate the seriousness of its purpose. As Tsai asserts, Brown used the Provisional Constitution to speak to multiple audiences and to fulfill multiple purposes: instilling order in the provisional nation he came to lead, communicating a sense of purpose to wealthy potential donors, and galvanizing African American and white supporters (*America's Forgotten Constitutions*, 86, 100). It was constitutive of a provisional national community even as it deconstructed America's founding documents and recent legal decisions.

Like the constitution produced by the Cherokee Nation, Brown's Provisional Constitution used the U.S. Constitution as a model but made significant alterations, including abolishing slavery and nullifying the *Dred Scott* decision. The preamble, which I quote in its entirety here, declared slavery to be an act of war and offered a much more specific vision of "We the People" than that outlined in the U.S. Constitution:

> Whereas slavery throughout its entire existence in the United States is none other than a most barbarous, unprovoked, and unjustifiable War of one portion of its citizens upon another portion, the only conditions of which are perpetual imprisonment and hopeless servitude or absolute extermination in utter disregard and violation of those eternal and self-evident truths set forth in our Declaration of Independence. Therefore,
>
> We, Citizens of the United States, and the oppressed people who, by a recent decision of the Supreme Court are declared to have no rights which the White Man is bound to respect, together with all other people degraded by the laws thereof, Do, for the time being, Ordain and establish for ourselves the following Provisional Constitution and Ordinances the better to protect our Persons, Property, Lives, and Liberties, and to govern our actions. ("Provisional Constitution," 26–27)

While the 1827 Cherokee Constitution highlighted the issue of territoriality, opening with a discussion of the Cherokee Nation's national borders, the Provisional Constitution reinterpreted the founding documents of the United States and reconfigured their relative silence on the subject of slavery. The second paragraph specifically recalled Chief Justice Taney's opinion in the *Dred*

Scott decision, but essentially declared it null and void by including both "citizens" and "oppressed people" as part of the community of allegiance of the new provisional nation. Article 1 followed up on this statement with an even more emphatic declaration that membership in this provisional nation was open to "[a]ll persons of mature age, whether Proscribed, oppressed, and enslaved Citizens, or of the Proscribed and oppressed races of the United States, who shall agree to sustain and enforce the Provisional Constitution and Ordinances of this organization, together with all minor children of such persons, shall be held to be fully entitled to protection under the same" ("Provisional Constitution," 27). Brown's conception of membership was capacious, including people of all races and extending rights and protections to children (another subject on which the U.S. Constitution was silent).

The governmental structure outlined in the Provisional Constitution resembled that of the United States in its broad strokes but was predicated on both a more radical popular sovereignty and a smaller, more flexible leadership. There were three branches of government, but the members of all three branches would be elected by the people. Brown's constitution abolished the Electoral College and the Senate. The legislative branch would have no more than ten members at any one time, which, combined with the president, the vice president, a five-person cabinet, and five members of the Supreme Court, would constitute the entire federal government. Such a governmental structure placed power in the hands of a very few individuals, yet rendered those individuals ultimately accountable to the people as a whole. It prevented the political beliefs of those in power from being replicated in the other branches; for example, it did not grant the president the power of appointing Supreme Court justices. Articles 13, 14, and 15 outlined procedures for the trial and impeachment of various members of the government. Thus, even as it represented a much more formal political architecture than that outlined in the Kansas covenant, the Provisional Constitution maintained some features of guerrilla operations, including a small, mobile leadership not linked to any particular space and capable of forming and reforming quickly. While this leadership was never fully put in place, the government still managed to function, with Brown and his followers adhering to the dictates of the constitution. According to Tsai, at the Chatham Convention two cabinet positions and two seats in Congress were filled. The members elected Brown to be commander in chief; J. H. Kagi (a white man) was named secretary of war; and Alfred Ellsworth and Osborne P. Anderson, both African American, were elected as congressmen of this provisional government, a move that enacted the nation's stance on race (*America's Forgotten Constitutions*, 85). Brown apparently asked Frederick Douglass to be the first president of the provisional nation, but Douglass declined.[47] Both he and Delany ultimately distanced themselves from Brown and his plans for the raid on Harpers Ferry.

The summer before the infamous raid, Brown produced a second national document, "A Declaration of Liberty by the Representatives of the Slave Population of the United States of America," which rearticulated the U.S. Declaration of Independence from an African American perspective. He dictated this document to his son Owen Brown while preparing for the attack on the armory at Harpers Ferry. Blending the Lockean view that sovereignty allowed for legitimate resistance against misuses of government with widespread understandings that sovereignty resided in the people (not the government), the "Declaration" took popular sovereignty to its logical extreme. In cases in which the government did not act according to the will of the people, the people could revise, and had a duty to revise, the government according to their wishes. Purporting to speak on behalf of the enslaved population, the document positioned enslaved people as "native and mutual citizens of a free Republic," alluding to the doctrine of jus soli citizenship, which links national belonging with place of birth ("Declaration of Liberty," in Stauffer and Trodd, *The Tribunal*, 38). Drawing on the language of the Declaration of Independence, it presumed that African Americans shared in the right to self-government authorized by America's founding documents. Not only had America violated its Revolutionary values by continuing as a slaveholding nation, claimed Brown's "Declaration," but its politicians also violated all people's rights by refusing to acknowledge antislavery petitions. The document implied that white people had also become disfranchised by the current government, which was no longer acting on behalf of their political interests. Speaking for enslaved people, the document asserted: "Regardless of our wishes, they 'declare themselves invested with power to legislate for us in all cases whatsoever.' They have abdicated government among us, by declaring us out of their protection, and waging a worse than cruel war upon us continually" (40). In a move that anticipated the attack to follow, this document echoed the Provisional Constitution's conception of slavery as a form of warfare that could and should be countered with force. It also reinforced the notion that because the United States had "abdicated" its responsibilities to African Americans and white Americans, the people were justified in forming their own government.

While Brown conceived of his provisional government as a way to circumvent state authority, he was tried for treason in a Virginia court after the raid on Harpers Ferry, and his provisional government was represented as a threatening *imperium in imperio*.[48] The transcript of the trial demonstrates the ways in which Virginia authorities reinterpreted Brown's provisional government and the Harpers Ferry raid as assaults on Virginia's sovereignty, in an attempt to link Brown, and by extension all Northern abolitionists, with violent attacks on states' rights.[49] The state claimed that Brown and his followers "did then and there feloniously and traitorously establish and set up, without authority of the Legislature of the Commonwealth of Virginia, a Government, separate from, and hostile to, the existing Government of said Commonwealth; and did then and there hold and exercise divers offices under said usurped Government."[50] Their attack on the federal arsenal at Harpers Ferry was, the indictment claimed, an act of war "for the purpose, end, and aim of overthrowing and abolishing the Constitution and laws of said Commonwealth, and establishing in the place thereof, another and different government, and constitution and laws hostile thereto" (*LTE*, 59). Thus, while Brown's documents specifically engaged the U.S. Constitution and Declaration of Independence and imagined the provisional government existing within the United States but outside of any particular state, Virginia authorities relocated Brown's nation within the state's own geopolitical boundaries for the purpose of the trial. This move echoed the efforts of the state of Georgia to relocate the Cherokee Nation within the state's territorial limits in response to the 1827 Cherokee Constitution, suggesting that Brown and his followers may not have been the only ones looking to the Cherokees for inspiration.

In his closing argument, Hiram Griswold, one of Brown's attorneys, worked to rearticulate Brown's relationship to Virginia. Brown should not be found guilty of treason, Griswold argued, because regardless of the location of Harpers Ferry, he was not a resident of Virginia: "this prisoner was not bound by any allegiance to this State, and could not, therefore, be guilty of rebellion against it" (*LTE*, 86). This argument was an attempt to remap the geographies of the case, removing Brown and his government from Virginia's jurisdiction, and to challenge the treason charge. Griswold went on to cite Brown's constitution as evidence that his provisional government did not constitute an imperium in imperio vis-à-vis the commonwealth of Virginia:

> It is said that there was an organized government, and that charge is sought to be sustained by evidence, particularly by a pamphlet that has been produced, and which was taken from the person of the prisoner. But, gentlemen, it would not necessarily follow that overthrowing the Commonwealth of Virginia was contemplated by anything which appears in that pamphlet. How many harmless organizations have existed in the world at countless times, surrounded with all the outside forms and machinery of government! aye, even as harmless things as debating societies have been so organized, congresses created, resolutions and laws discussed, and any one reading the bulletins and reports issued from time to time

from these associations would say, why here is a miniature government within the very limits of our State. (*LTE*, 86)

The Provisional Constitution was transformed in this argument from a nation-making document to the more general and benign-sounding genre of a "pamphlet," and the provisional government was described as "harmless" and likened to a "debating societ[y]." Griswold alluded to the ubiquity of written constitutions in the era to diminish the explicitly national aims of Brown and his followers. Any debating society or voluntary association could be viewed as a "miniature government" within a particular state, an argument that sought to subvert representations of the unique, treasonous qualities of Brown's efforts. Moreover, Griswold claimed that the documents offered no challenge to the commonwealth of Virginia because they made no specific reference to territory: "The pamphlet does not say what territory this association, or government, is to exercise jurisdiction over. Its proposed empire is not defined. It has fixed no territorial limits, and, therefore, if it means anything at all, it alludes to the government of the whole United States in general, and not to this State or any other in particular" (*LTE*, 87). Griswold sought to relocate Brown and his organization as outside of Virginia's jurisdiction and to frame the provisional government as having a political (not territorial) relationship with the United States, a move that served to reinforce federal rather than state sovereignty.

Returning to Griswold's point that not every organization with a constitution was a political entity, Samuel Chilton, Brown's other attorney, denied that Brown's organization constituted a nation at all. He suggested that the group "had a mere imaginary Government to govern themselves, and nobody else, just like governing a military company or debating society" (*LTE*, 90). Chilton's conception of "imaginary" here was linked with the argument that the government was solely composed of Brown and his followers. Because it did not possess territory nor extend its political jurisdiction over others, it did not constitute a "real" nation. Moreover, he concluded that its provisional status subverted any claims to nationhood: "Even if they intended to set up a government over the other, they did not do it" (90). Chilton drew on territorial conceptions of nationhood to defend Brown and his government from claims that they constituted a threatening imperium, but in so doing, he also subverted the group's ambitions. Brown had earlier rejected an insanity defense, but Chilton's statements worked against the kind of political leverage that Brown hoped to gain by acting as a provisional government.[51] While Brown's efforts at Harpers Ferry were thwarted, the subsequent trial and vast body of press coverage brought his provisional government widespread attention and further exposed fractures in the American nation.[52]

Delany and Douglass: Imperium in Imperio Reconsidered

Martin R. Delany and Frederick Douglass were both involved, to an extent, with Brown and the creation of the Provisional Constitution. The document was written at Douglass's home and possibly bore traces of his influence, and Delany had signed the letter of invitation to the Chatham Convention and attended it. Both men ultimately distanced themselves from Brown's violent guerrilla tactics, even as they wrote in support of his character. Douglass referred to him as an "old hero" and a "glorious martyr of liberty" and claimed that "[h]is daring deeds may cost him his life, but priceless as is the value of that life, the blow he has struck, will, in the end, prove to be worth its mighty cost."[53]

Before and after their involvement with Brown, both Delany and Douglass engaged rhetorics of imperium in imperio and worked with the political possibilities of interacting with the United States on national terms. While the two men collaborated on the editorship of the *North Star*, as Levine has pointed out, by the early 1850s their political perspectives had begun to diverge. Levine argues that these differences are often discussed in terms of Delany's interest in emigration versus Douglass's commitment to integration during the period in question.[54] However, such a binary constitutes a search for meaning rather than an attention to the effects of their arguments, which can best be understood in the context of the competing rhetorics of imperium in imperio that circulated during the 1850s. I argue that both Delany and Douglass strategically engaged rhetorics of imperium in imperio and deconstructed logics of popular sovereignty in attempts to reshape the political and, in Delany's case, geographic contours of the American nation. Like Brown and his provisional documents, they also explored the possibility that multiple nations could share a single territory and that individuals could maintain multiple and overlapping political relationships.

Martin Delany, whose views on nationhood were complicated and at times contradictory, envisioned African Americans as part of an ethnic nation existing within the United States and traversing its geopolitical borders, emphasizing relational networks rather than territorial possession as a national attribute. He used a domestic metaphor for nations in an 1849 article that appeared in the *North Star*, asserting that "[n]ations are but great families; each individual, citizen, or inhabitant, constitutes the members who compose that family."[55] As part of an argument that African Americans must focus on economic and political achievement, he wrote that, as in families, members of nations should "bear the same resemblance to the great leading traits which mark the enterprise of that people, as the individual members do to the family to which they belong."[56] Delany's novel *Blake; or, The Huts of America* (1859) based its revolutionary message in part on such ethnic conceptions of nationhood.[57] The titular character is able to spread his plans for revolt by word of mouth because of the relational networks that are already in place among African and African American people. This novel, described by Levine as "a Pan-African vision of black nationalism that means to combat and expose the limits of the U.S. nationalism espoused by blacks aligned with [Frederick] Douglass," constitutes one of the clearest endorsements of ethnic nationalism produced during the 1850s.[58] In the novel, the character Royer, also referred to as simply "the American," gives voice to the idea that Africans and African Americans share common origins. In "The Middle Passage," Royer and Captain Paul discuss the fact that two of the slaves aboard the ship seemed to recognize Blake. Royer asserts that it is entirely possible that the three know each other or are related: "'Negroes all know each other, you know; all uncles and aunts, brothers and sisters, and cousins,' replied the American. 'I never saw a Negro yet that wasn't acquainted with another Negro you could name; Negroes are all the same everywhere.'"[59] While on the surface this statement resonated with racist discourses that presented Africans and African Americans as interchangeable, the novel pressured such attitudes even as it emphasized the revolutionary potential of networks of relationality that exist among Africans as a "people." Abyssa, one of the slaves aboard the ship, who is from Sudan but has lived among the Ebo, recognizes Blake as a "civilized man" (224) and whispers the watchwords he has created. The novel argues that Africans and African Americans constitute a nation predicated on shared experiences and a common history, which white people cannot understand or contain.

Through its emphasis on black mobility as a national strategy, *Blake* links this nation not with the occupation of territory but with the ability to traverse territory. Martha Schoolman, who classifies the novel as "the quintessential North American geographic novel," suggests that "[b]y tracking its hero's movements across the Gulf of Mexico, it is widely argued, the novel acknowledges lines of kinship connection among enslaved and free Africans in the Western Hemisphere that have traditionally been elided by a myopic U.S. focus in accounts of African American culture."[60] In *Blake*, territory is important only insofar as it provides "space for action" (197). With his focus on mobility, Delany refashions legal definitions of African Americans as "moveable property," framing mobility as a source of power not a sign of inferiority. The individual members of this nation do not confront state power head on, but rather unsettle and destabilize it through their circulations. The novel's full title, *Blake; or, The Huts of America: A Tale of the Mississippi Valley, the Southern United States, and Cuba*, maps the numerous movements, both voluntary and involuntary, described by the text.

After his wife, Maggie, is sold to a couple headed for Cuba, Blake, who was educated in the West Indies and "decoyed" (*Blake*, 19) into bondage in Mississippi, escapes from slavery and travels throughout the South, circulating his plan for rebellion. His travels even take him to an "Indian Nation" near Fort Towson, Arkansas (85), before he eventually goes to Havana to reconnect with Maggie. While there he also meets his cousin Placido, a Cuban poet and revolutionary. While *Blake*, like other antislavery narratives, dramatizes the separation of families by the institution of slavery, it is also a novel about the formation and reformation of families and communities and the circulation of people and ideas. Blake's plan for revolution relies on the spread of information through the informal networks already in place among Africans and African Americans living in the United States. Despite the geographic area traversed in *Blake*, Katy L. Chiles cautions against reading Delany's work as simply transnational: "Rather than cleanly supplanting a national perspective with a transnational one, Delany presents a nation-state in which local, regional, national, and transnational figurations overlap and permeate each other." She further suggests that Delany's vision of nationhood stands as "the antithesis of an indivisible nation."[61] National affiliations in *Blake* are multiple, mobile, permeable, and, as Chiles suggests, divisible.

Delany engaged the concept of imperium in imperio most directly in his nonfiction works, particularly *The Condition, Elevation, Emigration, and Destiny of the Colored People of the United States*. African Americans, he argued, constitute a "nation within a nation," a status that links them with many other populations: "That there have in all ages, in almost every nation, existed a nation within a nation—a people who although forming a part and parcel of the population, yet were from force of circumstances, known by the peculiar position they occupied, forming in fact, by the deprivation of political equality with others, no part, and if any, but a restricted part of the body politic of such nations, is also true."[62] Here Delany drew on the concept of imperium in imperio although he used the common English translation of "nation within a nation." Delany used *nation* here to refer to both a disfranchised people and a political community; elsewhere he argued that while African Americans currently constituted the former, they should aspire to the latter form of nationhood. Like other peoples in "all ages" and in "almost every nation," African Americans were currently "restricted" by their enclosure within the United States. This rhetoric allowed Delany to challenge representations of African Americans as a political "anomaly," as was often suggested in discussions of imperium in imperio, and offer his own vision of shared experiences, which, while it made reference to race, insisted on relating to the United States on political rather than racial terms.

Delany deconstructed racist formulations of African Americans as an exception, a racialized political anomaly, by linking them with various populations across time and space and emphasizing their national status. While slavery has injured African Americans, they have not lost their nationality. Delany compared their position as a nation within a nation to that of "the Poles in Russia, the Hungarians in Austria, the Scotch, Irish, and Welsh in the United Kingdom, and . . . the Jews" (*Condition*, 42). Like Africans in America, these populations have suffered national injuries yet maintain hope of national regeneration. They are, he wrote, "scattered throughout not only the length and breadth of Europe, but almost the habitable globe, maintaining their national characteristics, and looking forward in high hopes of seeing the day when they may return to their former national position of self-government and independence, let that be in whatever part of the habitable world it may" (42). As in his fictional work, Delany emphasized multiple and overlapping affiliations as the norm rather than the exception, an effect of oppression rather than a signal of racial inferiority. He wrote in the appendix to *The Condition*, "[W]e have been, by our oppressors, despoiled of our purity, and corrupted in our native characteristics, so that we have inherited their vices, and but few of their virtues, leaving us in character, really a *broken people*" (221). Here his comments echoed Hosea Easton's accounts of the national injuries suffered by African and African American people and his hope for their national regeneration. Like Easton, Delany contended that despite the injuries that they have suffered, the nation he addressed could be reconstituted. He argued that while this nation, of which African Americans comprise a portion within the United States, had been "depriv[ed] of political equality," it was a nation that could be returned to its former status. Such statements functioned to subvert proslavery representations of racial inferiority through an insistence on political rhetorics of nationhood.

In a key speech delivered in 1854, Delany drew on rhetorics of popular sovereignty to emphasize the political claims of African American people. He argued in his keynote address to the National Emigration Convention of Colored Men, "Political Destiny of the Colored Race," that the "liberty of no man is secure, who controls not his own political destiny."[63] He emphasized throughout the speech the link between freedom and self-government. "A people, to be free, must necessarily be *their own rulers*; that is," argued Delany, "*each individual* must, in himself, embody the *essential ingredient* . . . of the *sovereign principle* which composes the *true basis* of his liberty" ("Political Destiny," 247). Even the act of choosing a representative was, for Delany, a form of self-government. He lamented that African Americans were denied the "right of inherent sovereignty" and could thus enjoy "neither. . . *freedom* nor *safety*" (248). Shifting into a medical metaphor, Delany argued that since African Americans had now identified this "great political disease," they must "discover and apply a *sovereign* remedy" in order to heal themselves as a nation (249, emphasis added). That "remedy," as Delany conceived of it in the mid-1850s, was emigration. As a nation within a nation, African Americans were inherently sovereign, yet that sovereignty could not be fully enacted under their present conditions. He argued that remaining a nation within the United States was not a long-term political option for African Americans.

While Delany differentiated his own conception of emigration—as voluntary and self-directed movement—from the paternalism of white American colonizationists, he shared some of their concerns with territoriality. However, his vision of nationhood ultimately worked to pressure U.S. geopolitical borders and promote his own conception of "America." In his discussions of place, he considered a number of different locations: the United States, Central and South America, and Africa. In one chapter of *The Condition . . . of the Colored People of the United States*, entitled "The United States Our Country," he declared: "We are Americans, having a birthright citizenship—natural claims upon the country—claims common to all others of our fellow citizens—natural rights, which may, by virtue of unjust laws, be obstructed, but never can be annulled. Upon these do we place ourselves, as immovably fixed as the decrees of the living God" (74). These "natural rights" and "birthright" claims upon which African Americans should remain "fixed" did not mean that they would remain geographically rooted within the territorial borders of the United States. In contrast, for Delany it was these rights and the inherent sovereignty that they implied that suggested that African Americans could form their own nation elsewhere. Moreover, "the improbability of ever attaining citizenship and equality of rights in this country" made such movement desirable ("Political Destiny," 254). His statements indicated his larger vision of the natural rights of African Americans and their multiple affiliations: African Americans were both Americans by birth and part of the African nation he discussed.

Delany ruled out both Canada and Liberia, two destinations proposed in previous emigration and colonization schemes, as possible locations for national regeneration. For him, Canada was not a workable location for a black nation because he did not see that black people could ever outnumber the white population. In his reading of Delany's views on citizenship, Glenn Hendler characterizes him as an advocate of "statistical citizenship" because Delany argued that black people must go to a place where they could represent the statistical majority.[64] To found a successful nation, Delany claimed in 1854, "our attention must be turned in a direction towards those places where the black and colored man comprise, by population, and constitute by necessity of numbers, the *ruling element* of the body politic" ("Political Destiny," 250). This suggests a vision of nationhood both ethnic and civic-territorial. However, Delany's writings indicate that there were other factors that contributed to his selection of an ideal place. Although black people would make up a statistical majority in Africa, Delany found Liberia to be geographically and climatologically "objectionable" (*Condition*, 185). He concluded this based on the fact that Liberia was located "in the *sixth degree* of latitude North of the equator, in a district signally unhealthy" (185). In addition to its geographic problems, Delany asserted that "Liberia is not an Independent Republic: in fact, *it is not* an independent nation at all; but a poor *miserable mockery*—a *burlesque* on a government—a pitiful dependency on the American Colonizationists" (185). Even though it occupied a discretely bounded territory, Liberia lacked the kind of political independence and decision-making power that Delany associated with sovereign nationhood; it pretended to be a nation rather than actually functioning as one. Its dependence on the United States and on the ACS indicated a kind of empty performance of sovereignty that he found to be unworkable. He turned his attention to Cuba, the Caribbean, and South America, places that he believed would be climatologically and politically more hospitable.

In his discussions of emigration, Delany worked to subvert representations of the United States as a single, homogenous, and territorially fixed state, expanding the concept of "America" to include North, South, and Central America. In Levine's reading, Delany "emphasiz[ed] the ways in which race challenges the very idea of the bordered nation" but also participates in rhetorics of Manifest Destiny and imperialism, which were well-established themes in U.S. political discourse.[65] I would add that Delany did not abandon the idea of a territorially bounded nation-state in his fictional and nonfictional works, but he also seemed to suggest that such borders were fluid rather than static. Challenging rhetorics of American exceptionalism, Delany worked to rhetorically separate "America" from the "United States" and suggested that America has always accommodated multiple nations. In *The Condition . . . of the Colored People of the United States*, he argued that "America" could accommodate the nation he envisioned because it was "designed by Providence as an asylum for all the various nations of the earth" (187). Levine highlights Delany's "mystical insistence that the destiny of U.S. blacks lies not in a return to Africa (as the colonizationists would have it) but in developing what Paul Gilroy terms an 'autonomous, black nation state' in Central and South America."[66] Delany noted that since its beginnings, "America," that is, both North and South America, had been a heterogeneous space, populated by people of various professions, classes, and races. Rather than arguing that God intended America for one specific people, as the Puritans did, Delany argued that the "'finger of God'" singled out the "American" continent as a place of refuge and as a distinctly multinational place (187). Here he also contested earlier arguments like those of Henry Highland Garnet, who claimed that African Americans should not emigrate because God had "planted" them in the United States.[67] America was exceptional for its multiplicity, according to Delany, not for its singularity or uniformity, and America did not correspond to the current geographic limits of the United States. He echoed these points in "Political Destiny of the Colored Race" in which he declared that "tribes of the black race" (267) were already living in Central America and the West Indies when the British and other Europeans arrived there, something he attributed to divine Providence. He concluded, "Upon the American continent, then, we are determined to remain, despite every opposition that may be urged against us" (268).

Delany's vision of African American popular sovereignty, in which sovereignty resides in the people and follows them wherever they go, unpacked both the emancipatory potential of popular sovereignty and the difficulties inherent in defining "the people." Outlining his plans for a new "American" nation, Delany described the people of the West Indies and Central and South America as "generous, sociable, and *tractable*" but not sovereign or self-governing ("Political Destiny," 268, emphasis added). Moreover, they were people who "now desire all the improvements of North America . . . [but] have no confidence in the whites of the United States" (268). In contrast, he believed that Indigenous Americans would "plac[e] every confidence in the black and colored people of North America" (268). Delany's sense of Indigenous Americans welcoming the "improvements" brought by African Americans resonated with the civilizing rhetorics of the ACS. Like the ACS visions of Liberia, he imagined that African Americans would form the ruling class of the nation he envisioned, differentiating them from the Indigenous peoples whom they would lead. Thus, while Delany linked sovereignty and self-government with African American people, he simultaneously elided that capacity in others. Delany's vision of a "colored" American nation paralleled in troubling ways the fights over popular sovereignty in the West and exposed in a new context the intellectual challenges associated with defining "the people." Even as it deconstructed several elements of midcentury American discourses of nationhood and sovereignty by emphasizing mobility and adaptability as national traits and by entertaining the possibility of multiple affiliations, Delany's formulation of a new "American" nation also was informed by territorial nation-state sovereignty and the logics of colonization.

Delany's consideration of an African American nation in East Africa reveals similar tensions surrounding issues of sovereignty. In an appendix to *The Condition . . . of the Colored People of the United States*, he highlighted the adaptability and mobility of African Americans: "There is one great physiological fact in regard to the colored race—which, while it may not apply to all colored persons, is true of those having black skins—that they can bear *more different* climates than the white race" (225). As part of his argument for emigration, Delany tried to transform black mobility, which many proslavery advocates framed in negative terms, into a positive value—a quality that uniquely enabled Africans and African Americans to be "'denizens of *every soil*'" and "'*lords* of terrestrial creation'" (226). God endowed the African race, he argued, with these qualities. They thus possessed the right of dominion and the ability to inhabit any climate, a form of God-given popular sovereignty. "Africa, to become regenerated," wrote Delany in his *Report of the Niger Valley Exploring Party*, "must have a national character, and her position among the existing nations of the earth will depend mainly upon the high standard she may gain compared with them in all her relations, morally, religiously, socially, politically, and commercially."[68] As with his plan for an "American" nation, Delany did not consider that Africans would not welcome the arrival of African American colonists and their presumed mandate to govern. Indigenous African peoples were not a focus in his vision of popular sovereignty. Rather, he was concerned with shifting the terms of the conversation from race to nation within the United States, a shift he believed would be more effective in generating political and social change.

Even though Delany's arguments about African Americans and nationhood can be seen as "conflicted,"[69] the salient points that emerge from his writings of the 1850s are his insistence on thinking and writing of African Americans in national terms and his framing of sovereignty as something that people can carry with them. African Americans, authorized by their natural rights and birthright claims to American citizenship, could and should consider moving elsewhere in order to enact the practices of sovereignty that he equated with nationhood. Regardless of where their nation was eventually planted, Delany argued that African American people must articulate their claims in national terms. He suggested that the "claims of no people, according to established policy and usage, are respected by any nation, until they are presented in a national capacity" (*Condition*, 221–222). He exhorted his readers to act on their capacity for sovereignty and self-government: "It is time we had become politicians, we mean, to understand the political economy and domestic policy of nations; that we had become as well as moral theorists, also the practical demonstrators of equal rights and self-government" (45). So in addition to making arguments about the immorality of slavery and the inherent humanity of the African race, Delany challenged his readers to think politically and to assert their national sovereignty by acting as "practical demonstrators of equal rights and self-government." Like the leaders of the Negro Convention movement, he called for the creation of a convention, one that would be attended by those of the highest intelligence rather than a gathering of the masses. The formation of such a convention, Delany implied, would further the politicization of African Americans and cement their national status. His arguments about the need for intelligent, qualified leaders—a kind of natural aristocracy—troubled his assertions of popular sovereignty and suggested that many of "the people" were not truly qualified to lead themselves. They required direction from those of "great worth and talents" (*Condition*, 218). Thus, even as Delany imagined African Americans carrying their God-given sovereignty into a transplanted nation, he also allowed for a kind of meritocracy in which the best and brightest would rise to the top. Here and elsewhere Delany revealed his understanding that in a post-Westphalian world, groups of people must style themselves as nations in order to communicate their political grievances to the international community.

Frederick Douglass had experienced firsthand the difficulties of being stateless in the 1850s and the irony that American extraterritorial sovereignty offered more protections to him as a slave than to him after his escape. Fearing that he would be captured and returned to his former master, Douglass embarked in 1845 for Ireland, a country whose experiences under British colonial rule had captured his attention. Douglass expressed tremendous sympathy for the Irish people, declaring in 1872 that he considered himself "something of an Irishman as well as a negro."[70] Yet, in earlier decades he was critical of comparisons of Irish suffering with that of enslaved African Americans, arguing that there was "no analogy between the two cases."[71] Moreover, he denounced the racial prejudices of Irish Americans who, he claimed, were "taught to believe that we eat the bread which of right belongs to them" and that "our adversity is essential to their prosperity."[72] One facet of the adversity that African Americans faced was made clear to Douglass when he traveled abroad. He wrote of his sense of alienation in a letter to William Lloyd Garrison dated 1 January 1846: "I hardly need say that, in speaking of Ireland, I shall be influenced by prejudices in favor of America. I think my circumstances all forbid that. I have no end to serve, no creed to uphold, no government to defend; and as to nation, I belong to none. I have no protection at home, or resting-place abroad. The land of my birth welcomes me to her shores only as a slave, and spurns with contempt the idea of treating me differently. So that I am an outcast from the society of my childhood, and an outlaw in the land of my birth. 'I am a stranger with thee, and a sojourner as all my fathers were.'"[73] Citing Psalm 39:12, Douglass positioned himself as a "stranger" and "sojourner," seen as a slave in America and an alien elsewhere. His declaration that he belonged to no nation was an acknowledgment that no sovereign power claimed his allegiance nor offered him protection. The irony of this, as he pointed out in an article for the *North Star*, is that if he were traveling *as a slave*, he would have the protection of the U.S. government. "A colored man who travels for the benefit of a white man," he wrote, "will have thrown over him the shield and panoply of the United States; but if he travels for his own profit or pleasure, he forfeits all the immunities of an American citizen."[74] Here he exposed the challenges inherent in the kind of mobility that Delany celebrated by arguing that the sovereignty of "the people" was highly situational and dependent on the recognition of other nations.

Although he did not share Delany's support for emigration in the 1850s, like Delany, Douglass engaged rhetorics of imperium in imperio as a means of gaining political leverage in works such as "The Present Condition and Future Prospects of the Negro People." In this 1853 address before the American and Foreign Anti-Slavery Society in New York City, he emphasized the sheer numbers of African Americans in the United States as proof that they were becoming a nation. In a rhetorical move that played on fears of an emergent African American nation, Douglass described free and enslaved people as a virtual nation that was in the process of being formed: "This people, free and slave, are rapidly filling up the number of four millions. They are becoming a nation, in the midst of a nation which disowns them, and for weal or for woe this nation is united. The distinction between the slave and the free is not great, and their destiny seems one and the same. The black man is linked to his brother by indissoluble ties. The one cannot be truly free while the other is a slave. The free colored man is reminded by the ten thousand petty annoyances with which he meets of his identity with an enslaved people, and that with them he is destined to fall or flourish. We are one nation, then" (253). Douglass's formulation of the nation here shared several similarities with that of Delany. Both conceived of nations as communities of people linked by a shared history, genealogy, and political potential, and both men distinguished national communities by the size of their population. Delany urged African Americans to emigrate to a place where they could constitute a majority, and Douglass cited the sheer numbers of African American people as proof of their potential nationhood in America. A body of people that large, he suggested, was a nation in the making. In addition to being a sizeable community with a shared history that created "indissoluble ties," African Americans shared a common destiny, which made them "one nation." Later in the address, Douglass again used the rhetoric of imperium in imperio to suggest the revolutionary potential of an African American nation: "Americans should remember that there are already on this continent, and in the adjacent islands, all of 12,370,000 Negroes, who only wait for the lifegiving and organizing power of intelligence, to mould them into one body, and into a powerful nation" ("Present Condition," 258). His emphasis on the scope of the emergent African American nation exerted a kind of rhetorical force on an audience already conditioned to view imperium in imperio as a political threat.

For Douglass, the sheer size of the African American population and the fact that it was an emergent nation complicated arguments for emigration. He expressed this belief in a letter to Harriet Beecher Stowe in 1853, which was later published in *Frederick Douglass' Paper*. Commenting on her representation of the Harris family's emigration to Liberia in *Uncle Tom's Cabin*, Douglass remarked: "The truth is, dear madam, we are *here*, and here we are likely to remain. Individuals emigrate—nations never."[75] For Douglass, conceiving of African Americans as a nation, a body of people, problematized colonization schemes. The African American nation, he argued at this point in his career, was deeply connected to America and could not just be transplanted permanently to another location. Russ Castronovo offers the following reading of Douglass's response to Stowe: "His words suggest the complexities of cultural resilience, implying that the American nation is not a single, monolithic entity but a composite gathering of nations within nations, or perhaps more properly given the prevailing antebellum racial hierarchy, a nation layered over nations. America's cultural sovereignty is disrupted by this recognition of its hybridity."[76] Douglass's response, with its insistence on framing African Americans as a nation within a nation, thus depicted America as a multinational entity in which people maintain multiple and sometimes overlapping political affiliations.

Although he echoed the rhetoric of imperium in imperio as part of an argument that nations never move, Douglass did make several attempts to redefine nationhood and sovereignty to include a more expansive area with more permeable borders. The nation that he presented in "The Present Condition and Future Prospects of the Negro People" did not occupy its own territory, and as a virtual nation, one that was in the process of becoming, it did not depend on territory for its power. Rather, this nation was suffused with potentiality. The broader definition that Douglass offered was explicitly national, but national in a sense that was not limited by geographic or current political borders. Despite his argument to Stowe that nations never emigrate, he, like Delany, credited the African American nation with a certain amount of mobility. Later in the same address he suggested that African Americans should not go to Africa because there are more convivial locations: "Other and more desirable lands are open to us. We can plant ourselves at the very portals of slavery. We can hover about the Gulf of Mexico. Nearly all the isles of the Caribbean Seas bid us welcome; while the broad and fertile valleys of British Guiana, under the sway of the emancipating Queen, invite us to their treasures, and to nationality" ("Present Condition," 258). His wording here is interesting. While African Americans could "plant" themselves in one location, they could also "hover" in another. Several locations offer the promise of "treasures" and "nationality," and what emerges from this passage is the power of potentiality, not a statist emphasis on territoriality. Focusing on Douglass's later interest in Haitian emigration during the 1850s and early 1860s, Levine argues that during this period, Douglass "imagines a unified black nationality in the American hemisphere," which "challenges the conventional view of Douglass as an African American nationalist who regularly sought to link that nationalism with his U.S. nationalism" (*Dislocating*, 181). Like Delany, Douglass's view of "America" was more expansive than we first suspected, encompassing, as Levine notes, the "American hemisphere." His rhetorics of national potential functioned to separate political capacity and ethnic ties from the possession of national space and challenged territorial narratives of American nationhood and sovereignty that relied on the language of chartered limits, title, and jurisdiction.

Douglass also argued that, as demonstrated by the lived experience of African Americans, people can and do have multiple affiliations with different forms of nations. In his famous 1852 address, "The Meaning of July Fourth for the Negro," Douglass followed his celebratory retelling of the American Revolution with a reminder that African Americans constituted a separate people who were not included in the American "people" whose independence was being celebrated that day: "Fellow-citizens, pardon me, allow me to ask, why am I called upon to speak here to-day? What have I, or those I represent, to do with your national independence? Are the great principles of political freedom and of natural justice, embodied in that Declaration of Independence, extended to us? and am I, therefore, called upon to bring our humble offering to the national altar, and to confess the benefits and express devout gratitude for the blessings resulting from your independence to us?"[77] Douglass here referred to his audience, which included many white abolitionists who had gathered to hear him speak in Rochester, New York, as "Fellow-citizens," yet he distanced himself and African Americans writ large from the national celebrations. He declared, "This Fourth [of] July is *yours*, not *mine*. *You* may rejoice, *I* must mourn."[78] Douglass highlighted the multiple national affiliations that African Americans maintained. In the case of those born in America, according to the principle of birthright citizenship, they were American citizens. Yet, they also shared genealogical ties with Africans. Subverting the binary view of imperium in imperio in which the emergent nation threatens the sovereignty of the host, Douglass reminded his audience that America was the threat. He also implied that not only is America the site of multiple nations, but individuals can and do maintain relationships with multiple entities.

While Delany suggested that African Americans' birthright claims to American citizenship authorized other forms of affiliation, in "The Claims of Our Common Cause" (1853), Douglass made a different argument for birthright citizenship. He said, "We would, first of all, be understood to range ourselves no lower among our fellow-countrymen than is implied in the high appellation of '*citizen*.'"[79] As a speech delivered at the Colored National Convention held in Rochester, New York, in 1853, Douglass's message functioned to instruct both white Americans and African Americans as to the nature of the African American claim to citizenship. He based his arguments on the notion of birthright citizenship and on the foundational documents of American politics: "By birth, we are American citizens; by the principles of the Declaration of Independence, we are American citizens; within the meaning of the United States Constitution, we are American citizens; by the facts of history, and the admissions of American statesmen, we are American citizens; by the hardships and trials endured; by the courage and fidelity displayed by our ancestors in defending the liberties and in achieving the independence of our land, we are American citizens."[80] Here Douglass drew on the rhetorical tradition employed by activists such as David Walker and Henry Highland Garnet, which based African Americans' citizenship on their economic, political, and emotional ties to the U.S. landscape. Their position as a nation within a nation, which he argued was the result of slavery and oppression, was not incompatible with their claims to birthright citizenship. The U.S. Constitution, he argued in 1854, established only two classes of people in America: "citizens" and "aliens."[81] Whether one was a citizen or not, Douglass asserted, was based on where one was born: U.S. citizens were those individuals born within the nation's territorial limits, while aliens were those who were born elsewhere. Because he was not an alien, Douglass claimed that he was, by default, a U.S. citizen. Moreover, his residence in the state of New York, which recognized his political rights, made him a federal citizen according to the U.S. Constitution. Thus, for Douglass, while slavery and oppression had positioned African Americans as a nation within a nation, the U.S. Constitution and other foundational documents acknowledged their citizenship. Like Brown did in his provisional documents, Douglass engaged the U.S. Constitution in order to make it speak differently on the subject of citizenship. In "The Present Condition and Future Prospects of the Negro People," he claimed that the proximity of the African American nation detracted from its political leverage. Douglass argued that while Americans were willing to listen to the plight of people from "distant nations," they did not listen to the woes of the African American nation in their midst. While Delany represented division as the norm in all nations and times, Douglass insisted that the position of African Americans was "anomalous, unequal, and extraordinary" because they were constructed as "aliens" in the land in which they were born ("Present Condition," 251).

Douglass also argued, however, that African Americans were not the only ones being victimized by what he read as a fundamental misunderstanding and manipulation of the concept of popular sovereignty, the "grand argument" that dominated conversations about the extension of slavery in the West. The issues inherent in the Kansas-Nebraska Act affected all American citizens. As U.S. citizens, the people who migrated to the territories were thought to carry their sovereignty with them, sovereignty that Douglass defined as "the right of the people to establish a government for themselves" ("Kansas-Nebraska," 308). He called for a return to the Revolutionary-era understandings of popular sovereignty as "the independent right of a people to make their own laws, without dictation or interference from any quarter" (308). This legislative independence, he claimed, was not being offered to the people of Kansas and Nebraska, who were, he contended, "as completely under the powers of the federal government as Canada is under the British Crown" (309). They were being deluded with rhetorics of complete independence and had only "the shadow" of control over one particular issue: slavery (309). Douglass here exposed the ways in which popular sovereignty had come to refer specifically to decision-making powers regarding slavery, a violation of the principles of the Revolution and a manipulation of white Americans' true relationship to the federal government. Like Delany, Douglass worked to unpack contemporary discourses of popular sovereignty and offered his own reading of the sovereignty of the people from that proposed by slavery apologists.

By the 1850s, African Americans had fully realized the strategic possibilities of framing themselves in national terms, and figures such as Delany and Douglass were working hard to establish African Americans as a nation. While they differed on specific points, both drew on this discourse to contribute to what William Wells Brown referred to as a national "reputation." In his 1863 work, *The Black Man: His Antecedents, His Genius, and His Achievements*, Brown asserted that nations learn from one another just like people do and that nations value their "reputation."[82] Reading Delany and Douglass along a binary of emigrationist-assimilationist obscures the ways in which both drew on the strategic value of rhetorics of nationhood and sovereignty in an attempt to shift conversations about race to conversations about political status. Their efforts functioned not to advance a single, coherent vision of nationhood but to complicate, challenge, and evacuate visions of a racially homogenous, territorially discrete, and indivisible American nation. Like John Brown and the members of the Chatham Convention, they engaged rhetorics of popular sovereignty and worked to write themselves into national and international political discourses in order to reframe the relationship between African Americans and the United States.

Conclusion

The 1850s were one of the most contentious decades in America's history, a flashpoint in which white Americans continued to look to the large-scale removal of nonwhite populations as the solution to internal division. Competing notions of the nature and location of sovereignty, how that sovereignty would circulate through western spaces, and who counted as "the people" led to fierce debates, violent conflicts, and ultimately civil war. Sovereignty, in many of these debates, emerged as inextricably linked to slavery. To limit white citizens' ability to "decide" matters related to slavery constituted an abrogation of their status as a sovereign people. As in earlier decades, some attempted to mitigate fears of internal division by projecting those fears onto the presence of a racial "nation" within the geopolitical borders of the United States. Even as it was becoming increasingly clear in the 1850s that there ultimately was no single American nation, white colonizationists and slavery apologists attempted to propose their respective solutions to America's problems in terms of the concept of imperium in imperio. The threatening potential of a nation of African Americans, they argued, could be mitigated through its removal or through the governance of slavery. Such rhetorics attempted to intervene in conversations about African American mobility as ways of connecting black people to particular spaces.

African American writers and orators turned to discussions of nationhood and sovereignty to reimagine ideas of black mobility and imperium in imperio. A variety of writers, including both emigrationists and integrationists, articulated their claims in national terms, exploring territorial, civic, and racial conceptions of nationhood. Many felt, as writer and politician Edward Wilmot Blyden did, that there was traction to be gained in nationalist arguments that was not available in discussions of cosmopolitanism. Blyden, who was born in the West Indies and emigrated to Liberia in 1850, wrote extensively about the need for all African people to think in national terms: "I believe nationality to be an ordinance of nature; and no people can rise to an influential position among the nations without a distinct and efficient nationality. Cosmopolitanism has never effected any thing, and never will, perhaps, till the millennium."[83] In their writings and speeches in the 1850s, both Delany and Douglass drew on rhetorics of divided sovereignty, of African Americans as a nation existing within and sometimes across the borders of the United States, and claimed for themselves the power to imagine different futures for both that nation and the United States. Although their views differed, both men worked to establish the national reputation of African Americans as a politicized population and not a racially marginalized group. They urged their African American audiences to think critically about terms such as *sovereignty*, *nationhood*, and *citizenship* and make their political claims be heard by the white American public. Throughout the decades to follow, African Americans continued to draw on imperium in imperio as a means of answering a series of key questions about their relationship to the United States during and after the Civil War: Should they work at integrating themselves into American political culture at whatever cost? Could they leverage the specter of internal revolution into greater political access within the United States? If they were denied access to American institutions, should they form their own? Should they consider leaving en masse and forming or joining another nation? What role would written constitutions play in their political efforts?

As John Brown and his Provisional Constitution suggest, imperium in imperio remained a potent way to think about national contingencies and to craft new conceptions of the United States. Taking a radical stance on popular sovereignty, he created a mobile, flexible, provisional U.S. government characterized by equal rights and abolition, which could, he argued, help the United States transition from a slaveholding nation to one in which all people were equal members. Like the constitution making of the Cherokees and the National Negro Convention movement, Brown's Provisional Constitution and "Declaration of Liberty" rearticulated key portions of America's founding documents to fit his own political agenda. He located his nation within the United States but outside of any particular state. Brown's government not only challenged territorial understandings of nationhood, but also, by its very existence, the notion that two nations could not occupy the same space. As Delany noted, Brown and the other Chatham members looked to the example of Native nations, specifically the Cherokees, as a working model of imperium in imperio. Just as supporters of African colonization were, perhaps, drawing on examples of Indian Removal, proponents of an African American nation found inspiration in Native polities and their strategic nation-to-nation relationship with the United States. While Brown's attack on Harpers Ferry forestalled any attempts to treat with the United States, his provisional government gestured toward the kinds of political possibilities being explored in the 1850s and early 1860s.

Another expression of those political possibilities, one diametrically opposed to Brown's position, was the CSA, which ratified its own written constitution in 1861, declared its break with the United States, and offered an alternative vision of slavery, territoriality, and imperium in imperio. Like the Cherokee Nation, the members of the Negro Convention movement, and Brown himself, the drafters of the Confederate Constitution turned for inspiration to the founding documents of the United States. Like many of these other groups, the founders of the Confederacy represented themselves as oppressed, likening their struggle against the North to that of the American colonists in the Revolutionary era. Yet, there were several key points that differentiated the CSA founders and the nation they formed from the other groups examined in this book. First, as Tsai notes, "Unlike many separatists of the past, disunionists were men of standing," who often "held elective or appointed office in the U.S. government or their states of residence" (*America's Forgotten Constitutions*, 119). They voted, owned property (including slaves), and exerted considerable political influence *in* U.S. political culture, and thus their political efforts must be differentiated from the tactics used by the other groups I examine. By 1861, the CSA's aim in declaring its national status was not to gain political traction in or in relation to the United States but to create a separate, slaveholding, territorial nation on the American continent. Moreover, despite its claims to racial distinction as a nation founded on whiteness, Confederates were not represented in broader public argument as a distinct racial other. Lincoln characterized them as "insurrectionary combatants" and framed their efforts as a "rebellion" rather than a national founding (qtd. in Tsai, *America's Forgotten Constitutions*, 143). However, as did many in the nineteenth-century political landscape, they acknowledged the power of the genre of the written constitution to communicate with the United States on a nation-to-nation basis and to articulate their views on sovereignty and nationhood.

The Confederate Constitution did not enshrine the visions of imperium in imperio offered by Calhoun and others in which the plantation was the foundation of the CSA's political system, opting instead to replicate certain aspects of federalism found in the U.S. Constitution.[84] Like Brown's Provisional Constitution, the CSA's constitution sought to rework the U.S. Constitution's rather vague references to slavery, with Brown explicitly prohibiting it and the Confederacy formally acknowledging its place in the nation it was creating. While, as many have noted, the U.S. constitution does not use the word *slave*, the Confederate Constitution uses some form of this word—"slave[s]," "slaveholding," "slavery"—ten times.[85] In a March 1861 address that became known as the "Cornerstone Speech," Alexander Stephens, the vice president of the CSA, announced, "The new constitution puts at rest, *forever*, all the agitating questions relating to our peculiar institution—African slavery as it exists among us—the proper *status* of the negro in our form of civilization."[86] Yet, the constitution was not without its critics, including officials from South Carolina, who were frustrated that the new constitution did not formally "entrench the plantation system, ensure the clout of larger slaveholding states, and reinvigorate the slave trade" (Tsai, *America's Forgotten Constitutions*, 141). It was also seen by some as not taking a strong enough stance on states' rights. Despite the importance of states' rights to Southern rhetoric, David P. Currie characterizes the Confederacy as a "looking-glass variant" of the United States.[87] He traces the ways in which sovereignty was uneasily divided between state and CSA authorities and the ways in which wartime exigencies pressured this vision of imperium in imperio. Unlike Brown's document, which was radical in its "utter silence about states" and its emphasis on a "single, national people," the Confederacy's constitution refashioned many aspects of divided sovereignty already present in the U.S. federal system while making explicit the role of slavery in the CSA (Tsai, *America's Forgotten Constitutions*, 92).

Ultimately, the Civil War produced a consolidation of power in the U.S. federal government and strengthened conceptions of federal sovereignty over that of the states. In the second half of the nineteenth century new tactics emerged in relation to Native and African American people that came to supplant large-scale and expensive removals of entire populations. Moreover, the United States was emerging as a global power and was a destination for increasing numbers of immigrants, not all of whom qualified for naturalization under current laws. As the next two chapters show, the presence of two of these populations in particular, the Irish and the Chinese, created new political, social, and economic exigencies for the United States. Irish and Chinese immigrants were framed as nations and were subject to administrative and legal forms of containment rather than to the kind of removal efforts that characterized U.S. responses to American Indian and free black people in the first half of the century. These immigrant groups also raised new questions about the implications of immigration and about understandings of extraterritorial sovereignty. As the United States extended its sovereign reach abroad, might other nations do the same? Would immigrant populations represent a division of American sovereignty through the introduction of foreign powers? Rhetorics of imperium in imperio played a key role in literary and cultural productions about Irish American and Chinese nations within the United States and in constructions of American nationhood and sovereignty.

CHAPTER FOUR

"An Irish Republic (on Paper)"

The Fenian Brotherhood, Virtual Nationhood, and Contested Sovereignties

THE CIVIL WAR divided America into two nations and pitted two divergent theories of sovereignty against one another: one that championed the sovereignty of the states versus one that argued for the primacy of federal sovereignty. One familiar story of the war is the triumph of federal sovereignty and the consolidation of power at the federal level. Yet, although the war is often discussed in terms of the political and military struggles between the North and South, other nations were involved as well, introducing new issues regarding extraterritorial sovereignty and political allegiance into this domestic crisis.

In addition to Native nations such as the Creek, Choctaw, Chickasaw, Osage, Comanche, and Cherokee, which eventually sided with the Confederacy, European states, particularly Britain, were drawn into the diplomatic fray. In an attempt to gain official recognition and support for the Confederate States of America (CSA), the South sent two Confederate emissaries, James Murray Mason and John Slidell, to Britain and France. In violation of international law and U.S. policy, Union captain Charles Wilkes of the USS *Jacinto* arrested these Confederate diplomats and their secretaries on board the British packet steamer *Trent* in 1861, a move that the Confederates hoped would draw Britain into the war. Britain claimed the seizure of the diplomats to be a violation of its national sovereignty, while President Abraham Lincoln and other Union leaders seethed at Britain's stance toward the Confederacy. To reduce the chances of Britain entering the war, the diplomats were released and allowed to continue their journey, which would prove unsuccessful in gaining meaningful support from Britain or France.¹

In the context of these competing sovereign claims and the shifting political terrain of the 1860s, as civil war threatened to boil over into transatlantic, international conflict, constructions of nationhood, national citizenship, and political allegiance were extremely fraught. This created both new exigencies and new opportunities for other groups in the United States, such as the Fenian Brotherhood, a group founded in 1858 as the American wing of the Irish Republican Brotherhood (IRB), and the Irish Republic that it claimed to lead. At various points in its history, the Fenian Brotherhood functioned as a secret society, a standing national army, and paramilitary insurgents. There was a brief period in the 1860s, however, when the Fenian Brotherhood acted as the government of the Irish Republic in America and, according to Thomas N. Brown "conducted itself as an important international power."[2]

Fenian literature, political practices, and military efforts, like those of John Brown and his followers, worked toward the formation of a provisional government within the United States. The Fenians drafted a written constitution that declared their national status in print even as they claimed no distinct territory. They referred to the Irish Republic as "virtually established,"[3] with *virtuality* signifying a particular kind of potentiality divorced from the occupation of a national space. The Fenians established their capital in New York's Union Square, issued letters of marque and reprisal, and made several unsuccessful attempts to invade Canada in order to strike a blow against Britain.[4] In addition to their written constitutions and published proceedings, the Fenians also produced a great deal of fiction and poetry celebrating the Fenian cause and chronicling its national exploits, including *Ridgeway: An Historical Romance of the Fenian Invasion of Canada*, which was published by James McCarroll in 1868 under the pseudonym of Scian Dubh. Like the nations I examined in previous chapters, the Fenians did not see their Irish Republic of America as a threat to American sovereignty and acted on the premise that multiple nations could share a single space. They pressured widely accepted dichotomies between domestic and foreign and between alien and citizen and questioned the relationship of territory to definitions of sovereignty and nationhood, even as debates about territory threatened to subvert their Irish Republic.[5]

The Fenians and their Irish Republic provide a rich site for exploring competing constructions of sovereignty, nationhood, and political allegiance at midcentury, a time when the United States was wracked by civil war at home and was extending its political reach abroad. In the last two chapters of *Divided Sovereignties*, I turn to groups that took up rhetorics of imperium in imperio as part of their attempt to relate to multiple nations on political terms and to enact multiple forms of political allegiance. In the case of the Fenians, they sought to engage both Britain and the United States on a nation-to-nation basis to gain political advantage. Historian Christian Samito describes the Fenians as a "pressure group" that worked to advance the cause of Irish freedom and rallied the larger Irish American community to press for greater political protections for naturalized and native-born Irish Americans.[6] While the Irish qualified for naturalized citizenship under U.S. law, they faced economic exclusions, nativist attempts to extend the waiting period for naturalization, and representations that territorialized them as a racial and religious underclass. In place of the kind of removal efforts faced by Native peoples and African Americans, Irish immigrants, particularly Catholic immigrants who came during the Great Famine years, experienced legal and administrative efforts to manage their collective behavior, specifically their political behavior and economic opportunities.

The Fenians framed their attempted invasions of Canada as a kind of war by proxy on behalf of their adopted country, but their political and military initiatives animated fears of an Irish imperium in the American press. Building on existing concerns about the political allegiances of naturalized citizens writ large and of Irish Americans in particular, critics of the Fenians returned to questions raised by Blackstone in his discussion of Catholics as an imperium in imperio in England, such as whether Catholics could be loyal citizens/subjects, whether their allegiance would be forever divided between secular and spiritual authorities, and whether it was possible for two sovereign entities to occupy the same space.[7] As I argue in this chapter, through the formation of the Irish Republic in America and transatlantic agitation, the Fenian Brotherhood shifted discussions of Irish Catholics from one of race and religion to one that included their political capacity as both American citizens and members of a virtual Irish Republic. Their Irish Republic constituted an argument that political allegiance and sovereignty could be divided, and their vision of an Irish nation in America that transcended the geopolitical borders of the United States pressured territorial understandings of nationhood and sovereignty. In so doing, they influenced the practice of American sovereignty in ways that they likely never anticipated. Even as they won greater protection for naturalized citizens, I contend that they also goaded the United States into more stridently asserting its territorial sovereignty at home and refusing to engage with other groups on national terms.

Naturalized Citizenship, Political Allegiance, and an Irish Catholic Imperium

The history of eighteenth- and nineteenth-century U.S. naturalization laws is inextricably linked to Irish immigration and fears of Irish radicalism. From

Harrison Gray Otis's infamous 1797 reference to "hordes of wild Irish" and hysterical accounts of the United Irishmen setting down roots in America to mid-nineteenth-century nativist efforts to extend the residency requirements, American political leaders created naturalization laws designed, in no small part, to manage the political behaviors of the Irish.[8] As immigration from Ireland increased due to the Great Famine (1845–1852), so too did warnings of the threat posed by Irish Catholics to American sovereignty. Attitudes toward the Irish were shaped by a complex set of transatlantic discourses about race, nation, and religion, as well as comparisons between the Irish and African Americans, with whom they shared urban spaces in the East. The political and social position of the Irish at midcentury was unique: they qualified for naturalized citizenship and were recognized as a powerful voting bloc but were still coded as unassimilable into the American body politic by many. The presence of large numbers of Irish immigrants in America and their agitation on behalf of Irish independence revived debates between Britain and the United States about the nature of sovereignty and political allegiance. Yet, this messy and contested political landscape also provided a space for groups such as the Fenian Brotherhood to create sovereignty-based arguments and practices that worked to renegotiate their collective relationships to America, Great Britain, and Ireland.

The status of naturalized American citizens, in the United States and abroad, was the subject of intense debate during the nineteenth century and highlighted challenges to the external sovereignty of the United States. In particular, U.S. sovereignty pressured and was pressured by the sovereignty of European nations that did not acknowledge expatriation as a right possessed by all individuals. The relationship between British sovereigns and their subjects was characterized as one of perpetual allegiance. While naturalization laws in British North America had been grounded originally in a similar doctrine of perpetual allegiance, the exigencies of the colonial project and the geographic distance from the metropole resulted in more flexible and varied applications. Immigration and naturalization laws were, as Aristide Zolberg writes, the "object of a perennial tug of war between the colonies and the metropole ever since the late seventeenth century, [and] the issue was propelled to the top of the political agenda in 1773 when Britain abruptly forbade its governors to assent to any new colonial naturalization acts."[9] American political and legal theorists worked to create national policies on immigration and naturalization in the context of shifting populations, territorial expansion, and engagements with foreign nations over issues of sovereignty. Beginning with the Naturalization Act in 1790 and continuing through the Naturalization Act of 1802, the "last major piece of legislation on this subject during the nineteenth century," political leaders in the newly formed American nation emphasized volitional rather than perpetual allegiance (Kettner, *Development*, 246).[10] The U.S. naturalization laws dictated that all free "white" persons who had lived in the United States for at least five years were eligible for citizenship, but whiteness, as Theodore Allen and Noel Ignatiev have suggested, was a category that had to be produced.[11] The position of Irish immigrants was complicated by a host of factors, including their numbers, perceptions of their racial and religious difference, and anxieties about their participation in American economic and political life.

The sheer quantity of Irish people who settled in America during the late eighteenth and nineteenth centuries created new political exigencies for both the United States and Great Britain. Irish immigrants pressured America's ill-defined naturalization laws and constituted a diasporic community with which Britain was forced to contend, albeit indirectly. Charles Fanning observes that "the Irish were easily the largest non-English immigrant group in America just after the Revolution."[12] By 1790 Irish immigrants or people of Irish descent comprised close to one-sixth of the total U.S. population of approximately three million people. The nineteenth century saw a dramatic rise in immigration, particularly from Ireland. In the 1850s the Irish comprised approximately 49 percent of all immigrants. More than four million Irish people came to America during the nineteenth century and became deeply involved in American public life. By 1855, 34 percent of the voting population in New York City were Irish and more than 145,000 Irish men served in the Civil War. It is important to recognize, however, the political, social, and religious differences that existed among Irish immigrants. While Ulster Protestants comprised the majority of eighteenth- and early nineteenth-century immigrants, Irish Catholics made up the largest percentage of the famine immigrants of the 1840s. Middle-class Irish immigrants were far less radical than those of lower socioeconomic backgrounds. In the wake of the famine migration and the tensions that arose during the Civil War, many Irish communities in America maintained at least some degree of antipathy toward Great Britain and, in the case of Irish Catholics, had concern about Anglo-American Protestants.[13]

Discussions of Irish Catholics in the wake of the mass migration of the famine years borrowed from British and Irish representations of Irish Catholics and blended rhetorics of racial and religious difference as part of a process that territorialized the Irish as an unassimilable nation within Protestant America. In *How the Irish Became White*, Ignatiev argues that Irish Catholics experienced both "racial" and "national" oppression in Ireland under English rule, a distinction that he notes, summarizing a point made by Allen, "turns on the composition of the group that enforces elite rule."[14] In the eighteenth century, Irish Catholics were, according to Ignatiev, labeled "native Irish, Celts, or Gaels (as well as 'Papists' and other equally derogatory names), and were regarded, and frequently spoke of themselves, as a 'race' rather than a nation" (*How the Irish Became White*, 35). The ruling group during this period was largely Ulster Protestants, but Ignatiev argues that the 1801 Act of Union "marked a turning point in British colonial policy in Ireland from racial to national oppression" (37). As Irish Catholics came to the United States in greater numbers, some Protestants portrayed the Irish as, in the words of historian Oscar Handlin, a "massive lump in the community, undigested, undigestible."[15] Such arguments represented Irish Catholics as crowding American cities, straining institutions, undercutting the value of American labor, and subverting American political culture. They also perpetuated racial stereotypes that linked Irish Catholics with African Americans, a connection that the Irish actively refuted. Ignatiev suggests that "[c]oming as immigrants rather than as captives or hostages undoubtedly affected the potential racial status of the Irish in America, but it did not settle the issue, since it was by no means obvious who was 'white'" (*How the Irish Became White*, 41). The Irish, he notes, lived and worked alongside African Americans in urban neighborhoods like New York City's Five Points. Accounts of "miscegenation" and "amalgamation" between the two groups circulated in the press, portraying both groups as racialized outsiders despite the difference in their legal and political status (i.e., Irish people could become citizens while African Americans could not). Ignatiev details the ways in which Irish immigrants engaged discourses of race to distinguish themselves from African Americans as part of an effort to claim "the privileges and burdens of whiteness" (59). He argues that while their skin color "made the Irish eligible for membership in the white race, it did not guarantee their admission; they had to *earn* it" (59).[16] Even as some Irish Americans engaged racist discourses and practices to distinguish themselves from African Americans, the Fenian Brotherhood sought to shift the terms of its own collective engagement with the United States and Great Britain from issues of race and religion to political and diplomatic concerns.

Anxieties about the Irish as a separate race or nation that could not be assimilated into white American society dovetailed with the anti-Catholic sentiments that circulated in nineteenth-century American public argument and framed Catholics as a threatening imperium. Such arguments echoed Blackstone's warnings about Catholics constituting an imperium in imperio in whatever country they resided: they would privilege the sovereignty of the pope over that of secular governments. One 1873 article in the *Christian Recorder* summarized the anti-Catholic position that had circulated in America for decades. In answer to the question, "Can Catholics be loyal citizens?" the writer declared that Catholic people could not be both loyal American citizens and active adherents to the Catholic faith. To be good Catholics, "[t]hey must remain an isolated people in the body of citizens an *imperium in imperio* with a paramount allegiance due to a foreign power."[17] David Brion Davis writes that opposition to Catholicism was "nourished by ethnic conflict and uneasiness over immigration in the expanding cities of the Northeast."[18]

As it was in England, American opposition to Catholicism was deeply interwoven with opposition to the Irish. During the peak years of Irish immigration, representations of the Irish as unassimilable fueled various forms of social/economic exclusion, and arguments about an Irish Catholic imperium informed nativist efforts to extend the residency requirements for naturalized citizenship. Scholars have debated the accuracy of accounts of No Irish Need Apply notices, yet stories of Irish people being prevented from working in certain factories or industries, such as banking in New England, suggest attempts to fix Irish immigrants in certain places within American society.[19] While the Irish were not the only immigrant population to include Roman Catholics, many in the Irish American community felt that such arguments were more often applied to Irish Catholics than to other populations. German immigrants, many of whom were Catholic, were held up as a model immigrant population compared with the Irish. David Noel Doyle argues that during the Philadelphia nativist riots in 1844, German Catholic neighborhoods were untouched.[20] Many Irish Americans contended that German Catholics were not subjected to the same levels of antagonism as Irish Catholics, and suggested that anti-Catholic arguments were yet another way of maligning the Irish. As one immigrant claimed in 1860, "The great majority of American people are, in heart and soul anti-Catholic, but more especially anti-Irish."[21] Suggesting that such feelings operated on a broader institutional level, an Irish correspondent in Louisville, Kentucky, wrote to Irish readers that America was governed by a "Protestant ascendency" not unlike that of Ireland.[22] Just as nativists returned to the language of imperium in imperio, which was by this point well established in discussions of religious *and* racial others, to frame Catholics, specifically Irish Catholics, as an internal threat, Irish immigrants filtered their experiences of oppression in America through the familiar dichotomy of Catholic-Protestant.

Members of the American Party, also known as the Know-Nothings, and others who harbored concerns over immigration and naturalization voiced their opposition to foreigners in general, but the Irish, particularly Irish Catholics, were frequent targets, because they were conceived to be religious and racial others and subjects of a monarchical government. Nativists contended that the Irish maintained their national character after settling in America and that the creation of Irish American military, religious, and social institutions threatened the political authority of the United States. Just as colonizationists warned that African Americans would always act as "Africans in America," proponents of extended residency requirements argued that the Irish could not easily abandon their political, religious, and social beliefs and would form separate national institutions in the United States that would subvert American political culture from within. In *Imminent Dangers to the Free Institutions of the United States through Foreign Immigration, and the Present State of the Naturalization Laws*, Samuel F. B. Morse warned that the Irish were forming separate institutions and military companies under the banner of Irish figures such as Daniel O'Connell. He wrote of the Irish: "[T]hey are men who having *professed* to become Americans, by accepting our terms of naturalization, do yet, in direct contradiction to their professions, clan together as a separate interest, and retain their foreign appellation."[23] He also distinguished the "naturalized *foreigner*" from the "naturalized *citizen*," with the former an individual who "professes to become an American, and still, being received and sworn to be a citizen, talks (for example,) of Ireland as 'his home,' as 'his beloved country,' resents any thing said against the Irish as said against him, glories in being Irish, forms and cherishes an Irish interest, brings hither Irish local feuds, and forgets, in short, all his new obligations as an American, and retains both a name and a feeling and a practice in regard to his adopted country at war with propriety, with decency, with gratitude, and with true patriotism."[24] Here Morse expressed the doctrine of perpetual allegiance in social and cultural terms and criticized the naturalized Irish American who "professes" to be an American while retaining his relationship to Ireland in "name," "feeling," and "practice." Such "naturalized *foreigners*," Morse argued, are a threat to the sovereignty of the United States and can never be fully assimilated into the framework of American political and social life. Critics of liberal immigration and naturalization policies used such arguments in the 1840s and 1850s to support waiting periods of up to twenty-one years for immigrants who desired naturalized citizenship. They praised birthright citizenship and feared the growing influence of what Irish leader Daniel O'Connell and other Young Irelanders had lauded in the 1840s as an "Irish nation in exile."[25]

Officially, the position of the American legal establishment was that naturalized citizens were subject only to the laws of the United States and owed their sole allegiance to their adopted country. Circulating throughout the debates over naturalization in the late 1850s and 1860s was the belief that political allegiance, like political sovereignty, could not be divided. Those citizens who acted on behalf of foreign interests within the jurisdiction of the United States risked being charged with a violation of U.S. neutrality. For example, in February 1856, members of the Robert Emmet Club of Cincinnati, a local branch of the Irish

Emigrant Aid Association of Ohio and a forerunner of the Fenian Brotherhood, were brought before Judge Humphrey Howe Leavitt in the Circuit Court of the Southern District of Ohio on charges that they violated the 1818 Neutrality Act. The charges stemmed from allegations that the defendants, all of whom were naturalized Irish Americans, were engaged in filibustering, or unauthorized military efforts against nations with which the United States was not at war. Judge Leavitt found the defendants not guilty of pursuing military actions against Britain and deemed that while their club's rhetoric might be inflammatory and imprudent, their actions did not constitute a violation of U.S. laws. However, near the end of his opinion in *United States v. Lumsden* (1856), Leavitt took an opportunity to comment on the issues of sovereignty and national allegiance that this case raised. Addressing the defendants and, by extension, all who participated in such organizations, Leavitt declared: "There can be no such thing as a divided national allegiance. The obligations of citizenship can not exist in favor of different nationalities at the same time" (26). Leavitt reinforced the sovereignty of the United States over all citizens—native-born and naturalized—"within the limits of the country" and upheld American constructions of voluntary citizenship as opposed to doctrines of perpetual allegiance (26).

In Leavitt's interpretation, the United States represented the supreme authority over all of its citizens. In turn, citizens must devote their undivided allegiance to the sovereign so long as they remained within the borders of the United States. While mere sentimental attachments to Ireland did not constitute a violation of U.S. laws, the judge used this case as an opportunity to suggest the problems associated with divided allegiance and, by extension, divided sovereignty. Divided allegiance is impossible, because such a duality would suggest that the United States and Ireland (or Britain) could both exercise sovereign power over naturalized Irish Americans on American soil, which would undercut the very meaning of sovereignty as the supreme political authority in a particular territory. In 1859 U.S. secretary of state Lewis Cass echoed similar sentiments in a letter to Joseph A. Wright, the U.S. ambassador to Prussia: "The moment a foreigner becomes naturalized his allegiance to his native country is severed forever," and he likened the process of naturalization to a kind of baptism, "a new political birth."[26]

Despite such descriptions, which framed naturalization as both a straightforward break and a quasi-religious experience, when naturalized citizens traveled abroad, particularly to their country of origin, their political position became quite complicated. The responsibilities of the U.S. government toward naturalized citizens who traveled abroad remained ill defined throughout the first half of the nineteenth century. Tensions between notions of voluntary and perpetual allegiance pervaded America's international *and* domestic policies. Despite the profound influence of Lockean formations of the social contract and the volitional elements of the relationship between government and the governed, British common-law doctrines of perpetual allegiance continued to exert some force in American jurisprudence and public discourse. The U.S. state and federal authorities framed expatriation as a natural right, but as Kettner argues, "[s]ome judges showed a great reluctance to diverge too widely from the old English notion of perpetual allegiance, though the traditional version of this doctrine was never applied in full force" (*Development*, 271). They also realized the challenges of enforcing American sovereignty and naturalization policies on foreign soil. According to Kettner, "By mid-century, the government's working policy seemed to be to extend diplomatic protection to naturalized citizens except in cases when the native government, within its own jurisdiction, sought to enforce obligations owed by the expatriate antecedent to his original departure" (271).[27]

The British doctrine of perpetual allegiance was at odds with American interpretations of volitional allegiance, which dictated that individuals could change their allegiance at will (with some limitations), but neither side was absolutely consistent in its adherence to or enforcement of a single policy. The mobility and transatlantic agitation of naturalized Irish Americans, combined with the tensions of the Civil War, brought these differences to the forefront of public attention.

The Fenian Brotherhood and the Irish Republic of America

The Fenian Brotherhood and the Irish Republic that it formed constituted a radical vision of imperium in imperio that sought to engage both the United States and Great Britain on a nation-to-nation basis to advance the cause of Irish freedom and, as their activities unfolded, to improve the political status of native-born and naturalized Irish American citizens. In so doing, they challenged representations of Irish Americans as a racial and religious other, acting as a nation that was uniquely capable of advancing both its own interests and those of the United States. In their attempt to reconfigure their relationship with the United States, the Fenians shared some similarities with the nations examined earlier in this book, but they had a broader international focus; they sought to capitalize on rising tensions between the United States and Great Britain during the Civil War to serve their own political ends.

When the Fenians established a provisional government in the 1860s, they rearticulated rhetorics of divided sovereignty and multiple political allegiances in order to characterize themselves as members of two nations—the United

States and the Irish Republic—that were temporarily sharing a single national space. Ultimately, however, fractures emerged in the ranks of the provisional government of the Irish Republic, with fault lines running between those who saw the lack of territory as a strategic advantage and those who asserted that land was necessary for nationhood (debates that resonated with those that had divided the Cherokee Nation). In the following section I chart the political and organizational shifts of the Fenian Brotherhood, the formation of the Irish Republic that it claimed to lead, and the ways in which this Irish Republic in America pressured both British and American constructions of nationhood, sovereignty, and political allegiance.[28]

Founded in 1858 by former members of the Young Ireland movement, John O'Mahony, Michael Doheny, and Michael Corcoran, as a successor of the Emmet Monument Association and as the American counterpart of James Stephens's Irish Republican Brotherhood, the Fenian Brotherhood hoped to create an independent Irish Republic in Ireland that would be free from British rule. Stephens dubbed the group the Irish Republican Brotherhood in America, but its American leader, O'Mahony, soon changed its name to emphasize the organization's connection with Irish military and literary history and to distinguish it from the IRB. O'Mahony, an ardent Irish nationalist, was an educated man with a keen interest in Irish literary culture. He had studied at the Sorbonne while exiled in France and had translated Geoffrey Keating's *History of Ireland* (ca. 1634) from Gaelic into English. Apparently unsatisfied with his group's position as the American wing of the Irish Republican Brotherhood, O'Mahony decided to change the group's name to the Fenian Brotherhood, an allusion to Fionn mac Cumhaill, the leader of the Fianna Eireann, a group of Celtic warrior-poets. The new name sought to evoke a national past and connect the group to the Celtic warrior ethos and to the literary project that would prove so important for the Irish Republic they founded.[29]

Initially, the structure of the Fenian Brotherhood resembled that of other groups, including the IRB, earlier transatlantic radical groups, and continental secret societies, but the Fenian organization soon underwent significant changes to assume a more public *national* character. The members of the IRB were organized at the local level into "circles," cells of up to eight hundred men who were each assigned the rank of captain, sergeant, or private. Each circle was led by a "centre." Stephens functioned as the group's leader or "head centre," and O'Mahony operated as the American head centre.[30] The Fenian Brotherhood began as an association of circles or cells functioning more or less independently under the auspices of a single authority. The decentralized structure emphasized mobility and worked against subversion from within, because individual members and local leaders knew very little about the group as a whole and could not betray the organization's plans. The Fenians later adopted a more complex and open organizational model. According to *The Fenians' Progress: A Vision*, the title of which alludes to John Bunyan's *Pilgrim's Progress* (1678), the Fenians took on a "new character" in 1863 and shed any pretext of secrecy.[31] Adopting a new, more open "character" helped the Fenians to avoid what historian Nancy J. Curtin identifies as "the contradictions involved in coupling secrecy with mass recruitment [that] plagued the United Irish movement throughout its so-called revolutionary phase."[32]

National conventions or congresses, as they would come to be called, were central to the formation of the Irish Republic in America. The Fenians held their first national convention in 1863 in Chicago and resolved that the group would be "divided into State, Organizations, Circles, and Sub-Circles, . . . [to be] presided over and governed respectively by State Centres, Centres and Sub-Centres."[33] O'Mahony was to continue as head centre, and the brotherhood also created a Central Council, made up of five men, and established the positions of treasurer and assistant treasurer. At the end of the three-day convention, the Fenian Brotherhood made a series of resolutions, the twelfth of which was: "We . . . do hereby proclaim the Republic of Ireland to be virtually established; and moreover, that we pledge ourselves to use all our influence, and every legitimate privilege within our reach to promote the full acknowledgement of its independence by every free government in the world."[34] During the Second Congress, held in Cincinnati, Ohio, in January 1865, the Central Council was increased from five to ten men. The published proceedings described the group in explicitly national terms, equating its hierarchy with a provisional government: "The Fenian Congress acts the part of a national assembly of an Irish Republic" (*PSN*, 5). In his address to the audience, O'Mahony asserted that the Irish Republic was "virtually at war with the Oligarchy of Great Britain" and would soon command a standing army ready to challenge the British (5). O'Mahony also referred to "the practice of self-government" and "our body politic," declaring that the group was now self-sustaining and not dependent on any particular members for survival (6).

Despite O'Mahony's optimistic pronouncements, the Fenian Brotherhood and the Irish Republic it claimed to lead were not immune to factionalism and internal division. Differences emerged surrounding the relationship between nationhood, land, and sovereignty.[35] O'Mahony wanted to use military efforts to provoke war between the United States and Britain. He emphasized that the Fenians' ability to serve as a catalyst for conflict between the United States and Britain, a conflict they could then join as part of an effort to liberate Ireland, was predicated on their current virtual status. Being everywhere and nowhere was key to inciting the kind of panic and anxiety on the part of the British that was necessary to escalating hostilities between Britain and the United States. Yet, while they were committed to provoking British anxieties, O'Mahony and his supporters did not conceive of the Fenians as terrorists or insurgents. They saw themselves as a legitimate nation waging war on an enemy state. William R. Roberts, a member of the Central Council elected at the Cincinnati Congress, critiqued what he saw as O'Mahony's inaction, classifying his approach as a "'drag chain' policy." Roberts, who came to lead a group known as the "men of action," or the Senate wing, argued that land was a precondition for sovereignty and nationhood.[36] Acting as a provisional government within the United States did not suffice; for Roberts and his followers, the Fenians had to occupy a space of their own as a base of military operations and in order for other nations to recognize them as belligerents. Later, in an article for the *Cincinnati Enquirer*, Roberts articulated this position: "The Irish Republic is yet ideal without a local habitation.... We must have some place for our government to raise a flag, build ships, issue letters of marque.... England could surround Ireland with a cordon of ships of war, but if we had a country with sea ports, we could send out ships to prey on her commerce, run blockade runners to Ireland, and get other nations to recognize our belligerency. If we haven't a country, our ships would be condemned as pirates."[37] Land here functioned symbolically and strategically; Roberts suggested Canada as a base of operations, as a place from which to launch attacks on Britain, and as a symbol of the sovereignty of the Irish Republic. Having territory of their own would, he hoped, make them belligerents rather than "pirates."

At the behest of Roberts and other members of the Central Council, the Fenian body politic underwent significant alterations during the Third Congress, held in Philadelphia in October 1865, which amplified the existing tensions between the two factions of the Fenian Brotherhood. At this meeting, attended by a reported six hundred delegates, the Fenian Constitution was revised to mirror that of the United States more closely, a move that brought the governance structure of the Fenian Brotherhood/Irish Republic more in line with the structure of the U.S. government. The symbolic importance of Philadelphia is worth noting.[38] The Fenians chose the site of the Continental Congress and the first U.S. national capital for their own political rebirth, thus linking their national history and political structure more closely with that of the United States. At the Philadelphia Congress, the position of head centre was abolished and the Central Council was dissolved. The new structure included a president, vice president, senate, and house of delegates. The vice president would be elected by the senate and would serve as its president. Under this new structure, the senate wielded significant power over the political and financial activities of the Fenian Brotherhood, giving final approval to cabinet appointments, handling fundraising and the appropriation of funds, fixing officers' salaries, and creating legislation.[39] The house of delegates also had power over matters such as the appropriation of funds. Together the house of delegates and the senate would function as the primary legislative body not only of the Fenian Brotherhood, but also of the entire Irish Republic. As the newly elected president, O'Mahony was allowed to choose cabinet officials for some positions—secretary of war, agent of the Irish Republic, bond agent, and correspondence secretary—but the new governmental structure limited his authority.[40]

A report given by Fenian treasurer Bernard Doran Killian highlighted the group's commitment to military action and international relations. At the Philadelphia Congress, he detailed his conversation with Secretary of State William Seward about the release of John Mitchel, an imprisoned Confederate Fenian, and about how the Andrew Johnson administration would respond to a Fenian strike on Canada.[41] During the negotiations, Killian held out the promise of extending the northern border of the United State to the St. Lawrence River should the Fenians be successful in their strike. Annexing Canada could help the United States augment its territory and would exact revenge for British aid to the Confederacy during the Civil War.[42] Even as they sought to challenge British imperial authority in Ireland and Canada, the Fenians engaged rhetorics of territorial conquest as part of their bid for U.S. support. Those in attendance at the Philadelphia meeting approved a military strike on Canada. Despite his initial criticism of such a raid as a "a mere diversion," which "[u]nless it drag the United States into war with England it can only end in defeat to those that engage in it," O'Mahony ultimately lent support to the plan "in the hope that it may lead to such a war."[43]

After the Philadelphia Congress, the gulf between the O'Mahony faction and the "men of action" widened, and the Irish Republic of America itself became an example of imperium in imperio with two rival governance structures and two constitutions. Roberts, Thomas Sweeny, and Killian established what became known as the "Fenian White House" in the Moffatt mansion near New York's Union Square, but this display of unity was short-lived.[44] The senate impeached O'Mahony over charges of financial impropriety, but he refused to recognize its authority and continued acting as leader of the Fenian Brotherhood. He held a meeting in New York in January 1866 in which six hundred of his supporters voted to reinstate the 1863 Constitution ratified in Chicago and declared their support for military action in Ireland rather than trying to strike at British interests in Canada. During this same period, Roberts and his supporters embarked on a tour of the Midwest, trying to generate support for their military efforts to seize land in Canada. Roberts called a Fourth Congress, which was held in Pittsburgh in February 1866, much of which focused on the plans of the Fenian secretary of war, General Thomas Sweeny, to launch a strike on Canada and on shoring up support for the Philadelphia Constitution. Thus, just as the United States was divided between the Union and the Confederacy, so too was the Irish Republic split between two rival factions.[45]

Despite the divisions in the Fenian Brotherhood, the two constitutions it produced agreed on a number of important points. The 1863 Constitution, ratified in Chicago and supported by O'Mahony and his followers, emphasized not territorial possession but the prevention of infiltration and the maintenance of a mobile, flexible governmental system. It framed the Fenians and their Irish Republic as compatible with and serving the interests of the United States, making an implicit argument that individuals could hold multiple political allegiances and that multiple nations could occupy the same territory. In a set of resolutions that accompanied the 1863 Constitution, the Fenians situated their organization as existing within and adhering to the laws of the United States, articulating their vision of two nations sharing the same national space. They declared that they would carry out their efforts on behalf of their "virtually established Irish Republic" without violating "the constitution and laws under which we live and to which all of us, who are citizens of the United States, owe our allegiance."[46] They emphasized their status as American citizens and insisted on engaging with the United States on political terms rather than as a racial or religious other. The rather vague definition of allegiance and citizenship contained in the U.S. Constitution contrasts sharply, however, with that of the Fenian Constitution, which extended membership in the Fenian Brotherhood to "Citizens of the United States of America, of Irish birth and lineage" and to "Irishmen and Friends of Ireland living elsewhere on the American Continent and in the Provinces of the British Empire, wherever situated."[47] Here the Fenians challenged the kind of either-or distinction articulated in *United States v. Lumsden*. They imagined their Irish Republic as headquartered "within the limits of the United States of America," but also suggested that their nation transcended geopolitical borders to include members in America, Ireland, and the British "Provinces."[48] The rest of this Fenian Constitution focused on organizational issues, and its structure of circles and centres suggested the influence of earlier Irish radical groups and the importance of secrecy and mobility to maintaining their national security.

The 1865 Constitution adopted in Philadelphia at the Third Congress echoed the U.S. Constitution more explicitly than the first but reframed its source text in order to make it accommodate multiple nations. In the 1865 Constitution, the Fenians referred to themselves throughout as the "Fenian Brotherhood of the United States" instead of just the Fenian Brotherhood, which suggests their understanding that their project of nation formation was compatible with a relationship to the United States.⁴⁹ The second constitution opened by rearticulating the U.S. Constitution's Preamble to fit the Fenians' national goals: "We, the Fenians of the United States and other portions of America, in order to form a more perfect union, establish justice, insure domestic tranquility, and secure the blessings of liberty for the Irish race in Ireland do ordain and establish this Constitution for the Fenian Brotherhood in the United States and other portions of America."⁵⁰ Here the Fenians imagined their own "more perfect union" transcending U.S. geopolitical borders and extending the political culture of the United States to the people of Ireland, a move that disrupted the relationship between sovereignty and national space. This blurring of territorial boundaries was furthered by Article 1, which, like the original Fenian Constitution of 1863, imagined a national body of members who transcended and traversed U.S. borders.⁵¹ The biggest change was the establishment of executive and legislative branches of government modeled on those of the United States. The sections dealing with the establishment of these branches and with cabinet positions revealed the group's focus on military and financial objectives. Theirs was a smaller, more mobile, and more centralized government than that of the United States, and the president had the sole authority to treat with other nations.

Like the first constitution, the 1865 document maintained an emphasis on secrecy and the prevention of the infiltration of British spies. Members had to follow certain procedures when corresponding with headquarters, and any members who moved to a new location had to provide letters of introduction. As in John Brown's provisional government, the Fenian Brotherhood created a centralized form of authority, even with a bicameral legislature, that made the government both more mobile and flexible and less open to espionage. Ultimately, like Brown's, the Fenian constitutions blended America's founding documents with their own sense that two nations could share a single territory in the name of spreading republicanism. The Fenian constitutions combined radical tactics honed in Ireland with American political rhetorics and created an Irish Republic in America that challenged widely held conceptions of the territorial nation-state. Neither the 1863 nor the 1865 document made any attempt to delineate a set territory for the provisional government, but merely located it under the protection of U.S. law.

Issues of territory and other factors distinguished the Fenians and their Irish Republic from the CSA, which was created at roughly the same time and also drew on America's founding documents. The CSA and the Fenians pursued very different courses in terms of American national space. The Fenians did not claim exclusive control of any space within the putative boundaries of the United States, and some in their ranks even hoped to augment the U.S. national space by adding Canada. In contrast, secession and the formation of the CSA reduced the amount of space that constituted the United States, and many of the debates leading up to secession hinged on control of the western territories.

There were several other key differences between the political philosophies and positions of the Fenians and the CSA. While some of its members were certainly native-born Americans, the official documents of the Fenian Brotherhood identified the group as *naturalized* citizens rather than as native-born Americans. As Mitchell Snay notes, both groups appealed to a kind of ethnic nationalism.[52] Yet unlike the Confederates, the Fenians were represented by nativists and others as racially and nationally other *before* they formed their own republic and attempted to reframe the terms of their engagement with the United States from issues of race and religion to those related to politics. In contrast, many outside of the South did not recognize the purported Anglo-Saxon origins of the Confederacy as distinct from the genealogy of the nation writ large. Most important, however, is that while the Confederacy based its right to nation formation on the sovereignty of the states, the Fenians appealed to their rights as individual citizens to work toward the establishment of an independent Ireland. This political vision of sovereignty, one informed by their position as *naturalized* Americans, distinguished them both from Confederate leaders and from the dominant political philosophy of Abraham Lincoln and many in the North. The Fenians also claimed that they were better positioned for such work than those in Ireland, because while associations such as the Fenian Brotherhood were illegal under British law, as naturalized citizens they had "repudiated" British laws upon becoming naturalized U.S. citizens. In the published proceedings from their first national convention, the Fenians defended their actions as the kind of "civic and social privilege" guaranteed to them by American law.[53]

A final key difference was the political position of the two groups in relation to Great Britain—the CSA hoped for British support while the Fenians decried the Confederacy's attempts to forge diplomatic ties with Great Britain. While some Irish Americans with links to the Fenians, such as John Mitchel, sided with the South, many Fenians fought for the Union army even as they railed at the thought of fighting for the abolition of slavery.[54] In the wake of the Trent Affair, the Fenians tried to make common cause with the Union by claiming that Britain represented a similar threat to both Irish and American sovereignty.

Even as the Fenians grappled with internal divisions, they sought to advance their cause and align themselves with the United States through military efforts. From 1866 to 1870, the Fenians made several attempts on Canadian lands;

O'Mahony was convinced to launch an ill-fated strike on Campobello Island because of the publicity and financial support garnered by the Roberts faction. It seemed that, like Roberts, many Fenians believed that the Irish Republic needed "to have territory before a state of belligerency could be recognized."[55] Other Fenian writers echoed Roberts's sentiments and characterized attacks on Canada as an attempt to gain a base of operations there from which to conduct the business of the Irish Republic. Fenian raids on Canada, then, were as much about the practice of sovereignty, defined as the exercise of political authority in a particular space, as they were about punishing Great Britain. An 1866 article published in the *New York Daily Tribune* by a "Special Correspondent" in Dublin echoed similar sentiments about a strike on Canada: "It will be a rising of British subjects to establish a government for themselves, to be called the Irish Republic of North America."[56] This correspondent went on to argue that seizing Canada was an opportunity for the Irish to demonstrate their capacity for self government, and if it did not prove successful, they could ask to become part of the United States. "Canada," the writer suggested, "will make two good sized States."[57]

Even as they viewed their republic as temporarily sharing American national space, Roberts and his followers' constructions of sovereignty were informed by their own unique sense of Manifest Destiny and the absorptive nature of republican governments. President Johnson and his administration initially did little to quell British anxieties or curtail the military and political efforts of the Fenians. In response to British calls for the U.S. government to put a stop to Fenian activities, Secretary of State Seward wrote to J. H. Burnley, the secretary of legation, that the government was not justified to take action against the Fenians and alluded to "the many well-founded complaints which this government has heretofore presented of aggressions committed by British subjects against the peace and sovereignty of the United States."[58] British aid to the Confederacy during the Civil War, Seward alleged, constituted an affront to U.S. "peace and sovereignty." His letter suggests that the United States was content to let the Fenians return the favor. In a later message to President Johnson, Seward offered the following explanation of the American response to British complaints: "[T]he entire inattention of Her Majesty's Government to our frequent and earnest representations concerning the naturalization question, and the irritations and exasperations which have attended the recent suspension of the habeas corpus render every form of expression, in reply to such complaints difficult and embarrassing to the Executive Authority."[59] Seward represented the Fenians as leverage that might be used to force Britain into changing its stance on naturalization and political allegiance. The threat of Fenian military strikes functioned to counterbalance British suspensions of the writ of habeas corpus in Ireland and Britain's refusal to acknowledge American political authority over naturalized U.S. citizens.

In addition to finding the Fenian threat politically useful in dealing with Britain, the Johnson administration was loath to alienate the Irish American vote by opposing the Fenians in advance of the 1868 election. British diplomat Sir Frederick Bruce wrote in May 1867 that "to the President and the administration the command of the Irish vote is essential with a view to the approaching elections, and they certainly will not hesitate to do anything agreeable to the Irish section of the population."[60] Samito's reading of the U.S. government's response to the Fenians emphasizes the fraught context of Reconstruction and the need to court "traditionally Democratic Irish American voters."[61] Thus, in dealing with the Fenian Brotherhood and its Irish Republic, the Johnson administration had to negotiate between the interests of British sovereignty and the sovereignty of the American people as it would be exercised in the upcoming election.

The Fenian ranks were swelled by Civil War veterans, as Samito has demonstrated, and by Fenian publications that regularly inflated the group's numbers and made optimistic predictions about the growth of the organization, which created a great deal of anxiety on both sides of the Atlantic. According to Neidhardt, only 82 delegates attended the first national convention in 1863, but over the next two years membership rose dramatically, an increase that has been linked to the large numbers of Irish Americans mustering out of the Union army. Neidhardt estimates the group's total membership at the time of the second convention to be approximately 10,000.[62] Other historical accounts suggest that in its heyday after the Civil War the Fenian Brotherhood boasted about 45,000 men, and it had a broad geographic reach, with circles in "eighteen states and three territories (Idaho, Colorado, and New Mexico)."[63] In some ways, however, the actual number of Fenian members was less important than the perceived strength of the group. The *New Haven Daily Palladium* cited published reports that placed the Fenians' total membership at nearly 2 million people. An 1865 article in the *New York Times* entitled "The Fenian Explosion: Brief Sketch of the Origins and Progress of the Movement" claimed that there were at that time more than 900 Fenian circles throughout the United States and Canada, with each one composed of between 100 and 500 men—putting the total number of Fenians anywhere from 90,000 to 450,000. Clearly anxious about the growing militarism of the Fenians, a letter to the editor of the London *Times* described the group as "half a million men" with more than a million dollars at their disposal.[64] The perceived strength of their numbers and resources and the capacity to create such anxiety were central to the Fenians' political leverage.

Fenian veterans found themselves at the center of a political and legal battle over issues of sovereignty and citizenship when several Union officers were arrested in Ireland in 1867 for bringing arms and men to aid in an Irish uprising. They included Col. John Warren and Col. William J. Nagle, who were arrested after the Fenian privateer *Erin's Hope* landed in Ireland. Warren was a naturalized Irish American, while Nagle was a native-born American, but Britain refused to recognize their status as Americans and charged them with treason as British subjects. Americans were incensed at what they regarded as an affront to U.S. sovereignty and the inconsistent application of British laws.[65] For example, although Britain had used the theory of perpetual allegiance to defend the impressment of sailors on American ships throughout the War of 1812, the Crown earlier had acknowledged the change in allegiance of the Revolutionary generation. As the author of an 1867 article entitled "*Only* an American Citizen," which circulated in the Fenian press, suggested, if Britain had truly subscribed to the doctrine of perpetual allegiance, Benjamin Franklin and George Washington would have been treated always as traitorous British subjects and not as American leaders and citizens. Perpetual allegiance proved a convenient means of exerting continued sovereignty over emigrants and challenging the sovereignty of the nations that received them. The author of "*Only* an American Citizen" argued that "the dictum [of perpetual allegiance] must manifestly be regarded as one of expediency, not of right, whose enforcement must be regulated by the amount of resistance offered to it."[66] Another article from that year challenged the United States to define the rights and responsibilities of naturalized citizens in response to the Fenian arrests. The author of this article in the *Irish News*, a Fenian journal, queried: "To which government do they [Irish Americans] owe allegiance? To the Queen of England, or to the United States? Which power are they bound to serve in case of war? Has the Queen of England a right to hang them for serving against their native country, or the United States a right to shoot them for not serving their adopted country?"[67] The writer questioned whether the sovereignty of the United States followed its citizens when they traveled abroad, or whether American citizens were subject to the sovereignty of whatever land they visited. The arrest and trial of naturalized and native-born American citizens gave the Fenians an opportunity to generate sympathy from the American public and to pressure U.S. authorities to act to protect the rights of U.S. citizens who were being, they felt, wrongfully treated as treasonous British subjects.

While many Americans expressed outrage at the British treatment of U.S. citizens in Ireland, various newspapers and magazines decried the military efforts of the Fenians as violations of their duties as American citizens and an example of imperium in imperio. An article in the *New York Times* in April

1866 asserted that "[i]t is not *England* that the Fenians are making war upon thus far, but the *United States*."⁶⁸ Fenian military efforts challenged the political authority of the United States, argued the anonymous author, and threatened to embroil the country in conflict with Great Britain, a nation with which America was currently at peace. The "Fenian organization" was denounced for its plans to attack Canada in a June 1868 article entitled "The Infamy of Radicalism" in the Walhalla *Keowee Courier*: "The Fenian organization, pledged to work for the delivery of Ireland from English rule, has grown to be quite formidable, and in fact its proportions are growing so colossal that, ere many months have flown, the attention of our Government will have to be seriously called to it. This '*Imperium* in *imperio*' may not, just now, be a cause of apprehension, but it is certainly a question fraught with interest how far it is compatible with the genius of our free institutions and a government based upon popular consent, to allow huge military organizations to be formed within its jurisdiction."⁶⁹ Appearing two years after the Battle of Ridgeway, one of the earliest Fenian attacks on Canada, this article framed the Fenians as an ongoing threat, a dangerous example of imperium in imperio, a "colossal" military presence within America's "jurisdiction" that was an affront to popular sovereignty and republican government. According to this line of argument, while the Fenians had created a virtual nation with porous borders, their presence within America's territorial limits made them the responsibility of the U.S. government. The author's rather inflated characterization of the Fenian membership may have reflected the Fenians' own exaggerated figures. Alternatively, perhaps it indicates the tendency of some members of the American press to equate all Irish Americans with the Fenians and their Irish Republic.

Just as some Fenian writers claimed that "[e]very Irishman is at heart a Fenian," non-Fenians sometimes conflated the larger body of Irish Americans with the radical Fenians, citing the political and military efforts of the Fenian Brotherhood as a rationale for restricting the Irish vote.⁷⁰ A February 1868 article in the *Christian Recorder*, an African American newspaper, challenged Fenian practices and allegiances: "What is their right of citizenship, and to what government do they really belong?" (qtd. in Samito, *Becoming American*, 189). Framing Fenians as "sworn subject[s]" of the Irish Republic in America and politically active U.S. citizens, the author offered a vision of what such divided sovereignty might do to American political culture: "perhaps hundreds of thousands of them . . . come up to our polls with their naturalization papers in their hands, people of another government, but allowed to use their Irish Catholic vote to press the policy of ours into their own" (189). Seeking to reinscribe divided sovereignty as a political impossibility, the author claimed that "either the 'Irish nation' is a myth, or the citizenship of these people is not American, and they have no more right to interfere in our politics than a subject of Russia" (189). A later article published in the *Milwaukee Sentinel*, entitled "Imperium in Imperio" and discussing Clan na Gael, successors to the Fenian Brotherhood, echoed these points and seemed to presume that all Irish Americans were also members of an Irish nation in America. The author noted the significant population of Irish Americans, most of whom were "voting and taking their full share of the direction of this Government."[71] However, "[a]t the same time, they propose to maintain an Irish government for the direction of the 'national affairs' upon the soil of the United States." The author concluded that such efforts constituted an attempt to provoke conflict between the United States and Britain and that "in working to this end, they [Irish Americans] are not loyal to the obligations which they assumed in becoming American citizens."[72] As in the article in the *Christian Recorder*, this piece framed the formation of an Irish nation within the United States as an affront to the political authority of the United States and a violation of the political relationship between the U.S. nation and its citizens. Echoing Blackstone, both pieces suggested that sovereignty could not be divided: two states could not share the same space, in terms of territorial space or the space of individual bodies. Naturalized immigrants must choose between their country of origin and the United States, a choice that the Fenian Brotherhood strenuously opposed.

Although the Fenians had commanded international attention in 1865 and 1866 as rumors of their planned attacks circulated, in the wake of the actual attacks, the group began to lose ground militarily and politically. O'Mahony's attempt to capture Campobello Island in 1866 did not meet its objectives, and neither did attacks on Canada that were launched in 1866, 1870, and 1871. Responding to increasing pressure from Great Britain, the Johnson administration had intervened to cut off the flow of men and supplies into Canada in advance of the 1866 Battles of Ridgeway and Fort Erie. Fenian general Sweeny, William Roberts, and several others were arrested, but never brought to trial after the adoption of a congressional resolution that asked that further legal actions against the Fenians not be pursued. The Fenians' Irish nation was linked with the Irish American vote and still wielded a certain amount of political leverage. America's political leaders were hesitant to bring the Fenians to trial for violating the neutrality laws. Yet, in the court of public opinion, damage had been done. James Gibbons, a Philadelphia printer and Fenian senator, declared in an 1868 letter that the attempt to found an Irish Republic had met with little success. Summing up the feelings of many, the *New York Times* dubbed the failed raids the "Fenian fizzle," and the group was described as "one of the greatest political nuisances of our day" by the *Christian Advocate*.[73] While the latter sought to portray the group as humorous, it also argued that the U.S.

government needed to put a stop to Fenian agitation. "Fenianism is organized among us," wrote the anonymous author for the *Christian Advocate*. "It has its President, its Cabinet Secretaries, its legislative councils, its military functionaries, and army. It is an *imperium in imperio* on the territory of our Republic."[74] While it might have been politically useful for the U.S. government to turn a blind eye to the Fenians during and immediately after the Civil War, this author claimed that such a position was now untenable. By 1871 the *New York Times* predicted the demise of the Fenian Brotherhood in an article called "Exeunt the Fenians": "If Fenianism could possibly be made more ridiculous than it now is, that desirable end would have been fully attained by the late abortive splutter at Fort Garry."[75] While the group's demise was more than a decade away, this article reveals that the Fenians, who had used the press to great advantage in the early years of their organization, had ceased to command the kind of attention on which their group depended for its political power.

Fenian arguments about the rending of allegiances and the choices that naturalized citizens must make challenged British theories of perpetual allegiance and the unbreakable bonds between sovereign and subject. Yet such arguments also failed to capture the political realities and perspectives of naturalized citizens and native-born Americans from immigrant families, who experienced the effects of divided sovereignty and felt the pull of divided allegiance. The lived experiences of many Irish immigrants emphasized that sovereignty was dividing the Irish; as the case of the Fenians imprisoned by the British made clear, their bodies were sites where sovereign powers were enacted and made manifest. Like other immigrant groups, they felt an emotional pull between their country of origin and the one in which they currently resided. They thus sought to frame that sense of divided allegiance in positive terms. Noted immigration historian Oscar Handlin suggests that "the meaningful question is not whether loyalties are divided, but whether they can be justified in terms acceptable to all Americans."[76]

The Fenians and their Irish Republic constituted one example of the ways in which Irish Americans worked to translate their lived experience of divided loyalties and competing sovereign claims into something that was understandable to their fellow Americans and politically advantageous to their cause. As part of this process of translation, they expressed their political position and strategic practices in terms of rhetorics of sovereignty and nationhood. By the mid-1860s, the Fenian Brotherhood had established many features of an Irish nation in America, including a presidency, a War Department, a senate, a capital, a flag, a written constitution, war bonds, letters of marque and reprisal, and what they claimed was a standing army ready to march on British North America. They also had an active literary culture that prominently helped Fenians to create a textual space in which to communicate and perform their own vision of national sovereignty.

Fenian Literature and Virtual Nationhood

Literature played an important role in the creation of the virtual Irish Republic and the articulation of Fenian constructions of sovereignty. The Fenian Brotherhood engaged in the kind of literary nation-building discussed by Anderson in *Imagined Communities*, which contends that printed texts are constitutive of the "imagined community" of the nation, allowing readers to conceive of themselves as a body politic. Such national communities, Anderson argues, are both "limited and sovereign" (6) as a result of the spread of print capitalism, which allows "rapidly growing numbers of people to think about themselves and to relate themselves to others, in profoundly new ways" (36). The texts produced by the Fenians addressed the members of a not yet actualized Irish Republic as well as audiences in Britain, Ireland, and the United States, and those authors sought to link their own national narrative to that of the United States. In his "Report of the Secretary of Civil Affairs," addressed to Fenian general John O'Neill, D. O'Sullivan referred to "the Irish nation, at home and in exile."[77] The *Irish Republic* argued for the presence of two Irelands: "For now there is another Ireland in existence and at work—the free Ireland of America—to accomplish national deliverance."[78] John Savage, an ally of O'Mahony, proclaimed the Irish to be a "distinct republic, within the American Republic."[79] These and other Fenian texts positioned the Irish Republic as a nation within the United States as part of the attempt to engage in international diplomacy, and they both appealed to and challenged widely held understandings of indivisible political allegiance and the nation as a bounded territorial space.

The Fenians sought to create and maintain the boundaries of their nation in print before it was actualized in space. Addressing the delegates gathered for the Second Congress of the Fenian Brotherhood in January 1865, O'Mahony asserted that "[f]ew men in America are still ignorant of the nature and object of this organization" and that any who still were could consult the group's published materials.[80] Anyone who wished to do so would have encountered a surprising amount of written works, ranging from newspapers and the published proceedings of Fenian conventions to poetry, song, and fiction. Fenian newspapers published in the United States included the New York *Irish-American*, New York *Irish Nation*, New York *Phoenix*, New York *Sunday Citizen*, New York *Irish Citizen*, the *Irish News*, New York *Irish People*, Boston *Pilot*, Chicago *Irish Republic*, the *Irish World*, and *Mooney's California Express*. Articles by and about the Fenians also appeared in other major publications of the era, such as Horace Greeley's *New-York Tribune*, the *New York Times*, the *Boston Pilot*, the *Philadelphia Inquirer*, San Francisco's *Daily Evening Bulletin*, Washington, D.C.'s *National Intelligencer*, the *St. Louis Republican, Harper's Weekly*, and *Frank Leslie's Illustrated Newspaper*. James Gibbons published the proceedings of the national conventions, which included public documents such as the Fenian Constitution and by-laws. Michael Scanlan, the editor of Chicago's *Irish Republic*, who was known as "the Fenian poet," published a book of poetry in 1866 called *Love and Land*, which contained some of the brotherhood's best-known verses. The *Fenian Songster* purported to offer the "national hymns" of the Irish nation (the songs were heard at Fenian meetings), and other poems and songs appeared in newspapers and periodicals.[81] Numerous speeches, pamphlets, and biographies of Fenian leaders also helped to spread Fenian political ideas. Works such as *The Fenians' Progress* and *The Fenian Catechism* by Bodkin alluded to the political and religious dimensions of sovereign power. Fictional works produced by and about the Fenians included Henry Llewellyn Williams's *The Fenian Chief; or, The Martyr of '65*, which focused on Fenian efforts in Ireland, and Scian Dubh/James McCarroll's *Ridgeway: An Historical Romance of the Fenian Invasion of Canada*. Reflecting on the Fenians and their activities in the 1860s in *Troublous Times in Canada*, John A. MacDonald, who served as Canada's first prime minister, observed that they "resolved to form an Irish Republic (on paper), as the Fenians were without territory until they captured it."[82] MacDonald's statement captured both the virtual nature of the Irish Republic and the Fenians' literary and territorial aspirations. Yet, like many others who have written about the Fenians, MacDonald measured the group's success by its military efforts and framed the organization as a failure because of its inability to claim a national space. He minimized the political leverage that the Fenians gained through their "Irish Republic (on paper)" and the ways in which political actualities occurred in response to their virtual nation.

Mediating the competing sovereign claims over their persons as naturalized U.S. citizens, throughout their published writings the Fenians articulated both a perpetual allegiance to Ireland and a volitional allegiance to the United States that could be synthesized in their affiliation with the Irish Republic. They made their case to readers, in part, in sympathetic terms, arguing that divided allegiance was natural and productive. While the Fenians professed their love for their "adopted country," they could not go anywhere without hearing the "cry of our famine stricken people" and continued to talk of Ireland as "home" and themselves as Irish citizens of the United States (*PSN*, 52, 48). In an address to the Senate wing of the Fenian Brotherhood in 1867, William Roberts used a familial metaphor to discuss the political allegiances of Irish Americans and to challenge notions that Fenian activities subverted the sovereignty of the United States. He argued against the notion that "because we love the mother that bore us, we cannot adore the bride of our choice."[83] Here Roberts echoed earlier discussions of perpetual and volitional allegiance and employed family relationships as metaphors in his description of Irish Americans as a collective entity. His example of a man's different relationships to his mother and wife suggested the possibility and the normativity of multiple allegiances. Further examples of the kind of constitutive rhetoric to which Anderson alludes are found throughout the published proceedings of the annual congresses and other official documents of the Fenian Brotherhood. Such documents told readers who the group *was* and what it *did*.

The Fenians used print media to publicize their claims to sovereign nationhood and to engage the United States and Britain on political terms. While the meetings themselves were held behind closed doors to protect the necessarily more secretive activities of the IRB, after each convention the proceedings were published in abridged form in various newspapers and in pamphlet form. In an address given at the "preliminary meeting" of the first national convention, O'Mahony, the head centre of the Fenian Brotherhood, asserted that it was time for the group to "declare our position, our object and our resources before the world, so that all the friends of Irish freedom may understand us" (*PFN*, 6). To make this declaration, the published proceedings included accounts of the various sessions that were held and the Fenian Constitution, by-laws, and resolutions. These portions spelled out the political claims of the Fenians and argued that the Fenians were not a secret society but rather an "association having for its object the national freedom of Ireland" through the creation of an independent Irish nation (31). They depicted this virtual Irish nation as public, distinct, and linked with a national past. There was also a section that asserted the "indestructability" of the Irish nation and claimed that the Irish were "one of the distinct nationalities of the earth" with an inherent right to self-government and self-possession (38).

Like the congressional proceedings, published reports from the Fenian circles helped readers conceive of the scope and activities of the Fenian Brotherhood and its virtual republic. Sent from locations such as Clarksville, New Jersey; Baltimore, Maryland; Charleston, South Carolina; Galveston, Texas; and San Francisco, California, these reports challenged constructions of the Fenians as a secret society by offering accounts of the members and their activities. The details of such reports were often mundane—election results, funds collected, public events organized—but occasionally suggested the perspectives that members had on the larger political issues facing the brotherhood. By perusing such documents, Irish Americans could imagine themselves as part of a community of readers and political actors existing within the United States, but "virtually at war" with Britain. To a wider audience, such documents attempted to position the Fenians' Irish Republic on an international stage alongside the United States and Great Britain.[84]

Fictional works by Fenian authors sought to demonize Great Britain in order to show common cause with the United States and to legitimate military action against British targets. James McCarroll's 1868 novel, *Ridgeway*, published under the pseudonym Scian Dubh (which means Black Knife), chronicles the international engagements of the Fenian Brotherhood and shows the ways in which they used fiction to rearticulate representations of the Irish as an oppressed racial and religious underclass. Since it is not well known today, a brief plot summary will help to illustrate the novel's engagement with the Fenian project.

The story opens in May 1866, roughly one month before the first Fenian attack on Canada, at a point when "astute politicians were struck with the formidable aspect of Fenianism in both hemispheres."[85] The novel introduces readers to Nicholas (Nick) Barry, a young Irish soldier in the British army, who is stationed in Canada and hopes to be discharged soon so that he can marry his sweetheart, Kate McCarthy. An orphan who has been sent to live with relatives in America, Kate's future prosperity is threatened by a chancery suit that seems likely to be decided in favor of the well-connected Anglo-Irish landowner Philip Darcy. The real action of the novel begins in a bar in Buffalo, New York, called the Harp, owned by Tom O'Brien, a Fenian leader. Nick meets a stranger named Greaves and reveals that he is about to apply for his discharge from the army. Through a conversation with Nick's superior officer, Greaves subverts this plan, and Nick decides to desert rather than to risk further separation from Kate. Greaves enlists the help of several accomplices and abducts Kate under the pretense of setting up a meeting with Nick. On the eve of the Fenian invasion, Nick has left the British army and risks arrest if he returns to British soil, but Kate is being kept at an unknown location in Canada. Nick joins the Irish Republican Army of the Fenians to strike a blow for Ireland and hopefully to rescue Kate. He achieves both of his goals and eventually learns that Greaves is none other than Philip Darcy, Kate's opponent in the chancery suit and a British spy. Greaves/Darcy also went by the name of Lauder and was Kate's unwanted suitor; Lauder tried to deceive Kate and secure her hand in order to ensure the success of his land claims. He is killed finally, and Nick and Kate are free to live happily ever after.

As a novel, *Ridgeway* drew on familiar generic conventions, featured a celebration of Fenianism and the Irish Republic in America, and borrowed plot elements from captivity narratives, seduction fiction, and historical romance. Its author sought to link Fenian literary culture to that of the United States. One of the many striking features of *Ridgeway* is its performance of its own historicity, a performance that was at odds with the recent events it dramatized. Although it was styled as a "historical" account of the Fenian invasion of Canada, the novel was published just two years after the events that it describes, but it appeals to history to provide justification for the Fenians and their military exploits. They were working toward a restoration of Irish nationhood, not merely filibustering.[86] Like Williams's *The Fenian Chief*, which was published the same year as the death of its titular chief, *Ridgeway*, to borrow a phrase from Shirley Samuels, represents a "popular history of the present moment."[87] *Ridgeway* commemorates a fictionalized historical past and "celebrate[s] ... the achievement of a possible future."[88] Like in many historical novels of its era, McCarroll set domestic intrigue against a backdrop of international turmoil. By styling it "an historical romance," the writer aligned his novel with works by popular and commercially successful authors such as Sir Walter Scott and James Fenimore Cooper, whose works, like *Ridgeway*, dramatized historical events and social development against a backdrop of conflict and division.[89]

To elucidate these conflicts and divisions, *Ridgeway*'s author presented national "types" that emphasized the distinctions between the American, Irish, and English national characters, and he portrayed the Irish Republic as a nation within the United States, not a domestic racial population. In the use of such types, *Ridgeway* resonated with other examples of American historical romance, such as those by Cooper. In *The Making of Racial Sentiment*, Ezra Tawil argues that Cooper and other authors of frontier romances drew distinctions between the different races based on "emotional rather than exclusively physical properties."[90] As I suggested in the second chapter, Cooper's types, like the ones presented in *Ridgeway*, can be seen as national rather than (or in addition to) racial, but they were developed and distinguished, as Tawil has suggested, by factors other than physiognomy, including emotionality, behavior, and character. In *Ridgeway*'s introduction McCarroll represented Ireland as England's "*Alma Mater*" and challenged racial formulations of Anglo-Saxon superiority (iii). Moving from a celebration of Ireland's history to a critique of England's crimes, McCarroll drew on racial discourses to frame the English as impure and devoid of history and culture. The English "invader" came from a "bastard nationality" without "a single drop of proud, pure blood" (v). Personified as "the hybrid offspring" of incontinent leaders, this "invader" was argued to be devoid of a pure lineage and had neither a "history nor past of his own" (v).

Framing England as the enemy of the Irish nation involved more than just listing political grievances, however. As the military drama of the novel unfolds, the body of Kate McCarthy, the novel's heroine, functions as a metonym for the Irish nation in ways that hearken back to similar conflations between a female body and the nation in the seduction novels of early America. Kate is threatened economically by a chancery suit and sexually by the physical advances of an unwanted suitor, who has sided with the English. The potential forced marriage with Darcy mirrors the forced union between Ireland and Britain, while the relationship of choice between Nick and Kate functions as an endorsement of the kind of volitional allegiance exercised in America. Kate's economic triumph and the preservation of her chastity are achieved, albeit indirectly, through the Fenians' military campaign. By associating Ireland with a vulnerable, virtuous woman and England with a treacherous predator, the novel played on readers' sympathies and echoed early American novels like the bestselling *Charlotte Temple*, in which a young girl falls prey to the advances of a British soldier.[91] Through narrative and numerous political asides, McCarroll in his novel framed the Irish nation within a nation as a distinct political community with the prerogative to distinguish between friends and enemies.[92] The narrator of *Ridgeway* suggests that groups like the Fenian Brotherhood cannot operate in Ireland, but that an Irish nation within a nation can be "[s]ecure beneath the ample folds of the glorious stars and stripes of the great Republic of America" (73).

Fenian texts characterized the relationship between the United States and the Irish Republic as two nations sharing the same space for the purposes of protection and mutual benefit, which resonated with the Fenian constitutions and challenged constructions of territorial sovereignty and indivisible allegiance. In one image of the "Fenian White House," the flag of the Irish Republic, the sunburst and harp, is shown flying below the Stars and Stripes. The relative position of the flags suggests that the sovereignty of the United States trumps that of the Irish Republic. A somewhat similar image appeared as the cover art for *The Fenians' Progress*, published in 1865. In the foreground sits Erin, dressed in green and holding her harp, while Columbia, holding the Stars and Stripes, stands slightly behind her. The green flag of the Fenians appears slightly behind the American flag, reinforcing its inferior position. While the two women look in opposite directions, the commingling of national symbols suggests the close relationship between the two nations and, perhaps, between the IRB and its American counterpart, the Fenian Brotherhood.[93]

Financial bonds issued by the Irish Republic offered a slightly different vision of the relationship that the Fenians imagined between the two nations. A bond from 1866 depicts a personification of Erin with the Fenian symbol of the harp pointing toward Ireland in the distance. A Union soldier places his sword at her feet, in a chivalric gesture that echoes the romantic imagery seen elsewhere in Fenian texts, while an Irish wolfhound sits at her side. The image represents the military might of the Union army in the service of the Irish nation and links the two in common cause.[94] The narrative of *The Fenians' Progress* supports such a reading: it opens with a dream vision in which the narrator encounters Lord Edward Fitzgerald, an Irish-born revolutionary involved with the uprising of 1798, and General Richard Montgomery, an Irish military leader who led the ill-fated American attempt to invade Canada in 1775. In this work, the narrator fights as part of a Fenian army led by these two Irish-born leaders, one representing Ireland and the other America. *The Fenians' Progress*, like other Fenian texts, was addressed to the provisional Irish Republic and enacted a form of sovereignty by aligning the Irish Republic with America in opposition to Britain. Framing the relationship in emotional terms, *The Fenians' Progress* asserts that "the hopes, interests, aspirations, and the very life of the Irish people are indissolubly wrapped up with the United States," and both must "flourish or decay together" (37). As argued in an 1864 lecture by Brigadier General James Kiernan, a Fenian, entitled *Ireland and America versus England*, government is the "emenation [sic]" of the will of the people and if the people want to work for Irish independence, they have that right.[95] Part of that effort, for Kiernan, involved expanding the territorial boundaries of the United States by seizing Canada. Employing language reminiscent of Manifest Destiny on behalf of the dispossessed Irish, Kiernan declared that republics are, by nature, "progressive" and "absorbent" and are destined to take over new land.[96] Fenian texts linked the political destinies of the United States and the Irish Republic, and imagined the Fenians serving America's territorial interests, even as the nation they claimed to lead, by its very existence, disrupted and deconstructed the integrity of U.S. borders.

Fenian texts appealed to U.S. history to argue for the legitimacy of the Fenian effort to form an Irish nation in the United States and to pursue military efforts in Canada. The narrator of *The Fenians' Progress* cast the history of Texas as the story of immigrants who established an independent nation within Mexico, fought for their independence, and then were recognized by the United States and incorporated into the Union. The text proclaims, "During the period of her independence, it cannot be doubted that Texas had a perfect right to build or purchase a navy, to raise an army, and for instance, if she had the wish and the strength to do so, to invade Cuba, destroy the Spanish power there, and give the people of that island a free and independent government" (36). Here, Texas's hypothetical right to invade Cuba, a right derived from its status as an independent nation, was linked explicitly with the Fenian attacks on Canada. The battle for Ireland was figured not as an internal revolution, but as an imperialist gesture toward spreading freedom and democracy abroad. The example of Texas did not mirror exactly the Fenian situation; however, the author used it to suggest that the United States had, in at least one other instance, recognized the sovereignty of a nation that emerged from within the territory of another. Moreover, the author drew on a version of Texas history to suggest that one of the rights inherent in sovereign nations is the right to invade other nations and change their system of government. Seen from this perspective, if the Irish Republican Army attacked Canada, it would be an exercise of Fenian rights, not a violation of U.S. sovereignty.

The Fenians cited their rights as Americans as authorizing their military actions; they also conveniently ignored certain laws, such as the 1818 Neutrality Act. In an 1866 speech, William Roberts made an emotional appeal for military action:

> On the borders of this great Republic, where you have made for yourselves a home and earned the right to think, act, and live in the spirit of the broadest freedom; where your prerogatives cannot be restricted or denied by faction, parties, or prejudice, so long as you are true to your own manhood and the spirit of the laws which guarantee your rights and insure to brave men their liberties; on the very borders of this Republic, near your very doors, flaunting in your faces its blood-stained emblem of authority, is a Government whose history is written in the blood of your race, whose wealth has been drawn from twenty generations of your robbed and slaughtered kindred, and whose influence and power has been gained by every infamy and crime which the most selfish and debased instincts could prompt or resort to.[97]

Fenians should be true to the "spirit" of American laws, but apparently should not worry too much about the particulars. Their dual allegiance and national affiliation seems to give the Fenians a certain amount of flexibility in terms of what laws they choose to obey. Roberts claimed that "the Neutrality laws cannot prevent" Fenians from organizing themselves into a military force. He reminded his listeners that "England's power is not confined to England or Ireland," but extends across national and geographic borders to Canada, India, and the Caribbean. Thus, that power could be attacked at any location, and neutrality was neither possible nor desirable.

Just as British national power extended beyond the national borders of England, Irish nationhood, according to Fenian texts, was expansive and mobile. Like the written constitutions and other official Fenian documents, fictional texts offered representations of a virtual Irish Republic characterized by territorial mobility and military prowess rather than the static occupation of territory. *The Fenians' Progress* framed Canada as "the true road to Irish nationality" and claimed that the "welfare and destiny of Canada" was, like that of the Irish, linked with the United States (25, 38). Canada emerged here not as a destination but as a "road," something to be passed through. This speaks to the mobility that often characterized Fenian constructions of nationhood, which framed the Irish Republic as moving from one location to another until it reached its ultimate goal of independence in Ireland. *Ridgeway* also dramatized the Fenian attack on Canada as freeing Canada from British rule and facilitating its absorption into the United States. It thus framed the Fenians as exercising sovereign power through moving across space rather than holding it. In one of many political asides in the novel, the narrator argues that while England has oppressed the Irish in Ireland, "outside and beyond her control or reach, another body of Irish, which has aptly been termed a nation within a nation," has developed in America (73). Here "nation within a nation" refers not to racial or cultural separatism but to the political and military capabilities of the Fenians' Irish Republic.

While the United States defined its sovereignty in the nineteenth century in terms of the occupation and political control of territory, this novel identifies Fenians and the Irish nation that they claimed to lead by their capacity to move across spaces and geopolitical borders. The Fenians are described in *Ridgeway* as an "invincible floating power" (71) with mobile military, executive, and literary components, which exerts its influence over territory not by staking out boundaries and statically possessing land, but rather by moving through and across it. The power of the Irish nation is not "walled in" by natural or political boundaries; Ireland is "alive and active in other lands, and so powerful outside her own borders, that there is no such thing as circumscribing her influence or operations in so far as they relate to her struggles for independence" (73). Personifying Fenianism as a warrior wielding a sword or halberd, the narrator states: "The mighty embodiments of Irish power and patriotism, yclept Fenianism, stalks forth through the empire with an uplifted glaive in its hand, and no one can say how soon or where the swift stroke of destruction shall fall" (17–18). The Fenians, leaders of the free Irish Republic in America, are not bound to any particular space, but are both everywhere and nowhere, frustrating British attempts to challenge them. Like Martin Delany, the Fenians argued that mobility was a strategic advantage through which nations could secure political advantage.

Such an emphasis on mobility and circulation was reinforced not only by the inflated accounts of Fenian membership, but also by the almost hyperpublic nature of Fenian circles, which regularly published reports of their meetings and activities in the American press. Far from maintaining a veil of secrecy, Fenian circles published their activities in newspapers such as the *Irish-American*, including treasury reports that detailed how much money had been collected. The mundane inner workings of the organization were cataloged in almost obsessive detail. The overall effect of such accounts was to emphasize the scope of the organization and the "citizenry" of the Irish Republic. With groups writing from states as far-flung as Massachusetts and California, the image of the brotherhood that emerged from the press was of a group that was dispersed and mobile, the kind of "floating power" described in *Ridgeway*, which could not be countered directly because there was no clear center or front line. Even a strike on the capital in New York City would not have eradicated the political structure nor the rank and file of the Irish Republic. In this way, representations of the Fenian Brotherhood and its Irish Republic emphasized not the Fenians' capacity to hold space, but their mobility, dispersal, and ability to traverse space.

Fenian texts challenged not only the relationship between nations and territory, but also the relationship between nations and time. As represented in Fenian texts, the Irish Republic was at once rooted in the historical past, existed in a provisional state in the present, and was forecasted to achieve its full potential in the future. In addition to making claims of perpetual existence, Fenian texts implicitly subverted teleological narratives of development, in which nations grow, achieve maturity, and then decay. Contrasting what he saw as England's decline with the reinvigoration of Ireland, Scanlan, the "Fenian poet," offered the following lines in the introduction to his *Love and Land*:

> England is growing old; Ireland's growing young.
> England is growing weak; Ireland's growing strong.[98]

These lines do not allude to a future state, but rather one that is returning to its youthful glory and strength. In a poem written to celebrate the so-called men of action, entitled "Roberts' Appeal," the speaker imagines a ghost army rising up to fight alongside the current generation for Ireland's freedom. The poem concludes: "We march forth in youth eternal, flanked by the Father and the Son."[99] Paradoxically, Ireland here is represented as both very old and ever young, and the speaker is not merely eulogizing what is lost, but putting such losses in the service of an as yet to be achieved future. For the Fenians, the Irish Republic could span both spatial and temporal borders, including people on both sides of the Atlantic and in both the past and present.

Conclusion

While the group eventually splintered, through their political, military, and literary efforts, the Fenians had successfully intervened in both national and international discussions of sovereignty, nationhood, and political allegiance. As Samito has noted, the efforts of the Fenian Brotherhood resulted in a strengthening of the rights of naturalized citizens both in the United States and when they traveled outside of its borders. Fenian agitation surrounding the high-profile trials of Irish Americans in Britain served to galvanize the American public in support of more defined rights for naturalized citizens, contributing to a "broad and popular movement [that] urged equal rights and protection for native and naturalized citizens, action to compel Britain to recognize expatriation rights, and affirmation of the power of the United States to define and protect its citizens" (Samito, *Becoming American*, 205). The Fourteenth Amendment and the Expatriation Act of 27 July 1868 were the U.S. government's answer to the Fenians and to African Americans and a formal acknowledgment that naturalized and native-born citizens enjoyed the same political rights. Negotiations with nations such as Britain and Prussia ensured that the sovereignty of the United States did not stop at its borders, but followed its citizens (native-born and naturalized) when they traveled abroad. The transatlantic movement of Fenians had forced the United States to rethink constructions of territorial sovereignty that linked authority to place. Returning to an earlier definition of sovereignty in which authority was linked to individuals, a model advocated by the Fenians, the United States exerted its authority over its citizens regardless of their geographic location.

The Fenians and their virtual Irish Republic also informed U.S. foreign and domestic policy in other ways. Shortly after the Battle of Ridgeway, President Johnson had issued a proclamation condemning the Fenians as "evil disposed persons."[100] In May 1870, following one of the Fenian raids on Canada, President Ulysses S. Grant told his cabinet that he would not allow the "organization of a Government within the U.S.," "the 'holding of a Congress,'" or the "assumption of the power to raise armies and fit out expeditions."[101] That the president of the United States had to expressly forbid the formation of a government within U.S. territorial borders speaks to the political force exerted by the Fenians and their virtual republic. Grant was particularly focused on the military aspects of such governments and issued the "Proclamation, against the Fenian Invasion of Canada," condemning "illegal military expeditions and enterprises" originating from within the United States.[102] Those who pursue such military efforts, he warned, will give up their right to the protection of the U.S. government. While it may have behooved the Johnson administration to initially encourage or ignore Fenian activities in order to gain political advantage over Britain during and after the Civil War, Grant faced different circumstances. In 1870, as states such as Virginia, Mississippi, and Texas were readmitted to the Union as part of Reconstruction, there was an emphasis on national unity and territorial sovereignty. The presence of other nations and armies within the U.S. borders constituted a threat to this vision of unity that could not be ignored. The Grant administration had no desire to repeat the military and diplomatic events of the preceding decade and sought to deny a vision of divided sovereignty in which the United States played host to other nations.

The Fenians were not the only group to which this message was addressed. An 1871 congressional act shifted the terms of engagement with Native nations from treaty making to legislation, a move that Bruyneel suggests eroded the nation-to-nation relationship and contributed to the "increased domestication [of Native nations] within the American political system."[103] Moreover, events taking place to the south may explain Grant's explicit denial of the United States as a site in which multiple nations could be housed. Following an 1868 uprising in Cuba against the Spanish, many Cuban migrants sought refuge in the United States and then continued their political efforts to gain belligerent status for Cuba. In a message to Congress, President Grant summarized the situation: "During the whole contest the remarkable exhibition has been made of large numbers of Cubans escaping from the island and avoiding the risks of war; congregating in this country, at a safe distance from the scene of danger, and endeavoring to make war from our shores, to urge our people into the fight which they avoid, and to embroil this Government in complications and possible hostilities with Spain."[104] Here and elsewhere Grant suggested that no other nation could operate within the territorial borders of the United States, a move that bolstered constructions of territorial sovereignty and gestured toward its fractures. Grant mapped such spatial concerns onto his denial of Cuban belligerency: "The insurgents hold no town or city; have no established seat of government; they have no prize courts; no organization for the receiving and collecting of revenue; no seaport to which a prize may be carried or through which access can be had by a foreign power to the limited interior territory and mountain fastness which they occupy. The existence of a legislature representing any popular constituency is more than doubtful."[105] The Fenians and their Irish Republic, however, had exhibited many of these features—a capital, a system for collecting revenue, and a legislature—and operated in a historical moment in which the interests of their virtual republic aligned, at least in part, with those of the United States.

Through their literary and military efforts, the Fenians styled themselves as a mobile Irish Republic that could be nurtured in the United States and then relocated to Canada and to Ireland itself. Their political force lay not in their ability to defend territory, but in their capacity to move through it. They intervened in contemporary debates about political allegiance, citizenship, and sovereignty, selectively adapting British and American legal thought to craft their own unique vision of divided sovereignty in which a virtual Irish Republic could exist temporarily within the United States. But as they mounted more and more unsuccessful military campaigns, their reputation and influence waned. Their critics turned to the familiar language of imperium in imperio to characterize the Fenian threat and to pressure the U.S. government to intervene.

Attacks on the Fenians and their Irish nation revealed continued anxieties about volitional allegiance and naturalization. Fenian leaders such as Michael Corcoran, an officer in the Union army who fought with the Sixty-Ninth New York, an all-Irish regiment, framed their own bodies as sites of divided allegiance and sovereignty. "One half of my heart is Erin's," wrote Corcoran in his captivity narrative, "and the other half is America's."[106] Could naturalized citizens really abandon their allegiance to their home country, or would they always be to some extent divided? If the latter were true, then the presence of such divided bodies exposed fissures in U.S. territorial sovereignty, places where political authority other than that of the United States could be exercised. Legislation passed during the 1860s, including the Fourteenth and Fifteenth Amendments, and treaties negotiated with foreign nations sought to mitigate concerns such as these, but did not completely erase them. As I show in the next chapter, issues surrounding the definition of U.S. citizenship and the nature and reach of American sovereignty remained subjects of intense debate.

CHAPTER FIVE

"China in the United States"
Extraterritorial Sovereignty, the Six Companies, and Rhetorics of a Chinese Imperium

IN THE WAKE of the Civil War and the passage of the Reconstruction amendments (1865–1870), definitions of U.S. citizenship were broadened to include African Americans, and greater protections were extended to naturalized citizens when they traveled abroad. As the United States attempted to heal the divisions of the previous few decades, the nation also looked outward and focused on extending its economic and political reach beyond its geopolitical borders. What Walter LaFeber has dubbed the "new empire" had already "moved with increasing authority into such extracontinental areas as Hawaii, Latin America, Asia, and Africa."[1]

With developments in theories of extraterritorial sovereignty, Americans began to expect that U.S. sovereignty would follow them when they traveled abroad. The Fenians and their Irish Republic raised troubling questions about divided sovereignty and allegiance related to naturalized citizenship. Fears of immigrants introducing the sovereignty of another nation were amplified by the large numbers of Chinese immigrants who began arriving during the gold rush years (1848–1855) and who, according to the terms of treaties negotiated with China, did not qualify for U.S. citizenship. Americans questioned what it would mean for the United States and, in particular, for California to host a large number of foreign nationals who owed allegiance to a foreign emperor. Charges that these immigrants constituted an imperium in imperio, led by what were popularly known as the Chinese Six Companies, a confederation of district associations formed by Cantonese immigrants, began to circulate at the state level and then were taken up in American public argument more broadly in the 1870s.² As leaders of and advocates for the Chinese community in the United States, the Six Companies were a stark reminder that extraterritoriality could be a two-way street: extending America's sovereignty abroad raised the possibility of divisions at home.

"A Chinese Ishmael," a short story published in 1899 by Sui Sin Far, offers one vision of the role that the Six Companies played in the Chinese community of California and, as Kate McCullough notes, "speaks to this view of the Chinese as a nation within a nation."³ The story focuses on two young lovers, Leih Tseih and Ku Yum, who are living and working in San Francisco's Chinatown and experiencing different forms of bondage. Leih Tseih owes the Six Companies for his passage to America and must work to repay that debt, while Ku Yum is a slave owned by a couple who wish to sell her to Lum Choy, an old enemy of her lover. When the young pair run away together, Lum Choy takes his grievances to the Six Companies for redress. Making his claim before the board of presidents, Lum Choy requests that the board "engage officers of the law to capture this lawless man, and ... prosecute him, as it is in order for the Six Companies so to do."⁴ When the board members respond that Leih Tseih has paid his debt and they have no authority to punish him for the "crimes" of which he has been accused, Lum Choy reacts with surprise that the Six Companies cannot exercise jurisdiction over someone whose passage they financed. The leaders of the Six Companies affirm that they cannot publicly violate American law and thus cannot involve themselves in Lum Choy's case. Nevertheless, they do suggest that there might be more covert channels through which his claims can be satisfied. In the end, the young lovers decide to commit suicide rather than face separation. As McCullough notes, the story "suggests that the Chinese Six Companies represents [sic] a sort of Chinese regulatory body at work within the United States, implying the existence of two national juridical systems."⁵

Sui Sin Far's story reflected many of the widely held fears about the presence of Chinese immigrants in California, including the belief that they were forming a separate judicial system within America's borders through which Chinese imperial law would be practiced on American soil. Arguments about a Chinese imperium in imperio revealed Americans' intense anxieties about extraterritorial sovereignty and their continuing concern about internal division. Like Irish immigrants, newcomers from China were territorialized as racially and religiously unassimilable into the American body politic, but unlike the Irish, their national separateness was reinforced by U.S. law. Because they were excluded from becoming U.S. citizens, Chinese immigrants remained Chinese subjects despite the fact that they lived and worked in the United States. Beginning in the 1850s, they were subject to a host of discriminatory state laws and practices that impacted their ability to work and their overall quality of life.

Like the Fenian Brotherhood, the Chinese Six Companies worked to engage two nations—in this case, China and the United States—on political terms and argued that multiple polities could, in some sense, share the same space. Through their political, legal, and literary efforts, the leaders of the various companies sought to adapt the organizational structures of the Chinese guilds and district associations to the exigencies of life in California. The Six Companies emphasized Chinese immigrants' status as foreign nationals protected by the treaties negotiated between China and the United States (and not subject to the authority of individual U.S. states) and drew on traditional modes of engaging sovereign power in their dealings with both U.S. and Qing officials. Moreover, like the Cherokees, African Americans, and Irish Americans, Chinese immigrants challenged racialized rhetorics of imperium in imperio and instead offered their own vision of divided sovereignty, which they represented as aligned with U.S. interests. Documents produced by the Six Companies and their supporters, including the written constitutions produced by the companies, challenged the exclusionary legal practices directed at Chinese immigrants, attempted to renegotiate their relationship to the United States and the general American public, and outlined their efforts to manage the lives of Chinese immigrants as part of their conception of divided sovereignty. The Six Companies were at the center of contests between state and federal authorities in the United States and between U.S. federal authorities and Qing officials. Their efforts to engage the U.S. federal government were, in a sense, successful, but that success came at great cost. Fear of a Chinese imperium, which was closely linked with the activities of the Six Companies in the minds of many white Americans, was among the factors that led to the 1882 Chinese Exclusion Act, an attempt to prevent the exercise of extraterritorial sovereignty on U.S. soil even as the United States extended its reach abroad.

Extraterritorial Sovereignty, Jurisdiction, and Visions of a Chinese Imperium in the West

Against a backdrop of intense domestic debates over how the nation would be "reconstructed" in the 1860s and 1870s and what the role of African Americans, American Indians, white women, and immigrant groups such as the Irish would be in the newly reforged United States, conversations about expatriation and the extension of U.S. jurisdiction onto foreign soil circulated as the United States negotiated various naturalization treaties with nations such as Great Britain and Prussia. Put another way, at the very moment when Congress was trying to concretize the domestic borders of the United States and to remake the bonds between the states, U.S. officials were troubling such borders by arguing for the extension of American sovereignty abroad. The U.S. government created a version of external state sovereignty that was not geographically limited and that followed its citizens as they traversed national borders. Such policies differed from earlier understandings of sovereignty, which focused on the perpetual relationship of individuals to a particular sovereign or to a particular place rather than on a nation's global political reach. Concerns about extraterritorial sovereignty were expressed in the popular press not only in relation to U.S. nationals traveling abroad, but also in relation to foreign nationals living and working in the United States, who were or might represent sites of foreign sovereignty on U.S. soil during the period of their residence. As in earlier cases, imperium in imperio provided a language for communicating a variety of cultural anxieties and for turning fears of internal division outward onto an "other" nation. In the 1870s, those anxieties crystallized around the threat that Chinese immigrants posed to federal, state, and municipal sovereignty, particularly in the state of California.

Sovereignty remained contested within the nation's territorial borders, and definitions of U.S. citizenship—both native-born and naturalized—remained the subject of debate as the United States began to extend its political authority abroad. Extraterritorial sovereignty gained real political force in the mid-nineteenth century through interactions between various nations and imperial China and became an important part of U.S. foreign and domestic policy. While the United States had negotiated treaties with North African nations after the Barbary Wars that guaranteed some degree of extraterritoriality, those treaties largely dealt with maritime concerns rather than the position of U.S. nationals living abroad. It was not until the 1840s that the United States began to accept the premise that nationals living outside of the United States should be subject to U.S. laws rather than to those of the nation in which they lived. As Samito has suggested, among the myriad effects of the transatlantic military and political efforts of the Fenian Brotherhood and their Irish Republic was the galvanizing of American public opinion on the need for the federal government to offer equal protections to U.S. citizens at home and abroad.[6] As a result of treaties with nations such as China, American citizens took U.S. sovereignty with them when they traveled to other nations, but such treaties also raised the possibility that resident or visiting aliens could introduce foreign sovereignty into the United States.

China played a key role in shaping the exercise of U.S. extraterritorial sovereignty and constitutes a key example of the challenges raised by extraterritoriality. The Treaty of Wanghia (1844), negotiated by Caleb Cushing, the ambassador to China under President John Tyler, established diplomatic relations between the United States and China and stipulated that U.S. nationals in China would be subject to U.S. extraterritorial sovereignty, not the laws of China. Sovereignty in the case of Americans in China was constructed as political rather than territorial. What mattered was not where one was living and working, but the nation into whose political community one was born. For example, Americans who committed crimes in China were subject to U.S. jurisdiction and tried according to U.S. laws. The Treaty of Burlingame, negotiated between the United States and China in 1868, also recognized the increasing flows of individuals, goods, and capital across geopolitical borders and, in the case of the United States, the importance of Chinese labor.[7] Article V of the treaty stated, "The United States of America and the Emperor of China cordially recognize the inherent and inalienable rights of man to change his home and allegiance, and also the mutual advantage of free migration and emigration of their citizens and subjects, respectively, from one country to the other, for purposes of curiosity, of trade, or as permanent residents."[8] Article VI specified the political status of each nation's citizens when they traveled to the other country. Each nation promised that the other's citizens/subjects would "enjoy the same privileges, immunities, and exemptions, in respect to travel or residence, as may there be enjoyed by citizens or subjects of the most favored nation" (6). However, they agreed that while this provision recognized the right of individuals to expatriate, "nothing herein contained shall be held to confer naturalization upon citizens of the United States in China, nor upon the subjects of China in the United States" (6). Thus, while Chinese citizens residing in the United States could enjoy certain rights related to "travel or residence," they could not become U.S. citizens. The same was true for U.S. citizens in China. Such individuals would retain an alien status no matter how long they resided in the nation in question. They were positioned geographically inside, but politically outside the body politic: temporary residents who existed outside of the temporality of naturalization and citizenship. As the flows of individuals between China and the United States increased, so did anxieties about what such individuals meant for the operation of state and federal political authority.

The number of Chinese immigrants who came to the West Coast of the United States in search of economic opportunities increased in the late 1840s because of a number of factors, including the aftereffects of the Opium Wars, the discovery of gold in California, and the rise of the contract labor system (popularly referred to in nineteenth-century American public argument as the "coolie trade"). In the same year that the Treaty of Guadalupe Hidalgo ceded Alta California to the United States, some in the United States began to consider the benefits of Chinese labor for the building of the transcontinental railroad and the growth of agriculture in the western United States. In the 1840s, it was mostly men who traveled to the United States from China, temporarily leaving their families to pursue economic opportunities. Although Chinese people had traveled to the Americas as early as the sixteenth century, the beginning of the California gold rush in 1848, as Xiao-huang Yin notes, provided the impetus for significant numbers of Chinese people to travel to the United States. Chinese immigrants were among the first to reach the gold mines in Sierra Nevada, and according to Yin, there were 325 Chinese "forty-niners."[9] The number of Chinese immigrants in California rose to 25,000 by 1852, and by 1860 the Chinese constituted the largest foreign-born ethnic group. During the 1860s Chinese laborers were imported from China by the Central Pacific Railroad to aid in the completion of the transcontinental railroad. As the gold rush subsided and work was completed on the transcontinental line, Chinese workers sought employment in other fields and many moved to large cities such as San Francisco. In 1882, the year that the Chinese Exclusion Act was passed, the Chinese population of the United States numbered about 150,000. Yin estimates that including those who came to the United States and later returned to China, the total number of Chinese people who "took the Gold Mountain trip from 1849 to 1882" was somewhere between 322,000 and 400,000 (*Chinese American Literature*, 15).[10] Cantonese merchants, who would play an important role in the development of the Six Companies, were also among the early migrants.

Reactions to Chinese immigrants in California were mixed during the nineteenth century. According to Yin, "Although prejudice lived side by side with opportunity in frontier towns and mining camps in general, free competition and tolerance prevailed in the first few years of the Gold Rush" (*Chinese American Literature*, 15). He cites the participation of Chinese people in events such as Fourth of July celebrations and the San Francisco memorial for President Zachary Taylor as evidence of the role they played in the life of many communities. Yin also quotes California governor John McDougal, who in January 1852 called the Chinese "one of the most worthy classes of our newly adopted citizens—to whom the climate and character of these lands are particularly suited" (16). McDougal's praise must be understood in the context of the naturalization laws of the 1850s, which limited naturalization to white people. Thus, when he spoke of "newly adopted citizens," he did not refer to the actual political status of the Chinese, but merely their residence in the community. In the later nineteenth century, labor groups and "anticoolie clubs" voiced their opposition to Chinese laborers and became active forces in California politics in an attempt to forestall competition with Chinese workers. Chinese immigrants faced oppressive working conditions, racial prejudice, and violence, and the challenges that they faced were well documented. Increasing numbers of Chinese immigrants, a weakening U.S. economy, and complaints from American labor interests, such as the Working Men's Party of California, the National Labor Union, the Knights of Labor, and the American Federation of Labor, contributed to the enactment of exclusionary measures at state and federal levels.[11]

The precarious legal position of Chinese immigrants in America was especially apparent in California, already the site of political and legal struggles between the United States, Mexico, and American Indian nations such as the Cahuillas.[12] California began to implement legislative policies that sought to restrict the economic and political opportunities of Chinese immigrants in the early 1850s. Responding to complaints regarding Chinese miners and other laborers, state leaders passed a number of measures that imposed economic hardships on foreign-born individuals who did not qualify for U.S. citizenship, measures that included a tax on foreign miners, landing taxes on ships that transported such individuals, and capitation taxes on Chinese laborers. In May 1852 California's legislature passed a foreign miner's license tax that required a $3 payment from every foreign miner who did not (or could not) intend to become a U.S. citizen. Subsequently, An Act to Discourage the Immigration to This State of Persons Who Cannot Become Citizens Thereof was passed in 1855, which levied a $50 per person tax on anyone transporting to California individuals who were ineligible for citizenship. An 1862 law, An Act to Protect Free White Labor against Competition with Chinese Coolie Labor and Discourage Immigration of the Chinese into the State of California, involved a capitation tax of $2.50 per month on all Chinese people living in the state with some exceptions for mining and work in certain other industries. Fearing the implications for Chinese immigrants and American Indian people, the California legislature voted against the Fifteenth Amendment to the U.S. Constitution. State leaders also passed laws to restrict the entry of Chinese women into the state, thereby reducing the number of babies born to Chinese parents who might qualify for birthright citizenship under the Fourteenth Amendment. Cities such as San Francisco also created municipal laws to regulate Chinese labor and control the activities of Chinese immigrants. Many of these state and municipal laws were not enforced or later were challenged as violations of the Constitution and/or the treaties negotiated between the United States and China.[13] Such challenges highlighted the continued tensions between local, state, and federal authorities and the ongoing debates surrounding whether the power to regulate immigration and naturalization resided in the states or in Congress.

Chinese immigrants in California faced judicial as well as legislative discrimination. In an 1854 case, *People v. Hall*, a California judge interpreted section 14 of the act of 16 April 1850, which prohibited African American or American Indian people from testifying against whites, as also prohibiting the testimony of Chinese. In his opinion, the chief justice of the California Supreme Court, Hugh Murray, argued that "Indian," "Negro," and "mulatto" are "generic" terms meant to refer to the full spectrum of nonwhite people.[14] The intention of the legislature, he contended, was to exclude all nonwhite people from testifying against white people, and so it "adopted the most comprehensive terms to address every known class or shade of color" (20). The Chinese were specifically excluded from participating in California courts of law because they had been "marked as inferior" and because they were presumed to be biased and incapable of abandoning their own national concerns (21). Murray wrote of the Chinese as an "anomalous spectacle of a distinct people, living in our community, recognizing no laws of this State, except through necessity, bringing with them their prejudices and national feuds" (21). Using language that resonated with critiques of the position of the Cherokee Nation in Georgia, Murray's opinion framed the Chinese as a form of imperium in imperio, a "distinct" people living within but not subject to U.S. jurisdiction. They should not provide testimony in American courts because, he argued, they did not follow American laws and would represent the intrusion of a foreign power, the Chinese emperor, into American jurisprudence.[15]

It should be noted that such judicial exclusion did not meet with universal approbation, but generated harsh criticism from the Chinese American community in California and from visitors to the state. In an account of his travels in California in 1861, which were included in *Roughing It*, Mark Twain decried the judicial exclusion of Chinese immigrants and the abuses that they suffered at the hands of some Americans: "Any white man can swear a Chinaman's life away in the courts, but no Chinaman can testify against a white man. Ours is the 'land of the free'—nobody denies that—nobody challenges it. [Maybe it is because we won't let other people testify.]."[16] Here Twain connected the legal exclusion of the Chinese to a broader critique of the American legal system: America's legal and political fictions were not challenged because those who would offer such challenges were prevented from speaking through established legal channels. Representations of America as the "land of the free" were, Twain suggested, made possible by the unfreedom of groups such as the Chinese, who were not only legally excluded, but also physically abused. He claimed that while he was writing his reflections on the Chinese, children were stoning a Chinese man to death in the city (*Roughing It*, 820). By juxtaposing his meditations on current legal proscriptions with violent actions perpetrated by children—with the apparent sanction of observing adults—Twain hinted at the effects such laws had on the broader community and the impacts they would have on the nation's future. Twain concluded this chapter with the assertion that not everyone in California was opposed to the Chinese, a message that he directed specifically to his Eastern readers. He wrote that "[n]o Californian *gentleman or lady* ever abuses or oppresses a Chinaman, under any circumstances." Rather, such acts were committed by the "scum of the population" and their children: "they, and naturally and consistently, the policemen and the politicians, likewise, for these are the dust-licking pimps and slaves of the scum, there as well as elsewhere in America" (825). Despite Twain's assertion that not everyone in California was against the Chinese, political rhetoric continued to emphasize the so-called Chinese question and suggested to Eastern readers that antipathy toward the Chinese was not just the province of labor organizers and "scum." Such rhetoric focused with increasing frequency on the role of the Chinese Six Companies and included charges that the group imported slave labor and constituted a separate government within the territorial limits of California.

The growing antipathy toward the Chinese on the West Coast informed congressional debates about U.S. citizenship and naturalization laws. During the debates over the Fourteenth and Fifteenth Amendments several congressmen used the rhetoric of imperium in imperio to identify perceived threats to their state that might result from a more expansive policy on jus soli (birthright citizenship). In his discussion of the Fourteenth Amendment and birthright citizenship, Senator George H. Williams, a Republican from Oregon, claimed that Chinese immigrants in the West were forming "an imperium in imperio—China in the United States."[17] This line of argument countered attempts by Massachusetts senator Charles Sumner and others to expand the naturalization laws to include Chinese immigrants. The Fourteenth Amendment changed the composition of the American political community within its territorial limits and formalized a version of the extraterritorial sovereignty that followed U.S. nationals abroad, but the political position of Chinese immigrants remained the subject of treaty negotiations, a matter of foreign rather than domestic policy and the exclusive purview of the federal government.

In this contentious political landscape of the postwar period, both Republicans and Democrats vied for the support of Western voters and labor interests, turning to the "Chinese question" as a means of wooing both audiences through the representation of the Chinese as a common enemy. As historian Andrew Gyory argues, "Chinese immigrants . . . became pawns in a political system characterized by legislative stalemate and presidential elections decided by razor-thin margins."[18] They became "the indispensable enemy not to workers but to politicians" (15), who used the issue of Chinese immigration to distract voters from other issues and to appeal to public concerns. Public attention was galvanized by rhetorics that linked Chinese contract labor with chattel slavery. Anti-Chinese rhetoric blurred the distinction between voluntary immigration and importation. Having just purged slavery from the South, many Americans had little interest in seeing the institution revived in the West. Decrying Massachusetts factory owner Calvin T. Sampson's efforts to break a strike by bringing in Chinese laborers, Alexander Troup, the vice president of the National Labor Union, was quoted in a *New-York Tribune* article as proclaiming, "We have abolished the slavery of the black man, but these capitalists are endeavoring to resurrect it."[19] Chinese contract labor and, for some, all Chinese labor was coded as another iteration of chattel slavery, but one with the potential to unite the nation in common cause rather than divide it in another civil war. According to Saxton, the Chinese were positioned as a common enemy that could unite Republicans and Democrats; he notes that "[b]y 1876 both major parties had adopted anti-Chinese clauses in their national platforms."[20]

Among the fullest expressions of the anti-Chinese position and fears of a Chinese imperium were those articulated during California Senate hearings on Chinese immigration. In April 1876 the California Senate appointed a committee of seven senators to investigate issues surrounding Chinese immigration into the state, and many witnesses were asked about the Six Companies' role vis-à-vis the Chinese in California. Several witnesses represented the Six Companies as a benevolent organization or mutual aid society meant to help immigrants with the transition from China to the United States. Leung Cook, the president of the "Ning-yeung [Ning Yung] Company," insisted that the Six Companies merely assisted new immigrants in finding employment and adjusting to American life.[21] Rev. Otis Gibson, a former missionary to China, denied that the Six Companies constituted a separate judicial authority: "The six companies, so far as the people are concerned, are arbiters."[22] Gibson suggested that when the Six Companies could not settle a case, they referred it to the American court system. Gibson's sentiments were reinforced by another witness, E. J. Lewis, who had served in the California Assembly and Senate. He claimed that the Six Companies served a valuable function for Chinese immigrants and helped them adjust to their new surroundings: "Coming to a strange country, ignorant of our laws, language, and customs, they find these companies an absolute necessity."[23] Like Gibson, Lewis portrayed the Six Companies as intermediaries between Chinese immigrants and American institutions, not threats to American sovereignty. He noted that when asked, the Six Companies maintained that they did not have the power to regulate criminal activities and served in a merely advisory capacity. Lewis concluded that

San Francisco's Chinatown was a blight and should be removed, but he did not frame the Six Companies as a danger to American political life.

Others who testified before the Senate committee, however, came to different conclusions and represented the Chinese in California as subject to a foreign government, a Chinese imperium that existed within American territorial borders. Matt Karcher, who served as the chief of police in Sacramento for four years, argued that the Six Companies "have their own tribunals where they try Chinamen, and their own laws to govern them. In this way, the administration of justice is often defeated entirely, or, at least, to a very great extent."[24] He articulated the common concern that the Six Companies essentially constituted a separate government, wielding judicial, legislative, and executive authority over the Chinese immigrant community in the United States. While *People v. Hall* expressed fears that the Chinese would subvert American law from within and thus sought to exclude them, Karcher maintained that the presence of the Chinese disrupted the exercise of American law in a different sense. By setting up their own parallel judiciary and legislative systems, they prevented the enforcement of American law within the space of Chinatown, an affront to state and municipal sovereignty.

A memorial sent the following year by the California Senate to the U.S. Congress, which, as its title suggested, sought to elucidate the "social, moral, and political effect of Chinese immigration," synthesized many of the points raised during the Senate hearing. This text, written by a Senate committee, highlighted the presence of a virtual Chinese government within the state of California, drawing on the familiar rhetoric of imperium in imperio to make its supporters' case and heighten fears of subversion from within:

> A graver difficulty still is developed in the existence among the Chinese population of secret tribunals unrecognized by our laws and in open defiance thereof, an imperium in imperio that undertake[s] and actually administer[s] punishment, not infrequently of death. These tribunals exercise the power of levying taxes, commanding masses of men, intimidating interpreters and witnesses, enforcing perjury, punishing the refractory, removing witnesses beyond the reach of process, controlling liberty of action, and preventing the return of Chinese to their homes in China. In fact, there exists amongst us tribunals and laws alien to our form of government and which practically nullify and supersede both National and State authority.[25]

The committee enumerated all of the powers exercised by the "secret tribunals," which included not only the power to render judicial decisions, but also the power to make and enforce laws. According to the Senate committee, this

Chinese legal system, operating on the West Coast of America, was subverting the authority of state and federal laws and threatening the very foundation of American territorial sovereignty—the exercise of political and judicial authority within a bounded space.

The arguments that emerged from the 1876 U.S. congressional hearings, which were published in 1877, represent an important archive of anti-Chinese sentiments and echoed many of the arguments that were made in the California hearings. By the time the California Senate's memorial was published in 1877, issues surrounding Chinese immigration had been established as a national issue rather than as merely state and local concerns.[26] In 1874, President Grant had suggested that he would support anti-Chinese legislation, and two years later a congressional committee launched an investigation of the Chinese in California. The Joint Special Committee to Investigate Chinese Immigration traveled to San Francisco and held a series of hearings over the course of eighteen days with the goal of ascertaining "the character, extent, and effect of Chinese immigration."[27] The committee was composed of six congressmen—three members of the Senate and three members of the House—and was chaired by Oliver P. Morton, a senator from Indiana. Like the California Senate committee, the joint congressional committee explored whether the Chinese Six Companies constituted an imperium in imperio and operated a separate political and judicial system within California. The committee questioned the nature of the Six Companies and the role they played in relation to Chinese immigration.

Near the beginning of the report, Frank Pixley, a journalist and a former attorney general of California, suggested that the Six Companies served a variety of purposes, some benevolent and some commercial. He then testified that he could offer proof that the Six Companies had organized "secret tribunals exercising a criminal and civil jurisdiction, an *imperium in imperio*" (*Report of the Joint Special Committee*, 24). The Six Companies, he argued, made their own laws, held their own courts, and passed their own sentences, which could include death sentences. According to Pixley, Chinese immigrants were subject to the laws of the Six Companies and remained under their authority as long as they remained in the United States. These organizations exercised the prerogative of sovereignty over a population that, as noncitizens, occupied a liminal position in relation to the U.S. government and the individual states. In an appendix to the report, S. V. Blakeslee, a minister and the editor of the *Pacific*, made a comparison between "coolyism" and African slavery. Slavery, he contended, broke the bonds between African people and prevented them from forming a coherent community within the United States, whereas "coolyism" fostered such development. "Already they have a perfect government among themselves distinct from our own," he claimed, "with their laws, their secret courts of trial, and their police, executive, and other officers, the object of which is to perpetuate their race peculiarities, their clanship interests, and their religion, with terrible sanctions of law, even the death penalty, to enforce their regulations." He went on to say that the Chinese were "managing a perfect and increasingly efficient '*imperium in imperio*,' to enforce obedience to their requirements, however adverse to American interests or government" (1242). The Chinese, he suggested, had formed a working shadow government within California and exercised sovereignty and jurisdiction over the Chinese community.

As further proof of the dangers of this Chinese imperium, the anti-Chinese witnesses claimed that immigrants from China did not adopt any of the practices of American citizens and did not pursue citizenship. Ignoring the limitations that U.S. naturalization laws put on nonwhite immigrants, Pixley asserted that Chinese immigrants "take no step in the direction of citizenship" and claimed that there was no known case of a Chinese person in America desiring to become a citizen (*Report of the Joint Special Committee*, 17). The report concluded from the evidence presented that the Chinese "do not desire to become citizens of this country, and have no knowledge of or appreciation for our institutions" (vii). They might not currently wish to vote in U.S. elections, but the report raised the concern that allowing them to vote would have disastrous consequences: "To admit these vast numbers of aliens to citizenship and the ballot would practically destroy republican institutions upon the Pacific coast, for the Chinese have no comprehension of any form of government but despotism, and have not the words in their own language to describe intelligibly the principles of our representative system" (vii). Chinese immigrants were framed as doubly threatening: they could not be incorporated into American society without destroying its republican character, but their current status had led to the formation of their own separate government. By exercising sovereignty over Chinese people and the spaces they inhabited in America, their shadow government represented a threat to municipal, state, and federal authority and, according to some witnesses interviewed by state and federal leaders, constituted a dangerous example of divided sovereignty. The joint committee argued that if left unchecked, Chinese immigrants would threaten to turn the states along the Pacific Coast into "practically provinces of China rather than States of the Union" (viii). They not only had brought a foreign influence to U.S. shores, the committee determined, but also threatened to transform the West Coast into a foreign space beyond the reach of American territorial sovereignty.

Witnesses proposed that what made the situation of the Chinese unique from that of other noncitizens and allowed for the rule of the Six Companies was their concentration in urban communities. Chinatowns were represented as dangerous extensions of China within the larger United States in ways that revealed continued concern with managing the relationship of "other" nations to the American landscape. In the report, California senator Frank McCoppin described San Francisco's Chinatown as being "as foreign as any quarter of Canton or Peking, and its inhabitants are governed by the 'six companies' rather than by the municipality" (*Report of the Joint Special Committee*, 11). As miniature foreign nations operating within the state of California, Chinatowns were represented as disrupting the exercise of state and federal sovereignty, which could not penetrate these densely populated foreign spaces. According to McCoppin, the Chinese were a "pagan horde," temporary residents who maintained their distinct national identity and who could not be incorporated into American society (10). Such arguments about the foreign nature of Chinatowns and their residents contributed to the process through which the Chinese were territorialized as a racially "other" nation operating within a contained urban space, which, in turn, opened up arguments for their further containment and exclusion.

As in the California Senate hearings, San Francisco's Chinatown, the headquarters of the Six Companies, became the locus of many political arguments about the political status of the Chinese. In a speech before the U.S. House of Representatives in 1878, Congressman Horace Davis of California emphasized the foreign qualities of Chinatown:

> The Chinese quarter of San Francisco occupies from seven to eight small blocks in the heart of the city, in which are densely packed about twenty thousand human beings, which form two-thirds of its Chinese population. To pass into this quarter from the adjoining streets is like entering a foreign country. The streets are thronged with men in foreign costume; the buildings are decorated with strange and fantastic ornaments; the signs and advertisements are in queer, mysterious characters; the objects exposed for sale are new and strange; the ear hears no familiar sound, but is assailed with an incomprehensible jargon, and the very smells that pour from the cellars and open doors are utterly foreign and marvelous.[28]

Davis drew a sharp contrast between Chinatown and the surrounding community through his use of adjectives such as "foreign," "strange," "fantastic," "queer," "mysterious," and "incomprehensible" to describe the sensory experience of walking through the neighborhood. The visitor, Davis asserted, was "assailed" by the newness and strangeness of the experience. He represented Chinatown as more than an ethnic enclave, but rather as a foreign space that was not governed by American law, a nation within a nation. Moreover, when Chinese people operated outside of the space of Chinatown, they functioned,

Davis suggested, as a kind of contagion and introduced foreign sovereignty into the American political community. The Chinese immigrant in mining camps and other communities was "utterly an alien in the body-politic, and like some foreign substance in the human body, breeding fever and unrest till that system is relieved of its unwelcome presence" (3). He credited the Chinese with "the formation of what is almost a foreign government in the very heart of the State" (6). Within the space of a few pages, Davis demonstrated two of the perspectives of those opposed to Chinese immigration: individual Chinese people infiltrated and contaminated American communities, while large groups of Chinese immigrants formed their own separate states. Both scenarios, he implied, were threats to American political authority.

Many critiques of Chinese immigration drew on racist representations of "Mongolian" inferiority, rhetorics that would come to be associated with the "yellow peril" and labor concerns, which dovetailed with the theme of the Chinese forming a separate nation on the West Coast. One of the leading voices in this discussion was Henry George, a journalist, lecturer, political economist, and two-time New York mayoral candidate. George, who had been a prospector in his youth, was staunchly opposed to Chinese immigration and even recorded physical altercations with Chinese people in his diary. In "The Chinese in California," a letter that appeared in the *New-York Tribune* on 1 May 1869, George produced what Roger Daniels contends might be the first expression of a key element of "yellow peril" rhetoric: a Chinese invasion of the United States.[29] George claimed that unlike African Americans, who were by then eligible for U.S. citizenship, the Chinese would never assimilate into American society. George turned to history and essentialist arguments about national traits to distinguish the Chinese from other groups that had eventually claimed the right to vote. African Americans were, he contended, blank slates when they were forced into slavery and thus were shaped by American institutions. Previous arguments about African Americans' lack of political history were here reworked in their favor. The Chinese, in contrast, would have to "unlearn" their "civilization and history," a task that George framed as nearly impossible.[30] One of his chief concerns was what he saw as the Chinese propensity for forming their own institutions in the United States: "They have a great capacity for secret organizations, forming a State within a State, governed by their own laws; and there is little doubt that our courts are frequently used by them to punish their own countrymen, though more summary methods are oftentimes resorted to."[31] Here George used an English translation of imperium in imperio, but the point remained the same: Chinese immigrants in the West had established their own government and exercised their own political and judicial authority in a manner that subverted municipal, state, and federal jurisdiction. They were subject to Chinese sovereignty and brought that sovereignty with them when they settled in California, forming an outpost of China in the United States.

George drew on the rhetoric of imperium in imperio even more explicitly in later writings. He claimed that the Chinese could not be held accountable to American law, particularly in spaces such as San Francisco's Chinatown, which he called a "perfect miniature China."[32] Within the spaces of Chinatowns, the Chinese Six Companies maintained a separate legal system that prevented Chinese immigrants and their children from fully assimilating into American culture. George expanded on this point in an article for the *Cyclopedia of Political Science*, linking the Chinese imperium to the political situation in China. The weakness of the Chinese government, he asserted, led to "extralegal association" and the formation of secret societies and guilds. Expanding on this point, he wrote, "By virtue of this capacity for organization, the Chinese in a foreign country really constitute an *imperium in imperio*, really live under a Chinese government of their own—a government which finds ample means to enforce its own laws and regulations. This is as notorious on the Pacific Coast of the United States as it is in every other part of the world to which the Chinese have gone in any numbers. Without the aid of American law, and in spite of American law, Chinese regulations are enforced."[33] Here George contended that Chinese immigrants brought these organizations into foreign countries and created the architecture of a Chinese imperium. George explicitly referenced the presence of a "Chinese government" with "ample means to enforce its own laws and regulations." The presence of this government, he proposed, subverted the operation of American law because it enforced its own laws regardless of the function of local, state, and federal laws in relation to the Chinese. He reiterated throughout his writings that the spaces occupied by Chinese immigrants within the territorial limits of the United States were foreign spaces, subject to foreign laws, which U.S. laws could not penetrate. The United States must address the presence of this "government," George argued, because it had created jurisdictional conflicts between state and federal authorities and had introduced a foreign legal system into American national space.

Some fictional works of the era also offered dire warnings about a Chinese imperium and vitriolic critiques of Chinese people and culture. Atwell Whitney's 1878 novel, *Almond-Eyed: A Story of the Day*, pits the handsome, moral, and long-suffering Job Stearns against the nefarious Deacon Spud, the owner of a starch factory and a supporter of Chinese labor; his son, Simon; and the Chinese themselves, led by Ah Chung. Like George's letter, the novel anticipates in a number of ways the anxieties associated with the "yellow peril": Chinese laborers force white Americans out of the labor market, bring with them the pestilence of smallpox, and introduce vices such as gambling and opium smoking into what is represented as a previously upright Protestant community. Using an agricultural metaphor, the novel likens Chinese institutions to the tobacco plant, which, when planted in a field, makes the soil unfit for other plants. "On some of the best soil of America are Chinese institutions planted," observes the narrator of *Almond-Eyed*. Chinese immigrants, the novel suggests, "plant" their own institutions in America and subvert the republican institutions that ensure the survival of American democracy.[34]

Editor and author Pierton W. Dooner's *The Last Days of the Republic* argues even more explicitly that Chinese institutions in America constitute an extension of the Chinese government. This narrative traces the history of Chinese immigration to the United States up to the point of its publication and then offers a "history of the future" that includes a Chinese takeover of U.S. state and federal governments and a war between white Americans and Chinese immigrants.[35] Among the first steps that the Chinese take in their conquest of America is the formation of the Six Companies, which are described as an extension of the Chinese government. To facilitate the movement of Chinese people to America, "[c]ompanies were organized, ostensibly as private enterprises, but virtually chartered, controlled and directed by the central government at home. These were known in America as the Chinese Six Companies . . . whose agents were commissioned by the Emperor; and . . . exercised the functions of legislative and judicial officers as well as virtual governors of the Chinese people in America" (28). According to this argument, through the formation of these organizations, the Chinese emperor is able to establish a "virtual" presence in America, with officers who make and enforce laws and exercise control over the Chinese people in the United States. Elsewhere, the text refers to a "trans-Pacific government for the emigrant" (54) and represents the Six Companies as a "sub-government" (63) existing within the state of California. It is through the efforts of the Chinese Six Companies that a Chinese imperium forms on the West Coast: "It was in this way that a government within a government was established; or, in other words, that the jurisprudence of China became the law of her people in California" (61). Drawing on the rhetoric of divided sovereignty, Dooner's text, like others of the period, discusses Chinese immigrants as "a government within a government," a body of people living within the jurisdiction of the United States, but operating under the laws of imperial China. The extension of Chinese sovereignty within the space of the United States is represented as a precursor to a political and military takeover. While labor issues and racial stereotypes figure prominently in this text, the emphasis is on the Chinese not merely as a separate racial group or a source of cheap labor, but rather as a separate political entity poised to subvert the sovereignty of the United States and create discord between state and federal authorities.

People on both sides of the so-called Chinese question pointed to the problems inherent in having large numbers of individuals in the United States who were not eligible for citizenship and not subject to U.S. jurisdiction. Questions remained, however, as to what to do in order to satisfy federal, state, and local interests. Beginning soon after the issue of Chinese immigration was taken up by Congress in 1870, critics of the Chinese imperium suggested that the United States could take one of two approaches to solving the problem of divided sovereignty: either allow Chinese to become naturalized American citizens or restrict their entrance into the United States. In an 1873 argument that resonated with early American critiques of "taxation without representation," M. B. Starr, the author of *The Coming Struggle*, claimed that the Chinese would not continue to pay such taxes once they became "civilized" unless they were allowed to participate fully in American political life. Starr contended that the liminal status of Chinese immigrants—who lived within the territorial borders of the United States, were subject to its taxes and some of its laws, but remained subjects of China—could not continue without threatening to destabilize American political life.[36] As previously mentioned, Sumner had tried to change U.S. laws in order to facilitate the naturalization of Chinese immigrants, but his efforts were soundly defeated. Fears of how the franchise would further Chinese conquest of the United States were articulated by California officials, federal authorities, and others. A greater restriction on Chinese immigration emerged as the favored solution to what was perceived as a dangerous division of sovereignty, the growth of a Chinese imperium in California. A new treaty was negotiated with China in 1880 and ratified the following year; it allowed for the restriction of immigration, which, in turn, paved the way for later legislation.[37] In discussions of the Chinese in California, the Chinese Six Companies emerged as an extension of the Chinese government, a kind of virtual nation that governed Chinese immigrants and operated outside of U.S. law.

The Chinese Six Companies and the Division of Sovereignty

The Six Companies was the term used by Americans to denote a confederation of companies, or district associations, which were one of several types of organization to which Chinese immigrants could belong. While many of the records of the Six Companies were apparently lost in the 1906 San Francisco earthquake and the fires that followed, the group produced a wealth of documents, including written rules and constitutions, articles published in newspapers and other periodicals, letters, petitions, and legal documents. Despite the amount of literature they produced and the influence that they exerted, historian Yucheng Qin notes that the Six Companies have been neglected in studies of both nineteenth-century China and Chinese America. Qin's work reveals how the Six Companies "stepped into the void created by the slow and ineffective responses from the Qing government" to address the racism experienced by Chinese immigrants and prompted "the nationalist turn of China's approach to foreign relations in the nineteenth century."[38] In the context of ongoing concerns about imperium in imperio and the division of sovereignty, I focus here on the development of the Chinese Six Companies on the West Coast, their engagement with American political culture and the genre of the written constitution, and their exercise of political and judicial authority, which they framed as aligned with rather than an affront to the sovereignty of the United States.

Chinese immigrants to the United States brought with them several types of voluntary associations that served various purposes in the community. As Daniels suggests in *Asian America*, the "family association or clan (that is, all those who had a common last name and thus a putative common ancestor), was the primary associational focus" for Chinese immigrants.[39] Additionally, Chinese immigrants might also have belonged to district associations, which functioned like "guilds" or "native-place" associations, the first of which were formed in the early sixteenth century (Qin, *Diplomacy of Nationalism*, 8–9). Such groups provided support for Chinese people from a particular region who had left their place of origin. They oversaw the burials of members, provided places of worship, served as arbiters and mediators in disputes between members, advocated for members in their dealings with nonmembers, and exercised judicial authority over members. The leaders of the companies were elected officials, and members paid yearly dues to support the efforts of the association. Some companies worked cooperatively and formed confederacies to work toward common goals. In discussing the role of the Chinese Six Companies, Daniels characterizes it as an "umbrella organization," a confederacy that exercised authority over the various district associations.[40] A third type of organization was the secret societies known as *tongs*, groups that apparently had some connections to the Triad Society in China and, in the United States, prompted concern regarding their possible involvement with illicit activities such as gambling, drugs, and prostitution.[41] Many Chinese immigrants were involved in family and district associations, and the companies played a central role in community formation as immigrants found themselves in unfamiliar and sometimes hostile surroundings.

All three of these types of organization had their roots in China, with the companies or district associations tracing their descent from Chinese guilds. Qin notes the "extragovernmental activism" pursued by the guilds in nineteenth-century China and their contributions to Chinese cultural and political life during the Ming and Qing dynasties (*Diplomacy of Nationalism*, 11). Nineteenth-century Americans who had spent time in China emphasized the importance of guilds to Chinese society. In his testimony before the California Senate in 1876, F. F. Low, a minister plenipotentiary from the United States to the emperor of China, explained the importance of guilds to Chinese society: "The Chinese people are made up of guilds, of all sorts and kinds, and rule, in this manner, everything sold—as tea, silks, etc., even to the transportation on wheelbarrows."[42] Low's sentiments were echoed in the testimony of W. J. Shaw, who had visited China. When asked if the power of the guilds or companies exceeded that of the "central government," Shaw responded that "these guilds or companies are formed as . . . sort of mutual protection societies. The members have a strong feeling for their companies, and would be ready to obey any reasonable request, and sometimes any unreasonable request."[43] Although Shaw framed the guilds as "mutual protection societies," he also emphasized the power wielded by these organizations. When questioned, Shaw implied that the guilds exercised greater authority than the Chinese government and suggested that if such organizations were imported to the United States, there was reason to believe that they would operate in a similar fashion. His comments implied that if Chinese immigrants brought the guild system to America, these guilds would pose a challenge to federal, state, and municipal authorities through their command of immigrant populations.

When they traveled to foreign countries, Chinese immigrants took the concept of the district association with them and established similar organizations wherever they settled. Immigrants created such organizations in Malaysia, Singapore, and America. The Kong Chow (Gangzhou) Company was among the first to be established in the United States, sometime between 1849 and 1851, along with the Sam Yup (Sanyi) Company, which was established in 1851. The Sze Yap (Siyi) Company was formed shortly thereafter, as were the Yeoung Wo (Yanghe) Company and Hip Kat (Xieji) Company, which later changed its name to the Yan Wo (Renhe) Company. Not long after its formation, the Sze Yap Company began to splinter, with some former members establishing the Ning Yung (Ningyang) Company in 1854. In the United States the companies functioned very much as they had in China. Like their Chinese predecessors, they worked to help members maintain ties with their places of origin and to provide various forms of aid. The companies provided members with temporary housing, a place of worship, medical care, burial services, postal services, leisure and recreation, and mediation when disputes arose between members of a single company or among members of different companies. Membership in a particular company was determined by the district in which one had lived in China and was—according to the documents produced by the various companies—voluntary. They disputed the claim that they regulated the importation of laborers and prostitutes, and instead suggested that immigrants from a given district were expected, upon arrival in the United States, to report to the appropriate company if they sought the protection of that organization. Members paid an entrance fee to belong to a company, although people could gain an exemption if they were ill or out of work. Individual companies elected officials to deal with internal and external business and hired staff to maintain the headquarters.[44]

Like guilds and district associations in China, the companies sometimes banded together to create confederacies based on regional ties and common interests. The Four Houses, which Qin describes as a "federal organization" composed of the four oldest companies in San Francisco, was formed in 1853 (*Diplomacy of Nationalism*, 28). The Four Houses transformed into the Five Companies later that same decade. These groups were predecessors of the Chinese Six Companies—the Kong Chow (Gangzhou) Company, Sam Yup (Sanyi) Company, Yeoung Wo (Yanghe) Company, Ning Yung (Ningyang) Company, Hop Wo (Hehe) Company, and Yan Wo (Renhe) Company—which, despite its sobriquet, included between four and eight companies during the nineteenth century. The records of the Six Companies' founding have been lost and the precise year of the group's creation is unknown, but scholars note that references to the group and its activities suggest that it was formed before 1860. While additional companies were added later, the name Six Companies stuck for many Americans and was used by the group in writings directed to American audiences. A new organization, known in English as the Chinese Consolidated Benevolent Association, which included some of the Six Companies' officers, was founded in 1882 and formally incorporated in 1901.[45]

The Six Companies responded to the exigencies of life in America and organized its own bicameral legislative body. All Chinese immigrants were eligible for membership in the Six Companies, even if they were not originally from one of the districts associated with one of the companies in the confederation. The Six Companies maintained records of the names and addresses of all Chinese people living in the United States, which gave them a certain amount of access to and leverage over Chinese people, who, because of their status as noncitizens, were not accounted for in many municipal, state, and federal records in the United States. The leadership of the Six Companies was drawn from that of the various member companies and included a board of presidents and a board of directors. The board of presidents was composed of the presidents of the companies, and leadership of the board rotated among its members in such a way as to allow each man to serve as president of the Six Companies at least once during his tenure as president of his own company. The board of directors was made up of representatives from each of the companies, and the number of representatives allotted to each company varied according to the company's overall membership—one representative for every five hundred members. The leadership of the Six Companies also retained American lawyers to advise them on legal matters and hired lobbyists to represent them in Sacramento. The boards, sometimes referred to as a "congress," had a permanent headquarters in San Francisco's Chinatown and oversaw a wide variety of activities, including collecting money from immigrants and sending it back to their relatives and friends in China, providing medical care and burial services, and maintaining a place of worship. As Qin notes in his discussion of the history and operations of the Six Companies, "[l]ike other *huiguan*, the Six Companies was a combined charitable, mutual-aid, and self-defense society, in addition to serving as a judicial system for dealing with both internal disputes and external assaults" (*Diplomacy of Nationalism*, 46).[46]

Like the other groups I have examined, the Six Companies drafted written rules and constitutions in order to communicate their authority and maintain internal order through the production of what Jameson calls a "social code." Despite the loss of the original records, historical accounts and translations of these documents provide a sense of the nature of the Six Companies' constitutions. William Hoy describes the constitution of what was originally the Five Companies, which established the governmental structure of the organization: a "sort of board of presidents," who took turns serving as the president of the entire group.[47] A translation of one company's constitution appeared in the *Oriental; or Tung-ngai san-luk*, edited by Rev. William Speer, a former missionary to China, and associate editor Lai Sai (or Lee Kan), which was one of the earliest newspapers published in both Chinese and English in the United States.[48] A translation of the constitution and "rules" of the Yeoung Wo Company (referred to as Yeung Wo by Speer) provides an example of the kind of constitutional documents produced by the Six Companies. Speer published a copy of the constitution and rules to correct misconceptions about the companies and to demonstrate "in a plain and convincing way the intelligence and capability" of the Chinese.[49] This speaks to the dual function of constitutions, which in this case worked to relate to an audience of nonmembers and to regulate the behavior of members. It opened with the following statement:

> Since it is necessary for the government of such associations, and the promotion of the common good, that some rules should be adopted, we, members of the Yeung-wo Company, now dwelling in a foreign country, have established those

which follow. Those which formerly existed in a general form we deem it necessary to draw up in a new and definite shape, and to publish them to all men, since successive immigrations have become less substantial in their character, and troubles have sprung up like thorns. They are in conformity with the customs of the foreign country in which we are sojourning. We trust they will be exactly observed by common consent. They were adopted ... on a fortunate day of the ninth month of the year 1854.[50]

Territorial concerns played no role in this constitution, which focused instead on legal and administrative authority as exercised over Chinese members in America, a move that challenged binaries of foreign and domestic as well as conceptions of indivisible sovereignty within a bounded space.

This document positioned the company as separate from yet complementary to both the United States and China, and created a set of governing principles for a population that was not addressed in the U.S. Constitution. A series of "general regulations" were listed, which included entrance fees, the procedure for those who wished to return to China, and the rules governing behavior in the company's headquarters. These rules suggested that the company functioned as an arbiter in disputes between members and worked to adjudicate disputes between members and other institutions or individuals. Complaints about members of other companies should be referred to the agent of the Yeoung Wo Company, and, if necessary, agents of the various companies would work together to solve the dispute. The rules demonstrated an awareness that regulating the behavior of Chinese nationals provided political leverage to the company, offering it a means of configuring its members' collective relationship with China and the United States. The constitutions produced by the Six Companies, individually and collectively, were a first step in achieving this kind of political leverage, which they later hoped would inform the political practices of the Qing dynasty. Indeed, as Qin suggests, the Six Companies saw written constitutions as central to China's relationship to the United States and other nations. He describes a petition that the Six Companies sent "to Prince Tao and the Qing Court at the beginning of the twentieth century," which asserted "that it was essential to have a national assembly and a constitution to meet the challenges of the national crisis" (*Diplomacy of Nationalism*, 3).

The Yeoung Wo Constitution positioned the company's efforts as subordinate to and in service of America's constitutional and judicial efforts but addressed Chinese immigrants in ways that the American legal and political culture did not. The judicial functions of the company were framed as beneficial to American law, not a threat to its authority. The fourth object of the company was described thusly:

> Disputes between miners and others are settled at the company houses without the expense, delay, and trouble of a resort to our courts of law. A friendly arbitration is held before a meeting of their company, or before a joint committee of the five companies, where the case is more difficult, or when persons of different districts are involved. The proceedings on these occasions are generally calm, judicious, and satisfactory to the disputants. In former days, encouraged by the examples of lynching among our own people, the companies sometimes took the law in their own hands so far as to inflict corporal punishment upon offenders in their houses, but such practices are now disclaimed by them. Those doings are now past, and offenders are handed over by them to our courts, in cases which their counsels cannot adjust.[51]

Here the companies were shown to ease the burden on the American court system by reducing the number of minor disputes that the courts had to adjudicate. The document worked to distance the "friendly," "calm," and "satisfactory" proceedings of the companies from the violent and arbitrary image of them that circulated in the American press. It was the lynchings committed by white Americans, the translator suggested, that persuaded the companies to practice corporal punishment. Thus, while discussions of the Six Companies that circulated in American newspapers and political debates often emphasized the frequency with which they meted out the death penalty, here such punishment was framed as an anomaly that was adopted from American practices.

In later writings directed toward an American audience, representatives of the Six Companies carefully distinguished between arbitration and the formation of a shadow judicial system in a rhetorical move meant to deflect charges of a threatening Chinese imperium. William Hoy, who served as secretary for the Six Companies and published a history of them in 1942, characterizes the group as a "general board of arbitration" and notes that the anti-Chinese prejudice that pervaded the California legal system caused Chinese immigrants to place greater faith in the judgments of the Six Companies.[52] The Six Companies, he suggests, exercised authority over a population that could not testify against white people in California courts and were often not addressed by U.S. federal law.

Rather than emphasizing their juridical authority and their ability to order the death of anyone who broke the rules, the Six Companies emphasized their concern with and regulation of the lives and movements of Chinese immigrants. While representatives of the Six Companies vehemently denied that they were involved with the "coolie trade" and involuntary labor, as Claudia Sadowski-Smith suggests, they did participate in the "credit-ticket system" and "took on the immigrants' passage debt, helped immigrants find work in the United States, negotiated their terms of labor, and ensured the repayment of their debt."[53] Qin points to evidence that the Six Companies were involved with the financing of Chinese laborers' passage to the United States and actively worked to dissuade immigrants when the environment in California became less welcoming (*Diplomacy of Nationalism*, 140). Representatives from the Six Companies met new immigrants as they arrived in America and took them to the appropriate company. They kept registries of the names and addresses of all Chinese immigrants, which as Lawrence Douglas Taylor Hansen notes, allowed them to "exercis[e] a degree of control over their whereabouts."[54] According to Stanford Lyman, if a Chinese immigrant did not align with a company, the consequences could be severe. The Six Companies could "withhold financial aid, order social ostracism, render a punitive judgment in a suit brought before its tribunal, and arrange for false charges and incriminating testimony in public courts."[55] The Six Companies also regulated the movements of immigrants, particularly their ability to return to China. As stated in the Yeoung Wo rules, that company could prevent a member from returning to China if that member had outstanding debts, thus denying them an "exit permit."[56] Through their concern for and intervention in the lives of members and nonmembers, the Six Companies exercised a form of control associated with the modern nation-state that Foucault identifies as biopower, structuring the lives of Chinese immigrants rather than merely meting out punishment.[57] The Six Companies recognized that such practices could serve as a bargaining chip in their engagements with the U.S. government and imperial China.

In addition to regulating the affairs of Chinese immigrants, the Six Companies also served an external function, lobbying the U.S. government on behalf of Chinese immigrants in the absence of a formal Chinese legation and working to engage state and federal officials on political terms. As Takaki notes, representatives from the Six Companies successfully advocated for provisions for Chinese immigrants during the negotiation of the Burlingame Treaty in 1868. As I discuss later in this chapter, their written documents reminded American authorities of those treaty terms and called on them to honor them. They also met with a congressional delegation in 1869 to protest state laws, such as the miner's tax and prohibitions on Chinese testimony. Takaki cites the 1870 Civil Rights Act, which extended judicial rights to all persons, regardless of skin color or country of origin, as proof of the Six Companies' effectiveness in lobbying on behalf of Chinese immigrants.[58] In the 1860s and early 1870s, the Six Companies and their allies were able to successfully appeal to federal authorities in their struggles with California. In the absence of diplomatic representation, the Six Companies brought the authority of the Chinese government to bear in issues surrounding the treatment of Chinese nationals, functioning not as a secret society but as an agent of Chinese diplomacy.

Realizing that the political status of Chinese immigrants in the United States was linked to both the presence of a formal legation and the recognition of a Chinese nation-state, the Six Companies lobbied the Qing dynasty for the establishment of a diplomatic presence. Like the other groups I examine, the Six Companies realized the importance of engaging the United States on national terms rather than as a racial or ethnic group. In their 1876 "A Memorial of the Chinamen to the President," addressed to President Grant, leaders of the Six Companies began by noting that they wrote "in the absence of any Consular representative."[59] Here and elsewhere, as Qin notes, representatives of the Six Companies took on some of the usual functions of a formal legation, advocating on behalf of Chinese subjects, representing (to an extent) the interests of the Qing dynasty, and serving as intermediaries between the Qing dynasty and the U.S. government. Qin observes that when an official from China visited California, representatives from the Six Companies asked the official to broach the subject of a legation with the Chinese government, even suggesting that they would contribute financially to the establishment of a diplomatic presence. The Qing dynasty finally appointed an ambassador in 1878, when Chen Lambin was appointed the first Chinese minister to the United States.[60] In an interview with a reporter, Minister Lambin asserted that the embassy would "'supersede' the authority and influence of the Six Companies" (qtd. in Qin, *Diplomacy of Nationalism*, 99). This comment suggested that the Six Companies had indeed been serving in a governmental function or were perceived as such by the Qing dynasty. But even after the establishment of the Chinese consulate in the United States, the Six Companies continued to function in much the same ways as they did before, exercising internal authority over Chinese immigrants and operating externally as an intermediary between Chinese immigrants, the Chinese imperial government, and various authorities in the United States.

In addition to pushing for a greater Chinese diplomatic presence in the United States, the Six Companies also challenged discriminatory state and local laws. Responding to the proposed taxes on foreign miners in 1853, the heads of the Four Houses, a precursor to the Six Companies, had their attorney request a meeting with the Congressional Committee on Mines and Mining Interests. A series of interviews were held in San Francisco and recorded in the committee's report. Charles McClain notes, "The committee's report of these interviews offers compelling evidence of the well-developed political sensitivity of the Chinese community leadership even at this early date."[61] Company leaders provided demographic information on the Chinese community and challenged accounts of "coolie" labor and forced servitude. On behalf of Chinese immigrants, they also communicated to the committee a list of grievances. McClain argues that these grievances were presented in a manner that "appealed to the committee's sense of justice and equity" and its economic interests, suggesting that fair treatment of the Chinese might lead to increased trade between the two countries.[62] Letters written by Rev. A. W. Loomis, who replaced William Speer as the head of the San Francisco mission to the Chinese, detailed discussions between him and the Six Companies' leadership. Responding to their request, he suggested that they write petitions and seek counsel from a qualified attorney. In a letter to the Board of Foreign Missions, Loomis revealed that he had found an attorney to work with the Six Companies and that the leaders and this attorney had already worked out an agreement. The Six Companies supported various test cases to challenge the constitutionality of discriminatory laws such as San Francisco's cubic-air ordinance and its queue-cutting ordinance.[63] Thus, in addition to lobbying both the Qing imperial government and U.S. state and federal authorities on behalf of the Chinese communities, the leaders of the Six Companies also worked to shape U.S. judicial culture. Working with American lawyers, they challenged California laws as unconstitutional because they were an infringement of federal sovereignty by regulating immigration and international commerce. While they were accused of maintaining their own separate judicial system, the Six Companies' leaders deftly used the U.S. court system to shape the relationship between Chinese immigrants and the United States.

The Chinese Six Companies were discussed in various ways throughout the second half of the nineteenth century, and one of the charges against them was that they constituted a nation within a nation and functioned as an extension of imperial Chinese sovereignty within the United States. The Six Companies carefully positioned their organization as akin to the trade unions and mutual aid societies found throughout the United States during this period. Yet, they did exercise both political and judicial authority over the immigrant population in ways that sought to manage their daily lives: settling disputes, meting out punishments, and intervening in the lives of immigrants from the moment they left China until the time they decided to return. Moreover, the Six Companies' leaders understood the importance of framing their grievances in national terms and of belonging to a nation that would protect their interests even as they sidestepped charges that their organization was threatening an imperium within the United States. In a historical moment when the United States was extending its extraterritorial sovereignty by exerting authority over U.S. nationals when they traveled abroad, the Six Companies lobbied for the Qing dynasty to do the same. As Qin argues in regard to the impact of the Six

Companies on Chinese politics, "the Chinese Six Companies in California responded to racist challenges by organizing [their] own community, developing modern nationalism, and teaching the Qing dynasty how modern nationalism should be pursued diplomatically" (*Diplomacy of Nationalism*, 1).

The next section will examine how, in the absence of a formal legation, the literary and political practices of the Six Companies worked to shift the terms of engagement with the United States from race to nation and depicted a particular version of divided sovereignty.

The Six Companies, Extraterritorial Sovereignty, and Chinese Literature in America

Because they were denied access to American political culture and legal systems, the Chinese Six Companies adapted the institutional form of the district association to create a type of divided sovereignty that would attend to the needs of immigrant people and exert pressure on the Chinese and American state and federal governments. They engaged in strategic practices that mirrored the kind of extraterritorial sovereignty that the U.S. government exerted over its nationals in China. Also, beginning in the 1850s, when some of the earliest discriminatory laws against the Chinese were passed in California, the leaders of the companies turned to print media to circulate their arguments. Denied the opportunity to testify in court, they took their case to the American public, engaging U.S. authorities on political terms in an attempt to refigure their collective relationship to the United States. While it is true that there were relatively few newspapers produced by Chinese immigrants during the nineteenth century, the Six Companies and their advocates worked through various channels to influence public opinion, challenge discriminatory laws and practices, and narrate the political status of Chinese immigrants in America. As part of this narration, the Six Companies and their allies resisted racialized representations of the Chinese that positioned them as akin to African American and American Indian people, who were increasingly framed in American law and public argument as domestic racial groups, and as a racialized imperium. Appealing to the terms of the Burlingame Treaty, the leaders of the Six Companies worked to shift the discussion from one of race to one of nationhood, sovereignty, and treaty rights in which the interests of the Six Companies were aligned with (rather than opposed to) those of the United States.

In addition to their strategic engagements with American law, leaders of the Six Companies and the network of American advisors that they created attempted to shift the terms of the debate over Chinese immigration and reshape the mode of engagement between Chinese immigrants and American authorities through their use of print media. In an 1874 publication entitled *The Chinese Question from a Chinese Standpoint*, produced by the Six Companies, the authors lamented the limited presence that Chinese immigrants had in American newspapers. "Unfortunately for us," they wrote, "our civilization has not attained to the use of the daily press—that mighty engine for molding public sentiment in these lands—and we must even now appeal to the generosity of those, who perhaps bear us no good will, to give us a place in their columns to present our cause."[64] There were Chinese-language and bilingual newspapers published in California during the second half of the nineteenth century, but their circulations and influence were limited. The list of early Chinese-language papers includes *Golden Hills' News*, the *Oriental* (edited by Speer and Lai Sai), the *California China Mail and Flying Dragon*, *Tang-Fan Gongboa/The Oriental*, and the *Sacramento Daily News*. Some of the earliest newspapers were published by missionaries, as in the case of *Golden Hills' News* and the *Oriental*, and many had relatively short runs.[65] In the absence of a truly national Chinese American press in the mid-nineteenth century, representatives from the companies and their allies turned to American papers. While not a great deal of writings produced by Chinese immigrants survive from the nineteenth century, particularly when compared with the volume of material produced *about* Chinese immigrants by American writers, the Six Companies and other advocates of the Chinese community recognized the importance of print in maintaining a sense of collective allegiance. Moreover, since they were denied the right to testify in California's courts, they took their case before the court of public opinion.

Memorials and petitions were an established means for inferiors to address their superiors and to request redress of grievances in the nineteenth century in both China and the United States.[66] In *Signatures of Citizenship*, Susan Zaeske defines the petition as "a request for redress of grievances sent from a subordinate (whether an individual or a group) to a superior (whether a ruler or representative)."[67] Zaeske notes that this genre "is characterized by a humble tone and an acknowledgement of the superior status of the recipient" (3). While this genre originated as a way for individuals to address their sovereign about personal matters, "over time the meaning and function of petitioning changed drastically" (3). Generally speaking, this was true in both Qing China and nineteenth-century America. During the Qing dynasty, there were well-established protocols for the circulation of memorials, with the expectation being that most petitions from individuals would be directed to local officials and then gradually moved up the ranks if they were not addressed. There were some circumstances, however, in which the emperor could be addressed directly or memorials could bypass local officials and address those at a higher level, a situation that was, as Ho-fung Hung notes, likened by one emperor to "children's complaints to their grandparents about their parents." Such complaints were likely to be framed in terms of Confucian notions of filial piety even as they critiqued local officials. As Hung suggests, "a common remedy for powerless subjects abused by local officials was to travel all the way to Beijing to appeal to the emperor as their grand patriarch, hoping that he would sympathize with their plight and penalize corrupt local officials."[68]

In Britain, the right of petition was thought to derive from the Magna Carta. Petitioners acknowledged their own inferiority with respect to the addressee, but the genre of the petition carried the expectation that the addressee was bound to consider the grievance described in the document. Petitions joined writers and rulers into a web of requests and obligations and became an established way for subjects to place demands on sovereign power. During the colonial period in America, the petition was used by individuals to address colonial assemblies and by the assemblies themselves to articulate their concerns to Parliament. Zaeske argues that the rise of popular sovereignty and the increasing power of public opinion informed the practice of petitioning: "The radical potential of petitioning multiplied significantly when groups, rather than individuals (as in original practice), began to direct their grievances not only to governing bodies but also to the public" (*Signatures of Citizenship*, 12). In the nineteenth-century United States, groups that were prevented from becoming citizens often turned to the petition as a vehicle for requesting redress of grievances from government officials and for publicly airing their concerns. For prosperous Chinese merchants who could speak and write in both English and Chinese, memorials were a logical vehicle to communicate their grievances to government officials and the American people.

An 1852 message from California governor John Bigler framed the conflict between state and federal authorities over issues of Chinese immigration and prompted some of the earliest writings from leaders of California's Chinese community and the forerunners of the Six Companies. In his message, Bigler argued that Chinese immigration to California should be restricted through taxation and that Congress should prohibit contract labor and the "coolie trade." He distinguished Chinese immigrants from European immigrants, who were capable of becoming U.S. citizens according to the naturalization laws of the time, creating a racial distinction that the leaders of the Chinese community would work tirelessly to refute. He noted that the phrase "free white person" had been interpreted to exclude African Americans, American Indians, and Asian peoples and claimed that to his knowledge, no Asians had become naturalized U.S. citizens.[69] In a rhetorical move that foreshadowed

People v. Hall (1854), Bigler linked African Americans, American Indians, and Asian peoples as populations unqualified for citizenship and ineligible to testify in U.S. courts. On a broader level, he represented them as incapable of being assimilated into the U.S. body politic. Anticipating that some might see his stance as a violation of the Treaty of Wanghia, Bigler asserted that this treaty did not specify the "civil or political privileges" that were to be granted to Chinese immigrants in the United States, but rather focused on commercial relations and property rights ("Governor's Special Message"). Bigler argued that states have the right to discourage the immigration of populations that they find undesirable and could appeal to federal authorities for stronger prohibitions, but were not bound to wait for the federal government's approval to take action. He appealed both to earlier constructions of state sovereignty and to the notion that Asian immigration was a new issue that might require "departures from precedents" ("Governor's Special Message"). His message foreshadowed the struggles between state and federal sovereignty that would emerge throughout the debates over Chinese immigration and the multiple interpretations of extraterritorial sovereignty that circulated at midcentury. While scholars have generally focused on the struggles between the Northern and Southern states during Reconstruction, Western states such as California emerged as proponents of state sovereignty on issues of immigration and citizenship.[70]

Governor Bigler's message prompted several responses from the leadership of California's district associations, which were at that time not yet consolidated into the Six Companies, responses that challenged his characterizations of the Chinese and disputed his constructions of state sovereignty. The first such document, "Letter of the Chinamen to His Excellency, Gov. Bigler" (1852), was published in numerous local and national venues, including the *Daily Alta California*, the *San Francisco Herald*, the *Sacramento Daily Union*, and *Littell's Living Age*, and drew on Chinese and American conventions of petitioning. Its authors, Hab Wa and Tong Achick, positioned themselves as writing on behalf of the Chinese in California. While little is known about Hab Wa, Tong Achick had close ties with the Six Companies. He had been educated in American schools and, as Yin notes, would later serve as an "interpreter and translator in court for the Chinese Six Companies." He also published translations of the "testimony of the leaders of the Six Companies ... in 1853 and 1854" (*Chinese American Literature*, 20). This letter opened by expressing the writers' "sorrow" over the governor's recent letter.[71] They stated that after considering his comments and talking among themselves, they had determined to write a "decent" and "respectful" appeal "pointing out to your Excellency some of the errors which you have fallen into about us" ("Letter of the Chinamen," 32). The tone was of supplicants to an authority with greater political power, but the authors claimed a certain kind of moral force and superior knowledge. While this letter adhered to many of the conventions of the petition, Yin notes that it differed from contemporary Chinese petitions in significant ways: "Unlike traditional petitions by civilians to government officials in imperial China, the letter's opening was unusually straightforward" (*Chinese American Literature*, 19). He characterizes this letter as "direct" and "firm" in contrast to the "round-about way" and "humble style" of Chinese petitions (19). Yet the authors were subtle in offering their corrective to Bigler. They "do not presume" to address American law, but instead subtly reminded Bigler (and the newspaper's readers) that the relationship between the United States and China was governed by treaties, not by state officials ("Letter of the Chinamen"). This evasion was more than just the authors' avoidance of a topic with which they were presumably less familiar than the governor, but rather constituted a veiled suggestion that Bigler and the California legislature did not exercise ultimate authority over Chinese nationals living in the United States. By reminding him of the importance of treaties and nation-to-nation negotiations between the United States and China, the authors suggested that Bigler should not overstep the boundaries of his authority.

Norman Asing (also known as Sang Yuen), who characterized himself as a naturalized U.S. citizen and a member of the Yeoung Wo Company, also responded to Bigler's message in a letter published in the *Daily Alta California*, offering an appeal to morality, a challenge to specific policies, and an insistence on the political.[72] Acknowledging Bigler's superior position, Asing referenced his multiple affiliations as a "Chinaman," a "republican," a "lover of free institutions," and a citizen of the United States.[73] He addressed Bigler in his official capacity as governor and reminded him that his words carried weight with the legislature and the general public. The real force of Asing's argument came from his appeals to American history, republican civic virtue, and the Confucian ideal that subjects could hold their leaders morally accountable for their actions. Drawing on America's revolutionary past, he likened California's attempt to restrict Chinese immigration to Britain's attempts to control immigration to and definitions of citizenship in the American colonies. This comparison made implicit the connections between Bigler's opposition to the Chinese and the tyranny of King George III, framing both instances as threats to American sovereignty and aligning Chinese immigrants with colonial Americans. While Asing began the letter by speaking as an individual, in the middle he shifted into speaking for the Chinese community in America and turned to issues of race: "And we beg to remark, that so far as the history of our race in California goes, it stamps with the test of truth the fact that we are not the degraded race you would make us. We came amongst you as mechanics or traders, and following every honorable business of life" ("To His Excellency"). Asing strove to convince the governor and, by extension, the reading public that the Chinese should not be classified by whites as racial others but rather "are as much allied to the *African* race and the red man as you are yourself" ("To His Excellency"). He likened the color of Chinese people's skin to that of Europeans but then dismissed the idea that America's founding documents were grounded in racial hierarchy: "nor do we consider that your Excellency, as a Democrat, will make us believe that the framers of your declaration of rights ever suggested the propriety of establishing an aristocracy of *skin*" ("To His Excellency"). Here Asing deliberately read racial concerns out of America's founding documents. It was after taking on the voice of the Chinese community that Asing's tone became less conciliatory. Early in the text, he acknowledged the governor's influence on policy and public opinion, but he subsequently shifted to a discussion of the limitations placed on Bigler and other state officials: "It is out of your power to say, however, in what way or to whom the doctrines of the Constitution shall apply. You have no more right to propose a measure for checking immigration, than you have the right of sending a message to the Legislature on the subject" ("To His Excellency"). Here Asing reminded Bigler of his position as a state official who lacked the power to reinterpret the terms of the Constitution and to dictate the terms of immigration. As a naturalized citizen of the United States, Asing employed the genre of the petition to appeal to Bigler not to enact restrictions on Chinese immigration and to correct his racist views of Chinese people. Yet he also reminded the governor that the Chinese are a foreign population over whom federal officials, not state officials, exercise ultimate authority. Asing's ethos as a petitioner was predicated on both political inclusion and national exclusion, and he spoke both for himself and for the Chinese community in America, which he sought to frame in national rather than racial terms. By publishing the letter in a California newspaper, Asing addressed not only Bigler as a state official, but also the broader political community of "the people."

Bigler's message prompted a third letter entitled *Remarks of the Chinese Merchants of San Francisco on Governor Bigler's Message*, which was written by Lai Chun-chuen and published on behalf of the members of the Hak-sheung Ui-kun, or Chinese Merchants Association.[74] Written before the consolidation of the Six Companies and the ratification of the Burlingame Treaty, these remarks, which functioned as a petition, alluded to discussions of restricting Chinese immigration. It addressed Bigler, the California legislature, and "the People" of the state of California. While this petition addressed Bigler in a conciliatory manner as "His Excellency," it also, in a sense, went over his head to address those who put him in office. Citing Confucius, Lai Chun-chuen suggested that "all nations are really the same," having both virtuous and corrupt members.[75] These remarks distinguished between issues over which the state could claim jurisdiction and questions of immigration, which were under the purview of the U.S. government. Responding to the claim that the Chinese were responsible for the gambling and prostitution that occurred in California, this text noted that such practices were illegal in China and detested by Chinese merchants living in the United States. While they abhorred such practices, the merchants had found it impossible to enforce Chinese laws in the United States and urged Bigler to enact laws forbidding these vices. Like Hab Wa, Tong Achick, and Norman Asing, Lai also challenged racist representations of Chinese immigrants, even as he employed racial stereotypes to distinguish Chinese people from Native American and African American people (*Remarks*, 5). Lai concluded the merchants' petition with a request that also delivered a veiled warning. He appealed to state lawmakers to prevent "the rabble" from harassing Chinese immigrants, calling on the state to regulate the behavior of its citizens rather than focusing on legislating immigration (6). If such protections could not be enacted, provisions should be made for immigrants to return to China or for the city of San Francisco to accommodate an influx of "several tens of thousands of Chinese immigrants" (6). Here the petitioners raised the specter of mass immigration on the scale of which California legislators had been warning. Lai created a somewhat false dichotomy between a mass exodus of Chinese immigrants—a significant economic blow—and a mass entrance that would challenge the political, economic, and legal status quo of San Francisco. Here, as in earlier pamphlets and petitions, the author sought to subtly direct the legislative actions of the state and drew key distinctions between state and federal sovereignty with regard to the Chinese community.

As the Chinese Six Companies began to play an increasingly prominent role as spokespeople for Chinese immigrants in the 1860s, they reiterated their arguments that they were well positioned to regulate the Chinese community. Such arguments were grounded in their knowledge of the Chinese language and culture as well as American law. In an 1862 article in the *Sacramento Daily Union*, entitled "Notice to the Public," the leaders of what were then the Five Companies detailed a legal case in which a Chinese man was falsely accused of murder on the basis of a forged letter. This ploy was successful, they argued, because the forger knew that American judges would be unable to read Chinese characters. Arguing that the "Chinese alone are able to distinguish the different handwritings of their countrymen," the leaders of the Chinese companies argued for a role for themselves in the American legal system: facilitating the implementation of American law among the Chinese population.[76] The leaders of the companies argued that the challenge of enforcing those laws among the Chinese population required their assistance. Yet, because Chinese people could not testify in California courts, the leaders of the companies presented their appeal to the American people directly, using the popular press as a vehicle for their petition. Using a similar tactic, a memorial that appeared in the *Daily Alta California* in June 1868 suggested that all women in Hong Kong who wished to come to the United States should be required to obtain an "authenticated seal of the Six Companies" before boarding ships so as to prevent prostitutes from traveling to the United States.[77] This memorial, published during the negotiation of the Burlingame Treaty, projected the authority of the Six Companies across the Pacific to what was then a British colony. In their appeal to the American public, the memorialists framed the Six Companies as uniquely positioned to protect American interests abroad, exercising a kind of legal authority even within a space defined as British. They sought, as did their predecessors, to carve out a role for themselves that was complementary to the American legal and political culture, exercising a form of sovereignty over Chinese people without challenging that exercised by U.S. state and federal authorities.

After the passage of the Burlingame Treaty with its fuller articulation of extraterritorial sovereignty, the Chinese companies grew more explicit in their calls to federal authorities to restrain the states from extending their jurisdiction over Chinese immigrants. One notable example is "A Remonstrance from the Chinese in California to the Congress of the United States" (1868), reportedly written by a man named Pu Chi and translated and published by Speer in *The Oldest and Newest Empire*. In this document, the petitioners expressed their belief that "the conduct of the officers of justice here has been influenced by temporary prejudices and that your honorable government will surely not uphold their acts."[78] They called on Congress to address twelve topics of import to the Chinese community in California: "We earnestly pray that you would investigate and weigh them; that you would issue instructions to your authorities in each State that they shall cast away their partial and unjust practices, restore tranquility to us strangers, and that you would determine whether we are to leave the country or to remain" ("A Remonstrance," 589). The opening of this petition was explicit in its appeal to federal authority over that of the states, contrasting the treatment that Chinese immigrants in the United States had received with that of foreigners in China. The authors leveled harsh criticism against the U.S. Supreme Court for its prohibition on Chinese testimony:

> Why, then, is this burden laid upon us Chinese alone? Suppose there be false witness borne, are the judges of your honorable country blind and stupid, so that they

cannot discern it and estimate testimony at its value? Because here and there a Chinese or two has proved a perjurer, shall it prejudice our entire nation? Shall this degrade us beneath the negro and the Indian? This is a great injustice, such as is not heard of in our Middle Kingdom! It injures your fair name. Every nation under heaven mocks at you. Hence it is not alone we Chinese that suffer, but blessings are lost thereby to your own land. (596)

The authors here upbraided Congress for the "injustice" and moral outrages that had been perpetrated against the Chinese and suggested that the world was watching America's treatment of Chinese immigrants. They engaged rhetorics of racial hierarchy to distinguish their own national status from that of supposedly inferior racial groups and to advance their political claims.

After requesting several specific legal actions, including prohibitions on Chinese prostitution and gambling, the authors suggested the role that the Chinese companies and their leaders could play in the implementation of U.S. law. They noted that the influx of immigrants into the United States brought both virtuous and vicious individuals from all nations: "Among our Chinese there are some bad people; and only the Chinese can know who they are. If you will permit the Chinese merchants, they will prepare private statements as to such persons, vouching for them by the signature of their names. Thus rogues may be justly punished, and will understand that the laws are to be respected, and will be deterred from the commission of crimes; and they will return to the ways of virtue" ("A Remonstrance," 601–602). As in earlier petitions, the merchant leaders of the companies suggest a vision of divided sovereignty in which they could complement the U.S. legal system by identifying criminals who were unknowable to American authorities. They were not usurping American legal authority nor exercising Chinese sovereignty, but rather were facilitating the identification and punishment of criminals who would otherwise escape notice. They also requested that if Congress did not wish Chinese immigrants to mine in the United States, they set a date three years hence when Chinese immigrants could cash in their property and return to China. If such a plan were to be enacted, they also desired that no additional immigrants would be allowed to enter the United States. However, if Chinese immigrants were to be allowed to mine, then Congress should instruct the court system to allow Chinese testimony and prevent infringements of their rights (602–603). Here as elsewhere the leaders of the companies appealed to federal legislative authority, suggesting a greater role for Chinese leaders in adjudicating legal cases and calling for changes to state and federal policies that discriminated against Chinese immigrants. They framed their particular version of divided sovereignty as a boon to U.S. political and legal institutions, helping them to regulate the activities of a foreign population whose language most Americans neither spoke nor wrote.

As anti-Chinese sentiment increased in the 1870s, the Six Companies were increasingly under attack in the press, and they addressed themselves to President Grant and both houses of Congress in attempts to remedy their situation. They framed a memorial as a response to both the congressional investigation and the California Senate hearing on Chinese immigration that occurred in 1876. Noting that they were not given the opportunity to provide the "Chinese Side of the Question" to the California Senate committee, they used this memorial as an opportunity to plead their case. They denied their involvement in procuring involuntary Chinese labor and forming a shadow judiciary.[79] In a separate memorial to President Grant, the petitioners made similar denials: "These Six Companies were originally organized for the purpose of mutual protection and care of our people coming to and going from this country. The Six Companies do not claim, nor do they exercise any judicial authority whatever, but are the same as any tradesmen's or protective and benevolent societies" ("Memorial of the Chinamen to the President," 26). Here the writers distanced themselves from any kind of "judicial authority," including that which they had earlier claimed to wield, framing their organization as akin to "tradesmen's or protective and benevolent societies" (26). Unlike earlier memorialists, they suggested that all Chinese immigrants take their claims to American courts in civil and criminal matters. Antagonism against the Chinese, the writers suggested, increased around the time of "state and general elections" (26) They appealed to the president and, by extension, to Congress to abide by the terms of "the treaty of amity and peace" between the two nations and to protect the rights of Chinese immigrants. "But, if the Chinese are considered detrimental to the best interests of this country," the memorialists concluded, "and if our presence here is offensive to the American people, let there be a modification of existing treaty relations between China and the United States, either prohibiting or limiting further Chinese immigration, and, if desirable, requiring also the gradual retirement of the Chinese people now here from this country" (26). On one level, such a statement can be read as endorsing a Chinese exodus from the United States and restricting further immigration. Yet, it is also important to note the emphasis on treaty negotiations, which, by definition, recognized Chinese sovereignty and constituted a formal agreement between China and the United States. The petitioners here proposed renegotiating the treaty as an alternative to unilateral U.S. decisions on Chinese immigration policies.

To protect the interests of Chinese immigrants and maintain their own prominence in the community, the Chinese Six Companies formed a kind of nation within a nation. They performed strategic practices of external sovereignty usually reserved for foreign diplomats and represented the interests of the Qing dynasty in the United States, or at least their version of those interests. Throughout the 1860s and 1870s, the Six Companies attempted to reframe the "Chinese question" from one of race to one of political status, continually reminding political figures and the general public that they were foreign nationals whose treatment was governed by the terms of treaties. They also modeled a form of internal sovereignty within the Chinese community. Barred from testifying in U.S. courts and faced with discriminatory laws, the Six Companies established their own system of arbitration and population management and volunteered their services to American authorities. They positioned themselves as uniquely able to translate between two cultures with different languages and different legal systems. The judicial authority exercised by the Six Companies was, they claimed, supportive of American sovereignty and not a threat to American law. As Chinese immigration became a national issue and as concerns about a Chinese imperium intensified, they shifted back to rhetorics of benevolence and voluntary association. Through their written works, which synthesized elements from both Chinese and American political cultures, they worked to build and maintain a community and to advocate for their political claims to state and federal authorities and to "the people."

Conclusion

As the United States worked to reconstruct itself in the wake of the Civil War and extended its extraterritorial sovereignty abroad, fears arose about the consequences of extraterritorial sovereignty as recognized in treaties such as those with China. If U.S. sovereignty followed its citizens as they traveled abroad, then it stood to reason that the sovereignty of other nations followed foreign nationals when they resided in the United States. The political position of Chinese immigrants in America revealed these anxieties and the continued struggles between state and federal authorities over questions of sovereignty. In this contentious political landscape, the Chinese Six Companies functioned as a kind of nation within a nation, mediating between a series of competing political interests, and regulating the lives of their members. They synthesized Chinese and American political culture in order to construct the collective relationship of Chinese in America to both China and the United States.

The internal authority that they wielded was both judicial and administrative in nature, and the nation that they formed was not explicitly territorial. Indeed, they scrupulously denied charges that the Six Companies was a shadow government even as they framed themselves as a system that operated alongside and complemented U.S. legal and political institutions. At the same time, they continually reminded American officials that they were not a "domestic" racialized population, such as African Americans and American Indians (according to the logic of the time), but foreign nationals whose treatment was governed by treaty rights. They framed their claims in terms of their national status in order to shift the terms of the debate from racial inferiority to political rights. Positioned in the interstices of Chinese and American laws, they framed themselves as arbiters and translators who mediated between two populations with significant cultural and linguistic differences.

The exclusion laws of the 1880s demonstrated a significant shift in American constructions of sovereignty as it related to immigrant populations. In the struggles between the state of California and the federal government over the right to regulate and legislate immigrant populations, during which the Six Companies played a key role, the federal government emerged the winner. However, this did not lead to more legal protections for Chinese immigrants; in fact, quite the opposite occurred. In 1882, Congress passed the Chinese Exclusion Act, the "first federal law ever passed banning a group of immigrants solely on the basis of race or nationality," a law that was renewed three times by the first decade of the twentieth century (Gyory, *Closing the Gate*, 1). The exclusion laws of the 1880s suggested the direction the federal government planned to take. Regulating and managing immigration had been understood historically as a prerogative of sovereignty, but the *exclusion* of populations was something new. It was argued that the United States had to repeal the Burlingame Treaty, because the terms of that treaty were in violation of its sovereign right to exclude immigrants. In a letter to Tsui Zwo Yin, China's foreign minister, Assistant Secretary of State William Wharton explained the link between sovereignty and exclusion. The exclusion of Chinese people, he argued, was the result of the cultural and political differences between the two nations: "It is the inherent prerogative of sovereignty to take cognizance of such incompatibilities and to provide special conditions for the toleration of the unassimilable element in the national community."[80]

Scholars have proposed a number of answers to the question of why Congress took such unprecedented steps to exclude the Chinese. Gyory offers the following summary: "Historians have identified three forces behind the Chinese Exclusion Act: pressure from workers, politicians, and others in California, where most Chinese had settled; a racist atmosphere that pervaded the nation in the nineteenth century; and persistent support and lobbying by the national labor movement" (*Closing the Gate*, 1). All of these factors likely contributed to the exclusion laws. Yet, as I have suggested, constructions of the Chinese as a foreign nation in the United States, an effect of extraterritorial sovereignty and global commerce that the country did not want to acknowledge, also gave rhetorical force to arguments for the exclusion of Chinese immigrants. In a period in which fictions of national reconstruction faced constant challenges and borders were becoming more porous, fears of imperium in imperio circulated in political discourse and public argument as part of the narrative justification for the legislative exclusion of other nations deemed to be politically and racially unassimilable.

CONCLUSION

Becoming Minority Nations in Nineteenth-Century America

In *Negotiations*, a collection of interviews and essays that address many of the concepts that have concerned Gilles Deleuze throughout his career, he turns to the topic of politics and, in an interview entitled "Control and Becoming," responds to the question of "[h]ow can a minority becoming be powerful." As he considers this question, Deleuze offers a corrective to notions that the distinction between the minority and the majority is a statistical one and characterizes the difference as one of creativity versus conformity:

> The difference between minorities and majorities isn't their size. A minority may be bigger than a majority. What defines the majority is a model you have to conform to: the average European adult male city-dweller, for example.... A minority, on the other hand, has no model, it's a becoming, a process. One might say the majority is nobody. Everybody's caught, one way or another, in a minority becoming that would lead them into unknown paths if they opted to follow it through. When a minority creates models for itself, it's because it wants to become a majority, and probably has to, to survive or prosper (to have a state, be recognized, establish its rights, for example). But its power comes from what it's managed to create, which to some extent goes into the model, but doesn't depend on it. A people is always a creative minority, and remains one even when it acquires a majority: it can be both at once because the two things aren't lived out on the same plane.[1]

In this quotation, Deleuze emphasizes the creative power of minorities, the ways in which they have no "model[s]" but only generate them for strategic advantage ("to become a majority"). As I have argued, in nineteenth-century

America, nationhood was such a model, which various groups sought to create for themselves in order to gain political advantage. During this time, Cherokees, African Americans, Irish Americans, and Chinese immigrants recognized that nationhood was the model of the majority, and they acted on the notion that to "survive or prosper" required engaging the United States (and, in some cases, other nations) as nations. They enacted powerful forms of minority becoming—crafting written constitutions that were both creative and disruptive, engaging America's founding documents, and, in the process, changing those documents to be more inclusive. They employed print media as part of their efforts to counter processes that attempted to territorialize them as domestic racial inferiors, and they positioned themselves in international political debates. Some of the nations examined in this book achieved a permanent political status, while others did not; the Cherokee Nation exists today, while the Irish Republic of the Fenian Brotherhood is a distant memory. But we should not judge success solely in terms of longevity, but rather should, as Deleuze suggests, turn our attention to the effects of their creative processes. The engagements between the United States and these "other" nations shaped constructions of nationhood, sovereignty, and citizenship in various, contradictory, and sometimes surprising ways during the nineteenth century.

I now return to Griggs and his 1899 novel as a means of both concluding these discussions and opening up new questions. M. Guilia Fabi locates Griggs's *Imperium in Imperio* in the context of utopian literature and suggests that Griggs even drew his title from one of the bestselling utopian works of the nineteenth century, Edward Bellamy's *Looking Backward, 2000–1887*.[2] In Bellamy's novel, women comprise a separate part of the military and political system of the year 2000, and the narrator observes that they form "a sort of imperium in imperio."[3] Griggs may have known Bellamy's work, but, as I have suggested, the story of imperium in imperio is much larger than these two writers. Yet, like Bellamy's novel, in which a nineteenth-century protagonist travels to the future to reflect on the past, Griggs's novel is at once retrospective and forward looking. It draws on the broader history of imperium in imperio in American literature and public argument in its dramatization of a black nation within the United States, but also anticipates twentieth-century iterations and the emergence of majority models other than the nation-state.

Even before Griggs published *Imperium in Imperio*, African Americans were noting the ways in which a separate black nation in the United States was being represented as desirable by white Americans and how the phrase "nation within a nation" was becoming increasingly wedded to concepts of racial separatism. Many of these observations were circulating in Christian churches and other religious venues. The phrase appeared frequently in writings by African American ministers and public figures as they struggled to deal with Jim Crow laws and the failed promises of Reconstruction. In the words of a Methodist minister and editor, Rev. Benjamin Tanner, in 1876, "The ultimatum the nation presents to the American colored man of Negro descent is that he shall build up an *imperium in imperio*."[4] Whereas earlier rhetorics of imperium in imperio had warned of the dangers of divided sovereignty, segregation promoted the creation of separate institutions among the African American community and a logic of separate but equal. Tanner continued, "An *imperium in imperio* is the nation[']s demand. Everything separate and apart. No coming in. Schools, churches, hotels, railcars, workshops, and even cemeteries,—of each and all there must be a brace; at least, in so far forth as it pertains to the technical Negro. Nor does it hesitate to go to the astounding length of having two armies! A white one and a black one."[5] Such demands were not placed, Tanner argued, on other groups, but only were required of African Americans and would have dangerous consequences for the nation as a whole. "It is not, then," Tanner insisted, "the best thing for the nation to insist that an eighth of all its people shall be, practically, 'a nation within a nation.' Not, indeed, if liberty and republicanism are to be preserved."[6]

Tanner's concerns were reiterated by Frederick Douglass, who described African Americans as a nation within a nation in his earlier writings. However, in "The Nation's Problem," a speech delivered to the Bethel Literary and Historical Society in April 1889, Douglass rejected this formulation. He addressed "the error that union among ourselves is an essential element of success in our relations to the white race" and deconstructed the familiar adage that "united we stand and divided we fall" (Foner, *Frederick Douglass*, 732). Instead, Douglass argued that "our union is in weakness" (732). He urged African Americans not to divide themselves into separate communities and not to create separate institutions. Such tactics, Douglass claimed, led only to further exclusion and alienation, while a "few colored people scattered among large white communities are easily accepted by such communities, and a larger measure of liberty is accorded to the few than would be to the many" (732). Returning to Blackstonian rhetorics, Douglass argued, "A nation within a nation is an anomaly. There can be but one American nation under the American government, and we are Americans" (732). Here Douglass defined a nation within a nation in terms of both political division and racial separatism, asserting that both were obstacles in African Americans' quest for social acceptance and political rights. In the context of Jim Crow, thinking of African Americans in national terms no longer seemed productive to Douglass.

Just three years before the publication of Griggs's novel, Booker T. Washington engaged the subject of an African American imperium in a speech delivered before the 1896 Presbyterian Home Mission rally at Carnegie Hall in New York City. He warned white Americans of what would happen if they did not promote the industrial education and economic uplift of African Americans:

> Within the next two decades it will be decided whether the negro, by discarding antebellum ideas and methods of labor, by putting brains and skill into the common occupations that lie at his door, will be able to lift up labor out of toil, drudgery and degradation into that which is dignified, beautiful and glorified. Further, it will be decided during this time whether he is to be replaced, crushed out as a helpful industrial factor, by the fast spreading trades unions and thousands of foreign skilled laborers that even now tread fast and hard upon his heels and begin to press him unto death. This question is for your Christian church to help decide. And in deciding, remember that you are deciding, not alone for the negro, but whether you will have eight millions of people in this country, or a race nearly as large as Mexico, a nation within a nation that will be a burden, a menace to your civilization, that will be continually threatening and degrading your institutions, or whether you will make him a potent, emphatic factor in your civilization and commercial life.[7]

Playing on the larger history of racial anxieties associated with imperium in imperio and racial separatism, Washington attempted to gain support for his cause by leveraging the threat of a black nation forming within the United States. He emphasized the size of the African American population and claimed that they would become a "menace" and "be continually threatening and degrading your institutions" if they were not assisted. What he hoped for was economic integration, not separatism.

Griggs, a Methodist minister who was likely familiar with such conversations taking place in religious circles, was writing in a period of transition. Throughout the nineteenth century, rhetorics of imperium in imperio had been employed in American literature and public argument as a way of coding a variety of peoples as a political anomaly, geographic impossibility, and racialized threat. Yet, as I have shown, this particular language also provided a tool for groups that sought to renegotiate their political position vis-à-vis the United States. Griggs's *Imperium in Imperio* was published at a time in which American political culture and understandings of sovereignty and power were changing. His novel imagines a scenario in which African Americans can claim territory, raise money, build a government and a military, and launch a military attack on the United States. Yet, such a direct confrontation between two territorially based nations was growing increasingly unlikely in the America of the 1890s, as the practices of U.S. sovereignty were shifting from territorial control to the kind of biopower that Foucault discusses in his lecture series *"Society Must Be Defended."* Earlier engagements between the United States and "other" nations had taken up the project of removing those groups from within America's putative borders. In the wake of the Reconstruction amendments, America's citizenry was more diverse, and most white Americans recognized that African Americans, American Indians, and immigrants were part of the political landscape. They could not be removed en masse nor completely shut out of the nation's political culture.

Sovereignty in America had also become invested in the management of populations and the positioning of them in particular places within the nation's geopolitical borders. Jim Crow laws, the Dawes Act, and various other strategies led to new forms of containment and racial discrimination, and the deployment of certain forms of sovereign power grew less frequent. Conditions shifted to those that resemble what Foucault describes: "[W]e see the appearance of a State racism: a racism that society will direct against itself, against its own elements and its own products. This is the internal racism of permanent purification, and it will become one of the basic dimensions of social normalization."[8] In other words, instead of removal, this form of "State racism" acts through absorption, management, and normalization. That we now think of imperium in imperio in terms of racial separatism, particularly as it relates to African Americans, was not a foregone conclusion in 1787. Rather, I would suggest that it is an effect of the ways in which this particular rhetorical trope evolved in response to shifting constructions of sovereignty from the control of territory to the management of populations' behavior within that territory.

While it might be tempting to read Griggs's novel, with his vision of armed military conflict and bounded national space, as denoting the end of a certain conception of direct, national confrontation, it can more fully be appreciated as a turning point. In many ways *Imperium in Imperio* is a novel that reflects back on the nineteenth century. It is set in the nineteenth century and draws on the political vocabulary of the nineteenth century in its depiction of the transition from slavery to freedom, the failed project of Reconstruction, and issues of territoriality, race, nationhood, sovereignty, internal division, and collective allegiance. Yet those issues did not disappear as the new century began, and in this way Griggs's novel can also be read as gesturing toward the concerns of future generations.

Our own historical moment is animated by versions of these same conversations, from immigration and its impact on American politics and culture to the forms of territorial and economic containment that many face in America's urban centers. As in the century on which Griggs's novel reflects, minority groups (in the Deleuzian sense) in twenty-first-century America are both acted on by processes of territorialization and normalization and engaged in powerful creative efforts to form new models and new modes of collective engagement.

NOTES

Abbreviations

African Repository and Colonial Journal (ARCJ)
American Colonization Society (ACS)
American Periodicals Series Online (APS)
Bell, *Minutes of the Proceedings of the National Negro Conventions* (MP)
California Digital Newspaper Collection (CDN), http://cdnc.ucr.edu/cgi-bin/cdnc
Confederate States of America (CSA)
Fenian Brotherhood Records and O'Donovan Rossa Personal Papers (FBR)
Library Company of Philadelphia (LCP)
Library of Congress (LOC)
The Life, Trial, and Execution of Captain John Brown (LTE)
Making of America Online, Cornell University Library (MOA)
Milledgeville Historic Newspapers Online (MHN)
Moulton, *Papers of Chief John Ross* (PJR)
Nineteenth-Century U.S. Newspapers Online (NCN)
Proceedings of the First National Convention of the Fenian Brotherhood Held in Chicago, Illinois, November 1863 (PFN)
Proceedings of the Second National Congress of the Fenian Brotherhood Held in Cincinnati, Ohio, January 1865 (PSN)
ProQuest Historical Newspapers Online (PHN)
Uncle Tom's Cabin (UTC)

Introduction

1. Griggs, *Imperium in Imperio*, 190. All subsequent references to the novel are from the Arno edition and cited parenthetically in the text. Griggs's life and work have generated renewed critical attention. Some notable examples include Chakkalakal and Warren, *Jim Crow*; Coleman, *Sutton E. Griggs*; Levander, "Sutton Griggs"; Karafilis, "Oratory"; Knadler, "Sensationalizing Patriotism"; Johnson, "Return"; and Fabi, "Desegregating."

2. McDonald, *States' Rights*, viii. Coleman connects Griggs's title to Martin Delany's

reference to African Americans as a "nation within a nation" in *The Condition, Elevation, Emigration, and Destiny of the Colored People of the United States* (1852). See Coleman, *Sutton E. Griggs*, 19. Others have linked Griggs's novel with Edward Bellamy's *Looking Backward: 2000–1887*, which also uses the phrase *imperium in imperio*, locating both novels in the utopian tradition. See Fabi, "Desegregating," 115.

3. For a brief treatment of African Americans' engagement with rhetorics of imperium in imperio in discussions of race in nineteenth-century America, see Zuck, "Martin R. Delany." Studies of the twentieth-century African American literature and culture surrounding Marcus Garvey's Back to Africa movement and the Black Power movement of the 1960s and 1970s often link *imperium in imperio* to racial separatism. See, for example, Dawson, *Black Visions*; and Woodard, *Nation within a Nation*. For discussions of Griggs's vision of *imperium in imperio* and racial separatism, see Williams, "Moving Up," 95; Gillman, *Blood Talk*, 110; and Winter, *American Narratives*, 104. In his analysis of the novel, Coleman reads the characters of Belton and Bernard as embodying "Black nationalism within the United States" and "Black separatism within the borders of the United States" (*Sutton E. Griggs*, 70).

The phrase *imperium in imperio* was used to describe a wide range of entities in nineteenth-century literature and public argument, including newspapers, Freemasons, trade unions, organized crime, secret societies on college campuses, and Mormons. It had a brief career as the state motto of Ohio and was used to sell tractors. For other examples of rhetorics of *imperium in imperio*, see "American Student Life," *Continental Monthly* 2.3 (1862): 266–273; "Trade Unions and the Chinaman," *New York Evangelist* 41.28 (1870): 4; "The Knights of Labor," *Independent* 38.19 (10 June 1886): 17; "The Mormon Imperium in Imperio," *Independent* 37.1934 (24 December 1885): 19–20; "The Third Avenue Railroad," *Independent* 38.1952 (29 April 1886): 20. All available at APS.

4. Arac, *Emergence*, 2–3.

5. I use the term *Irish Americans* to indicate that during the nineteenth century Irish immigrants were eligible to become naturalized U.S. citizens, and many members of the Fenian Brotherhood, discussed in chapter 4, were naturalized citizens. This contrasts with the status of Chinese immigrants in California, who, with some exceptions, were not eligible for citizenship.

6. See Hutchison, *Apples and Ashes*, 10–11. For more on the political culture of the Confederacy, see Faust, *Creation*; Escott, *After Secession*; McCurry, *Confederate Reckoning*; and Hanlon, *America's England*.

7. Kazanjian's use of the term *flashpoint* refers to a "process by which someone or something emerges or bursts into action or being ... *and* it refers to the powerful effects of that emergence or transformation" (*Colonizing Trick*, 27). Hereafter this source is cited parenthetically in the text.

8. Examples of classic works that exemplify this nationalist approach include McDowell, *American Studies*; Matthiessen, *American Renaissance*; Miller, *Errand*; and Bercovitch, *American Jeremiad*. For oft-cited examples of American political and intellectual history, see Parrington, *Main Currents*; Hartz, *Liberal Tradition*; Bailyn, *Ideological Origins*; Wood, *Creation of the American Republic*; Appleby, *Liberalism and Republican-*

ism; and McDonald, *States' Rights*. Examples of social historians and literary scholars who have focused on the political practices of a broad range of Americans include Wilentz, *Chants Democratic*; and Waldstreicher, *In the Midst*.

9. Gross, "Death Is So Permanent," 72. Fishkin describes the "transnational turn" and the growing scholarly focus on "contact zones" in more detail in "Crossroads of Culture." Influential studies on black nationalism include Stuckey, *Ideological Origins*; Moses, *Classical Black Nationalism* and *Golden Age*; and Gordon, *Black Identity*. For examples of studies of American Indian nations and nationalism, see Walker, *Indian Nation*; Konkle, *Writing*; Wilkinson, *Blood Struggle*; Weaver, Womack, and Warrior, *American Indian Literary Nationalism*; Weaver, *Other Words*; Rifkin, *Manifesting America*; and Nelson, *Progressive Traditions*.

10. Scholarship in this vein is extensive. For representative examples of transnational, hemispheric, and transamerican studies, see the work of Pease and Kaplan, Fluck, Gilroy, Levander and Levine, Rowe, Giles, Goudie, Huang, Gruesz, Brickhouse, and Schoolman. Levine's reassessment of American literary nationalism and his attention to "the vexed connections (and disconnections) between race and nation" have been of particular value to this book, especially his consideration of the contributions of African Americans to American literary nationalism and his examination of the "regional, trans-American, and transnational dimensions" of American literary nationalism" (*Dislocating*, 5). Schoolman frames *Abolitionist Geographies* as "an experiment in thinking about the archive of abolitionist spatial practice beyond the familiar stories of sectionalism and Manifest Destiny" and, in so doing, rethinks some of the assumptions of hemispheric approaches to literary study (1). As a challenge to the conflation of transatlantic and transnational, Rifkin recounts a discussion of Native nations and transnational American studies in *Manifesting America*, 22–25.

11. Deloria and Lytle, *The Nations Within*.

12. Hanlon, *America's England*, ix.

13. Ibid., 12.

14. Giles makes this point in *Atlantic Republic*, 72. Hanlon's discussion of his work as both exemplifying the Civil War focus that Giles critiques and offering the kind of international context for which Giles calls can be found in the introduction to *America's England*, 11–12.

15. For a survey of the concept of tribal sovereignty and its various meanings, see Cobb, "Understanding," 115–131. On the question of whether sovereignty has a cultural element in addition to its political and legal implications, see ibid., 118. Here she quotes Alfred's assertion that "[s]overeignty today ... is conceived as a wholly political-legal concept" (118). Cobb offers a definition of sovereignty as "a nation's power to self govern, to determine its own way of life, and to live that life—to whatever extent possible—free from interference," a definition that also, for Cobb, works for the concept of tribal sovereignty (118). Discussions of American Indian and tribal sovereignty include Deloria, "Intellectual Self-Determination"; Deloria and Lytle, *The Nations Within*; Vizenor, *Wordarrows*; Wilkins and Lomawaima, *Uneven Ground*; Wilkins, *American Indian Sovereignty*; Alfred, *Peace*; Kidwell and Velie, *Native American Studies*; Lyons,

"Rhetorical Sovereignty"; Bruyneel, *Third Space*; Byrd, *Transit of Empire*; and Barker, *Sovereignty Matters*. A number of scholars have helped to establish law and literature as a vibrant arena of literary studies. See especially Wald, *Constituting Americans*; Thomas, *Civic Myths*; Dimock, *Residues of Justice*; Crane, *Race, Citizenship, and Law*; Berlant, *Queen of America*; Cheyfitz, "Savage Law"; King, *Race, Theft, and Ethics*; and Rifkin, *Manifesting America*.

16. Greiman, *Democracy's Spectacle*, 48. Hereafter this source is cited parenthetically in the text.

17. DeLombard, *In the Shadow*, 4. Subsequent references are cited parenthetically in the text.

18. Elmer, *On Lingering*, 3–4. Hereafter this source is cited parenthetically in the text.

19. See Slauter, *The State*; and Beaumont, *Civic Constitution*.

20. Beaumont, *Civic Constitution*, 2, 6.

21. Foucault, "Nietzsche, Genealogy, History," 146.

22. Beaumont, *Civic Constitution*, xv.

23. For a sustained discussion of the development of identity politics and its relationship to formalism, see Sánchez-Arce, "Identity and Form." Space does not permit a comprehensive list of identity-based criticism. Representative examples of book-length scholarship from the late twentieth and twenty-first centuries include Gordon, *Black Identity*; Zafar, *We Wear the Mask*; Allen, *Blood Narrative*; Nelson, *Progressive Traditions*; Hertzberg, *Search*; Grice, *Negotiating Identities*; Jacobs, *Mexican American Literature*; Kerkering, *Poetics*; McCullough, *Regions of Identity*; and Armstrong, *Forging Gay Identities*.

24. For more on "territorial representation" as a form of "social inscription," see Deleuze and Guattari, *Anti-Oedipus*, 184–192.

25. These definitions are quoted and discussed in Hudson, "From 'Nation' to 'Race.'" Samuel Johnson's 1755 edition of his *Dictionary* defines *race* as "a family ascendancy," "a family descendancy," "a generation; a collective family," and "a particular breed." Similarly, the *Oxford English Dictionary* suggests that early uses of *nation* also evoked familial relations or descent, in addition to referencing a particular political institution. Hudson writes that British dictionaries such as Randle Cotgrave's *Dictionarie of the French and English Tongues* (1611) and Nathan Bailey's *An Universal Etymological Dictionary* (1721) contained definitions similar to those of Johnson. For more on natural history and the development of racial theory, see Wheeler, *Complexion of Race*. She argues that "skin color emerges as the most important component of racial identity in Britain during the third quarter of the eighteenth century" (9).

26. For a sustained discussion of Jefferson's thoughts on race and nation, see Onuf, *Jefferson's Empire*.

27. Rafinesque, "Primitive Black Nations of America."

28. Morton, *Crania Americana* and *Crania Aegyptiaca*. Numerous scholars have focused on Morton and the rise of scientific racism. For more on his categorization of races, see, for example, Menand, "Morton, Agassiz," 110; and Fabian, *Skull Collectors*, 83.

29. Tawil, *Making of Racial Sentiment*, argues for the use of the term *human variety* rather than *race* to describe conceptions of human difference in the eighteenth century (9–10).

30. Jordan's *White over Black* remains a central work on the development of constructions of race in America from the sixteenth century through the early nineteenth. On the fluidity of racial thought in early America and an exploration of the belief that people could become a different race, see Chiles, *Transformable Race*, 3–22. Dana Nelson (*The Word*, 13) locates the beginnings of the shift toward more essentialist notions of racial difference earlier, in the mid-seventeenth century. Overviews of the concept of creole degeneracy include Bauer and Mazzotti, *Creole Subjects*; and Kupperman, "Introduction." For a summary of Wheeler's argument, see her introduction to *Complexion of Race*, "The Empire of Climate," 1–48.

31. Emphasizing the link between territory and political form in contemporary understandings of the state, Robert Jackson defines a *state* as "a defined and delimited territory, with a permanent population, under the authority of a government" (*Sovereignty*, 5–6).

32. Anderson, *Imagined Communities*, 6; Waldstreicher, *In the Midst*, 142. For more on how Americans represented Benjamin Franklin in the formation of national culture, see Mulford, "Figuring Benjamin Franklin."

33. Smith, *National Identity*, 11. My thanks to Carla J. Mulford for introducing me to Smith's work.

34. Smith, *National Identity*, 12. See also Smith, *Ethnic Origins of Nations*. Smith and Anderson are just two voices in a vibrant and ongoing conversation about what nations are and how they developed. For alternative perspectives, see Balibar, "The Nation Form"; Wallerstein, "Construction of Peoplehood"; Gellner, *Nations and Nationalism*; and Hroch, "From National Movement."

35. For more on the construction of national identity through printed texts, holidays, and public events, see Waldstreicher, *In the Midst*.

36. Elliott, "Sovereignty," 194.

37. For an additional discussion of supremacy and the etymology of sovereignty, see Jackson, *Sovereignty*, 19–21.

38. Philpott, *Revolutions in Sovereignty*, 4.

39. Bederman, *Classical Foundations*, 109.

40. For more on the evolution of sovereignty, see Pocock, *Machiavellian Moment*; Robbins, *Eighteenth-Century Commonwealthman*; Clark, *Language of Liberty*; and Raustiala, *Does the Constitution*. MacMillan explores the ways in which conceptions of sovereignty were informed by imperialist efforts in *Sovereignty and Possession*. Elmer, *On Lingering*, focuses on racialized constructions of sovereignty that developed through encounters between Europeans, African Americans, and American Indians, while Rosen, *American Indians*, and Ford, *Settler Sovereignty*, focus on sovereignty and Native peoples. For overviews of conceptions of sovereignty, see Jackson, *Sovereignty*; and Bartleson, *Genealogy of Sovereignty*. In the twentieth and twenty-first centuries, a number of important theories of sovereignty have emerged that demonstrate a shift away

from an emphasis on the control of space. In *Political Theology*, Schmitt emphasizes the role of "decisionism" in sovereignty. Foucault's *Discipline and Punish* and "Society Must Be Defended" address various forms of power, including sovereign power, disciplinary power, and biopower. With the growth of global capitalism, Hardt and Negri argue in *Empire*, "sovereignty has taken a new form, composed of a series of national and supranational organisms united under a single logic of rule. This new global form of sovereignty is what we call Empire" (xii). Agamben has argued that sovereignty is wedded to power over what he calls "bare life" and the ability to decide on the "state of exception." In *Homo Sacer*, he contends, "[A]n act is sovereign when it realizes itself by simply taking away its own potentiality not to be, letting itself be, giving itself to itself" (46). See also Agamben, *State of Exception*.

41. Bailyn, *Ideological Origins*, 24.

42. Bailyn, *Ideological Origins*, 26–27, discusses sources for American understandings of sovereignty. Bederman discusses sovereignty and classical thought in *Classical Origins*.

43. "Popular Sovereignty," in Tocqueville, *Democracy in America*, 1:63. For a sustained reading of Tocqueville and popular sovereignty, see Greiman, *Democracy's Spectacle*, 36–74.

44. Brown, *Walled States*, 21–22.

45. It is related to another term, *dominium*, defined as "the right to possess and rule territory" within a given jurisdiction. For more, see MacMillan, *Sovereignty and Possession*, 6.

46. Blackstone, *Commentaries*, 1:49. For more on Blackstone's influence, see Lutz, "Relative Influence."

47. Blackstone, *Commentaries*, 4:114. For more on Blackstone's conceptions of sovereignty, see Lubert, "Sovereignty and Liberty."

48. 6 Geor. III, c. 12 (1766), qtd. in Kettner, *Development*, 132. Hereafter references to Kettner are cited parenthetically in the text. In *Ideological Origins*, Bailyn observes, "The condition of British America by the end of the Seven Years' War was therefore anomalous: extreme decentralization of authority within an empire presumably ruled by a single, absolute, undivided sovereign" (204).

49. Otis, *Rights*, 17.

50. Otis, *Vindication*, 18.

51. Bailyn, *Ideological Origins*, 205. The current thinking Bailyn mentions is a quotation from Grotius. For more on the logic of Otis's arguments, see ibid., 205–207.

52. Otis, *Vindication*, 4.

53. Bland qtd. in Bailyn, *Ideological Origins*, 211.

54. Dickinson, *Letters*, 12–13.

55. Ibid., 21.

56. Wood, *Creation of the American Republic*, 352. Hereafter this source is cited parenthetically in the text.

57. Bailyn, *Ideological Origins*, 209.

58. Seabury qtd. ibid., 223.

59. Galloway, "Reply," qtd. ibid.
60. Iredell, *To the Inhabitants*, 217.
61. Ibid., 219.
62. Johnstone, *Governor Johnston[e]'s Speech*, 13.
63. Clinton, *Brief History*, qtd. in Bederman, *Classical Foundations*, 104.
64. Bederman, *Classical Foundations*, 105.
65. For a reading of the Articles of Confederation, see Wood, *Creation of the American Republic*, 354–363.
66. Publius, "No. XX," in *Federalist Papers*, 102.
67. "To George Washington," 1:287.
68. For more, see Barksdale, *The Lost State*.
69. Qtd. in Bederman, *Classical Foundations*, 133.
70. Publius, "No. XV," in *Federalist Papers*, 74.
71. Merriam, *History of American Political Theories*, 259; "To Thomas Jefferson" (24 October 1787), 347.
72. Adams qtd. in Walsh, *Political Science*, 267. During the ratification debates, even while many conceded that sovereignty could be defined as supreme authority, arguments arose among representatives of the various states about where sovereignty resided. McDonald, *E Pluribus Unum*, recounts that "[s]ome held that sovereignty, the whole power, devolved upon Congress, others that it devolved upon the states, still others that it devolved upon the whole people, the people of the states, and even the people of the towns" (190).
73. As Clark notes in *Language of Liberty*, James Wilson, a Supreme Court justice and professor of law at the College of Philadelphia, "identified as 'the *vital* principle' of the American constitution the doctrine that 'the supreme or sovereign power of the society resides in the citizens at large'; a doctrine that Blackstone, denying Locke, 'treated as a political chimera, existing only in the minds of some theorists, but, in practice, inconsistent with the dispensation of any government upon earth'" (129).
74. *Chisholm v. Georgia*, 434.
75. Madison, "Sovereignty," 4:394.
76. "Letter from V. du C— to His Father," 296.
77. Ibid.
78. Tocqueville, *Democracy in America*, 182. Subsequent references to this source are cited parenthetically in the text.
79. Calhoun, *A Disquisition*, 146.
80. As Kettner has suggested, Anglo-American formulations of popular sovereignty begged the question: "Who are 'the People'?" (*Development*, 285).
81. Some examples are discussed in Tsai's *America's Forgotten Constitutions*. Tsai's work focuses on eight written constitutions, produced by groups ranging from the Republic of Indian Stream (1832–1835) to the Pacific Northwest Homeland (2006).
82. Paine, *Rights of Man*, 89.
83. Goldie and Wokler, *Cambridge History*, 610.
84. Beeman, *Penguin Guide*, 136.

85. Paley, *Essay*, 1.
86. Jameson, *Political Unconscious*, 84.
87. Adams, "Thoughts on Government," 235. Adams is quoting Livy via James Harrington here. See Sellers, *American Republicanism*, 127.
88. Paine, *Four Letters*, 15.
89. *Constitution of the American Anti-Slavery Society*, Articles 2, 3. For more on the Hebrew Ladies Sewing Circle, see *Constitution and By-Laws*.
90. Here I expand on a point made by Slauter in *The State as a Work of Art* that constitutions were texts that "created the conditions for their own preservation" (25). He goes on to say that "written constitutions created governments that would guarantee the various rights declared on paper not simply because they were on paper but because the texts . . . explicitly created mechanisms for protecting those rights (a government that checked itself) or because the constitution had created conditions under which citizens could rely on extratextual protections (such as the scale of the republic)" (25).
91. Jameson, *Archaeologies*, 36.
92. As Tsai has noted in the introduction to *America's Forgotten Constitutions*, "In establishing the American republic, the Founders unleashed a pair of seductive ideas: popular sovereignty and written constitutionalism" (2).
93. For more on the Confederate Constitution, see McCurry, *Confederate Reckoning*, 78; Currie, "Through the Looking-Glass"; and Tsai, *America's Forgotten Constitutions*, 118–151.
94. By "domestic" I mean that most such confrontations, even those with European nations, happened in North America. An obvious exception would be the Barbary Wars. My understanding of extraterritoriality is drawn from Raustiala, who defines it as instances in which "domestic law extends beyond sovereign borders" (*Does the Constitution*, 5).
95. Albrecht-Crane, "Style, Stutter," 143. Deleuze and Guattari elaborate on *territorialization* and *reterritorialization* in *A Thousand Plateaus* and *Anti-Oedipus*.
96. I am not the first to note the connections between Indian Removal and African colonization. See, for example, Guyatt, "Outskirts"; and Apap, "Let No Man." In this book, I expand on this connection and chart the transition from Removal to management and containment.
97. Here and elsewhere, I draw my understanding of the terms *virtual* and *actual* from the work of Lévy and his reading of Deleuze. Lévy asserts that the "virtual is by no means the opposite of the real. On the contrary, it is a fecund and powerful mode of being that expands the process of creation, opens up the future, injects a core of meaning beneath the platitude of immediate physical presence" (*Becoming Virtual*, 16).

Chapter One. "In the Heart of So Powerful a Nation"

1. I draw the phrase "securing [of] the Revolution" from Buel, *Securing*.
2. Levine, *Dislocating*, 67. Subsequent references to this source are cited parenthetically in the text.

3. Arac, *Emergence*, 3.

4. Here I draw on Arac's use of the phrase "national narrative" in *Emergence* to refer to fictional and nonfictional works that "told the story of the nation's colonial beginnings and looked forward to its future as a model for the world" (2–3).

5. The chapter in Lawrence, *Studies in Classic American Literature*, on James Fenimore Cooper's *Leather-Stocking Tales* is an early example of this line of inquiry. More recent studies include Berkhofer, *White Man's Indian*; Deloria, *Playing Indian*; Scheckel, *Insistence*; and Bellin, *Demon of the Continent*.

6. Tawil, *Making of Racial Sentiment*, 2.

7. Levine summarizes critical assessments of Cooper's frontier novels in "Temporality." See, in particular, 164–165. He cites the work of Bellin, Gaul, Cheyfitz, and Scheckel as examples of scholarship that argues for Cooper's endorsement of Removal based on the "temporal overlap" between his fiction and the legal and political efforts to dispossess Native peoples (164). Levine counters that Cooper's contemporaries did not draw similar conclusions and notes that Cooper was often critiqued for his overly sympathetic portrayals of Native people. Through his reading of *The Deerslayer*, Levine concludes that "there is much in the Leatherstocking series that voices clear opposition to whites' racist violence against the Indians" (165).

8. Throughout this chapter, I discuss the Cherokee Nation led by Principal Chief John Ross (sometimes referred to as the Eastern Cherokees) and the "Old Settlers" or "Western Cherokees" who migrated to places such as present-day Arkansas, Texas, and Mexico in the decades before the Trail of Tears and created their own government. As Justice notes, "Today there are three federally recognized Cherokee governments—the Cherokee Nation and the United Keetoowah Band of Cherokee Indians in Oklahoma, and the Eastern Band of Cherokee Indians in North Carolina—with a combined citizenry of over 250,000" (*Our Fire Survives*, 23). As for the relationship of these three governments to their nineteenth-century predecessors, Justice writes that the Cherokee Nation in Oklahoma traces its origins to the emigrants led by Ross, while the United Keetoowah Band descends from the Old Settlers. The Eastern Band in North Carolina is composed of the descendants of those who stayed in the East (223–224n3).

9. Wald, *Constituting Americans*, 28.

10. While the Cherokees were the first to draft a written constitution, other Native nations soon followed. The first Choctaw Constitution was ratified in 1847, the Chickasaw Nation produced its first written constitution in 1860, and the Constitution of the Muskokee Nation was published in 1868.

11. For more on Knox's policy, dubbed "expansion with honor," see Denson, *Demanding*, 16–17. On the function of treaties, Berkhofer writes that early negotiations between the United States and American Indian peoples had two concerns: "the extinction of native title in favor of White exploitation of native lands and resources and the transformation of native lifestyles into copies of approved White models" (*White Man's Indian*, 135).

12. Deloria and Wilkins, *Tribes*, 26.

13. Ibid.

14. Ibid., 23. On the ways in which treaty negotiations testified to the U.S. government's ability to engage in international diplomacy and the supremacy of federal sovereignty, see Rifkin, *Manifesting America*, 41.

15. Rifkin, *Manifesting America*, 41.

16. Yarbrough, *Race*, 70.

17. The term *savage nation* is used frequently in eighteenth- and nineteenth-century Anglo-American representations of Native Americans, including Adair, *History*; and Heckewelder, *History, Manners, and Customs*.

18. Rifkin, *Manifesting America*, 48. For more on "imperial interpellation" and "translation," see ibid.; and Cheyfitz *Poetics of Imperialism*.

19. See, for example, Perdue, *Cherokee Editor*, 32.

20. For work that highlights the contrast between mixed-bloods and full-bloods, see scholarship by Perdue and by McLoughlin. It is worth noting, Justice suggests, that Cherokees traditionally defined membership in their polity in terms of matrilineal descent rather than according to racial standards of blood quantum. Thus, they did not distinguish between "full-blood" and "mixed-blood" people in the same fashion as did their white American contemporaries, who sought to map their own notions of racial hierarchy onto Native people. On the instability and complexity of terms such as *full-blood* and *mixed-blood*, see *Our Fire Survives*, xv. Nelson, *Progressive Traditions*, reminds us that "plenty of Cherokee mixed-bloods opposed removal, and more full-bloods than we imagine favored leaving." He also cites the example of the Old Settlers, "many of whom are often accounted among the most traditional members of the tribe, who had already departed for the Arkansas territory in the early 1800s" (149).

21. Nelson, *Progressive Traditions*, 138.

22. Justice coins the term "Chickamauga consciousness," which is named for "the nationalist resistance movement of the late eighteenth and early nineteenth centuries that was devoted to armed response to U.S. violence and expansion into ancestral territories" (*Our Fire Survives*, 30). This group was led by Tsiyu Gansini (Dragging Canoe). When Justice talks of Ross's "Chickamauga rhetoric," he is highlighting the principal chief's commitment to nationalism and resistance.

23. McLoughlin, *Cherokee Renascence*, xvii.

24. For the changes in Cherokee constructions of citizenship in 1809, see McLoughlin, Conser, and McLoughlin, *Cherokee Ghost Dance*, 75–77.

25. In her reading of the 1827 Constitution, Ford argues, "More than any other document, the Cherokee Constitution shows the extent to which Cherokees participated in, and to important degrees spurred on, the discourse of territoriality in Georgia and the United States" (*Settler Sovereignty*, 156). Ford highlights the role that the Cherokees played in redefining "Indian Country" as "a geographic space governed by Indian law" through their emphasis on defining the territorial boundaries of the nation (130).

26. "Constitution of the Cherokee Nation," *Cherokee Phoenix* 1.1 (28 February 1828), available in the Ayer Collection.

27. "Constitution of the State of Georgia," in *Digest*, 906.

28. Garrison discusses this interpretation of the commerce clause in chapters 4, 5, and 6 of *Legal Ideology*.

29. "Constitution of the Cherokee Nation."

30. For more on Cherokee conceptions of race in the nineteenth century and exclusions of African Americans from citizenship, see Yarbrough, *Race*, 11.

31. "Constitution of the Cherokee Nation."

32. Vattel, § 5, "Unequal Alliance," in *Law of Nations*, 1:1. Like Blackstone's *Commentaries*, Vattel's *Law of Nations* was cited frequently in the political debates of the nineteenth century in the United States. While his definition of *sovereignty* as indivisible "political authority" was not new, Vattel contributed a number of key ideas about the ways in which states might ally themselves with one another without sacrificing their individual sovereignty. Examples included not only a federal republic, in which "several sovereign and independent states may unite themselves together by a perpetual confederacy," but also the relationship that weaker states might form with stronger ones for the purposes of protection. Such states, he argued, do not cease to be sovereign even though they might make various concessions to the stronger state— tribute, military support, and so forth. He also envisioned a more extreme situation wherein one nation might transfer its sovereignty, according to the terms of an agreement, to a more powerful nation. See Vattel, *Law of Nations*, 1:1. For more on the uses of Vattel in American political thought, see Bederman, *Classical Foundations*, 109–110.

33. Walker, *Indian Nation*, 113.

34. Konkle, *Writing*, 43.

35. *Caldwell v. Alabama* qtd. in Garrison, *Legal Ideology*, 164.

36. Banner, *How the Indians Lost*, 171.

37. Qtd. in Dale and Litton, *Cherokee Cavaliers*, xv.

38. The legacy of the Yazoo fraud haunted Georgia politics for nearly twenty years after the cession of lands to the federal government. For more on the Yazoo fraud, see Abernathy, *The South*; Lamplugh, *Politics*; Phillips, *Georgia and State Rights*; and Young, "Exercise of Sovereignty." Discussing *Fletcher v. Peck* as a prelude to the Cherokee cases, Norgren, *Cherokee Cases*, asserts that Chief Justice John Marshall "invented the category of occupancy title and needed a legal justification for his confection" (89).

39. Lumpkin, *Removal*, 55. While published after the Cherokee Removal had been effected, this work constitutes a collection of many of Lumpkin's speeches, correspondence, and public discourse on the Cherokees in Georgia, much of which was published during his tenure as a congressman.

40. Ibid., 55–56.

41. Konkle, *Writing*, 44.

42. Forsyth, "Legislature of Georgia," *Niles' Weekly Register* 35.898 (1828): 222, APS.

43. Lumpkin, *Removal*, 189.

44. Prucha, *Great Father*, 189.

45. "The Indians," *Southern Recorder*, 20 March 1830, MHN.

46. "The Georgia Question," *Southern Recorder*, 20 January 1831, MHN.

47. "An Examination of the Cherokee Question," rptd. in *Federal Union*, 19 April 1832. The original title of this article as it appeared in the *Washington Globe* was "An Examination of the Indian Question" (31 March 1832). Available through MHN.

48. The *Western Recorder* reprinted Jeremiah Evarts's William Penn essays in 1830,

including No. XXIII, which engages the argument of imperium in imperio. See "Present Crisis in the Condition of the American Indians: No. XXIII," *Western Recorder* 7.5 (2 February 1830): 1. The same newspaper also reprinted from the *New York Observer*, with the signatures of several men, Evarts's *Brief View* as "Indian Claims," *Western Recorder* 6.50 (15 December 1829): 1–2. Both texts are available through APS. For an overview of Cass's response to Evarts in the *North American Review*, see Andrew, *From Revivals to Removal*, 206–207.

49. "Indian Colonization," *Columbian Star and Christian Index* 1.11 (12 September 1829): 171–172, APS.

50. Some scholars have made the link between the logics of African colonization and the Indian Removal policy, which, as Guyatt notes, have historically been studied separately ("Outskirts," 987). See also Apap, "Let No Man."

51. Eaton, "The Secretary of War to the Cherokee Delegation [copy]," *Niles' Weekly Register* 36.926 (13 June 1829): 258, APS.

52. Ibid., 259.

53. Jackson, "President Jackson on Indian Removal," 47. Hereafter, this source is cited parenthetically in the text.

54. Perdue and Green, *Cherokee Nation*, 63. For more on Jackson's emphasis on the bill and the debate that followed, see ibid., 61–63.

55. Ibid., 61–62.

56. Evarts, "No. XXIII," in *Cherokee Removal*, 180. All references to Evarts's writings are from this edition.

57. A writer for the *American Monthly Magazine* likewise referred to arguments regarding the "inconvenience" of a Cherokee *imperium*, suggesting this was part of a broader discourse. See "Indian Reports in Congress, Indian Speeches, &c," *American Monthly Magazine* 2.9 (December 1830): 610, APS.

58. Evarts, "No. XXIII," in *Cherokee Removal*, 179–180.

59. Evarts, "No. XV," ibid., 128.

60. Evarts, *Brief View*, 204.

61. Ibid., 205–206.

62. Campbell, *Memorial*, 14.

63. Ibid.

64. "The *North American Review* for Jan. 1830," 3:154–155.

65. Evarts, *Brief View*, 204.

66. *Cherokee Nation v. Georgia*, 3.

67. Ibid., 9.

68. Ibid., 43.

69. Ibid., 130.

70. Ibid., 131.

71. Garrison, *Legal Ideology*, 132.

72. *Cherokee Nation v. Georgia*, 130–131 (emphases in original).

73. Ibid., 161.

74. Wald, *Constituting Americans*, 24.

75. The dissenting opinion was attributed to Thompson, while a note at the end indicated that Justice Story concurred with this opinion. Subsequent references will be made to Thompson's opinion with the understanding that it also represents the thoughts of Justice Story.

76. *Cherokee Nation v. Georgia*, 199.

77. In the chapter "The Removal Rhetoric of Elias Boudinot and John Ross," Nelson presents the construction of Boudinot and Ross as embodying a binary of assimilationist-traditionalist, particularly as they approached the Removal crisis. He examines the ways in which both figures engaged rhetorics and practices that can be identified with "progressive" and "traditional" approaches. See Nelson, *Progressive Traditions*, 165–200. Additional examples of scholarship on Ross and Boudinot are Schneider, "Boudinot's Change"; Teuton, "Cities of Refuge"; Ross-Mulkey, "The *Cherokee Phoenix*."

78. Ross, "Annual Message" (24 October 1831), in *PJR*, 1:229.

79. "To Hugh Montgomery" (20 July 1830), in *PJR*, 1:193.

80. Ibid.

81. Konkle, *Writing*, 44.

82. "Annual Message" (13 October 1828), in *PJR*, 1:142.

83. Editorial, *Cherokee Phoenix* (17 June 1829), in Perdue, *Cherokee Editor*, 108.

84. "Constitution of the Cherokee Nation."

85. "To the Senate and House of Representatives" (27 February 1829), in *PJR*, 1:155.

86. Editorial, *Cherokee Phoenix* (21 December 1831), in Perdue, *Cherokee Editor*, 145. Like Hosea Easton and others, Boudinot cited Acts 17:26 as a refutation of racist arguments for polygenesis. See Boudinot, Editorial, *Cherokee Phoenix* (17 September 1831), in Perdue, *Cherokee Editor*, 140.

87. Ross and his followers are sometimes referred to as the National or Patriot Party, while the Ridge-Boudinot faction is also known as the Treaty Party because of their involvement with the 1835 Treaty of New Echota.

88. "To Hugh Montgomery" (16 April 1828), in *PJR*, 1:136.

89. Perdue and Green, *Cherokee Nation*, 20.

90. "John Ridge to Major Ridge and Others" (10 March 1835), in Dale and Litton, *Cherokee Cavaliers*, 12. On Ross's offer to Jackson, see Perdue and Green, *Cherokee Nation*, 103.

91. "To Messrs. Ross and Others" (5 February 1836), in Perdue, *Cherokee Editor*, 198.

92. Editorial, *Cherokee Phoenix* (28 January 1829), in Perdue, *Cherokee Editor*, 105. Perdue notes that while Boudinot had initially opposed Removal, by the spring of 1832 his name was included on a pro-Removal petition. For more on Boudinot's changing stance, see Perdue, *Cherokee Editor*, 25–26.

93. Editorial, *Cherokee Phoenix* (28 January 1829), in Perdue, *Cherokee Editor*, 105.

94. "To the Editor of the *Cherokee Phoenix*," in Perdue, *Cherokee Editor*, 172.

95. Ibid., 174.

96. Ross, "An Address to a General Council of the Cherokees" (10 June 1839), in *PJR*, 1:712–713.

97. "To Ross and George Lowry" (14 June 1839), in *PJR*, 1:714–715.

98. "Imperium in Imperio," *Cherokee Advocate* (10 February 1882).

99. Maxey qtd. in Burton, *Indian Territory*, 44. For more on the bill, see ibid., 44–45. The *Cherokee Advocate* was published by the Cherokee Nation from 1844 to 1906 and had several different editors, including members of the Boudinot and Ross families. For a brief overview of the newspaper's history, see Littlefield and Parins, *American Indian and Alaska Native Newspapers and Periodicals*, 63–75.

100. The phrase also appeared as part of debates about the political status of Cherokee people in the Republic of Texas in the 1830s. For more, see Clark, *Chief Bowles*, 92.

Chapter Two. "And Ethiopia Shall Stretch Forth Her Hands"

1. Kennedy and Parker, *Official Report*, 19.

2. Ibid. While the accuracy of the document and the nature of the conspiracy have been debated by later scholars, the *Official Report* conveys Southern whites' deep-seated fear of slave rebellion and the potential of free black people to foment such rebellion. For more on the scholarly debate surrounding the conspiracy and the extent to which the *Official Report* can be said to represent the perspectives and actions of Vesey and his coconspirators, see Levine, *Dislocating*, 80–87.

3. Egerton, *He Shall Go Out Free*, 130–131.

4. Rifkin, *Manifesting America*, 38.

5. Act of 6 March 1820, chap. 22, § 8, 3 Stat. 548 (1820).

6. For a summary of the debates over Missouri's entrance into the Union, see Levine, *Dislocating*, 74–80; Smith, *Civic Ideals*, 175–181; and Hammond, *Slavery*, 55–75.

7. Smith, *Civic Ideals*, 175.

8. Qtd. in "Missouri—Citizenship," in *Abridgment of the Debates of Congress*, 7:39.

9. Qtd. ibid., 692.

10. Jefferson, "Laws," in *Notes*, 185. For more on definitions of slaves as "chattel property," which have their roots in ancient Rome, see Davis, "Slavery," 124–126.

11. News of the Gabriel plot prompted the Virginia assembly to suggest that James Madison, then the governor of Virginia, communicate secretly with Thomas Jefferson as to whether or not "persons obnoxious to the laws or dangerous to the peace of society may be removed." This led to a series of closed-door communications about the possibility of removing free African Americans. Not long after the Nat Turner rebellion, the state of Maryland authorized the acquisition of land in Africa for the colonization of free blacks. See "Colonization of People of Color from Virginia," in *American State Papers*, 37:464–465. Ford offers an overview of Virginia's response to the Gabriel plot and Maryland's efforts in the wake of the Nat Turner rebellion in *Deliver Us from Evil*, 88, 359.

12. "Facts Respecting Slavery: An Extract," *Boston Recorder and Religious Telegraph* 11.51 (22 December 1826), 204, APS.

13. *An Essay of the Late Institution*, 34.

14. Hall, *Earth into Property*, 99.

15. "St. Domingo," *Literary Magazine* 2.15 (December 1804): 655, APS.

16. Ibid., 657.
17. Seabrook, *Concise View*, 4.
18. Staudenraus, *African Colonization*, 104.
19. The ACS was inspired in part by a group of men in Washington who were discussing the ideas of Thomas Jefferson. Its early proponents included Robert Finley (credited with founding the organization), Charles Fenton Mercer, Elias B. Caldwell, Henry Clay, Francis Scott Key, and Bushrod Washington. In 1816, Paul Cuffee, a businessman and activist of African American and American Indian ancestry, led a group of thirty-eight people from America to Sierra Leone, a British colony. For a brief summary of Cuffee and the rise of the ACS, see Howe, *Political Culture*, 135–136. More on the history of Sierra Leone and the involvement of Olaudah Equiano can be found in Carretta, *Equiano*. The ACS assisted with the foundation of Liberia, the American answer to Sierra Leone, in 1821–1822 and was involved with the colony until it declared its independence in 1847. For the history of colonization, see Staudenraus, *African Colonization*; and Castiglia, *Interior States*, 101–135. Onuf discusses Jefferson's conception of an "African nation" and his thoughts on colonization in *Jefferson's Empire*, 147–188.
20. Charles Carroll Harper, "Address of C. C. Harper," *ARCJ* 2.6 (August 1826): 188–189, APS.
21. Rev. Stephen Foster, "An Essay for the Fourth of July," *ARCJ* 3.12 (February 1828): 374, APS.
22. "Annual Meeting of the American Colonization Society," *ARCJ* 2.11 (January 1827): 329, APS.
23. "Colonization and Anti-Slavery Societies," *Christian Watchman* 14.31 (2 August 1833): 132, APS. Hereafter this source is cited parenthetically in the text.
24. "Annual Meeting," *ARCJ* 2.11 (January 1827): 329, APS.
25. Ibid., 329.
26. "Annual Meeting of the Colonization Society," *ARCJ* 1.1 (March 1825): 16, APS.
27. "Colonization Society of New Jersey," *ARCJ* 1.9 (November 1825): 281, APS. As Kazanjian argues in *Colonizing Trick*, such discourse suggested the workings of a "racial governmentality," an attempt to regulate populations that "renders the very idea of a racially and nationally codified population as that which it seeks to address" (115). He writes that "colonized black Americans are to be objects of an experiment in Enlightenment governmentality; they are to be rendered, represented, and maintained 'free'" by the United States (123). The imperialist dimensions of women's colonization literature has been noted by Ryan, "Errand into Africa"; Kaplan, "Manifest Domesticity"; and Taketani, "Postcolonial Liberia." Kazanjian also discusses the imperialist logics of colonization in *Colonizing Trick*, 89–138.
28. Castiglia, *Interior States*, 104.
29. Ibid.
30. McDonald devotes a chapter to what he calls the "Era of Mixed Feelings," and Sean Wilentz offers a chapter called "Era of Bad Feelings." See McDonald, *States' Rights*, 71–96; and Wilentz, *Rise of American Democracy*, 182–217. They discuss issues such as the financial panic of 1819; continuing debates about the extension of slavery

into the West; disagreements over the national bank, paper money, and protective tariffs; and various other rifts that occurred between the War of 1812 and the election of Andrew Jackson in 1828.

31. Adams qtd. in Walsh, *Political Science*, 267.

32. On this kind of constitutive rhetoric, McGee writes: "'The people' therefore are not objectively real in the sense that they exist as a collective entity in nature; rather, they are a fiction dreamed by an advocate and infused with an artificial, rhetorical reality by the agreement of an audience to participate in a collective fantasy" ("In Search," 240).

33. My use of the term *protonationalist* here is drawn from Moses's *Classical Black Nationalism*. He argues that what he calls "classical black nationalism ... reached its fullest expression in the years from 1850 to 1925" and can be "defined as the effort of African Americans to create a sovereign nation-state and formulate an ideological basis for a concept of a national culture" (2). Although he credits Robert Alexander Young, David Walker, and Maria Stewart with attempting to forge an image of African Americans as a people (or nation), the fact that they did not advocate the formation of a separate nation prevents them from being classified as classical black nationalists according to his definition.

34. Gordon, *Black Identity*, 5.

35. Dawson, "Black Public Sphere," 382.

36. Moses has written and edited several standard works on black nationalism, including *Classical Black Nationalism* and *Golden Age*. Other important considerations of black nationalism include Stuckey, *Ideological Origins*; Adeleke, *UnAfrican Americans*; and Van Deburg, *Modern Black Nationalism*. On transnational and transatlantic literatures and cultures, see Gilroy, *Black Atlantic*. On race, nation, and cosmopolitanism, see Nwankwo, *Black Cosmopolitanism*; and Aravamudan, *Tropicopolitans*. For a reading of cosmopolitanism more broadly, see Appiah's *Cosmopolitanism*.

37. See Brooks, "Prince Hall," 197–216. Brooks focuses explicitly on what she views as an early chapter in the history of black nationalism and Ethopianism: the work of Prince Hall and John Marrant. She examines how these ideas flourished in the context of Masonic orders. For more on Haynes, see Saillant, *Black Puritan, Black Republican*. For more on the early history of black nationalism and its major figures, see Gordon, *Black Identity*, 73. He notes that Bustill was a former slave and a member of the Free African Society who became Philadelphia's first African American schoolteacher. John Marrant can be considered the first ordained African American preacher in the United States. Prince Hall founded Boston's African Masonic Lodge. Liele "founded the first black Baptist churches in Georgia" and was succeeded by Bryan (Gordon, *Black Identity*, 73). Absalom Jones and Richard Allen were leaders of Philadelphia's African American community and founders of the Bethel African American Methodist Episcopal Church.

38. Hammon, "A Winter Piece," 4.

39. Wheatley, "On Being Brought," 13.

40. See Hammon, "A Winter Piece," 8. For more on Hammon's theological perspectives, see May, *Evangelism and Resistance*, 24–48. He notes the influence that Ham-

mon's Anglican masters had on his thinking: "Hammon's views on slavery, along with other religious signposts, signal the influence of colonial Anglican traditions. At the root of Hammon's Calvinism lay a strong emphasis on an interpretation of the strict doctrine of God's complete sovereignty: God controlled everything, and if blacks lived under the yoke of slavery, then that was the will of God and would not change unless his plan called for it" (26).

41. Brooks's concept of a "usable past" was developed in his 1918 essay, "On Creating."

42. Oson, *A Search for Truth*, n.p.

43. Newman, *Freedom's Prophet*, refers to Allen and others in his subtitle as "Black Founding Fathers" and discusses the formation of the Free African Society, which he describes as "one of the first examples of the idea that free blacks were a nation within a nation"(61). For more on Prince Hall and Freemasonry, see "Prince Hall," in Newman, Rael, and Lapsansky, *Pamphlets of Protest*, 44.

44. For discussions of the development of African American churches and periodicals, see Woodson, *History*; Lincoln, *Black Church*; Campbell, *Songs of Zion*; Bailey, *Race Patriotism*; and Levine, *Dislocating*, 87–95. Moss writes of African American education in *Schooling Citizens*, while Mjagkij provides entries on various nineteenth-century philanthropic organizations and mutual aid societies in *Organizing Black America*.

45. On the importance of print to African American protest, see Newman, Rael, and Lapsansky, *Pamphlets of Protest*, 1.

46. Walker, "Address," 79–80. Levine discusses Walker's call for readers of the *Appeal* to "see" his address printed in *Freedom's Journal*. See Levine, *Dislocating*, 101.

47. Walker, "Address," 81.

48. Ibid.

49. Ibid., 82.

50. Bruce discusses Grice's role in the conventions in *Origins*, 177.

51. For more on the development of the Negro Convention Movement, see Bell, *Survey*, 10–37. Newman, Rael, and Lapsansky use the term "quasi-political bodies" in their introduction to William Hamilton's "Address to the National Convention of 1834," in *Pamphlets of Protest*, 110.

52. Bell, *Minutes*.

53. Yingling, "No One Who Reads," 316–317.

54. "Title of This Journal," *Colored American*, 4 March 1837, in "One Year of the *Colored American*," National Humanities Center, http://nationalhumanitiescenter.org/pds/maai/community/text6/coloredamerican.

55. Ibid.

56. "Minutes and Proceedings ... First Annual Convention," in *MP*, 4–5.

57. Douglass, "Letter to C. H. Chase," *North Star*, 9 February 1849, in Foner, *Frederick Douglass*, 128.

58. Phan, *Bonds*, 2.

59. "Declaration of Sentiment," in *Minutes ... Fourth Annual Convention*, in *MP*, 29. Hereafter this source is cited parenthetically in the text.

60. "To the American People," in *Minutes . . . Fifth Annual Convention*, in *MP*, 25. Hereafter this source is cited parenthetically in the text.

61. In his discussion of the development of transatlantic political discourse, Clark notes that the "two dominant idioms of discourse . . . were law and religion" (*Language of Liberty*, 11).

62. Bercovitch, *American Jeremiad*, 4.

63. Miller, *New England Mind*, 1:14.

64. Bercovitch, *American Jeremiad*, 48.

65. Moses, *Black Messiahs*, 30–31. Subsequent references to this source are cited parenthetically in the text.

66. Howard-Pitney, *African American Jeremiad*, 13.

67. Gordon, *Black Identity*, 33.

68. Hall, "Charge," in Newman, Rael, and Lapsansky, *Pamphlets of Protest*, 45.

69. Saunders, "An Address" (1818), in Newman, Rael, and Lapsansky, *Pamphlets of Protest*, 82.

70. Ibid.

71. Raboteau, "Ethiopia," 401.

72. Smith, *Conjuring Culture*, 58.

73. Gillman, *Blood Talk*, 50. See also Sundquist, *Wake the Nations*, 560–561; and Moses, *Golden Age*, 23–24.

74. Young, *Ethiopian Manifesto*, 86. All quotations are from the version edited by Newman, Rael, and Lapsansky and are cited parenthetically in the text.

75. For a discussion of Walker's engagement with the U.S. Constitution, see Kazanjian, *Colonizing Trick*, 9.

76. Walker, *Appeal*, xxvi. All references to Walker's *Appeal* are to the version edited by Sean Wilentz and are hereafter cited parenthetically in the text.

77. Linebaugh and Rediker, *Many-Headed Hydra*, 299. Discussions of Walker as a black nationalist can be found in Moses, *Golden Age*; Gordon, *Black Identity*; and Levine, *Dislocating*. An article by Apap focuses on Walker's "nationalistic geographical imagination" ("Let No Man," 322).

78. The full title of the *Appeal* refers to the "coloured citizens of the world" while Walker referred to the "coloured citizens of this country" in article 4 (47).

79. Stewart, "An Address" (27 February 1833), in Richardson, *Maria W. Stewart*, 58.

80. Moses, *Classical Black Nationalism*, 90.

81. Ibid., 69. Yet, for Moses, Walker did not fit the definition of "classical black nationalism" because he did not argue for "a separate nation-state."

82. In the nineteenth century, *people* was often used interchangeably with the word *nation* to indicate "the whole body of citizens of a country, regarded as the source of political power or as the basis of society; *esp.* those qualified to vote in a democratic state, the electorate," according to the *Oxford English Dictionary*.

83. Moses, *Classical Black Nationalism*, 68.

84. Glaude's *Exodus!* offers a book-length study of the importance of the Exodus

story to nineteenth-century African Americans. See also Smith, *Conjuring Culture*, 55–80.

85. Apap, "Let No Man," 321.
86. Ibid., 322, 329–330.
87. Stewart, "Address," in Richardson, *Maria W. Stewart*, 64.
88. Stewart, "Religion," ibid., 34–35.
89. Stewart, "Address," ibid., 64. Adeleke mentions Walker's work in the context of the "labor theory of nationality" in *UnAfrican Americans* (39). He characterizes the work of later writers—such as Martin Delany, Henry Highland Garnett, and William Wells Brown—as engaging this theory.
90. Easton, *Treatise*, in Price and Stewart, *"To Heal the Scourge,"* 101. Subsequent references to Easton's work are to this edition.
91. Easton, *Treatise*, 67. Saunders stated, "And now, in the true spirit of the religion of that beneficent Parent, who has made of one blood all nations of men who dwell upon the face of the whole earth, many persons of different regions and various nations, have been led to the contemplation of the interesting relations in which the human race stand to each other" ("An Address," in Newman, Rael, and Lapsansky, *Pamphlets of Protest*, 82).

Chapter Three. *"Space for Action"*

1. Delany to Douglass (18 April 1853), in *Martin Delany*, 232. As Delany noted in this letter, he originally made this statement in a letter dated 22 March 1853. For critical discussions of *Uncle Tom's Cabin*, race, nation, and genealogy, see Weinstein, *Family*, 24–25; Riss, "Racial Essentialism"; Dillon, *Gender of Freedom*, 225–235; and Jackson, *American Blood*, 74–75. For a reassessment of the novel's relationship to colonization, see Schoolman, *Abolitionist Geographies*, 144–160.
2. On Delany's use of imperium in imperio to reconfigure current constructions of sovereignty and to foster the creation of racial and ethnic identity, see Zuck, "Martin R. Delany."
3. Qtd. by Chandler, "Speech" (4 April 1854), 29.
4. The Supreme Court's decision in the case of *Prigg v. Pennsylvania* (1842) reinforced the constitutional rights of slaveholders in cases where their slaves had fled to other states and declared that states could not intervene in the retrieval of slaves. Authority was said to reside in the federal government in cases involving fugitives, and as Supreme Court justice Story asserted in his opinion, states could not be compelled to enforce federal law in cases where that law ran counter to state laws. As McDonald notes (*States' Rights*, 135), several Northern states—Massachusetts, Vermont, New Hampshire, Pennsylvania, and Rhode Island—soon passed laws that barred state officials from assisting in the capture or return of persons claimed to be fugitive slaves. Such laws allowed Northern states to circumvent what they saw as the intrusion of both the federal government and the Southern slave power within the limits of their partic-

ular states. The Fugitive Slave Act of 1850, however, took control of fugitive slaves entirely out of the hands of state officials and made it an exclusively federal issue. As many argued at the time, the Fugitive Slave Act made slavery a national institution and limited the sovereignty of individuals and states that opposed slavery. Holman Hamilton's *Prologue to Conflict* remains a definitive study of the forces that shaped the Compromise of 1850 and how this legislation brought the nation closer to civil war. For more on the Fugitive Slave Act and its impact on African Americans, see Horton and Horton, "A Federal Assault." For a focused examination of the Anthony Burns case, see Pease and Pease, *Fugitive Slave Law*. Wald discusses literary reactions to the Fugitive Slave Act in *Constituting Americans*, 89, 153, 164. Thomas engages literary responses, including those of Harriet Beecher Stowe and Herman Melville, at length in *Cross Examinations*.

5. For more on popular sovereignty and the separation of powers in the eighteenth century, see Wood, *Creation of the American Republic*, 445–453. In his chapter on emergent social movements in the nineteenth century, Formisano charts the transition from the sovereignty of the people in Washington's administration through the populism that informed Jackson's and Van Buren's presidencies. Tracing changing conceptions of "the people," he notes that the sovereignty of the people was initially associated with representative democracy, not with the idea that the people would actually govern themselves. See *For the People*, 65–68.

6. Webster, "Second Reply" (26–27 January 1830), in *Abridgment of the Debates of Congress*, 7:431.

7. For brief discussions of Cass and popular sovereignty, see Carey, *Parties*, 94; and Zarefsky, *Lincoln*, 21.

8. Zarefsky, *Lincoln*, 10.

9. Johannsen credits Douglas with a "sincere belief" in popular sovereignty in *Frontier*, 20. For more on the connection between the Kansas-Nebraska Act and Douglas's railroad interests, see Hodder, "Railroad Background"; Huston, *Stephen A. Douglas*, 65.

10. For more on the passage of the Kansas-Nebraska Act and a breakdown of the voting by parties, see Carey, *Parties*, 185–186.

11. Chandler, "Speech," 28.

12. Ibid.

13. Benton, "Speech of Mr. Benton" (25 April 1854), in *Remarks of Mr. English*, 6.

14. Goode, "Speech of Hon. William O. Goode" (19 May 1854), ibid., 12.

15. Ibid.

16. Smith, *Civic Ideals*, 265.

17. Wald, *Constituting Americans*, 41.

18. Clegg, *Price of Liberty*, 3.

19. "A Transplanted Republic," *African Repository* 28.1 (January 1852): 24, APS.

20. Treaty with Liberia, 21 October 1862. For more, see U.S. Department of State, *Catalogue of Treaties*, 66. On the influence that Southern slaveholders had on the failure of the United States to recognize Liberian or Haitian sovereignty until 1862, see Popkin, *Concise History*, 154. For more on Jefferson's views on recognizing Haiti, see Matthewson, "Jefferson."

21. Ryan, "Errand into Africa," 565.
22. Ibid., 574–575.
23. See, for example, chapter 5 of Hale's *Liberia*, entitled "The Planting of the Nation." Kaplan, "Manifest Domesticity," 592, discusses Hale's campaign for the establishment of Thanksgiving as a national holiday in the context of the Mexican-American War and the project of national unification.
24. Ryan discusses Hale's belief that colonization would lead to the creation of "two strong nations" in "Errand into Africa," 565–566.
25. Traubel, *With Walt Whitman*, 5; Reynolds, *Whitman's America*, 49.
26. See, for example, Reynolds, *Whitman's America*; and Klammer, "Slavery and Abolition."
27. Whitman, "Prohibition of Colored Persons" (1858), 201.
28. Reynolds, *Whitman's America*, 48.
29. Whitman, "Prohibition of Colored Persons," 201.
30. Calhoun, speech (10 January 1838), in Mackitrick, *Slavery Defended*, 19.
31. Smith, "Lectures," 154.
32. McTyeire, *Duties*, 92.
33. Ibid., 93.
34. Fitzhugh, *Sociology*, 45.
35. Ibid., 37–38.
36. See the chapter "The Nomadic Beggars and Pauper Banditti of England," in Fitzhugh's *Cannibals All!*, 204–217.
37. Qtd. in Webb, *Life and Letters*, 101.
38. Qtd. in Stauffer and Trodd, *The Tribunal*, 42. All subsequent references to Brown's writings are from this collection and are cited parenthetically in the text. For a brief overview of the Chatham Convention, see Tsai, *America's Forgotten Constitutions*, 85.
39. For a detailed history of Brown's constitution and a reading of the document itself, see Tsai, *America's Forgotten Constitutions*, 83–117. Tsai frames Brown's vision as "ethical sovereignty," which he juxtaposes with the "racial sovereignty" expressed in the *Dred Scott* case (84). He also highlights Brown's lack of concern for territory and the recognition of other qualifications for nationhood (90). Hereafter this source is cited parenthetically in the text.
40. Frank [Frances] A. Rollin, *Life and Public Services of Martin R. Delany*, qtd. in Levine, *Martin R. Delany*, 331.
41. Ibid.
42. Tsai links Brown's conception of nationhood with another nation formed within the borders of the United States, Étienne Cabet's socialist Icarian nation (1848–1895), insofar as both "envisioned multiple political communities occupying the same space for the foreseeable future" and "believed that the political order's legitimacy did not depend on control of any particular parcel of land" (*America's Forgotten Constitutions*, 90).
43. Reynolds, *John Brown*, 252.
44. Brown, "Provisional Constitution and Ordinances for the People of the United States" (8 May 1858), in Stauffer and Trodd, *The Tribunal*, 37. Other sources, including

Reynolds, offer slightly different wordings of this article. Reynolds cites Article 46 as proof of Brown's desire to change the American political culture, not to overthrow the government itself (*John Brown*, 252).

45. This idea is proposed by Tsai, *America's Forgotten Constitutions*, 91.
46. Douglass, *Life and Times*, 276.
47. Ibid., 100.
48. As Tsai has noted, the Provisional Constitution played a prominent role in the trial of Brown and four of his alleged coconspirators (*America's Forgotten Constitutions*, 103).
49. For a discussion of how Brown's attack on Harpers Ferry inflamed discussions of states' rights and sectional tensions, see Reynolds, *John Brown*, 337–338. Reynolds claims that by insisting on trying Brown in Virginia, Governor Henry Wise was making a statement in support of state sovereignty. He also details widespread claims of Northern involvement.
50. *LTE*, 59. All subsequent quotations from Brown's trial are drawn from this source and are cited parenthetically in the text.
51. On Brown's rejection of an insanity defense, see Reynolds, *John Brown*, 38.
52. In his biography of Brown, Reynolds examines the vast amount of coverage that Brown's actions and subsequent trial generated, much of which excoriated him as a villain. Northern and Southern papers discussed his exploits in vivid detail, with some dismissing him as a "madman" and others lamenting that his experiences in Kansas had "shattered" his mind. Reynolds asserts that it was the Transcendentalists, most notably Henry David Thoreau, who were responsible for the recuperation of Brown's reputation (*John Brown*, 337–347).
53. Douglass, "Capt. John Brown Not Insane," in Foner, *Frederick Douglass*, 374–375. Douglass also gave a speech entitled "John Brown" at Storer College in Harpers Ferry (ibid., 633–648). The section on Brown from Rollin's biography of Delany is included in Levine, *Martin R. Delany*, 328–331.
54. Levine discusses their relationship and political differences in *Martin Delany, Frederick Douglass*. He also complicates the ways in which the two have been framed as diametrically opposed on issues of emigration and assimilation.
55. Delany, "Political Economy," in Levine, *Martin R. Delany*, 149.
56. Ibid., 150.
57. For a succinct summary of what is known of the publication history of *Blake*, see Schoolman, *Abolitionist Geographies*, 9. She notes that the novel did not appear in book form until it was edited by Floyd Miller, having only been published in serial form during Delany's lifetime. *Blake* was partially serialized in 1859 and reprinted in 1861–1862. Floyd Miller, in his introduction to the first book-length edition (1970), suggests that Delany might have begun the novel as early as 1852, although we can only speculate about the precise chronology of Delany's composition (Miller in Delany, *Blake*, xix).
58. Levine, *Martin Delany, Frederick Douglass*, 190. Levine notes that Miller's edition shortened the novel's original title, *Blake; or, The Huts of America: A Tale of the Mississippi Valley, the Southern United States, and Cuba*, which more fully demonstrates its transna-

tional concerns (*Martin Delany, Frederick Douglass*, 191, 290). For more on *Blake* and transnationalism, see Clymer, "Martin Delany's *Blake*."

59. Delany, *Blake*, 225. Subsequent references are cited parenthetically in the text.

60. Schoolman, *Abolitionist Geographies*, 1–2.

61. Chiles, "Within and Without," 325.

62. Delany, *Condition*, 42. Subsequent references are cited parenthetically in the text.

63. Delany, "Political Destiny," in Levine, *Martin R. Delany*, 247. Subsequent references are cited parenthetically in the text.

64. Hendler, *Public Sentiments*, 55–62.

65. Levine, *Martin Delany, Frederick Douglass*, 64.

66. Ibid., 67.

67. Garnet, *Past and Present*, 25. For more on Delany's response to Garnet's and Douglass's claims that African Americans should not leave the United States, see Levine, *Martin Delany, Frederick Douglass*, 67–68. Like Delany and Douglass, Garnet's position on emigration was complicated and changed over time. Bell, *Survey*, 133–134, emphasizes Garnet's later support for emigration. Garnet's 1860 "Address at Cooper's Insitute" argues for the missionary potential of the African Civilizing Society that he founded but asserts that African Americans do not have to emigrate to gain political and civil rights. For an excerpt of this address, see Moses, *Classical Black Nationalism*, 142–144.

68. Delany, *Report*, in Levine, *Martin R. Delany*, 351.

69. Levine describes Delany's position in *The Condition* as "conflicted" (*Martin Delany, Frederick Douglass*, 69).

70. Douglass qtd. in McFeely, *Frederick Douglass*, 280.

71. "Lecture on Slavery, No. 1" (1 December 1850), in Foner, *Frederick Douglass*, 169.

72. Douglass, "Present Condition" (11 May 1853), in Foner, *Frederick Douglass*, 256. Hereafter this source is cited parenthetically in the text.

73. "To William Lloyd Garrison" (1 January 1846), in Foner, *Frederick Douglass*, 17.

74. Douglass, "Government and Its Subjects," in Foner, *Frederick Douglass*, 146–147.

75. Douglass, "To Harriet Beecher Stowe" (8 March 1853), in Foner, *Frederick Douglass*, 216–217. Douglass's letter to Stowe is also discussed in Levine, "*Uncle Tom's Cabin*," 82.

76. Castronovo, "As to Nation," 250.

77. "Meaning of July Fourth," in Foner, *Frederick Douglass*, 194.

78. Ibid.

79. Douglass, "The Claims," in Foner, *Frederick Douglass*, 264.

80. Ibid. Bell, *Minutes*, 3–57, includes an account of this convention.

81. Douglass, "Kansas-Nebraska," in Foner, *Frederick Douglass*, 299. Hereafter this source is cited parenthetically in the text.

82. Brown, *The Black Man*, 44.

83. Blyden, *Liberia's Offering*, v.

84. For a detailed reading of the Confederate Constitution, see Currie, "Through the Looking-Glass."

85. Escott, *The Confederacy*, 7. See also Rubin, *Shattered Nation*, 100.
86. "Sketch," in Cleveland, *Alexander H. Stephens*, 721.
87. Currie, "Through the Looking-Glass," 1258.

Chapter Four. "An Irish Republic (on Paper)"

1. Symonds, *Lincoln and His Admirals*, provides a comprehensive account of the Trent Affair and the reaction in Washington (71–100). On American Indians and the Civil War, see Confer, *Cherokee Nation*; and Hauptman, *Between Two Fires*.

2. Brown, *Irish American Nationalism*, 39. Mitchell Snay has described the Irish nation imagined by the Fenians as future focused, a state in the making: "Fenian national identity rested upon the belief that Ireland had once been a nation, but that its nationalism had been destroyed by the English" (*Fenians*, 151). For Snay, the nation-making project of the Fenians was about "restoration" rather than "creation."

3. This was said during the first national convention. See *Special Commission . . . , Trial of Thomas Clarke Luby*, 219–220, qtd. in D'Arcy, "The Fenian Movement," 38.

4. Brown, *Irish American Nationalism*, briefly discusses these and other activities as proof that the Fenians functioned as an "international power" (39). See also Fenian Brotherhood, "Letters of Marque and Reprisal," box 2, folder 9, FBR.

5. For histories of the Fenian Brotherhood and the IRB, see D'Arcy, "The Fenian Movement"; Jenkins, *Fenians and Anglo-American Relations* and *Fenian Problem*; Neidhardt, *Fenianism*; Ramón, *Provisional Dictator*; and Snay, *Fenians*, 43–48, 55–57, 62–67, 86–90, 124–131, 150–153, 171–172.

6. Samito, *Becoming American*, 120. The gains the Fenians made for naturalized citizens both within the United States and when they traveled abroad are explored in depth at 194–218.

7. Despite the presence of Irish Protestants, anxieties about an Irish imperium tended to equate Irish with Catholic.

8. For more on Otis's "Wild Irish" speech, see Clark, *Irish in Philadelphia*, 15.

9. Zolberg, *Nation by Design*, 25.

10. Through the nineteenth century, *Calvin's Case*, or the *Case of the Postnati* (1608), exerted a profound influence on British understandings of subjectship and perpetual allegiance. Lord Coke, who was the chief justice of the Court of Common Pleas at the time of the case, made the famous argument "once a subject always a subject." Later legal theorists such as Blackstone supported Coke's interpretation and asserted that as soon as an individual was born in the British Empire, that individual owed natural or perpetual allegiance to the sovereign. Lord Coke qtd. in Kettner, *Development*, 50.

11. See Allen, *Invention*; and Ignatiev, *How the Irish Became White*.

12. Fanning, *Exiles of Erin*, 3.

13. For more on immigration and population statistics, see Snay, *Fenians*, 52–54; Fanning, *Exiles of Erin*, 2; and Brown, *Irish American Nationalism*, 17–19. Brown addresses the development of Irish American communities and the relationship of Irish Catholics to Anglo-American Protestants (19–48). On the "class and cultural diversity of nineteenth-century Irish-American behavior" (187), see Walsh, "A Fanatic Heart."

14. Ignatiev, *How the Irish Became White*, 35 (hereafter this source is cited parenthetically in the text). Ignatiev cites the work of Theodore Allen in his understanding of the difference between "racial" and "national" oppression.

15. Handlin, *Boston's Immigrants*, 60. For more on the critiques levied against Irish Catholic immigrants, their difficult material circumstances, and the ways in which they were treated as an undifferentiated mass to be managed, see Samito, *Becoming American*, 15–16.

16. Ignatiev discusses Irish Americans' attitudes toward slavery, their support of the Democratic Party, and their participation in riots in New York City. See, especially, *How the Irish Became White*, 7–14, 69, 88–99. Ignatiev and others have pointed out the ways in which Irish Americans sought to produce a "white" identity so as to separate themselves from African Americans and gain political and social advantages. For more on African American and Irish experiences in American cities and fears of "amalgamation," see Ignatiev, *How the Irish Became White*, 21, 41. There has been a great deal of work on the influence of physiognomy and scientific racism on visual and textual representations of the Irish, such as Thomas Nast's cartoons in *Harper's Weekly* and written accounts that conflated African Americans and Irish immigrants using terms such as "smoked Irish." For a summary of representations of the Irish as a distinct race, see Kenny, "Race." Book-length studies include Duffy, *Who's Your Paddy?*; Jacobson, *Whiteness*; Curtis, *Apes and Angels*; and Knobel, *Paddy and the Republic*.

17. "The Voice of Our Exchanges," *Christian Recorder* (27 February 1873), at Accessible Archives.

18. Davis, "Some Themes," 205–206.

19. See Dolan, *Irish Americans*, 96. "No Irish Need Apply" (ca. 1860) was a popular song of the 1860s that dramatized the challenges faced by an Irish immigrant seeking employment. For a discussion of the debates surrounding No Irish Need Apply signs, see Duffy, *Who's Your Paddy?*, 81.

20. Doyle, "The Irish in North America," 200.

21. Anonymous Irish immigrant qtd. in Miller, *Emigrants and Exiles*, 323.

22. The remarks of this anonymous author from Kentucky are quoted in "The Irish in America," *Ripley Bee*, 15 November 1856, NCN. An earlier author reported the use of this phrase in discussions of the Philadelphia riots of 1844 in an article entitled "The Fearful Riots and Outrages in Philadelphia," *New York Daily Tribune*, 10 May 1844. "Nativism," the writer asserted, "assumes that this is a *Protestant* country." A copy is available online through the LOC's Chronicling America website. Opposition by the Catholic clergy to the Fenian Brotherhood was discussed during the second national convention (*PSN*, 53).

23. Morse, *Imminent Dangers*, 14.

24. Ibid., 24.

25. On O'Connell's discussions of an "Irish nation in exile," see McCaffrey, *Textures*, 133. For more on the influence of the Know-Nothings during the 1850s, see Samito, *Becoming American*, 17–20.

26. Cass to Joseph A. Wright (8 July 1859), in U.S. Department of State, *Messages*, 135.

27. In 1840, while serving as U.S. minister to Prussia, Henry Wheaton articulated the notion that naturalized U.S. citizens reverted to being subjects of their country of origin when they traveled to that country. He wrote to a naturalized U.S. citizen of Prussian origin who had traveled to his home country and was being forced into military service: "Had you remained in the United States, or visited any other foreign country, (except Prussia,) on your lawful business, you would have been protected by the American authorities.... But, having returned to the country of your birth, *your native domicile and natural character* revert, (so long as you remain in the Prussian dominions,) and you are bound in all respects to obey the laws exactly as if you had never emigrated." See Wheaton to Johann P. Knocke, Berlin (24 July 1840), in U.S. Department of State, *Papers*, 1293.

28. For more on the organization of the IRB and possible connections with other groups, such as the Freemasons and the Carbonari, see Ramón, *Provisional Dictator*. She notes, "It has not yet been settled how much this structure [of the IRB] and its later development" was informed by other organizations and how much Stephens created himself (81). In "Modern Ireland: An Introductory Survey," Reilly calls the Fenians a "secret oath-bound organization" that, like earlier groups such as the United Irishmen, was structured into small circles or cells with the aim of "thwarting infiltration by informers" (96).

29. For more on O'Mahony's biography, the Fianna Eireann, and the formation and naming of the Fenian Brotherhood, see D'Arcy, "The Fenian Movement," 10–14; and Neidhardt, *Fenianism*, 6–7.

30. For more on the structure of the IRB and the Fenian Brotherhood, see Ramón, *Provisional Dictator*, 89–90; and Neidhardt, *Fenianism*, 5.

31. *The Fenians' Progress*, 45. Subsequent quotations from this source are cited parenthetically in the text. A copy of this work is available at LCP.

32. Curtin, *United Irishmen*, 62.

33. "Resolutions," in *PFN*, 42.

34. Qtd. in *Special Commission . . . , Trial of Thomas Clarke Luby*, 219–220, qtd. in D'Arcy, "The Fenian Movement," 38. The twelfth, thirteenth, and fourteenth resolutions were excised in the published proceedings of the conference because they were deemed "injudicious." See *PFN*, 38–39.

35. The split between the O'Mahony wing and the Senate wing is described in D'Arcy, "The Fenian Movement," 39, 102–130; Walker, *The Fenian Movement*, 49–80; and Campbell, *Ireland's New Worlds*, 108. While trouble had been brewing for some time, D'Arcy claims that the break was precipitated by O'Mahony's assumption of the power to issue the bonds of the Irish Republic (103). In addition to differing perspectives on the destiny of the Fenian Brotherhood, the two factions were distinguished by other political differences. As Rutherford has noted in volume 2 of his *Secret History*, "O'Mahony was a [D]emocrat; the Roberts party were nearly all Republicans" (233).

36. For more on Roberts and his supporters' use of the phrases "drag chain" and "men of action," see D'Arcy, "The Fenian Movement," 39.

37. Roberts, *Cincinnati Enquirer* (1 February 1866), qtd. in Walker, *The Fenian Movement*, 72.

38. In "A Kindred and Congenial Element," Lynch remarks, "The fact that the constitutional conventions of both the Fenian Brotherhood (1865) and the United Irishmen (1880) took place in Philadelphia was not lost to contemporary pundits" (81). For more on the 1865 Congress, see Neidhardt, *Fenianism*, 28; and D'Arcy, "The Fenian Movement," 78–81.

39. A copy of the 1865 Constitution can be found in *The Fenians' Progress*, 68–91.

40. The written proceedings of the Philadelphia convention have apparently not survived, but descriptions can be found in D'Arcy, "The Fenian Movement," 78–81; and Neidhardt, *Fenianism*, 28.

41. Killian's meeting with Seward and Mitchel's involvement with the Fenians are discussed in McGovern, *John Mitchel*, 192–193. For more on Killian's efforts with the Johnson administration, see D'Arcy, "The Fenian Movement," 84–85; and Walker, *The Fenian Movement*, 53, 81, 117–118. Walker describes an envoy that included Roberts and Killian, who were sent to Washington "to wait upon and treat with the President and his Cabinet on the part of the Fenian Brotherhood to make with the American authorities whatever arrangements they might deem conducive to the success of the Fenian Brotherhood" (qtd. in *The Fenian Movement*, 53). Roberts's allusion to "glorious, glorious news" led some to hope that American aid would be forthcoming (qtd. ibid.).

42. D'Arcy quotes from a letter that Killian wrote to Seward on 18 November asking, among other things, his opinion on "the organization of a Republic on the farther side of our North Eastern Boundary line and South of the St. Lawrence" ("The Fenian Movement," 85).

43. Instructions to John Mitchel (10 November 1865), qtd. in D'Arcy, "The Fenian Movement," 84.

44. On the "Fenian White House" and the impeachment of O'Mahony, see "The Fenian Explosion," *New York Times*, 13 December 1865, PHN; and D'Arcy, "The Fenian Movement," 81, 103–104.

45. For more on the shifting organizational structure of the Fenian Brotherhood, see D'Arcy, "The Fenian Movement," 107–118.

46. "Resolutions," in *PFN*, 31.

47. "Constitution and By-Laws," in *PFN*, 46.

48. Ibid., 46.

49. See "The Constitution of the Fenian Brotherhood, 1865," in *The Fenians' Progress*, 70, 72, 75.

50. Ibid., 68.

51. Ibid., 69–70.

52. Both groups are discussed in the chapter "Ethnic and Racial Nationalisms" in Snay's *Fenians*, 114–138.

53. On Fenian claims that they "repudiated" British laws upon becoming naturalized Americans, see *PFN*, 34. One of the resolutions passed at the first national convention declared that the group would not take direction from foreign leaders, because to do so would render them "unworthy of participating in the great political privileges, wherewith the naturalized citizens of America are invested" (see *PFN*, 35).

54. On Mitchel's connections with Fenianism and the Confederacy, see McGovern,

John Mitchel. For a discussion of Irish American participation in the Civil War, including that of the Fenians, see Samito, *Becoming American*, 26–35, 103–133. In *Normans and Saxons*, Watson notes that in the midst of growing tensions in the 1850s, some Southern writers framed the North and South as "two scientifically different races" (17); however, in the 1840s, many Americans "saw themselves as members of a common American race" (25). He argues that Southerners frequently employed racial arguments to argue for secession (28). For more on how Northern writers, such as George Perkins Marsh, Ralph Waldo Emerson, and Theodore Parker, wrote of Anglo-Saxon influence on American culture, but did not frame the North and South as separate races or nations, see 120–125. For more on Confederate nationalism and political culture, see Escott, *After Secession*; Faust, *Creation*; and Gallagher, *Confederate War*. Ignatiev discusses the 1863 New York riots, often mischaracterized as "draft riots," as evidence of Irish antipathy toward abolition and their focus on improving their own political status even at the expense of African Americans. See *How the Irish Became White*, 88–89.

55. Walker, *The Fenian Movement*, 55.

56. "Fenians in Ireland: Their Hopes and Fears . . . ," *New York Daily Tribune*, 28 January 1866. Copy available in FBR, box 3, folder 9, item 2.

57. Ibid.

58. Seward to Mr. Burnley (20 March 1865), in U.S. Department of State, *Diplomatic Correspondence*, 2:104.

59. Secretary Seward to Johnson (27 August 1868), qtd. in D'Arcy, "The Fenian Movement," 305.

60. Bruce to Lord Stanley (20 May 1867), in D'Arcy, "The Fenian Movement," 258.

61. Samito, *Becoming American*, 184. Subsequent references to this source are cited parenthetically in the text.

62. For more on the attendance at the Fenian conventions, see Neidhardt, *Fenianism*, 12–13, 15. Neidhardt also highlights the development of the Fenian Sisterhood, led by Ellen O'Mahony, the sister of Fenian leader John O'Mahony.

63. Snay, *Fenians*, 55–56. Additional accounts of Fenian membership can be found in Samito, *Becoming American*, 120–121.

64. "The Fenian Brotherhood Is Indeed a Powerful Organization . . . ," *New Haven Daily Palladium*, 2 August 1864; "The Fenian Explosion," *New York Times*, 13 December 1865; Fitz Herbert, "The Fenian Brotherhood in America: To the Editor of the London *Times*," rptd. in *New York Herald*, 30 January 1865. This letter was also reprinted in the *Leeds Mercury*, 18 January 1865; see *British Newspapers, 1600–1900* (online).

65. For more on these incidents, see Samito, *Becoming American*, 194–205.

66. "*Only* an American Citizen," *Irishman*, rptd. in *Irish News*, 30 November 1867, LOC.

67. "Under Which King, Bezonian?," *Irish News*, 23 November 1867, LOC.

68. "The Fenians vs. Our Government," *New York Times*, 21 April 1866, PHN.

69. "The Infamy of Radicalism," *Keowee Courier*, 26 June 1868, LOC, Chronicling America website.

70. An American Fenian, "Ireland for the Irish," *Littell's Living Age* 95.1230 (28 December 1867): 773, APS.

71. "Imperium in Imperio," *Milwaukee Sentinel*, 7 May 1883, NCN.

72. Ibid.

73. James Gibbons to Francis Gallagher, Philadelphia (24 July 1868), qtd. in Clark, "Letters from the Underground," 85. The *New York Times* published several articles whose titles included references to the "Fenian fizzle." See, for example, 18 March, 6 April, 27 April, and 28 April 1866, PHN. See also "The Fenian Nuisance," *Christian Advocate* 45.22 (2 June 1870): 172, APS.

74. "The Fenian Nuisance," 172.

75. "Exeunt the Fenians," *New York Times*, 19 October 1871, PHN.

76. Handlin, "America Recognizes Diverse Loyalties," qtd. in Brown, *Irish American Nationalism*, 28.

77. "Report of the Secretary of Civil Affairs," O'Sullivan to Gen. O'Neill (23 November 1868), rptd. in *Proceedings of the Senate and the House of Representatives of the Fenian Brotherhood*, 41.

78. *Irish Republic*, 4 May 1867, qtd. in Snay, *Fenians*, 153.

79. Savage, *Fenian Heroes and Martyrs*, 66.

80. O'Mahony, "Preliminary Meeting," in *PSN*, 5.

81. Mitchel had established the New York *Citizen* in 1854, but his later newspaper, the *Irish Citizen*, was critical of the Fenians. See D'Arcy, "The Fenian Movement," 3, 266. Gibbons held many positions in the Fenian Brotherhood, including state centre for Pennsylvania, a member of O'Mahony's Central Council, temporary president after O'Mahony's impeachment, and vice president under John O'Neill in 1868. Michael Scanlan's brother John was also a Fenian and a poet. Other references to Fenianism include Cobbe, "The Fenian 'Idea'"; and "The Fenians," *All the Year Round* (21 October 1865): 300–304. The final line of Walt Whitman's poem "Old Ireland," as it appeared in the *New York Leader*, has been taken by some to be a reference to the Fenian Brotherhood. For more, see Krieg, *Whitman and the Irish*, 108. Examples of articles include "The High Court of Fenian Judicature," *New York Times*, 11 December 1865, PHN; and "Fenianism—Why Is It?," *Putnam's Magazine*, May 1868, 543–548, APS.

82. MacDonald, *Troublous Times*, 11.

83. Roberts qtd. in Samito, *Becoming American*, 188.

84. Reports from Fenian circles appeared regularly in the *Irish-American*. For example, a report dated 28 March 1866 in the *Irish-American* discussed the allegiances of the Sarsfield circle of the Fenian Brotherhood. The group decided to side with Col. Roberts and Gen. Sweeny. See also "To the Editors of the *Irish-American*," *Irish-American*, 21 April 1866; and "Meeting Minutes, Buffalo, N.Y., February to July 1869," box 1, Francis B. Gallagher Collection of Fenian Brotherhood Records (MC 14).

85. Dubh, *Ridgeway*, 1. Subsequent references are cited parenthetically in the text.

86. This blurring of boundaries between past and present did not go unchallenged. In an article entitled "Fenianism—Why Is It?" that appeared in *Putnam's Magazine* in May 1868, the author questioned the creation of the Fenian Brotherhood and the ar-

gument that the group was an effect of the "mourning of its [Ireland's] lost nationality" (543). The author claimed that the Irish did not have the kind of nationality possessed by Scotland and merely projected an image of unified nationhood onto a much messier past.

87. Samuels, *Reading*, 97.

88. Ibid. A copy of *The Fenian Chief* is available at LCP.

89. Here I draw on Lukács's conception in *The Historical Novel*. As Samuels has suggested in *Reading*, "The articulation of nationalism in fictional narratives tends to appear as a dynamic set of relations between families and their interactions with forms of government" (93).

90. Tawil, *Making of Racial Sentiment*, 2.

91. For more on *Charlotte Temple* as a political allegory, see Davidson, "Introduction," xi–xii; and Barnes, "Novels." In *Importance*, 31–64, Tennenhouse challenges allegorical readings of Charlotte as a metonym of America and instead argues that the novel suggests anxieties about maintaining cultural connections with England.

92. In referring to the distinctions drawn in *Ridgeway* between "friend" and "enemy," I reference the work of Carl Schmitt, who cites the process of distinguishing between friend and enemy as central to politics, a process that he links with the decision-making power of sovereignty. See, in particular, *The Concept of the Political*.

93. Another image of Fenian headquarters appeared in the 23 December 1866 issue of *Harper's Weekly*.

94. Bonds of the Irish Republic from the 1860s, signed by John O'Mahony and issued in denominations of ten, twenty, and fifty dollars, are held in box 3, folder 5, FBR.

95. Kiernan, *Ireland and America*, 10. As Snay has noted in *Fenians*, "America provided the setting in which Fenians forged their distinctive diaspora nationalism. In America, an Irish 'nation' could materialize that would one day restore Irish nationality to Ireland" (140). Snay emphasizes that the Irish nation was "a state to be achieved" (152), which was a position held by many. Yet, as I have suggested, texts by and about the Fenians also referred to them as the provisional government of the Irish Republic.

96. Kiernan, *Ireland and America*, 11.

97. "Address of William R. Roberts, President, F. B. to the Fenian Brotherhood and Irishmen of America Headquarters, Fenian Brotherhood, 706 Broadway, 1 Nov. 1866," n.p., box 1, folder 17, Francis B. Gallagher Collection of Fenian Brotherhood Records (MC 14).

98. Scanlan, "Dedication," in *Love and Land*, iv.

99. Scanlan, "Roberts' Appeal," in *Love and Land*, 262.

100. "By the President of the United States of America. A Proclamation," in *The Fenian Raid*, 93.

101. Grant qtd. in D'Arcy, "The Fenian Movement," 359.

102. "President Grant's Proclamation against the Fenian Raid in Canada, Issued May 24, 1870," in McPherson, *Political History*, 544.

103. Bruyneel, *Third Space*, 66.

104. Grant, "To the Senate and House of Representatives," in Richardson, *A Compilation*, 65.

105. Ibid., 67.
106. Corcoran, *Captivity*, 22.

Chapter Five. "China in the United States"

1. LaFeber, *New Empire*, 1.
2. Nineteenth-century Americans used the term *company* instead of the Mandarin *huiguan* and referred to the larger organization as the Chinese Six Companies. For more on terminology, see Qin, *Diplomacy of Nationalism*, 45 and 141 (where he discusses the Zhonghua huiguan as "the Chinese national *huiguan*"). For the romanization of Chinese words in this chapter, I follow my source material (particularly in the case of proper names), and I include the Cantonese and Mandarin transliterations of the company names. Hoy and Lai use the Cantonese names, while Qin and Ling use both Cantonese and Mandarin. I follow Ling in using both Cantonese and Mandarin names (with the Mandarin in parentheses) and in the spelling of the Cantonese names of the Six Companies.
3. McCullough, *Regions of Identity*, 242.
4. "A Chinese Ishmael," 46. *Overland Monthly* lists the author as Sui Sin Fah, but I use the more conventional spelling.
5. McCullough, *Regions of Identity*, 243.
6. For more on the Fenians and greater protections for naturalized citizens, see Samito, *Becoming American*, 194–218. Ruskola discusses the Barbary treaties and the history of diplomatic relations between the United States and China in *Legal Orientalism*.
7. For more on the political position of U.S. citizens in nineteenth-century China, see Scully, *Bargaining*; and Raustiala, *Does the Constitution*, 68–81. On the Burlingame Treaty specifically, see McClain, *In Search of Equality*, 30–31.
8. Burlingame Treaty, 5–6. Hereafter this source is cited parenthetically in the text.
9. Yin, *Chinese American Literature*, 12. Hereafter this source is cited parenthetically in the text. For a brief discussion of the Chinese in the Americas in the sixteenth century, see Qin, *Diplomacy of Nationalism*, 16.
10. Yin, *Chinese American Literature*, cites a figure for total immigration at 322,000 and suggests in a footnote that the higher number of 400,000 is offered in K. Scott Wong's "Transformation of Culture," 207. For more on Chinese immigration, see Gyory, *Closing the Gate*, 7; Kanazawa, "Immigration"; Chung, *In Pursuit of Gold*. The sharp rise in immigration was due both to California's economic promise and to the difficulties facing China. Some parts of China, particularly Guangdong province, were still feeling the effects of the Opium Wars (1839–1842) and the Treaty of Nanjing (1842). The opening of the port of Canton to the West and the Taiping Rebellion (1850–1864) also contributed to the economic and political instabilities that encouraged large numbers of Chinese people to consider migrating to America. On the factors motivating Chinese immigration to the United States, see Yin, *Chinese American Literature*, 13–14.
11. For more on the development and influence of "anticoolie clubs," see Saxton, *Indispensible Enemy*, 67–91. Saxton's work is one of the fullest treatments of the argu-

ments that organized labor—groups such as the Working Men's Party, the Knights of Labor, and various trade unions and leagues—raised against the Chinese in California.

12. For more on the competing visions of sovereignty in California both before and after 1848, see Rifkin, *Manifesting America*, 149–196. Formally, the Treaty of Guadalupe Hidalgo that had ended the Mexican-American War had allowed for the division of sovereignty and the exercise of volitional allegiance within Alta California, stipulating that Californios could choose to become U.S. citizens or retain their Mexican citizenship. The terms of the treaty specified that, in either case, their lands would be protected. In practice, however, as Rifkin and others have noted, the Californios, the Cahuillas, and the lands they occupied were, to use a term that Rifkin frequently employs, "incorporated" into U.S. territorial sovereignty.

13. On California's attitudes and policies toward the Chinese, including the miner's tax and other taxes, see Sandmeyer, *Anti-Chinese Movement*, 40–56. On the 1862 labor law specifically, see Takaki, *Strangers*, 82. Other laws required smallpox vaccines for all Chinese immigrants landing in San Francisco and prohibited the disinterment of Chinese people who died in the United States.

14. "The People, Respondent v. George W. Hall, Appellant," in Odo, *Columbia Documentary History*, 19–20. Hereafter this source is cited parenthetically in the text.

15. For additional analysis of *People v. Hall*, see Takaki, *Strangers*, 102.

16. Twain, *Roughing It*, 820. Subsequent references to this source are cited parenthetically in the text. Twain also wrote an article praising the Burlingame Treaty: "The Treaty with China," *New-York Tribune*, 28 August 1868.

17. *Congressional Globe*, 40th Cong., 3rd sess. (5 February 1869): 901.

18. Gyory, *Closing the Gate*, 15 (subsequent references to this source are cited parenthetically in the text). Gyory positions his argument as an alternative to both the "California thesis," which argued that California workers, politicians, and residents brought the issue of Chinese immigration to a national stage, and those who argued that Chinese exclusion was the result of racist ideologies that circulated at the national level.

19. "Coolies vs. Crispins," *New-York Tribune*, 18 June 1870, LOC, Chronicling America website.

20. Saxton, *Indispensible Enemy*, 105. Saxton and others point to the presidential election of 1876 as a watershed moment when anti-Chinese sentiment rose to national prominence. Smith, *Civic Ideals*, notes that during the 1870s "Southern Democrats quickly sought to build a new South-west coalition of white supremacists, rendering Republican support for racial equality ever more politically perilous" (317).

21. *Chinese Immigration* (1876), 64, LCP.

22. Gibson qtd. ibid., 26.

23. Lewis qtd. ibid., 45.

24. Karcher qtd. ibid., 128.

25. *Chinese Immigration* (1877), 4–5.

26. Scholars disagree as to whether anti-Chinese sentiments predated the arrival of Chinese immigrants in significant numbers and circulated nationally, or developed in response to particular conditions in California and then were brought to a national

stage by California labor organizers. For a summary of the two positions, see Gyory, *Closing the Gate*, 6–8. Republican leaders began to shift their focus toward the issue of Chinese immigration in the late 1860s, and, as Roger Daniels notes in *Asian America*, "the first significant congressional debate about the rights of Chinese in the United States ... occurred in 1870" (43).

27. *Report of the Joint Special Committee*, iii. Hereafter, this source is cited parenthetically in the text.

28. Davis, "Chinese Immigration," 4, LCP. Hereafter this source is cited parenthetically in the text.

29. Daniels, *Asian America*, 39.

30. George, "The Chinese in California," *New-York Tribune*, 1 May 1869, in Wenzer, *Henry George*, 169. This article is also known by the alternate title "The Chinese on the Pacific Coast." For more on George and the Chinese, see Takaki, *Strangers*, 108–110.

31. George, "The Chinese in California," 170.

32. George, "John Stuart Mill," *Oakland Daily Transcript*, 20 November 1869, in Wenzer, *Henry George*, 177.

33. George, "Chinese Immigration," *Cyclopedia of Political Science* (1881–1882), in Wenzer, *Henry George*, 224.

34. Whitney, *Almond-Eyed*, 104.

35. Dooner, *Last Days of the Republic*, 84. Hereafter this source is cited parenthetically in the text.

36. Starr, *Coming Struggle*, 9–10.

37. Arguments against Chinese citizenship emerged during the joint committee's interviews in California. For a discussion of these, see Daniels, *Asian America*, 43–44. For more on the 1880 treaty, see ibid., 55.

38. Qin, *Diplomacy of Nationalism*, 2. Hereafter this source is cited parenthetically in the text.

39. Daniels, *Asian America*, 24.

40. Ibid. For more on the function of the huiguan or district associations, see Qin, *Diplomacy of Nationalism*, 9–10.

41. For more on nineteenth-century fears of the tongs, see Chin, *Chinatown Gangs*, 5. Ling and Austin (*Asian American History and Culture*, 237) distinguish between the many tongs that functioned as "peaceful mutual aid societies" and the "fighting tongs."

42. Low qtd. in *Chinese Immigration* (1876), 5.

43. Shaw qtd. ibid., 17.

44. Hoy provides a brief history of the development of the Six Companies in *Chinese Six Companies*. See also "The Chinese Companies," in Speer, *The Oldest and Newest Empire*, 554–571; Qin, *Diplomacy of Nationalism*, 27–37, 45–56; Pfaelzer, *Driven Out*; and Gyory, *Closing the Gate*, 288n18. Lai, *Becoming Chinese American*, 42, disputes the widely held understanding that the Kong Chow (Gangzhou) Company was the first to be formed in the United States. The name of the Yeoung Wo Company is alternatively spelled Yeong Wo.

45. For specifics on the Four Houses and their transition to the Five Companies, see

Qin, *Diplomacy of Nationalism*, 27–28. On the loss of the Six Companies' records and the founding of the Chinese Consolidated Benevolent Association, see ibid., 44–45, 103. Qin and others sometimes refer to the Six Companies as the Chinese Consolidated Benevolent Association. See ibid., 1.

46. On the legal function of the companies, see McClain and McClain, "The Chinese Contribution," 4–5.

47. Hoy, *Chinese Six Companies*, 11. He discusses later revisions on 27–30.

48. For more on Speer, Lai Sai, and the *Oriental*, see Gonzáles and Torres, *News for All the People*, 131. Lai Sai is also referred to as Lee Kan and Lai Sam. See also Hutton and Strauss Reed, *Outsiders*, 77.

49. The English translation was published in "The Chinese Companies: Their Internal Order," *Oriental; or, Tung-ngai san-luk*, 1 March 1855. This constitution and the rules circulated widely and are also quoted in Speer, *The Oldest and Newest Empire*, 557–565; and Hauser and Hauser, *The Orient*, 300–301. Here, I refer to the version published in Speer's *The Oldest and Newest Empire*.

50. Qtd. in Speer, *The Oldest and Newest Empire*, 557–558.

51. Qtd. ibid., 569.

52. Hoy, *Chinese Six Companies*, 20, 8.

53. Sadowski-Smith, "Unskilled Labor Migration," 783.

54. Hansen, "The Chinese Six Companies," 41.

55. Lyman, "Conflict," 480.

56. For more on exit permits, see Pfaelzer, *Driven Out*, 25.

57. For more on Foucault's conception of biopower, see his *"Society Must Be Defended."*

58. For more on the Six Companies, the Burlingame Treaty, and the 1870 Civil Rights Act, see Takaki, *Strangers*, 114

59. Lee Ming How et al., "A Memorial of the Chinamen to the President," *Independent* 28.1437 (15 June 1876): 26. This text was also printed in *Friends' Intelligencer* 33.18 (24 June 1876): 276–278, APS. It is also referred to as "A Memorial from Representative Chinamen in America to President U.S. Grant." See Yung, Chang, and Lai, *Chinese American Voices*, 18–23. Hereafter references to the "Memorial" as published in the *Independent* will be cited parenthetically in the text.

60. For more on the Six Companies' efforts to persuade the Qing government to appoint a legation, see Qin, *Diplomacy of Nationalism*, 94–97.

61. McClain, "Chinese Struggle," 541.

62. Ibid., 542.

63. For more on the test cases brought by the Six Companies, see McClain and McClain, "Chinese Contribution." On Loomis's role in helping them find an attorney, see McClain, "Chinese Struggle," 552.

64. Yong et al., *The Chinese Question*, 286.

65. For a comprehensive bibliography of Chinese American newspapers and periodicals, see Lo and Lai, *Chinese Newspapers*. For more on early Chinese-language newspapers in San Francisco, see Chen, *Chinese San Francisco*, 73–75.

66. As a number of scholars have noted, numerous terms were used during the Qing

dynasty (and at other periods in Chinese history) to describe memorials. Among other factors, the context, audience, and kind of complaint determined which term was appropriate. Here I use the terms *memorial* and *petition* interchangeably as part of my general discussion of the complaint system in China. For more detailed discussions of memorials and Chinese imperial government, see Bartlett, *Monarchs and Ministers*; and Wu, *Communication*.

67. Zaeske, *Signatures of Citizenship*, 3. Hereafter this source is cited parenthetically in the text.

68. Hung, *Protest with Chinese Characteristics*, 101, 1.

69. "Governor's Special Message," *Daily Alta California*, 25 April 1852, CDN. Hereafter this source is cited parenthetically in the text.

70. A notable example of scholarship that deals with Chinese immigrants, African Americans, and Reconstruction is Aairm-Heriot, *Chinese Immigrants*.

71. Hab Wa and Long [Tong] Achick, "Letter of the Chinamen to His Excellency, Gov. Bigler," *Littell's Living Age* 34.424 (29 April 1852): 32–34, MOA. Copies of this letter were also printed in the *Daily Alta California*, 30 April 1852; the *San Francisco Herald*, 30 April 1852; and the *Sacramento Daily Union*, 29 April 1852. Hereafter this source is cited parenthetically in the text.

72. According to Yung, Chang, and Lai, Asing "may indeed have been a naturalized citizen because although the 1790 Naturalization Law limited naturalization to 'free white persons,' some eastern courts were willing to naturalize Chinese" (*Chinese American Voices*, 11n1).

73. Norman Asing, "To His Excellency Gov. Bigler," *Daily Alta California*, 5 May 1852, CDN. Hereafter this source is cited parenthetically in the text.

74. This is indicated in a "Notice" that precedes Lai, *Remarks of the Chinese Merchants*.

75. Lai, *Remarks of the Chinese Merchants*, 3. Hereafter this source is cited parenthetically in the text.

76. "Notice to the Public—From the President [and] Directors of the Five Chinese Companies of the State of California," *Sacramento Daily Union*, 26 August 1862, CDN.

77. "A Memorial," *Daily Alta California*, 18 June 1868, CDN.

78. "A Remonstrance from the Chinese in California," 589. Subsequent references to this source are cited parenthetically in the text.

79. *Memorial of the Six Chinese Companies*, 2, 13.

80. "Mr. Wharton to Mr. Tsui" (10 December 1892), in *Executive Documents*, 5:42.

Conclusion

1. Deleuze, *Negotiations*, 173–174. My thanks to Abram Anders for introducing me to this source.

2. Fabi, "Desegregating," 115.

3. Bellamy, *Looking Backward*, 361.

4. Tanner, "The Nation's Ultimatum," *Christian Recorder*, 6 January 1876, at Accessible Archives. Tanner was a prominent figure in the AME Church and edited the *Christian Recorder*. For more on Tanner's life and work, see Seraile, *Fire in His Heart*.

5. Tanner, "The Nation's Ultimatum."
6. Ibid.
7. Washington, "Address of Booker T. Washington," qtd. in "Presbyterian Home Mission Rally," *New York Observer and Chronicle* 74.11 (12 March 1896): 350, APS. Coleman discusses Griggs, Booker T. Washington, and imperium in imperio in *Sutton E. Griggs*, 57–59. He also briefly discusses the novel's publication history and reception. Tanner, Washington, and Griggs are also briefly discussed in Zuck, "Martin R. Delany," 48–51.
8. Foucault, *"Society Must Be Defended,"* 62.

BIBLIOGRAPHY

Court Cases

Caldwell v. Alabama. 6 Stew. & P. 327 (Ala. 1831)
Calvin's Case. 7 Coke Report 1a, 77 ER 377 (1608)
Cherokee Nation v. Georgia. 30 U.S.(5 Peters 1) (1831)
Chisholm v. Georgia. 2 U.S. (2 Dallas 419) (1793)
Dred Scott v. Sandford. 60 U.S. (19 Howard 393) (1857)
Fletcher v. Peck. 10 U.S.(6 Cranch 87)(1810)
Goodell v. Jackson ex dem. Smith. 20 Johns. 693 (N.Y. 1823)
People v. Hall. 4 Cal. 399 (1854)
Prigg v. Pennsylvania. 41 U.S. (16 Peters 539) (1842)
United States v. Lumsden et al. 26 F. Cas. 1013 (1 Bond 5) (C.C.S.D. Ohio 1856)
Worcester v. Georgia. 31 U.S.(6 Peters 515)(1832)

Libraries and Archives

Edward E. Ayer Collection. Newberry Library, Chicago, Ill.
Fenian Brotherhood Records and O'Donovan Rossa Personal Papers. American Catholic History Research Center and University Archives, Catholic University, Washington, D.C.
Francis B. Gallagher Collection of Fenian Brotherhood Records, 1862–1870. MC 14. Philadelphia Archdiocesan Historical Research Center, Wynnewood, Pa.
Library Company of Philadelphia
Library of Congress

Published Sources

Aairm-Heriot, Najia. *Chinese Immigrants, African Americans and Racial Anxiety in the United States, 1848–1882*. Champaign: University of Illinois Press, 2003.
Abernathy, Thomas P. *The South in the New Nation, 1789–1819*, vol. 4: *A History of the South*. Baton Rouge: Louisiana State University Press, 1961.

Abridgement of the Debates of Congress, from 1789 to 1851 by the Author of the Thirty Years' View [Thomas Hart Benton]. Vol. 7. New York: Appleton, 1858.

Adair, James. *The History of the American Indians Particularly Those Nations Adjoining to the Missisippi [sic] East and West Florida, Georgia, South and North Carolina, and Virginia*... London: E. Dilly, 1775.

Adams, John. "Thoughts on Government." In *The Portable John Adams*, edited by John Patrick Diggins, 233–242. New York: Penguin, 2004.

Adeleke, Tunde. *UnAfrican Americans: Nineteenth-Century Black Nationalists and the Civilizing Mission*. Louisville: University Press of Kentucky, 1998.

Agamben, Giorgio. *Homo Sacer: Sovereign Power and Bare Life*. Translated by Daniel Heller-Roazen. Palo Alto, Calif.: Stanford University Press, 1998.

———. *State of Exception*. Translated by Kevin Attell. Chicago: University of Chicago Press, 2008.

Albrecht-Crane, Christa. "Style, Stutter." In *Gilles Deleuze: Key Concepts*, edited by Charles J. Stivale, 121–140. Montreal: McGill-Queen's University Press, 2005.

Alfred, Taiaiake. *Peace, Power, and Righteousness: An Indigenous Manifesto*. Don Mills, Ont.: Oxford University Press, 2008.

Allen, Chadwick. *Blood Narrative: Indigenous Identity in American Indian and Maori Literary and Activist Texts*. Durham, N.C.: Duke University Press, 2002.

Allen, Theodore W. *The Invention of the White Race: The Origin of Racial Oppression in Anglo-America*. Vol. 2. New York: Verso, 1997.

American State Papers. Washington, D.C.: Gales and Seaton, 1834.

Anderson, Benedict. *Imagined Communities: Reflections on the Origins and Spread of Nationalism*. London: Verso, 1983.

Andrew, John A., III. *From Revivals to Removal: Jeremiah Evarts, the Cherokee Nation, and the Search for the Soul of America*. Athens: University of Georgia Press, 2007.

Apap, Chris. "'Let No Man of Us Budge One Step': David Walker and the Rhetoric of African American Emplacement." *Early American Literature* 46.2 (2011): 318–350.

Appiah, Kwame Anthony. *Cosmopolitanism: Ethics in a World of Strangers*. New York: Norton, 2010.

Appleby, Joyce. *Liberalism and Republicanism in the Historical Imagination*. Cambridge, Mass.: Harvard University Press, 1992.

Arac, Jonathan. *The Emergence of American Literary Narrative, 1820–1860*. Cambridge, Mass.: Harvard University Press, 2005.

Aravamudan, Srinivas. *Tropicopolitans: Colonialism and Agency, 1688–1804*. Durham, N.C.: Duke University Press, 1999.

Armstrong, Elizabeth. *Forging Gay Identities: Organizing Sexuality in San Francisco, 1950–1994*. Chicago: University of Chicago Press, 2002.

Ashworth, John. *Slavery, Capitalism, and Politics in the Antebellum Republic*, vol. 2: *The Coming of the Civil War*. New York: Cambridge University Press, 2007.

Bailey, Julius. *Race Patriotism: Protest and Print Culture in the A.M.E. Church*. Knoxville: University of Tennessee Press, 2012.

Bailyn, Bernard. *The Ideological Origins of the American Revolution*. Cambridge, Mass.: Harvard University Press, 1967.
Balibar, Étienne. "The Nation Form: History and Ideology." In *Race, Nation, Class: Ambiguous Identities*, edited by Étienne Balibar and Immanuel Wallerstein, 86–106. London: Verso, 1991.
Banner, Stuart. *How the Indians Lost Their Land: Law and Power on the Frontier*. Cambridge, Mass.: Harvard University Press, 2005.
Barker, Joanne, ed. *Sovereignty Matters: Locations of Contestation and Possibility in Indigenous Struggles for Self-Determination*. Lincoln: University of Nebraska Press, 2005.
Barksdale, Kevin. *The Lost State of Franklin: America's First Secession*. Louisville: University of Kentucky Press, 2009.
Barnes, Elizabeth. "Novels." In *History of the Book in America*, vol. 2: *An Extensive Republic: Print, Culture, and Society in the New Nation, 1790–1840*, edited by Robert Gross and Mary Kelley, 440–448. Chapel Hill: University of North Carolina Press, 2010.
Bartleson, Jens. *A Genealogy of Sovereignty*. Cambridge: Cambridge University Press, 1995.
Bartlett, Beatrice S. *Monarchs and Ministers: The Grand Council in Mid Ch'ing China, 1723–1920*. Berkeley: University of California Press, 1991.
Bauer, Ralph, and José Antonio Mazzotti, eds. *Creole Subjects in the Colonial Americas: Empires, Texts, Identities*. Chapel Hill: University of North Carolina Press, 2009.
Beaumont, Elizabeth. *The Civic Constitution: Civic Visions and Struggles in the Path toward Constitutional Democracy*. New York: Oxford University Press, 2014.
Bederman, David J. *The Classical Foundations of the American Constitution*. New York: Cambridge University Press, 2008.
Beeman, Richard. *The Penguin Guide to the United States Constitution: A Fully Annotated Declaration of Independence, U.S. Constitution and Amendments, and Selections from the Federalist Papers*. New York: Penguin, 2010.
Bell, Howard Holman. *Minutes of the Proceedings of the National Negro Conventions, 1830–1864*. New York: Arno and the New York Times, 1969.
———, ed. *A Survey of the Negro Convention Movement, 1830–1861*. New York: Arno, 1969.
Bellamy, Edward. *Looking Backward: 2000–1887*. Boston: Ticknor, 1888.
Bellin, Joshua David. *The Demon of the Continent: Indians and the Shaping of American Literature*. Philadelphia: University of Pennsylvania Press, 2001.
Bercovitch, Sacvan. *The American Jeremiad*. Madison: University of Wisconsin Press, 1978.
Berkhofer, Robert, Jr. *The White Man's Indian: Images of the American Indian from Columbus to the Present*. New York: Knopf, 1978.
Berlant, Lauren. *The Queen of America Goes to Washington City: Essays on Sex and Citizenship*. Durham, N.C.: Duke University Press, 1997.

Blackstone, William. *Commentaries on the Laws of England.* 4 vols. 1765–1769. Reprint, Chicago: University of Chicago Press, 1979.

Blyden, Edward Wilmot. *Liberia's Offering: Being Addresses, Sermons, etc.* New York: John A. Gray, 1862.

Bodkin, D. G. *The Fenian Catechism: From the Vulgate of St. Lawrence O'Toole.* New York: Frank McElroy's Steam Printing Rooms, 1867.

Brickhouse, Anna. *Transamerican Literary Relations and the Nineteenth-Century Public Sphere.* New York: Cambridge University Press, 2004.

Brooks, Joanna. "Prince Hall, Freemasonry, and Genealogy." *African American Review* 34.2 (2000): 197–216.

Brooks, Van Wyck. "On Creating a Usable Past." *Dial* 64 (1918): 337–341.

Brown, Thomas N. *Irish American Nationalism, 1870–1890.* Philadelphia: Lippincott, 1966.

Brown, Wendy. *Walled States, Waning Sovereignty.* New York: Zone, 2010.

Brown, William Wells. *The Black Man: His Antecedents, His Genius, and His Achievements.* Boston: R. F. Wallcut, 1863.

Bruce, Dickson D. *The Origins of African American Literature, 1680–1865.* Charlottesville: University of Virginia Press, 2001.

Bruyneel, Kevin. *The Third Space of Sovereignty: The Postcolonial Politics of U.S.–Indigenous Relations.* Minneapolis: University of Minnesota Press, 2007.

Buel, Richard. *Securing the Revolution: Ideology in American Politics, 1789–1815.* Ithaca, N.Y.: Cornell University Press, 1972.

Burlingame Treaty. *English and Chinese Text of the Burlingame Treaty.* 1868. Reprint, San Francisco, Calif.: N.p., 1879.

Burton, Jeffrey. *Indian Territory and the United States, 1866–1906.* Norman: University of Oklahoma Press, 1997.

Byrd, Jodi A. *The Transit of Empire: Indigenous Critiques of Colonialism.* Minneapolis: University of Minnesota Press, 2011.

Calhoun, John C. *A Disquisition on Government, and a Discourse on the Constitution and Government of the United States.* New York: Appleton, 1854.

Campbell, James T. *Songs of Zion: The African Methodist Episcopal Church in the United States.* New York: Oxford University Press, 1995.

Campbell, Malcolm. *Ireland's New Worlds: Immigrants, Politics, and Society in the United States and Australia, 1815–1922.* Madison: University of Wisconsin Press, 2008.

Campbell, Robert. *Memorial: Robert Campbell to the President and Members of the Senate of the State of Georgia.* Savannah, Ga.: N.p., 1829.

Carey, Anthony Gene. *Parties, Slavery, and the Union in Antebellum Georgia.* Athens: University of Georgia Press, 1997.

Carretta, Vincent. *Equiano, the African: Biography of a Self-Made Man.* Athens: University of Georgia Press, 2005.

Castiglia, Christopher. *Interior States: Institutional Consciousness and the Inner Life of Democracy in the Antebellum United States.* Durham, N.C.: Duke University Press, 2008.

Castronovo, Russ. "'As to Nation, I Belong to None': Ambivalence, Diaspora, and Frederick Douglass." *American Transcendental Quarterly* 9 (1995): 245–260.

Chakkalakal, Tess, and Kenneth W. Warren, eds. *Jim Crow, Literature, and the Legacy of Sutton E. Griggs*. Athens: University of Georgia Press, 2013.

Chandler, Joseph R. "Speech of Joseph R. Chandler." In *Remarks of Mr. English, of Indiana, and Other Proceedings, upon the Occasion of the Introduction and Reference of the House Bill to Organize the Territories of Nebraska and Kansas*. Washington, D.C.: Congressional Globe Office, 1854.

Chen, Yong. *Chinese San Francisco 1850–1943: A Transpacific Community*. Palo Alto, Calif.: Stanford University Press, 2000.

Cheyfitz, Eric. *The Poetics of Imperialism: Translation and Colonization from "The Tempest" to "Tarzan."* New York: Oxford University Press, 1991.

——. "Savage Law: The Plot against American Indians in *Johnson and Graham's Lessee v. M'Intosh* and *The Pioneers*." In *Cultures of U.S. Imperialism*, edited by Amy Kaplan and Donald E. Pease, 109–128. Durham, N.C.: Duke University Press, 1993.

Chiles, Katy L. *Transformable Race: Surprising Metamorphoses in the Literature of Early America*. New York: Oxford University Press, 2014.

——. "Within and Without Raced Nations: Intratextuality, Martin Delany, and *Blake; or, The Huts of America*." *American Literature* 80.2 (2008): 323–352.

Chin, Ko-lin. *Chinatown Gangs: Extortion, Enterprise, and Ethnicity*. New York: Oxford University Press, 1996.

Chinese Immigration: The Social, Moral and Political Effect of Chinese Immigration: Policy and Means of Exclusion: Memorial of the Senate of California to the Congress, and an Address to the People of the United States. Prepared by a Committee of the Senate of California. Sacramento, Calif.: State Printing Office, 1877.

Chinese Immigration: The Social, Moral, and Political Effect of Chinese Immigration: Testimony Taken before a Committee of the Senate of the State of California, Appointed April 3, 1876. Sacramento, Calif.: State Printing Office, 1876.

Chung, Sue Fawn. *In Pursuit of Gold: Chinese American Miners and Merchants in the American West*. Champaign: University of Illinois Press, 2011.

Clark, Dennis. *The Irish in Philadelphia: Ten Generations of Urban Experience*. Philadelphia: Temple University Press, 1973.

——. "Letters from the Underground: The Fenian Correspondence of James Gibbons." *Records of the American Catholic Historical Society of Philadelphia* 81.2 (1970): 83–87.

Clark, J. C. D. *The Language of Liberty, 1660–1832: Political Discourse and Social Dynamics in the Anglo-American World*. Cambridge: Cambridge University Press, 1994.

Clark, Mary Whatley. *Chief Bowles and the Texas Cherokees*. Norman: University of Oklahoma Press, 1971.

Clegg, Claude A., III. *The Price of Liberty: African Americans and the Making of Liberia*. Chapel Hill: University of North Carolina Press, 2004.

Cleveland, Henry. *Alexander H. Stephens in Public and Private: With Letters and Speeches*. Philadelphia: National Publishing, 1866.

Clymer, Jeffrey. "Martin Delany's *Blake* and the Transnational Politics of Property." *American Literary History* 15.4 (2003): 709–731.
Cobb, Amanda J. "Understanding Tribal Sovereignty: Definitions, Conceptualizations, Interpretations." *American Studies* 46.3–4 (2005): 115–132.
Cobbe, Frances Power. "The Fenian 'Idea.'" *Atlantic Monthly* 17 (1866): 572–577.
Coleman, Finnie D. *Sutton E. Griggs and the Struggle against White Supremacy*. Knoxville: University of Tennessee Press, 2007.
Confer, Clarissa W. *The Cherokee Nation in the Civil War*. Norman: University of Oklahoma Press, 2007.
The Constitution of the American Anti-Slavery Society: With the Declaration of the Anti-Slavery Society Convention in September at Philadelphia in September, 1833, and the Address to the Public, Issued by the Executive Committee of the Society in September, 1835. New York: American Anti-Slavery Society, 1838.
Constitution of the . . . Anti-Slavery Society. Boston: Isaac Knapp, 1838.
Constitution and By-Laws of the Hebrew Ladies Sewing Circle of the City of Louisville Founded March 7, 1867. Louisville, Ky.: Bradley and Gilbert, 1867.
Cooper, James Fenimore. *The Last of the Mohicans: A Narrative of 1757*. Edited by Richard Slotkin. 1826. Reprint, New York: Penguin, 1986.
———. *The Pioneers: The Sources of the Susquehanna: A Descriptive Tale*. Edited by Donald Ringe. 1823. Reprint, New York: Penguin, 1988.
———. *The Prairie: A Tale*. Edited by Blake Nevius. 1827. Reprint, New York: Penguin, 1987.
Corcoran, Michael. *The Captivity of General Corcoran: The Only Authentic and Reliable Narrative of the Trials and Sufferings Endured during His Twelve Months Imprisonment in Richmond and Other Southern Cities*. Philadelphia: Barclay, 1865.
Crane, Gregg D. *Race, Citizenship, and Law in American Literature*. New York: Cambridge University Press, 2002.
Currie, David P. "Through the Looking-Glass: The Confederate Constitution in Congress, 1861–1865." *Virginia Law Review* 90.5 (2004): 1257–1399.
Curtin, Nancy J. *The United Irishmen: Popular Politics in Ulster and Dublin, 1791–1798*. 1994. Reprint, New York: Clarendon, 1998.
Curtis, L. Perry, Jr. *Apes and Angels: The Irish in Victorian Caricature*. 1971. Reprint, Washington, D.C.: Smithsonian Institution Press, 1997.
Dale, Edward Everett, and Gaston Litton. *Cherokee Cavaliers: Forty Years of Cherokee History as Told in the Correspondence of the Ridge-Watie-Boudinot Family*. 1939. Reprint, Norman: University of Oklahoma Press, 1995.
Daniels, Roger. *Asian America: Chinese and Japanese in the United States since 1850*. Seattle: University of Washington Press, 1988.
D'Arcy, William. "The Fenian Movement in the United States, 1858–1886." PhD diss., Catholic University of America, 1947.
Davidson, Cathy. "Introduction." In *Charlotte Temple* by Susanna Rowson. Edited by Cathy Davidson, xi–xxxiv. New York: Oxford University Press, 1986.
Davis, David Brion. "Slavery." In *The Comparative Approach to American History*, edited

by C. Vann Woodward, 121–134. 1968. Reprint, New York: Oxford University Press, 1997.

———. "Some Themes of Counter-Subversion: An Analysis of Anti-Masonic, Anti-Catholic, and Anti-Mormon Literature." *Mississippi Valley Historical Review* 47.2 (1960): 205–224.

Davis, Horace. "Chinese Immigration: Speech of Hon. Horace Davis, of California, in the House of Representatives, June 8, 1878." Washington, D.C.: U.S. Government Printing Office, 1878.

Dawson, Michael C. "The Black Public Sphere and Civil Society." In *The Oxford Handbook of African American Citizenship, 1865–Present*, edited by Henry Louis Gates Jr. et al., 374–399. New York: Oxford University Press, 2012.

———. *Black Visions: The Roots of Contemporary African-American Political Ideologies*. Chicago: University of Chicago Press, 2003.

Delany, Martin Robison. *Blake; or, The Huts of America*. 1859. Edited by Floyd Miller. Reprint, Boston: Beacon, 1970.

———. *The Condition, Elevation, Emigration, and Destiny of the Colored People of the United States*. 1852. Edited by Toyin Falola. Reprint, Amherst: Humanity Books, 2004.

Deleuze, Gilles. *Negotiations 1972–1990*. Translated by M. Joughin. New York: Columbia University Press, 1995.

Deleuze, Gilles, and Félix Guattari. *Anti-Oedipus: Capitalism and Schizophrenia*. Translated by Robert Hurley, Mark Seem, and Helen R. Lane. Minneapolis: University of Minnesota Press, 1983.

———. *A Thousand Plateaus: Capitalism and Schizophrenia*. Translated by Brian Massumi. Minneapolis: University of Minnesota Press, 1987.

DeLombard, Jeannine Marie. *In the Shadow of the Gallows: Race, Crime, and American Civic Identity*. Philadelphia: University of Pennsylvania Press, 2012.

Deloria, Philip J. *Playing Indian*. New Haven, Conn.: Yale University Press, 1998.

Deloria, Vine, Jr. "Intellectual Self-Determination and Sovereignty: Looking at the Windmills in Our Minds." *Wicazo Sa Review* 13.1(1998): 25–31.

Deloria, Vine, Jr., and Clifford M. Lytle. *The Nations Within: The Past and Future of American Indian Sovereignty*. Austin: University of Texas Press, 1984.

Deloria, Vine, Jr., and David E. Wilkins. *Tribes, Treaties, and Constitutional Tribulations*. Austin: University of Texas Press, 1999.

Denson, Andrew. *Demanding the Cherokee Nation: Indian Autonomy and American Culture, 1830–1900*. Lincoln: University of Nebraska Press, 2004.

Dickinson, John. *Letters from a Farmer, in Pennsylvania, to the Inhabitants of the British Colonies*. 1767. Reprint, London: J. Almon, 1774.

A Digest of the Laws of the State of Georgia: Containing All Statutes and the Substance of All Resolutions of a General and Public Nature . . . 2nd ed. Compiled by Oliver H. Prince. Athens, Ga.: Published by the Author, 1837.

Dillon, Elizabeth Maddock. *The Gender of Freedom: Fictions of Liberalism and the Literary Public Sphere*. Stanford, Calif.: Stanford University Press, 2004.

Dimock, Wai Chee. *Residues of Justice: Literature, Law, Philosophy*. Berkeley: University of California Press, 1996.

Dolan, Jay P. *Irish Americans: A History*. New York: Bloomsbury, 2008.

Dooner, Pierton W. *The Last Days of the Republic*. San Francisco, Calif.: Alta California Publishing House, 1880.

Douglass, Frederick. *The Life and Times of Frederick Douglass, from 1817 to 1882. Written by Himself*. Edited by John Lobb. London: Christian Age Office, 1882.

Downes, Paul. *Democracy, Revolution, and Monarchism in Early American Literature*. New York: Cambridge University Press, 2009.

Doyle, David Noel. "The Irish in North America, 1776–1845." In *Making the Irish American: History and Heritage of the Irish in the United States*, edited by J. J. Lee and Marion R. Casey, 171–212. New York: New York University Press, 2006.

———. "The Remaking of Irish America, 1845–1880." In *Making the Irish American: History and Heritage of the Irish in the United States*, edited by J. J. Lee and Marion R. Casey, 213–252. New York: New York University Press, 2006.

Dubh, Scian [James McCarroll]. *Ridgeway: An Historical Romance of the Fenian Invasion of Canada*. Buffalo, N.Y.: McCarroll, 1868.

Duffy, Jennifer Nugent. *Who's Your Paddy?: Racial Expectations and the Struggle for Irish American Identity*. New York: New York University Press, 2014.

Egerton, Douglas R. *He Shall Go Out Free: The Lives of Denmark Vesey*. Madison, Wis.: Madison House, 1999.

Elliott, Lorraine. "Sovereignty and the Global Politics of the Environment." In *Re-Envisioning Sovereignty: The End of Westphalia?*, edited by Trudy Jacobsen, Charles Sampford, and Ramesh Thakur, 193–209. Aldershot, England: Ashgate, 2008.

Elmer, Jonathan. *On Lingering and Being Last: Race and Sovereignty in the New World*. New York: Fordham University Press, 2008.

Ernest, John. *A Nation within a Nation: Organizing African Americans before the Civil War*. Lanham, Md.: Dee, 2011.

Escott, Paul D. *After Secession: Jefferson Davis and the Failure of Confederate Nationalism*. Baton Rouge: Louisiana State University Press, 1992.

———. *The Confederacy: The Slaveholders' Failed Venture*. Santa Barbara, Calif.: ABC-CLIO, 2010.

An Essay of the Late Institution of the American Society for Colonizing the Free People of Colour, of the United States. Washington, D.C.: Davis and Force, 1820.

Evarts, Jeremiah. *A Brief View of the Present Relations between the Government and People of the United States and the Indians within Our National Limits*. 1829. In *Cherokee Removal: The "William Penn" Essays and Other Writings*, edited by Francis Paul Prucha, 201–211. Knoxville: University of Tennessee Press, 1981.

———. *Cherokee Removal: The "William Penn" Essays and Other Writings*. Edited by Francis Paul Prucha. Knoxville: University of Tennessee Press, 1981.

Executive Documents of the Senate of the United States for the Second Session of the Fifty-Second Congress and the Special Session of the Senate Convened March 4, 1893. 9 vols. Washington, D.C.: U.S. Government Printing Office, 1893.

Fabi, M. Giulia. "Desegregating the Future: Sutton E. Griggs' Pointing the Way and American Utopian Fiction in the Age of Jim Crow." *American Literary Realism* 44.2 (2012): 113–132.

Fabian, Ann. *The Skull Collectors: Race, Science, and America's Unburied Dead*. Chicago: University of Chicago Press, 2010.

Fanning, Charles, ed. *The Exiles of Erin: Nineteenth-Century Irish-American Fiction*. 2nd ed. Chester Springs, Pa.: DuFour, 1997.

Faust, Drew Gilpin. *The Creation of Confederate Nationalism: Ideology and Identity in the Civil War South*. Baton Rouge: Louisiana State University Press, 1988.

Fenian Brotherhood. *Proceedings of the First National Convention of the Fenian Brotherhood Held in Chicago, Illinois, November 1863*. Philadelphia: James Gibbons, 1863.

———. *Proceedings of the Second National Congress of the Fenian Brotherhood Held in Cincinnati, Ohio, January 1865*. Philadelphia: James Gibbons, 1865.

———. *Proceedings of the Senate and the House of Representatives of the Fenian Brotherhood, in Joint Convention at Philadelphia, Pa., November 1868*. New York: D. W. Lee, 1868.

The Fenian Raid at Fort Erie, June the First and Second, 1866, with a Map of the Niagara Peninsula, Shewing the Route of the Troops, and a Plan of the Lime Ridge Battle Ground. Toronto: W. C. Chewett, 1866.

Fenian Songster. Philadelphia: Barclay, 1866.

The Fenians' Progress: A Vision. New York: John Bradburn, 1865.

Fishkin, Shelly Fisher. "Crossroads of Culture: The Transnational Turn in American Studies: Presidential Address to the American Studies Association, November 12, 2004." *American Quarterly* 57.1 (2005): 17–57.

Fitzhugh, George. *Cannibals All! or, Slaves without Masters*. Richmond, Va.: A. Morris, 1857.

———. *Sociology for the South; or, The Failure of Free Society*. Richmond, Va.: A. Morris, 1854.

Fluck, Winfried, Donald E. Pease, and John Carlos Rowe, eds. *Re-Framing the Transnational Turn in American Studies*. Hanover, N.H.: Dartmouth College Press, 2011.

Foner, Philip, ed. *Frederick Douglass: Selected Speeches and Writings*. New York: Lawrence Hill, 1950.

Ford, Lacy K. *Deliver Us from Evil: The Slavery Question in the Old South*. New York: Oxford University Press, 2009.

Ford, Lisa. *Settler Sovereignty: Jurisdiction and Indigenous People in America and Australia, 1788–1836*. Cambridge, Mass.: Harvard University Press, 2010.

Formisano, Ronald. *For the People: American Populist Movements from the Revolution to the 1850s*. Chapel Hill: University of North Carolina Press, 2008.

Foucault, Michel. *Discipline and Punish: The Birth of the Prison*. Translated by Alan Sheridan. New York: Vintage, 1977.

———. "Nietzsche, Genealogy, History." In *Language, Counter-Memory, Practice:*

Selected Essays and Interviews by Michel Foucault, edited by Donald F. Bouchard, 139–164. Ithaca, N.Y.: Cornell University Press, 1980.

———. *"Society Must Be Defended": Lectures at the Collège de France, 1975–1976.* Translated by David Macey. 1997. Reprint, New York: Picador, 2003.

Gallagher, Gary W. *The Confederate War*. Cambridge, Mass.: Harvard University Press, 1997.

Garnet, Henry Highland. *The Past and Present Condition, and the Destiny, of the Colored Race*. Troy, N.Y.: J. C. Kneeland, 1848.

Garrison, Tim Alan. *The Legal Ideology of Removal: The Southern Judiciary and the Sovereignty of American Indian Nations*. Athens: University of Georgia Press, 2002.

Gaul, Theresa Strouth. "Romance and the 'Genuine Indian': Cooper's Politics of Genre." *ESQ* 48 (2002): 159–186.

Gellner, Ernest. *Nations and Nationalism*. Ithaca, N.Y.: Cornell University Press, 1983.

Giles, Paul. *Atlantic Republic: The American Tradition in English Literature*. Oxford: Oxford University Press, 2006.

Gillman, Susan. *Blood Talk: American Race Melodrama and the Culture of the Occult*. Chicago: University of Chicago Press, 2003.

Gilroy, Paul. *The Black Atlantic: Modernity and Double Consciousness*. Cambridge, Mass.: Harvard University Press, 1993.

Glaude, Eddie S. *Exodus!: Race, Religion, and Nation in Early Nineteenth-Century Black America*. Chicago: University of Chicago Press, 2000.

Goldie, Mark, and Robert Wokler, eds. *The Cambridge History of Eighteenth-Century Political Thought*. Cambridge: Cambridge University Press, 2006.

Gonzáles, Juan, and Joseph Torres. *News for All the People: The Epic Story of Race and the American Media*. London: Verso, 2011.

Gordon, Dexter B. *Black Identity: Rhetoric, Ideology, and Nineteenth-Century Black Nationalism*. Carbondale: Southern Illinois University Press, 2003.

Goudie, Sean X. *Creole America: The West Indies and the Formation of Literature and Culture in the New Republic*. Philadelphia: University of Pennsylvania Press, 2006.

Greiman, Jennifer. *Democracy's Spectacle: Sovereignty and Public Life in Antebellum American Writing*. New York: Fordham University Press, 2010.

Grice, Helen. *Negotiating Identities: An Introduction to Asian American Women's Writing*. Manchester, England: Manchester University Press, 2002.

Griggs, Sutton E. *Imperium in Imperio: A Study of the Negro Race Problem: A Novel*. 1899. Reprint, New York: Arno, 1969.

Gross, Andrew S. "Death Is So Permanent: Drive Carefully." In *Re-Framing the Transnational Turn in American Studies*, edited by Winfried Fluck, Donald E. Pease, and John Carlos Rowe, 72–96. Hanover, N.H.: Dartmouth College Press, 2011.

Gruesz, Kirsten Silva. *Ambassadors of Culture: The Transamerican Origins of Latino Writing*. Princeton, N.J.: Princeton University Press, 2002.

Guyatt, Nicholas. "'The Outskirts of Our Happiness': Race and the Lure of Colonization in the Early Republic." *Journal of American History* 95.4 (2009): 986–1011.

Gyory, Andrew. *Closing the Gate: Race, Politics, and the Chinese Exclusion Act.* Chapel Hill: University of North Carolina Press, 1998.

Hale, Sarah Josepha. *Liberia; or, Mr. Peyton's Experiments.* New York: Harper and Brothers, 1853.

Hall, Anthony. *Earth into Property: Colonization, Decolonization, and Capitalism.* Montreal: McGill-Queen's University Press, 2010.

Hamilton, Alexander, James Madison, and John Jay. *The Federalist Papers.* Edited by Ian Shapiro. New Haven, Conn.: Yale University Press, 2009.

Hamilton, Holman. *Prologue to Conflict: The Crisis and Compromise of 1850.* Lexington: University Press of Kentucky, 1964.

Hammon, Jupiter. *A Winter Piece: Being a Serious Exhortation, with a Call to the Unconverted: and a Short Contemplation on the Death of Jesus Christ. Written by Jupiter Hammon, a Negro Man Belonging to Mr. John Lloyd, of Queen's Village, on Long Island, Now in Hartford.* Hartford, Conn.: Published by the Author, 1782. Early American Imprints, 1st ser., no. 17554 (microfilm).

Hammond, John Craig. *Slavery, Freedom, and Expansion in the Early American West.* Charlottesville: University of Virginia Press, 2007.

Handlin, Oscar. *Boston's Immigrants, 1790–1880: A Study in Acculturation.* Cambridge, Mass.: Harvard University Press, 1941.

Hanlon, Christopher. *America's England: Antebellum Literature and Atlantic Sectionalism.* Oxford: Oxford University Press, 2013.

Hansen, Lawrence Douglas Taylor. "The Chinese Six Companies of San Francisco and the Smuggling of Chinese Immigrants across the U.S.–Mexico Border, 1882–1930." *Journal of the Southwest* 48.1 (2006): 37–61.

Hardt, Michael, and Antonio Negri. *Empire.* Cambridge, Mass.: Harvard University Press, 2000.

Hartz, Louis. *The Liberal Tradition in America: An Interpretation of American Political Thought since the Revolution.* New York: Harcourt, Brace and World, 1955.

Hauptman, Laurence M. *Between Two Fires: American Indians and the Civil War.* New York: Free Press, 1995.

Hauser, Jeanette L., and Isaiah L. Hauser. *The Orient and Its People.* Milwaukee, Wis.: I. L. Hauser, 1876.

Heckewelder, John. *History, Manners, and Customs of the Indian Nations Who Once Inhabited Pennsylvania and the Neighboring States.* Philadelphia: A. Small, 1818.

Hendler, Glenn. *Public Sentiments: Structures of Feeling in Nineteenth-Century American Literature.* Chapel Hill: University of North Carolina Press, 2001.

Hertzberg, Hazel W. *The Search for an American Indian Identity: Modern Pan-Indian Movements.* Syracuse, N.Y.: Syracuse University Press, 1971.

Hodder, Frank Heywood. "The Railroad Background of the Kansas-Nebraska Act." *Mississippi Valley Historical Review* 12.1 (1925): 3–22.

Horton, James Oliver, and Lois E Horton. "A Federal Assault: African Americans and the Impact of the Fugitive Slave Law of 1850." In *Slavery and the Law,* edited by Paul Finkelman, 143–160. Lanham, Md.: Rowman and Littlefield, 2002.

Howard-Pitney, David. *The African American Jeremiad: Appeals for Justice in America.* Rev. ed. Philadelphia: Temple University Press, 2005.

Howe, Daniel Walker. *The Political Culture of the American Whigs.* Chicago: University of Chicago Press, 1979.

Hoy, William. *The Chinese Six Companies: A Short, General Historical Resumé of Its Origin, Function, and Importance in the Life of the California Chinese.* San Francisco, Calif.: Chinese Consolidated Benevolent Association, 1942.

Hroch, Miroslav. "From National Movement to the Fully-Formed Nation: The Nation-Building Process in Europe." In *Mapping the Nation,* edited by Gopal Balakrishnan, 78–97. London: Verso, 1996.

Huang, Yunte. *Transpacific Imaginations: History, Literature, Counterpoetics.* Cambridge, Mass.: Harvard University Press, 2008.

Hudson, Nicholas. "From 'Nation' to 'Race': The Origin of Racial Classification in Eighteenth-Century Thought." *Eighteenth-Century Studies* 29.3 (1996): 247–264.

Hung, Ho-fung. *Protest with Chinese Characteristics: Demonstrations, Riots, and Petitions in the Mid-Qing Dynasty.* New York: Columbia University Press, 2011.

Huston, James L. *Stephen A. Douglas and the Dilemmas of Democratic Equality.* Lanham, Md.: Rowman and Littlefield, 2007.

Hutchison, Coleman. *Apples and Ashes: Literature, Nationalism, and the Confederate States of America.* Athens: University of Georgia Press, 2012.

Hutton, Frankie, and Barbara Strauss Reed. *Outsiders in 19th-Century Press History: Multicultural Perspectives.* Bowling Green, Ohio: Bowling Green State University Popular Press, 1995.

Ignatiev, Noel. *How the Irish Became White.* New York: Routledge, 1995.

Iredell, James. *To the Inhabitants of Great Britain.* 1774. In *Life and Correspondence of James Iredell, One of the Associate Justices of the Supreme Court of the United States* by Griffith J. McRee, 1:205–220. New York: Appleton, 1857.

Jackson, Andrew. "President Jackson on Indian Removal." In *Documents of United States Indian Policy,* edited by Francis Paul Prucha, 47–48. Lincoln: University of Nebraska Press, 1975.

Jackson, Holly. *American Blood: The Ends of the Family in American Literature, 1850–1900.* New York: Oxford University Press, 2013.

Jackson, Robert. *Sovereignty: Evolution of an Idea.* Cambridge: Polity, 2007.

Jacobs, Elizabeth. *Mexican American Literature: The Politics of Identity.* New York: Routledge, 2006.

Jacobson, Matthew Frye. *Whiteness of a Different Color: European Immigrants and the Alchemy of Race.* Cambridge, Mass.: Harvard University Press, 1998.

Jameson, Fredric. *Archaeologies of the Future: The Desire Called Utopia and Other Science Fictions.* New York: Verso, 2005.

——— . *The Political Unconscious: Narrative as a Socially Symbolic Act.* Ithaca, N.Y.: Cornell University Press, 1981.

Jefferson, Thomas. *Notes on the State of Virginia.* In *The Portable Thomas Jefferson,* edited by Merrill D. Peterson, 23–232. New York: Penguin, 1975.

Jenkins, Brian A. *Fenian Problem: Insurgency and Terrorism in a Liberal State, 1858–1874.* Montreal: McGill-Queen's University Press, 2008.

———. *Fenians and Anglo-American Relations during Reconstruction.* Ithaca, N.Y.: Cornell University Press, 1969.

Johannsen, Robert Walter. *The Frontier, the Union, and Stephen A. Douglas.* Urbana: University of Illinois Press, 1989.

Johnson, Lynn R. "A Return to the Black (W)hole: Mitigating the Trauma of Homelessness in Sutton E. Griggs's *Imperium in Imperio.*" *Southern Literary Journal* 42.2 (2010): 12–33.

Johnstone, George. *Governor Johnston[e]'s Speech on American Affairs, on the Address in Answer to the King's Speech.* 1776. Reprint, Edinburgh: Privately printed, 1885.

Jordan, Winthrop D. *White over Black: American Attitudes toward the Negro, 1550–1812.* Chapel Hill: University of North Carolina Press, 1968.

Justice, Daniel Heath. *Our Fire Survives the Storm: A Cherokee Literary History.* Minneapolis: University of Minnesota Press, 2006.

Kanazawa, Mark. "Immigration, Exclusion, and Taxation: Anti-Chinese Legislation in Gold Rush California." *Journal of Economic History* 65.3 (2005): 779–803.

Kaplan, Amy M. *The Anarchy of Empire in the Making of U.S. Culture.* Cambridge, Mass.: Harvard University Press, 2005.

———. "Manifest Domesticity." *American Literature* 70.3 (1998): 581–606.

Karafilis, Maria. "Oratory, Embodiment, and U.S. Citizenship in Sutton E. Griggs's *Imperium in Imperio.*" *African American Review* 40.1 (2006): 125–143.

Kazanjian, David. *The Colonizing Trick: National Culture and Imperial Citizenship in Early America.* Minneapolis: University of Minnesota Press, 2003.

Kennedy, Lionel H., and Thomas Parker. *An Official Report of the Trials of Sundry Negroes, Charged with an Attempt to Raise an Insurrection in the State of South-Carolina: Preceded by an Introduction and Narrative: and, in an Appendix, a Report of the Trials of Four White Persons on Indictments for Attempting to Excite the Slaves to Insurrection.* Charleston, S.C.: James R. Schenck, 1822.

Kenny, Kevin. "Race, Violence, and Anti-Irish Sentiment in the Nineteenth Century." In *Making the Irish American: History and Heritage of the Irish in the United States,* edited by J. J. Lee and Marion R. Casey, 364–378. New York: New York University Press, 2006.

Kerkering, John D. *The Poetics of National and Racial Identity in Nineteenth-Century American Literature.* Cambridge: Cambridge University Press, 2003.

Kettner, James H. *The Development of American Citizenship, 1608–1870.* Chapel Hill: University of North Carolina Press, 1978.

Kidwell, Clara Sue, and Alan Velie. *Native American Studies.* Lincoln: University of Nebraska Press, 2005.

Kiernan, James Lawlor. *Ireland and America versus England: From a Fenian Point of View.* Detroit, Mich.: G. W. Pattison, 1864.

King, Lovalerie. *Race, Theft, and Ethics: Property Matters in African American Literature.* Baton Rouge: Louisiana State University Press, 2007.

Klammer, Martin. "Slavery and Abolition." In *Walt Whitman: An Encyclopedia*, edited by J. R. LeMaster and Donald D. Kummings, 640–643. New York: Garland, 1998.

Knadler, Stephen. "Sensationalizing Patriotism: Sutton Griggs and the Sentimental Nationalism of Citizen Tom." *American Literature* 79.4 (2007): 673–699.

Knobel, Dale. *Paddy and the Republic: Ethnicity and Nationality in Antebellum America*. Middletown, Conn.: Wesleyan University Press, 1986.

Konkle, Maureen. *Writing Indian Nations: Native Intellectuals and the Politics of Historiography, 1827–1863*. Chapel Hill: University of North Carolina Press, 2004.

Krieg, Joann P. *Whitman and the Irish*. Iowa City: University of Iowa Press, 2000.

Kupperman, Karen Ordahl. "Introduction: The Changing Definition of America." In *America in European Consciousness: 1493–1750*, edited by Karen Ordahl Kupperman, 1–29. Chapel Hill: University of North Carolina Press, 1995.

LaFeber, Walter. *The New Empire: An Interpretation of American Expansion, 1860–1898*. Ithaca, N.Y.: Cornell University Press, 1963.

Lai Chun-chuen. *Remarks of the Chinese Merchants of San Francisco on Governor Bigler's Message*. San Francisco, Calif.: Whitton Towne, 1855.

Lai, Him Mark. *Becoming Chinese American: A History of Communities and Institutions*. Walnut Creek, Calif.: Rowman AltaMira, 2004.

Lamplugh, George R. *Politics on the Periphery: Parties and Factions in Georgia, 1783–1806*. Newark: University of Delaware Press, 1986.

Lawrence, D. H. *Studies in Classic American Literature*. 1923. Reprint, New York: Penguin, 1977.

"Letter from V. du C— to His Father." 1825. In *The Atlantic Magazine*, 2:293–300. New York: E. Bliss and E. White, 1825.

Levander, Caroline. "Sutton Griggs and the Borderlands of Empire." *American Literary History* 22.1 (2010): 57–84.

Levander, Caroline F., and Robert S. Levine, eds. *Hemispheric American Studies*. New Brunswick, N.J.: Rutgers University Press, 2008.

Levine, Robert S. *Dislocating Race and Nation: Episodes in Nineteenth-Century American Literary Nationalism*. Chapel Hill: University of North Carolina Press, 2008.

———. *Martin Delany, Frederick Douglass, and the Politics of Representative Identity*. Chapel Hill: University of North Carolina Press, 1997.

———, ed. *Martin R. Delany: A Documentary Reader*. Chapel Hill: University of North Carolina Press, 2003.

———. "Temporality, Race, Empire, and Cooper's *The Deerslayer*: The Beginning of the End." In *The Oxford Handbook of Nineteenth-Century American Literature*, edited by Russ Castronovo, 163–178. New York: Oxford University Press, 2012.

———. "*Uncle Tom's Cabin* in *Frederick Douglass's Paper*: An Analysis of Reception." *American Literature* 64 (1992): 71–93.

Lévy, Pierre. *Becoming Virtual: Reality in the Digital Age*. Translated by Robert Bononno. New York: Plenum, 1998.

The Life, Trial, and Execution of Captain John Brown, Known as "Old Brown of Ossawatomie," with a Full Account of the Attempted Insurrection at Harpers Ferry: Compiled from Official and Authentic Sources. New York: R. M. DeWitt, 1859.

Lincoln, C. Eric. *The Black Church in the African American Experience.* Durham, N.C.: Duke University Press, 1990.

Linebaugh, Peter, and Marcus Rediker. *The Many-Headed Hydra: The Hidden History of the Revolutionary Atlantic.* Boston: Beacon, 2000.

Ling, Huping. *Chinese Chicago: Race, Transnational Migration, and Community since 1870.* Palo Alto, Calif.: Stanford University Press, 2012.

Ling, Huping, and Allan W. Austin. *Asian American History and Culture: An Encyclopedia.* New York: Routledge, 2010,

Littlefield, Daniel F., Jr., and James W. Parins. *American Indian and Alaska Native Newspapers and Periodicals, 1826–1924.* Vol. 1. Westport, Conn.: Greenwood, 1984.

Lo, Karl, and H. M. Lai. *Chinese Newspapers Published in North America, 1854–1975.* Washington, D.C.: Center for Chinese Research Materials, Association of Chinese Research Libraries, 1977.

Lubert, Howard L. "Sovereignty and Liberty in William Blackstone's *Commentaries on the Laws of England.*" *Review of Politics* 72.2 (2010): 271–297.

Lukács, Georg. *The Historical Novel.* Translated by Hannah Mitchell and Stanley Mitchell. 1937. Reprint, Lincoln: University of Nebraska Press, 1983.

Lumpkin, Wilson. *The Removal of the Cherokee Indians from Georgia.* 1907. Reprint, New York: Augustus M. Kelley, 1971.

Lutz, Donald S. "The Relative Influence of European Writers on Late Eighteenth-Century American Political Thought." *American Political Science Review* 78.1 (1984): 189–197.

Lyman, Stanford M. "Conflict and the Web of Group Affiliation in San Francisco's Chinatown, 1850–1910." *Pacific Historical Review* 43.4 (1974): 473–499.

Lynch, Timothy G. "A Kindred and Congenial Element: Irish-American Nationalism's Embrace of Republican Rhetoric." *New Hibernia Review* 13.2 (2009): 77–91.

Lyons, Scott Richard. "Rhetorical Sovereignty: What Do American Indians Want from Writing?" *College Composition and Communication* 51.3 (2000): 447–468.

MacDonald, John A. *Troublous Times in Canada.* Toronto: W. S. Johnston, 1910.

Mackitrick, Eric L. *Slavery Defended: The Views of the Old South.* Englewood Cliffs, N.J.: Prentice Hall, 1963.

MacMillan, Ken. *Sovereignty and Possession in the English New World: The Legal Foundations of Empire, 1576–1640.* New York: Cambridge University Press, 2006.

Madison, James. "Sovereignty." In *Letters and Other Writings of James Madison,* 4:390–395. Philadelphia: Lippincott, 1865.

———. "To George Washington" (16 April 1787). In *Letters and Other Writings of James Madison,* 1:287–292. Philadelphia: Lippincott, 1865.

———. "To Thomas Jefferson" (24 October 1787). In *Papers of James Madison,* vol. 10 (27 May 1787–3 March 1788), edited by Robert A. Rutland and William M. E. Rachal, 206–214. Chicago: University of Chicago Press, 1977.

Matthewson, Tim. "Jefferson and the Nonrecognition of Haiti." *Proceedings of the American Philosophical Society* 140.1 (1996): 22–48.

Matthiessen, F. O. *American Renaissance: Art and Expression in the Age of Emerson and Whitman.* New York: Oxford University Press, 1968.

May, Cedrick. *Evangelism and Resistance in the Black Atlantic, 1760–1835.* Athens: University of Georgia Press, 2008.

McCaffrey, Lawrence J. *Textures of Irish America.* 1992. Reprint, Syracuse, N.Y.: Syracuse University Press, 1998.

McClain, Charles J. "The Chinese Struggle for Civil Rights in Nineteenth Century America: The First Phase, 1850–1870." *California Law Review* 72.4 (1984): 529–568.

———. *In Search of Equality: The Chinese Struggle against Discrimination in Nineteenth-Century America.* Berkeley: University of California Press, 1994.

McClain, Charles J., and Laurene Wu McClain. "The Chinese Contribution to the Development of American Law." In *Entry Denied: Exclusion and the Chinese Community in America, 1882–1943,* edited by Sucheng Chan, 3–24. Philadelphia: Temple University Press, 1991.

McCullough, Kate. *Regions of Identity: The Constructions of America in Women's Fiction, 1885–1914.* Palo Alto, Calif.: Stanford University Press, 1999.

McCurry, Stephanie. *Confederate Reckoning: Power and Politics in the Civil War South.* Cambridge, Mass.: Harvard University Press, 2010.

McDonald, Forrest. *E Pluribus Unum: The Formation of the American Republic, 1776–1790.* New York: Penguin, 1972.

———. *States' Rights and the Union: Imperium in Imperio, 1776–1876.* Lawrence: University Press of Kansas, 2002.

McDowell, Tremaine. *American Studies.* Minneapolis: University of Minnesota Press, 1948.

McFeely, William S. *Frederick Douglass.* New York: Norton, 1991.

McGee, Michael. "In Search of 'the People': A Rhetorical Alternative." *Quarterly Journal of Speech* 61 (1975): 235–249.

McGovern, Bryan P. *John Mitchel: Irish Nationalist, Southern Secessionist.* Knoxville: University of Tennessee Press, 2009.

McLoughlin, William G., with Walter H. Conser Jr. and Virginia Duffy McLoughlin. *The Cherokee Ghost Dance: Essays on the Southeastern Indians, 1789–1861.* Macon, Ga.: Mercer University Press, 1984.

———. *Cherokee Renascence in the New Republic.* Princeton, N.J.: Princeton University Press, 1986.

McPherson, Edward. *The Political History of the United States of America during the Period of Reconstruction.* 3rd ed. Washington D.C.: James Chapman, 1880.

McTyeire, Holland Nimmons. *Duties of Christian Masters.* Edited by Thomas O. Summers. Nashville, Tenn.: Southern Methodist Publishing House, 1859.

Memorial of the Six Chinese Companies: An Address to the Senate and House of Representatives of the United States. San Francisco, Calif.: Alta California Publishing House, 1877.

Menand, Louis. "Morton, Agassiz, and the Origins of Scientific Racism in the United States." *Journal of Blacks in Higher Education* 34 (2001): 110–113.

Merriam, Charles. *A History of American Political Theories.* New York: Macmillan, 1903.

Miller, Kerby A. *Emigrants and Exiles: Ireland and the Irish Exodus to North America.* Oxford: Oxford University Press, 1985.

Miller, Perry. *Errand into the Wilderness.* 1956. Reprint, Cambridge, Mass.: Harvard University Press, 2009.
———. *The New England Mind: The Seventeenth Century.* 1939. Reprint, Cambridge, Mass.: Harvard University Press, 1961.
Mjagkij, Nina, ed. *Organizing Black America.* New York: Routledge, 2003.
Morse, Samuel F. B. *Imminent Dangers to the Free Institutions of the United States through Foreign Immigration, and the Present State of the Naturalization Laws: A Series of Numbers Originally Published in the New York Journal of Commerce in 1835.* New York: E. B. Clayton, 1835.
Morton, Samuel. *Crania Aegyptiaca; or, Observations on Egyptian Ethnography, Derived from Anatomy, History, and the Monuments.* Philadelphia: J. Pennington, 1844.
———. *Crania Americana: or, A Comparative View of the Skulls of Various Aboriginal Nations of North and South America.* Philadelphia: J. Dobson, 1839.
Moses, Wilson Jeremiah. *Black Messiahs and Uncle Toms: Social and Literary Manipulations of a Religious Myth.* University Park: Pennsylvania State University Press, 1993.
———, ed. *Classical Black Nationalism: From the American Revolution to Marcus Garvey.* New York: New York University Press, 1996.
———. *The Golden Age of Black Nationalism, 1850–1925.* 1978. Reprint, New York: Oxford University Press, 1988.
Moss, Hillary J. *Schooling Citizens: The Struggle for African American Education in Antebellum America.* Chicago: University of Chicago Press, 2010.
Moulton, Gary E., ed. *The Papers of Chief John Ross, 1807–1839.* 2 vols. Norman: University of Oklahoma Press, 1985.
Mulford, Carla J. "Figuring Benjamin Franklin in American Cultural Memory." *New England Quarterly* 72.3 (1999): 415–443.
———, ed. *The Power of Sympathy and The Coquette* by William Hill Brown and Hannah Webster Foster. New York: Penguin, 1996.
Neidhardt, Wilfried S. *Fenianism in North America.* University Park: Pennsylvania State University Press, 1975.
Nelson, Dana D. *The Word in Black and White: Reading "Race" in American Literature, 1638–1867.* New York: Oxford University Press, 1992.
Nelson, Joshua B. *Progressive Traditions: Identity in Cherokee Literature and Culture.* Norman: University of Oklahoma Press, 2014.
Newman, Richard. *Freedom's Prophet: Bishop Richard Allen, the AME Church, and the Black Founding Fathers.* New York: New York University Press, 2008.
Newman, Richard, Patrick Rael, and Philip Lapsansky, eds. *Pamphlets of Protest: An Anthology of Early African-American Protest Literature, 1790–1860.* New York: Routledge, 2013.
Norgren, Jill. *The Cherokee Cases: Two Landmark Federal Decisions in the Fight for Sovereignty.* 1996. Reprint, Norman: University of Oklahoma Press, 2004.
"The *North American Review* for Jan. 1830: Article III." In *The Spirit of the Pilgrims,* 3:141–161. Boston: Peirce and Parker, 1830.
Nwankwo, Ifeoma Kiddoe. *Black Cosmopolitanism: Racial Consciousness and*

Transnational Identity in the Nineteenth-Century Americas. Philadelphia: University of Pennsylvania Press, 2005.

Odo, Franklin, ed. *The Columbia Documentary History of the Asian American Experience.* New York: Columbia University Press, 2002.

Onuf, Peter. *Jefferson's Empire: The Language of American Nationhood.* Charlottesville: University of Virginia Press, 2000.

Oson, Jacob. *A Search for Truth; or, An Inquiry for the Origin of the African Nation: An Address, Delivered at New-Haven in March, and at New York in April, 1817. By Jacob Oson, a Descendant of Africa. Published for, and by the Request of, Christopher Rush, a Descendant of Africa.* 1817. http://oieahc.wm.edu/wmq/Jan07/Hall.pdf.

Otis, James, Jr. *Rights of the British Colonies Asserted and Proved.* Boston: J. Almon, 1764.

——. *A Vindication of the British Colonies.* 1765. Reprint, Boston: J. Almon, 1769.

Paine, Thomas. *Four Letters on Interesting Subjects.* Philadelphia: Styner and Cist, 1776.

——. *The Rights of Man, for the Use and Benefit of All Mankind.* 1791. Reprint, London: Daniel Isaac Eaton, 1795.

Paley, William. *An Essay upon the British Constitution: Being the Seventh Chapter of the Sixth Book of "The Principles of Moral and Political Philosophy."* London: R. Faulder, 1792.

Parrington, Vernon Louis. *Main Currents in American Thought: The Colonial Mind, 1602–1800.* 1927. Reprint, Norman: University of Oklahoma Press, 1987.

Pease, Donald E., and Amy Kaplan, eds. *Cultures of U.S. Imperialism.* Durham, N.C.: Duke University Press, 1993.

Pease, Jane H., and William Henry Pease. *The Fugitive Slave Law and Anthony Burns: A Problem in Law Enforcement.* Philadelphia: Lippincott, 1975.

Perdue, Theda, ed. *Cherokee Editor: The Writings of Elias Boudinot.* 1983. Reprint, Athens: University of Georgia Press, 1996.

Perdue, Theda, and Michael D. Green. *The Cherokee Nation and the Trail of Tears.* New York: Penguin/Viking, 2008.

Pfaelzer, Jean. *Driven Out: The Forgotten War against Chinese Americans.* Berkeley: University of California Press, 2008.

Phan, Hoang Gia. *Bonds of Citizenship: Law and the Labors of Emancipation.* New York: New York University Press, 2013.

Phillips, Ulrich Bonnell. *Georgia and State Rights.* 1902. Reprint, Macon, Ga.: Mercer University Press, 1984.

Philpott, Daniel. *Revolutions in Sovereignty: How Ideas Shaped Modern International Relations.* Princeton, N.J.: Princeton University Press, 2001.

Pocock, J. G. A. *The Machiavellian Moment: Florentine Political Thought and the Atlantic Republican Tradition.* Princeton, N.J.: Princeton University Press, 1975.

Popkin, Jeremy. *A Concise History of the Haitian Revolution.* West Sussex, England: Wiley-Blackwell, 2012.

Price, George R., and James Bremer Stewart. *"To Heal the Scourge of Prejudice": The Life and Writings of Hosea Easton.* Amherst: University of Massachusetts Press, 1999.

Prucha, Francis Paul. *The Great Father: The United States Government and the American Indians*. Lincoln: University of Nebraska Press, 1984.
Qin, Yucheng. *The Diplomacy of Nationalism: The Six Companies and China's Policy toward Exclusion*. Honolulu: University of Hawai'i Press, 2009.
Raboteau, Albert J. "'Ethiopia Shall Soon Stretch Forth Her Hands': Black Destiny in Nineteenth-Century America." In *African American Religious Thought: An Anthology*, edited by Cornel West and Eddie S. Glaude Jr., 397–413. Louisville, Ky.: Westminster John Knox, 2003.
Rafinesque, Constantine Samuel. "The Primitive Black Nations of America." *Atlantic Journal and Friend of Knowledge* 1.3 (1832): 85–86.
Ramón, Marta. *A Provisional Dictator: James Stephens and the Fenian Movement*. Dublin: University College Dublin Press, 2007.
Raustiala, Kal. *Does the Constitution Follow the Flag?: The Evolution of Territoriality in American Law*. New York: Oxford University Press, 2009.
Reilly, Eileen. "Modern Ireland: An Introductory Survey." In *Making the Irish American: History and Heritage of the Irish in the United States*, edited by J. J. Lee and Marion R. Casey, 63–147. New York: New York University Press, 2006.
Remarks of Mr. English, of Indiana, and Other Proceedings, upon the Occasion of the Introduction and Reference of the House Bill to Organize the Territories of Nebraska and Kansas. Washington, D.C.: Congressional Globe Office, 1854.
"A Remonstrance from the Chinese in California to the Congress of the United States." Translated by William Speer. In *The Oldest and Newest Empire* by William Speer, 588–604. San Francisco, Calif.: H. H. Bancroft, 1870; Hartford, Conn.: S. S. Scranton, 1870.
Report of the Joint Special Committee to Investigate Chinese Immigration. Report 689, 44th Cong., 2nd sess., 1876. Washington, D.C.: U.S. Government Printing Office, 1877.
Reynolds, David S. *John Brown, Abolitionist: The Man Who Killed Slavery, Sparked the Civil War, and Seeded Civil Rights*. New York: Vintage, 2005.
———. *Walt Whitman's America: A Cultural Biography*. New York: Knopf, 1995.
Richardson, James. *A Compilation of the Messages and Papers of the Presidents*. Vol. 7. Washington, D.C.: Published by the Authority of Congress, 1898.
Richardson, Marilyn. *Maria W. Stewart: America's First Black Woman Political Writer*. Bloomington: Indiana University Press, 1987.
Rifkin, Mark. *Manifesting America: The Imperial Construction of U.S. National Space*. New York: Oxford University Press, 2009.
Riss, Arthur. "Racial Essentialism and Family Values in *Uncle Tom's Cabin*." *American Quarterly* 46.4 (1994): 513–544.
Robbins, Caroline. *The Eighteenth-Century Commonwealthman: Studies in the Transmission, Development, and Circumstance of English Liberal Thought from the Restoration of Charles II until the War with the Thirteen Colonies*. Cambridge, Mass.: Harvard University Press, 1959.
Rosen, Deborah A. *American Indians and State Law: Sovereignty, Race, and Citizenship, 1790–1880*. Lincoln: University of Nebraska Press, 2007.

Ross-Mulkey, Mikhelle Lynn. "The *Cherokee Phoenix*: Resistance and Accommodation." *Native South* 5.1 (2012): 123–148.
Rowe, John Carlos. *The New American Studies*. Minneapolis: University of Minnesota Press, 2002.
Rubin, Anne Sarah. *A Shattered Nation: The Rise and Fall of the Confederacy, 1861–1868*. Chapel Hill: University of North Carolina Press, 2007.
Ruskola, Teemu. *Legal Orientalism*. Cambridge, Mass.: Harvard University Press, 2013.
Rutherford, John. *The Secret History of the Fenian Conspiracy: Its Origin, Objects, & Ramifications*. 2 vols. London: C. K. Paul, 1877.
Ryan, Susan M. "Errand into Africa: Colonization and Nation Building in Sarah J. Hale's *Liberia*." *New England Quarterly* 68.4 (December 1995): 558–583.
Sadowski-Smith, Claudia. "Unskilled Labor Migration and the Illegality Spiral: Chinese, European, and Mexican *Indocumentados* in the United States, 1882–2007." *American Quarterly* 60.3 (2008): 779–804.
Saillant, John. *Black Puritan, Black Republican: The Life and Thought of Lemuel Haynes, 1753–1833*. New York: Oxford University Press, 2003.
Samito, Christian G. *Becoming American under Fire: Irish Americans, African Americans, and the Politics of Citizenship during the Civil War Era*. Ithaca, N.Y.: Cornell University Press, 2009.
Samuels, Shirley. *Reading the American Novel, 1780–1865*. Hoboken, N.J.: Wiley-Blackwell, 2012.
Sánchez-Arce, Ana María. "Identity and Form in Contemporary Literature: An Introduction." In *Identity and Form in Contemporary Literature*, edited by Ana María Sánchez-Arce, 1–15. New York: Routledge, 2014.
Sandmeyer, Elmer. *The Anti-Chinese Movement in the United States*. 1939. Reprint, Champaign: University of Illinois Press, 1991.
Savage, John. *Fenian Heroes and Martyrs*. Boston: Patrick Donahoe, 1868.
Saxton, Alexander. *The Indispensible Enemy: Labor and the Anti-Chinese Movement in California*. Berkeley: University of California Press, 1971.
Saye, Albert B. *A Constitutional History of Georgia, 1732–1968*. 1948. Reprint, Athens: University of Georgia Press, 2010.
Scanlan, Michael. *Love and Land: Poems*. Chicago: Western News Company, 1866.
Scheckel, Susan. *The Insistence of the Indian: Race and Nationalism in Nineteenth-Century American Culture*. Princeton, N.J.: Princeton University Press, 1998.
Schmitt, Carl. *The Concept of the Political*. Expanded ed. Translated and edited by George Schwab. Chicago: University of Chicago Press, 2008.
———. *Political Theology: Four Chapters on the Concept of Sovereignty*. Translated by George Schwab. Cambridge, Mass.: MIT Press, 1985.
Schneider, Bethany. "Boudinot's Change: Boudinot, Emerson, and Ross on Cherokee Removal." *ELH* 75.1 (2008): 151–177.
Schoolman, Martha. *Abolitionist Geographies*. Minneapolis: University of Minnesota Press, 2014.
Schwab, George. "Introduction." In *Political Theology: Four Chapters on the Concept of Sovereignty* by Carl Schmitt. Cambridge, Mass.: MIT Press, 1985.

Scully, Eileen P. *Bargaining with the State from Afar: American Citizenship in Treaty Port China, 1844–1942.* New York: Columbia University Press, 2001.
Seabrook, Whitemarsh. *A Concise View of the Critical Situation and Future Prospects of the Slaveholding States.* Charleston, S.C.: A. E. Miller, 1825.
Sellers, Mortimer N. *American Republicanism: Roman Ideology in the United States Constitution.* New York: New York University Press, 1994.
Seraile, William. *Fire in His Heart: Bishop Benjamin Tucker Tanner and the A.M.E. Church.* Knoxville: University of Tennessee Press, 1998.
Slauter, Eric. *The State as a Work of Art: The Cultural Origins of the Constitution.* Chicago: University of Chicago Press, 2009.
Smith, Anthony D. *The Ethnic Origins of Nations.* Oxford: Basil Blackwell, 1986.
———. *National Identity.* Reno: University of Nevada Press, 1991.
Smith, Rogers. *Civic Ideals: Conflicting Visions of Citizenship in U.S. History.* New Haven, Conn.: Yale University Press, 1997.
Smith, Theophus H. *Conjuring Culture: Biblical Formations of Black America.* New York: Oxford University Press, 1994.
Smith, William A. "Lectures on the Philosophy and Practice of Slavery, as Exhibited in the Institution of Domestic Slavery in the United States, with the Duties of Masters to Slaves." Edited by Thomas O. Summers. Nashville, Tenn.: Stevenson and Evans, 1856. http://docsouth.unc.edu.
Snay, Mitchell. *Fenians, Freedmen, and Southern Whites: Race and Nationality in the Era of Reconstruction.* Baton Rouge: Louisiana State University Press, 2007.
Speer, William. *The Oldest and Newest Empire: China and the United States.* San Francisco, Calif.: H. H. Bancroft, 1870; Hartford, Conn.: S. S. Scranton, 1870.
Starr, M. B. *The Coming Struggle; or, What the People on the Pacific Coast Think of the Coolie Invasion.* San Francisco, Calif.: Excelsior Office, Bacon and Company, Book and Job Printers, 1873.
Staudenraus, P. J. *The African Colonization Movement, 1816–1865.* New York: Columbia University Press, 1961.
Stauffer, John, and Zoe Trodd. *The Tribunal: Responses to John Brown and the Harpers Ferry Raid.* Cambridge, Mass.: Harvard University Press, 2012.
Stephens, James. *Stephens' Fenian songster, Containing all the Heart-Stirring and Patriotic Ballads and Songs, as Sung at the Meetings of the Fenian Brotherhood.* New York, NY: William H. Murphy, 1866.
Stowe, Harriet Beecher. *Uncle Tom's Cabin; or, Life among the Lowly.* In *The Oxford Harriet Beecher Stowe Reader,* edited by Joan D. Hedrick, 78–405. New York: Oxford University Press, 1994.
Stuckey, Sterling. *The Ideological Origins of Black Nationalism.* New York: Beacon, 1972.
Sui Sin Fah [Far]. "A Chinese Ishmael." *Overland Monthly* 34.199 (1899): 43–49.
Sundquist, Eric. *To Wake the Nations: Race and the Making of American Literature.* Cambridge, Mass.: Belknap, 1993.
Symonds, Craig. *Lincoln and His Admirals.* New York: Oxford University Press, 2008.
Takaki, Ronald. *Strangers from a Different Shore: A History of Asian Americans.* Boston: Little, Brown, 1989.

Taketani, Etsuko. "Postcolonial Liberia: Sarah Josepha Hale's Africa." *American Literary History* 14.3 (2002): 479–504.
Tawil, Ezra. *The Making of Racial Sentiment: Slavery and the Birth of the Frontier Romance*. New York: Cambridge University Press, 2006.
Tennenhouse, Leonard. *The Importance of Feeling English: American Literature and the British Diaspora, 1750–1850*. Princeton, N.J.: Princeton University Press, 2007.
Teuton, Sean Kicummah. "Cities of Refuge: Indigenous Cosmopolitan Writers and the International Imaginary." *American Literary History* 25.1 (2013): 33–53.
Thomas, Brook. *Civic Myths: A Law and Literature Approach to Citizenship*. Chapel Hill: University of North Carolina Press, 2007.
———. *Cross Examinations of Law and Literature: Cooper, Hawthorne, Stowe, and Melville*. Cambridge: Cambridge University Press, 1987.
Tocqueville, Alexis de. *Democracy in America*. 1835. Translated by Arthur Goldhammer. Reprint, New York: Library of America, 2004.
Traubel, Horace. *With Walt Whitman in Camden*. Vol. 3. New York: Mitchell Kennerley, 1914.
Tsai, Robert L. *America's Forgotten Constitutions: Defiant Visions of Power and Community*. Cambridge, Mass.: Harvard University Press, 2014.
Twain, Mark. *The Innocents Abroad; Roughing It*. New York: Library of America, 1984.
U.S. Department of State. *Catalogue of Treaties: 1814–1918*. Washington, D.C.: U.S. Government Printing Office, 1919.
———. *Diplomatic Correspondence of 1865: Papers Relating to Foreign Affairs*. Vol. 2. Washington, D.C.: U.S. Government Printing Office, 1866.
———. *Messages of the President of the United States, Communicating, in Compliance with Resolutions of the Senate, Information Relative to the Compulsory Enlistment of American Citizens in the Army of Prussia, &c.* Washington, D.C.: George W. Bowman, 1860.
———. *Papers Related to the Foreign Relations of the United States*. Pt. II. Washington, D.C.: U.S. Government Printing Office, 1873.
Van Deburg, William L. *Modern Black Nationalism: From Marcus Garvey to Louis Farrakhan*. New York: New York University Press, 1997.
Vattel, Emmerich de. *The Law of Nations; or, Principles of the Law of Nature Applied to the Conduct of Affairs of Nations and Sovereigns*. 1758. Reprint, Philadelphia: P. H. Nicklin and T. Johnson, 1835.
Vizenor, Gerald. *Wordarrows: Native States of Literary Sovereignty*. 1978. Reprint, Lincoln: University of Nebraska Press, 2003.
Wald, Priscilla. *Constituting Americans: Cultural Anxiety and Narrative Form*. Durham, N.C.: Duke University Press, 1995.
Waldstreicher, David. *In the Midst of Perpetual Fetes: The Making of American Nationalism, 1776–1820*. Chapel Hill: University of North Carolina Press, 1997.
Walker, Cheryl. *Indian Nation: Native American Literature and Nineteenth-Century Nationalisms*. Durham, N.C.: Duke University Press, 1997.
Walker, David. "Address, Delivered before the General Colored Association at Boston."

1828. In his *Appeal in Four Articles*. Edited by Sean Wilentz, 79–83. New York: Hill and Wang, 1995.

———. *Appeal in Four Articles*. Edited by Sean Wilentz. 1829. Reprint, New York: Hill and Wang, 1995.

Walker, Mabel. *The Fenian Movement*. Colorado Springs, Colo.: R. Myles, 1969.

Wallerstein, Immanuel. "The Construction of Peoplehood: Racism, Nationalism, Ethnicity." In *Race, Nation, Class: Ambiguous Identities*, edited by Étienne Balibar and Immanuel Wallerstein, 71–85. London: Verso, 1991.

Walsh, Correa Moylan. *The Political Science of John Adams: A Study in the Theory of Mixed Government and the Bicameral System*. New York: Putnam, 1915.

Walsh, Victor A. "'A Fanatic Heart': The Cause of Irish American Nationalism in Pittsburgh during the Gilded Age." *Journal of Social History* 15.1 (1981): 187–204.

Watson, Ritchie Devon, Jr. *Normans and Saxons: Southern Race Mythology and the Intellectual History of the American Civil War*. Baton Rouge: Louisiana State University Press, 2008.

Weaver, Jace. *Other Words: American Indian Literature, Law, and Culture*. Norman: University of Oklahoma Press, 2001.

Weaver, Jace, Craig S. Womack, and Robert Allen Warrior. *American Indian Literary Nationalism*. Albuquerque: University of New Mexico Press, 2006.

Webb, Richard, ed. *The Life and Letters of Captain John Brown, Who Was Executed at Charlestown, Virginia, Dec. 2, 1859, for an Armed Attack upon American Slavery; with Notices of Some of His Confederates*. London: Smith, Elder, 1861.

Weinstein, Cindy. *Family, Kinship, and Sympathy in Nineteenth-Century American Literature*. New York: Cambridge University Press, 2004.

Wenzer, Kenneth C., ed. *Henry George: Collected Journalistic Writings*. Vol. 1. Armonk, N.Y.: Sharpe, 2003.

Wheatley, Phillis. "On Being Brought from Africa to America." In her *Complete Writings*. Edited by Vincent Carretta, 13. New York: Penguin, 2001.

Wheeler, Roxann. *The Complexion of Race: Categories of Difference in Eighteenth-Century British Culture*. Philadelphia: University of Pennsylvania Press, 2000.

Whitman, Walt. "Prohibition of Colored Persons" (*Brooklyn Daily Times*, 6 May 1858). In *A House Divided: The Antebellum Slavery Debates in America, 1776–1865*, edited by Mason I. Lowance, 201–202. Princeton, N.J.: Princeton University Press, 2003.

Whitney, Atwell. *Almond-Eyed: A Story of the Day*. San Francisco, Calif.: A. L. Bancroft, 1878.

Wilentz, Sean. *Chants Democratic: New York City and the Rise of the American Working Class*. New York: Oxford University Press, 1984.

———. *The Rise of American Democracy: Jefferson to Lincoln*. New York: Norton, 2005.

Wilkins, David E. *American Indian Sovereignty and the U.S. Supreme Court: The Masking of Justice*. Austin: University of Texas Press, 1997.

Wilkins, David E., and K. Tsianina Lomawaima. *Uneven Ground: American Indian Sovereignty and Federal Law*. Norman: University of Oklahoma Press, 2001.

Wilkinson, Charles F. *Blood Struggle: The Rise of Modern Indian Nations.* New York: Norton, 2005.
Williams, Andreá N. "Moving Up a Dead-End Ladder: Black Class Mobility, Death, and Narrative Closure in Sutton Griggs's *Overshadowed.*" In *Jim Crow, Literature, and the Legacy of Sutton E. Griggs,* edited by Tess Chakkalakal and Kenneth W. Warren, 88–110. Athens: University of Georgia Press, 2013.
Williams, Henry Llewellyn. *The Fenian Chief; or, The Martyr of '65.* New York: R. M. DeWitt, 1865.
Williams, Samuel Wells. *The Middle Kingdom: A Survey of the Geography, Government, Literature, Social Life, Arts, and History of the Chinese Empire and Its Inhabitants.* Vol. 2. New York: Scribner, 1882.
Winter, Molly Crumpton. *American Narratives: Multiethnic Writing in the Age of Realism.* Baton Rouge: Louisiana State University Press, 2007.
Wong, K. Scott. "The Transformation of Culture: Three Chinese Views of America." *American Quarterly* 48.2 (1996): 201–232.
Wood, Gordon S. *The Creation of the American Republic, 1776–1787.* 1969. Reprint, Chapel Hill: University of North Carolina Press, 1998.
Woodard, Komozi. *A Nation within a Nation: Amiri Baraka (Leroi Jones) and Black Power Politics.* Chapel Hill: University of North Carolina Press, 1999.
Woodson, Carter Godwin. *The History of the Negro Church.* Washington, D.C.: Associated Publishers, 1921.
Wu, Silas H. L. *Communication and Imperial Control in China: Evolution of the Palace Memorial System, 1693–1735.* Cambridge, Mass.: Harvard University Press, 1970.
Wu, William F. *The Yellow Peril: Chinese Americans in American Fiction, 1850–1940.* Hamden, Conn.: Archon, 1982.
Yarbrough, Fay A. *Race and the Cherokee Nation: Sovereignty in the Nineteenth Century.* Philadelphia: University of Pennsylvania Press, 2008.
Yin, Xiao-huang. *Chinese American Literature since the 1850s.* Urbana: University of Illinois Press, 2000.
Yingling, Charlton W. "No One Who Reads the History of Hayti Can Doubt the Capacity of Colored Men: Racial Formation and Atlantic Rehabilitation in New York City's Early Black Press, 1827–1841." *Early American Studies: An Interdisciplinary Journal* 11.2 (2013): 314–348.
Yong, Lai, et al. *The Chinese Question from a Chinese Standpoint.* Translated by Otis Gibson. San Francisco, Calif.: Cubrey, 1874. Rptd. in Otis Gibson, *The Chinese in America,* 285–292. Cincinnati, Ohio: Hitchcock and Walden, 1877.
Young, Mary. "The Exercise of Sovereignty in Cherokee Georgia." *Journal of the Early Republic* 10.1 (1990): 43–63.
Young, Robert Alexander. *The Ethiopian Manifesto.* 1829. In *Pamphlets of Protest: An Anthology of Early African-American Protest Literature, 1790–1860,* edited by Richard Newman, Patrick Rael, and Philip Lapsansky, 84–89. New York: Routledge, 2013.
Yung, Judy, Gordon H. Chang, and H. Mark Lai, eds. *Chinese American Voices: From the Gold Rush to the Present.* Berkeley: University of California Press, 2006.

Zaeske, Susan. *Signatures of Citizenship: Petition, Antislavery, and Women's Political Identity*. Chapel Hill: University of North Carolina Press, 2003.

Zafar, Rafia. *We Wear the Mask: African Americans Write American Literature, 1760–1870*. New York: Columbia University Press, 1997.

Zarefsky, David. *Lincoln, Douglas, and Slavery: In the Crucible of Public Debate*. 1990. Reprint, Chicago: University of Chicago Press, 1993.

Zolberg, Aristide. *A Nation by Design: Immigration Policy in the Fashioning of America*. 2006. Reprint, Cambridge, Mass.: Harvard University Press, 2008.

Zuck, Rochelle Raineri. "Martin R. Delany and Rhetorics of Divided Sovereignty." In *African American Culture and Legal Discourse*, edited by Lovalerie King and Richard Schur, 39–56. New York: Palgrave, 2009.

INDEX

★ ★ ★ ★

abolitionism. *See* Brown, John (abolitionist)
Adams, John, 23, 26; as Novanglus, 20
"Address at the African Masonic Hall" (M. W. Stewart), 95–96, 99
"Address before the Pennsylvania Augustine Society, An" (Saunders), 101, 239n91
Africa. *See* African colonization
African American nationhood: as being written into existence, 79–82, 236n32, 236n37; as ethnic, 82, 96–98, 121–122, 238n82; purpose of rhetoric, 70; sovereignty of God, 87, 91–96
African Americans: as alien but not foreign, 71; birthright citizenship and, 88–89, 108, 118, 125, 133; Cherokee and, 40; convenantal role of, 91–92, 93–94; free and enslaved, as one people, 130; as imperium in imperio, 123–125; Irish Americans / Irish immigrants and, 142, 144, 245n16; legal status, 7; as menace if not improved, 218; as multinational, 89, 123, 132–133; spiritual geography and Indian Removal, 88; as taking over section of United States, 74–75; as unassimilable, 76; as united, politicized, national body within federal system, 83–84, 115; as virtual nation, 29–30, 80, 81, 101, 111, 135. *See also* free black people; slaves and slavery
African colonization: African American nationhood and, 70; America as true home of African Americans, 76, 98–99, 100–101; American Colonization Society, 75–76, 235n19; American Indian peoples and, 47; Biblical Exodus story and, 98; versus emigration, 125; imperialism and, 77–78, 235n27; Liberia as destination, 109; in literature, 109–110; as necessary for development of African Americans, 111; sacralization of territory and actualization of sovereignty, 76–77; Turner rebellion and, 234n11; *Uncle Tom's Cabin*, 103–104; virtual nationhood and, 29
African Masonic Lodge, 82
African Methodist Episcopal (AME) Church, 82
African Repository, 109

Agamben, Giorgio, 226n40
Albrecht-Crane, Christa, 27–28
Alfred, Taiaike, 223n15
allegiance and sovereignty: existence of multiple political, 153; extraterritoriality and, 175–176; immigration and divided, 161; perpetual, 142–143, 146–147, 158, 244n10, 246n27; simultaneous existence of perpetual and volitional, 163–164; volitional, 142–143, 148
Allen, Richard, 80, 82, 99–100, 236n37
Allen, Theodore, 143
Almond-Eyed (Whitney), 190–191
America, as different than United States, 126–127, 132
"American Africanism," 78
American Colonization Society (ACS), 75–76, 235n19. *See also* African colonization
American Indian peoples: as alien but not foreign, 71; blood quantum, 37–38, 230n20; as citizens, 108; Civil War and, 139; constitutions, 229n10; desire to make more easily governable, 47; development of nationhood, 37, 39; as domestic dependent nations, 57; in national literature, 32–33, 229n7; as nonterritorial and movable, 34, 64; racialization of, 36, 40, 42; shift from treaty making to legislation, 173; sovereignty and industrial progress, 67
America's England (Hanlon), 5–6, 223n14
America's Forgotten Constitutions (Tsai), 8, 111, 228n92
Anderson, Benedict, 12–13, 83; *Imagined Communities*, 162
Anderson, Osborne P., 117
Apap, Chris, 98
Appeal in Four Articles (D. Walker), 83–84, 94–95, 96–98
Apples and Ashes (Hutchison), 4
Arac, Jonathan, 32
Articles of Confederation, 21, 22–23, 227n72
Asian America (Daniels), 193, 253n26
Asing, Norman, 206–207, 255n72

Atlantic Magazine, 24
Atlantic Republic (Giles), 223n14
Austin, Allan W., 253n41

Bailyn, Bernard, 14, 18, 226n48
Balibar, Étienne, 4
Banner, Stuart, 43–44
Beaumont, Elizabeth, 8, 10
Becoming Chinese American (Lai), 253n44
Bederman, David J., 14, 21
Bellamy, Edward, 216
Benton, Thomas Hart, 107
Bercovitch, Sacvan, 90
Berkhofer, Robert, Jr., 229n11
Bigler, John, 204–208
biopower, 199, 219
birthright citizenship: of African Americans, 88–89, 108, 118, 125, 133; Chinese immigrants and, 181
"Black Founding Fathers," 82
black jeremiads: defined, 90; early, 91–92; Ethiopian prophecy, 92–96; ethnic nationhood and, 96–98, 238n81; "two chosen people" argument, 90
Black Man, The (W. W. Brown), 134
black nationalism: *Appeal in Four Articles* as foundational text, 94–95; defining, 80, 236n33; need for separate political state, 238n81
Blackstone, Sir William, 17
Blake (Delany), 122–123, 242n57
Blakeslee, S. V., 186–187
blood quantum, 37–38, 230n20
Blyden, Edward Wilmot, 135
Boston Recorder and Religious Telegraph, 74
Boudinot, Elias, 28–29; Cherokee Nation as predating Georgia, 62; as embodiment of binary of assimilationist-traditionalist, 233n77; the people as constituting nation, 65; Removal position change, 64, 233n92; on Ross, 64; sovereignty of Cherokee as granted by God, 62–63; territory as not definition of nation, 64
Brief View of the Present Relations between the Government and People of the United States and the Indians within Our National Limits, A (Evarts), 51–52, 54
Brooks, Van Wyck, 81, 237n41
Brown, John (abolitionist): "Declaration of Liberty," 104, 114, 118; Delaney and, 117–118, 121; Douglass and, 115–116, 117–118, 121; ethical sovereignty, 114, 241n39, 241n42; Harpers Ferry, 118–120, 242nn48–49; reputation, 242n52. *See also* Provisional Constitution (1858)
Brown, John (Cherokee Old Settler), 66
Brown, Thomas N., 140
Brown, Wendy, 16
Brown, William Wells, 134

Bruce, Sir Frederick, 157
Bruyneel, Kevin, 173
Burlingame, Treaty of (1868), 179, 199, 209
Burnley, J. H., 156
Bustill, Cyrus, 80, 236n37

Cabet, Étienne, 241n42
Caldwell, Elias B., 235n19
Calhoun, John C., 24, 111–112
California: laws discriminating against Chinese immigrants, 181–183, 252n13; Senate hearings on Chinese immigrants, 184–186; Treaty of Guadalupe Hidalgo and, 252n12
"California thesis," 252n18
Campbell, Robert, 52–53
Canada: Fenian Brotherhood attacks, 151, 152, 155–156, 159, 160; fiction about Fenian Brotherhood attacks, 140, 163, 165–170, 179; as refuge for African Americans, 85; U.S. response to Fenian Brotherhood attacks, 172–173, 247n41
Cannibals All! (Fitzhugh), 113
Cass, Lewis, 106, 147
Castiglia, Christopher, 78
Catholics and Catholicism: all Irish Americans as, 244n7; German, 145; as imperium in imperio, 17, 141, 144–145
Chandler, Joseph R., 107
Chang, Gordon H., 255n72
Chatham Convention, 114, 115. *See also* Provisional Constitution (1858)
Cherokee: as always self-governing, 53; Compact of 1802 and, 44; currently recognized by federal government, 229n8; as ethnic nation, 59, 64, 65; as historical presence in its territory, 45, 53; nationalism, 37–38; traditional tribal membership, 37–38, 230n20
Cherokee Advocate, 67, 234n99
Cherokee Constitution (1827), 28–29; African Americans and, 40; citizenship linkage to territory, 40–41; God as granter of Cherokee sovereignty, 62; importance, 35; as inspiration for John Brown, 104, 136; as inspiration for Provisional Constitution, 104, 115; overview, 35; sovereignty of U.S. and Georgia and, 41–42; territorial assertions, 39–40, 230n25; U.S. and Georgia constitutions and, 40
Cherokee Constitution (1839), 66
Cherokee Nation: development, 38–39; as fraudulent nation, 46; location and value of territory, 51; as modern but not new, 61–62; as new form of existing government, 53; as not in territory of Georgia, 55–56; political capacity, 52; political split, 63, 233n87; as predating Georgia, 62; removal and newness of, 42, 45, 48–49; territoriality of citizenship, 39
—sovereignty of: as dangerous precedent, 49

INDEX

sovereignty of Georgia and, 44–45, 47–48, 55; sovereignty of United States and, 34, 42, 44–45, 46–47; treaties and, 35
Cherokee Nation v. Georgia (1831): arguments for Cherokee, 54–56, 58; dissent, 57–58, 233n75; Marshall opinion, 56–57
Cherokee Phoenix, 64, 233n92
Cheyfitz, Eric, 37
"Chickamauga rhetoric," 38, 230n22
Chickasaw Nation, 67, 229n10
Chiles, Katy L., 12, 123
Chilton, Samuel, 120
China: extraterritoriality of Chinese immigrants and, 176, 212; guilds, 194, 195; Six Companies and, 193, 197, 199–200, 201–202; treaties with, 178–179, 192, 211; use of memorials and petitions, 203–204, 205
Chinese American Literature (Yin), 180
Chinese Consolidated Benevolent Association, 195, 254n45
Chinese Exclusion Act (1882), 177, 213–214
Chinese Five Companies, 195, 196, 208–209
Chinese Four Houses, 195, 200–201
Chinese immigrants
—compared with colonial Americans, 206; Congressional hearings, 186–189; extraterritoriality and, 176, 212; Fourteenth Amendment debate and, 183; gambling by, 208; issue as political distraction, 183–184, 252n18, 252n20; newspapers, 203; positive responses to, 180; problem of Chinatowns, 187–189, 190; solutions suggested, 192; threat of massive numbers coming or leaving, 208; voluntary organizations, 193–195, 253n41. *See also* Chinese Six Companies
—discrimination against: American labor interests, 181, 252n11; California laws, 181–183, 252n13; in courts, 181–182, 198, 199; development, 252n26; exclusion, 177, 213–214; as imperium in imperio, 175–176, 185–190, 191–192; inability to become naturalized citizens, 175, 176, 179; leverage of Six Companies and, 195, 198; in literature, 190–192; motivating factors, 179–180, 251n10; racialization as others, 182, 189, 204–205, 206–207, 209–210; response of Chinese organizations, 200–201, 203, 205–206, 207–211; unassimilability, 176, 187–189, 205; "yellow peril" rhetoric, 189–190
"Chinese in California, The" (George), 189, 253n30
"Chinese Ishmael, A" (Sui Sin Far), 176
"Chinese on the Pacific Coast, The" (George), 253n30
Chinese Question from a Chinese Standpoint, The (Chinese Six Companies), 203
Chinese Six Companies, 176, 251n2, 254n45; appeals to federal government, 200–201, 206,
207, 209, 211; California Senate hearings, 184–186, 211; constitutions, 196–201; development, 193, 195, 253n44; functions, 190, 196–201, 208–209, 210, 212; in literature, 191; as partner of American government, 197–198, 199–200, 210–211, 212; as portrayed in Congressional hearings, 186–188; response to discrimination against Chinese immigrants, 200–201, 203, 205–206, 207–211; structure and membership, 193, 195–196
—works of: *The Chinese Question from a Chinese Standpoint*, 203; "A Memorial of the Chinamen to the President," 200, 211
Chisholm v. Georgia (1793), 23
Choctaw Constitution (1847), 229n10
Choctaw Nation, 67
Christian Advocate, 160–161
Christian Recorder, 144–145, 159–160
Christian Watchman, 76
Cincinnati Enquirer, 151
Citizen (New York), 249n81
citizenship: of African Americans, 7, 72, 88–89, 108, 133; of American Indian peoples, 108; birthright, 88–89, 108, 118, 125, 133, 181; Chinese immigrants and, 175, 176, 179, 222n5; in Fenian 1863 Constitution, 153; linkage to territory in Cherokee Constitution, 40–41; mobility and, 73–74; naturalized (*see* naturalized citizenship); in Provisional Constitution, 117; racialized, 78, 143, 222n5; states' rights, 205; statistical, 125; territory and, 39
"civic founders," 8
Civic Ideals (R. Smith), 252n20
civic-territorial nation: African colonization and, 109–110; Cherokee as, 59, 63–64; combined with ethnic, 125–126; defined, 13; as increasingly definition of nationhood, 34, 102, 151, 156, 173
Civil Rights Act (1870), 199
Civil War, 5–6, 139, 155, 156, 248n54. *See also* Confederate States of America (CSA); Confederate States of America Constitution
"Claims of Our Common Cause, The" (Douglass), 133
Clan na Gael, 160
Classical Black Nationalism (Moses), 236n33
Clay, Henry, 72, 235n19
Clegg, Claude Andrew, III, 109
Clinton, Robert, 21
Cobb, Amanda J., 223n15
Colonizing Trick, The (Kazanjian), 77–78, 235n27
Colored American, 86
Columbian Star, 46–47
Coming Struggle, The (Starr), 192
Commentaries on the Laws of England (Blackstone), 17
Compact of 1802, 44

Compromise of 1850, 106
Condition, Elevation, Emigration, and Destiny of the Colored People of the United States, The (Delany), 123–124, 125
Confederate States of America (CSA): as ethnic nation, 4, 155, 248n54; Great Britain and, 139, 155; racialization and, 137; *Trent* incident, 139
Confederate States of America Constitution, 26–27, 105, 137–138
Constitution of the Muskokee Nation, 229n10
constitutions: as attempts to relate politically and not racially, 7–8; Chinese Six Companies, 196–201; defining, 9; Fenian, 140, 151–155; generic features, 26, 228n90; Great Britain, 25–26; as instrument for laws to be measured against, 26; political jeremiads as, 90. *See also specific documents*
"Control and Becoming" (Deleuze), 215
Cook, Leung, 184
"coolie" trade, 183–184, 186, 198–199
Cooper, James Fenimore: *Leather-Stocking Tales*, 33, 229n7; *The Prairie*, 33
Corcoran, Michael, 149, 174
"Cornerstone Speech" (A. Stephens), 137–138
Cornish, Samuel, 82
cosmopolitanism, 80, 135
Crania Americana and Crania Aegyptiaca (S. Morton), 12
Creation of the American Republic, The (Wood), 19, 106
"credit-ticket system," 198–199
Cuffee, Paul, 235n19
culture: creation of national literature and, 32–33; as element of sovereignty, 6, 223n15; identity and, 4, 9–10; territory and, 13, 27–28. *See also* literature
Currie, David, 138
Curtin, Nancy J., 150, 168–170
Cushing, Caleb, 178–179
Cyclopedia of Political Science, 190

Daily Alta California, 206, 209
Daniels, Roger, 189; *Asian America*, 193, 253n26
D'Arcy, William, 246n36
Davis, David Brion, 145
Davis, Horace, 188–189
Dawson, Michael C., 80
decisionism, 226n40
Declaration of Independence, 70, 86, 87, 118, 133
"Declaration of Liberty by the Representatives of the Slave Population of the United States of America" (J. Brown), 104, 114, 118
"Declaration of Sentiment" (National Negro Convention movement), 87–88
Declaratory Act (1766), 17
Delany, Martin R., 29–30, 135–136; African Americans as ethnic, mobile nation, 121–123; African Americans as imperium in imperio, 123–125; Africans in Africa and, 128; America as different than United States, 126–127; Brown, John, and, 114, 117–118, 121; Chatham Convention and, 114, 115; on Cherokee Constitution, 104; nationhood as divisible and multiple, 123; politicization of sovereignty and nationhood, 128–129; on *Uncle Tom's Cabin*, 103–104
—works of: *Blake*, 122–123, 242n57; *The Condition, Elevation, Emigration, and Destiny of the Colored People of the United States*, 123–124, 125; "Political Destiny of the Colored Race," 124–125, 127; *Report of the Niger Valley Exploring Party*, 128
Deleuze, Gilles, 10; "Control and Becoming," 215; *Negotiations*, 215
DeLombard, Jeannine Marie, 6–7
Deloria, Vine, Jr., 5, 36
democracy, sovereignty in, 6, 7
Democracy in America (Tocqueville), 6, 7, 15, 24
Dessalines, Jean-Jacques, 74
Dickinson, John, 18–19
Dictionary of the English Language (S. Johnson), 11, 224n25
Dislocating Race and Nation (Levine), 79
divided sovereignty. *See* imperium in imperio
divine sovereignty. *See* sovereignty of God
Doheny, Michael, 149
dominium, defined, 226n45
Dooner, Pierton W., 191–192
Douglas, Stephen A., 106–107
Douglass, Frederick, 29–30, 135–136; all African Americans as one nation, 130–131; birthright citizenship of African Americans and, 133; Brown, John, and, 115–116, 117–118, 121; emigration and, 131–132; as multinationalist, 132–133; on self-segregation by African Americans, 217; travels abroad, 129–130; on U.S. Constitution, 86
—works of: "The Claims of Our Common Cause," 133; "The Meaning of July Fourth for the Negro," 132; "The Present Condition and Future Prospects of the Negro People," 130, 131–132, 133–134
Downes, Paul, 6
Dred Scott v. Sandford (1857), 108, 116–117
Dubh, Scian. *See* McCarroll, James
Duties of Christian Masters (McTyeire), 112

Easton, Hosea, 124; *A Treatise on the Intellectual Character and Civil and Political Condition of the Colored People of the United States*, 100–101
Easton, John, 47–48
Egerton, Douglas, 69
Elliott, Lorraine, 14
Ellsworth, Alfred, 117

Elmer, Jonathan, 7
emigration, 125–127, 128, 131–132, 243n67
empire: multiple sovereignties within, 19; single sovereignty within, 18, 226n48; United States as new, 175
Empire (Hardt and Negri), 226n40
England. *See* Great Britain
E Pluribus Unum (McDonald), 227n72
ethical sovereignty, 114, 241n39, 241n42
Ethiopian Manifesto, The (Young), 92–94
Ethiopian prophecy, 92–96
ethnic nations and ethnic nationalism: African Americans as, 82, 96–98, 121–122, 238n81; African colonization and, 109–110; Cherokee as, 59, 64, 65; combined with civic-territorial, 125–126; Confederacy as, 4, 155, 248n54; described, 13; of Fenians, 155; racial homogeneity and, 110–111; terminology, 238n82
Evarts, Jeremiah, 50–52, 54
"Exeunt the Fenians" (*New York Times*), 161
extraterritoriality: allegiance and, 175–176; of Chinese immigrants, 28, 176, 212; defined, 228n94; naturalized citizens and, 30, 178; sovereignty and, 147, 156–157, 158, 172, 201–202; treaties negotiating, 177–179

Fabi, M. Guilia, 216
Fanning, Charles, 143
Federalist Papers, The (Madison and Hamilton), 21, 23
federal system: enforcement of Fugitive Slave Act, 239n4; as imperium in imperio, 23, 24, 52–53, 56; sovereignty in, 3, 21–22, 107–108, 227n72; treaties with American Indian peoples as endorsement, 36; united, politicized, national African American body within, 83–84, 115
Federal Union, 46
Fenian Brotherhood (later Fenian Brotherhood of the United States), 30; Canada as base, 150, 151, 152, 155–156, 247n41; Canada in literature and, 140, 163, 165–170, 179; in common cause with United States against Great Britain, 166–168; constitutions, 140, 151–155; as ethnic nation, 155; founded, 140; Great Britain and, 150–151, 152, 156, 158, 166–168; as leverage for North for Civil War, 156–157; literary associations with United States, 166–167; literary references to, 249n81; membership strength, 157, 159–160, 170–171; national mobility, 114, 170; objectives, 150, 249n86; overview and structure, 149–150, 151–152, 246n28; as pressure group, 141; publication of conventions' proceedings, 164–165, 249n84; rights and responsibilities of citizenship and, 158–159, 247n53; rival factions, 151, 152–153, 246n36; territory and nationhood issue, 151; as threat to U.S. sovereignty, 158–159
Fenian Chief, The (H. L. Williams), 163

"Fenian Explosion, The" (*New York Times*), 157
Fenian Movement, The (M. Walker), 247n41
Fenians (Snay), 250n95
Fenian Songster, 163
Fenians' Progress, The (Curtin), 150, 168–170
Finley, Robert, 235n19
Fitzhugh, George, 113
Five Companies, 195, 196, 208–209
"flashpoints," 4, 222n7
Fletcher v. Peck (1810), 44, 231n38
Ford, Lisa, 239n25
foreign nationals, 197; as imperium in imperio, 175–176. *See* Chinese immigrants; Chinese Six Companies
Formisano, Ronald, 106, 240n5
Forsyth, John, 45, 50
Foster, Stephen, 75–76
Foucault, Michel, 199, 219; "Nietzsche, Genealogy, and History," 8–9; *Society Must be Defended*, 219
Four Houses, 195, 200–201
Franklin, Republic of, 21
Free African Society, 82, 237n43
free black people: African American terms to indicate, 85; as citizens, 72, 88–89; influence on slaves, 74; institutions created, 82–83; National Negro Convention as representative, 70, 85; as one nation with slaves, 130; as virtual nation, 71, 72, 75–76
Freedom's Journal, 82, 83–84
Free Republic of Franklin, 21
Frelinghuysen, Theodore, 49–50
Fugitive Slave Act (1850), 106, 239n4
full-bloods, 37–38, 230n20

Gabriel slave uprising plot, 73–74, 234n11
Galloway, Joseph, 20
Garnet, Henry Highland, 243n67
Garrison, Tim Alan, 55
George, Henry, 189–190; "The Chinese in California," 189, 253n30; "The Chinese on the Pacific Coast," 253n30
Georgia: Cherokee Nation as not in territory of, 55–56; Cherokee Nation as predating, 62; Cherokee Nation as threat to sovereignty of, 47–48; as indivisible sovereignty, 48; sovereignty of, as per Cherokee Constitution, 41–42; sovereignty of Cherokee Nation as at war with that of United States and, 44–45; sovereignty of Cherokee Nation as equal to, 55; as threat to sovereignty of Cherokee Nation, 60; Yazoo land scandal, 43–44, 231n38
Georgia State Constitution, 39
Gibbons, James, 160, 163, 249n81
Gibson, Otis, 184
Giles, Paul, 223n14
Gillman, Susan, 92
Gilroy, Paul, 80, 126

Goode, William O., 107–108
Gordon, Dexter B., 80, 90
Grant, Ulysses S., administration of, 172–173, 186
Great Britain: American Civil War and, 139, 155, 156; Chinese immigrants compared with colonial Americans, 206; Fenian Brotherhood and, 150–151, 152, 156, 158; Irish Americans and, 142, 143; perpetual allegiance, 148; policy in Ireland, 144; recognition of sovereignty of American Indian peoples, 36; sovereignty and Parliament, 17–20; sovereignty and religion, 17
Green, Michael D., 49, 50
Greiman, Jennifer, 6, 7
Grice, Hezekiah, 84
Griggs, Sutton E., 1, 216, 218–219
Griswold, Hiram, 119–120
Guadalupe Hidalgo, Treaty of (1848), 106, 252n12
Guattari, Félix, 10
Gyory, Andrew, 183, 213, 252n18

Hab Wa, 205–206
Haiti, 74–75, 109
Hale, Sarah Josepha, 109–110
Hall, Prince, 80, 82, 91–92, 236n37
Hamilton, Alexander, 20; *The Federalist Papers* (with Madison), 21, 23
Hammon, Jupiter, 236n40; "A Winter Piece," 80–81
Handlin, Oscar, 144, 161
Hanlon, Christopher, 5–6, 223n14
Hansen, Lawrence Douglas Taylor, 199
Hardt, Michael, 226n40
Harper, Charles Carroll, 75–76
Harpers Ferry, Va., 118–120, 242n48–49, 242n52
Hemphill, Joseph, 73
Hendler, Glenn, 125
Hip Kat (Xieji) Company, 194–195
Homo Sacer (Agamben), 226n40
Hopewell, Treaty of (1785), 38, 54
Hop Wo (Hehe) Company, 195
Howard-Pitney, David, 90
How the Irish Became White (Ignatiev), 143–144
Hoy, William, 196, 198
Hudson, Nicholas, 11
Hung, Ho-fung, 204
Huston, James L., 107
Hutchinson, Thomas, 19–20
Hutchison, Coleman, 4

Icarian nation, 241n42
identity, 4, 9–10. *See also* nationhood; racialization
Ignatiev, Noel, 245n16, 248n54; *How the Irish Became White*, 143–144
Imagined Communities (B. Anderson), 162
immigration: control as sovereign right, 205, 207, 208; divided allegiance and, 161; extraterritorial sovereignty and, 28, 30; states' rights, 205, 213

Imminent Dangers to the Free Institutions of the United States through Foreign Immigration, and the Present State of the Naturalization Laws (Morse), 146
imperialism and African colonization, 77–78, 235n27
imperium, defined, 17, 51
imperium in imperio: in Articles of Confederation, 21, 22–23, 227n72; as containment strategy, 71; defining, 2–3, 4, 17, 55–56, 222n3; eminent domain and, 67, 68; European examples, 52; positive, sentimental component, 60; racialized, 78–79
Imperium in Imperio (Griggs), 1, 216, 218–219
"Indian Country," 239n25
Indian Removal: African American attempts to distance selves, 88; arguments against, 34, 50–54, 54–58, 61–62, 63; arguments for, 34, 40, 42, 45, 46–49; Compact of 1802 and, 44; definition of nation, 59
Indigenous nations. *See* American Indian peoples
In the Shadow of the Gallows (DeLombard), 6–7
Iredell, James, 20
Ireland and America versus England (Kiernan), 168
Irish-American, 249n84
Irish Americans and Irish immigrants: all considered Catholic, 244n7; all considered members of Fenian Brotherhood, 159–160; changing nature of immigrants and, 143; habitations' proximity to African Americans, 142; identity as white, 144, 245n16; participation in Civil War, 155, 248n54; population numbers, 143; racial prejudices of, 129, 144; treatment in United States, 141; as unassimilable, 143–144, 145–146, 245n22; as virtual nation, 30
Irish Citizen, 249n81
Irish News, 158
Irish Republic, 162
Irish Republican Brotherhood (IRB), 140
Irish Republic in America, 122n2, 140, 162, 167, 250n94. *See also* Fenian Brotherhood
Irish Republic of America, 152

Jackson, Andrew, administration of, 48–49, 60–61
Jackson, Robert, 225n31
Jameson, Fredric, 26, 196
Jefferson, Thomas, 11; *Notes on the State of Virginia*, 73
jeremiads, 90
Johnson, Andrew, administration of, 156–157, 160, 172, 247n41
Johnson, Samuel, 11, 224n25
Johnstone, George, 20
Jones, Absalom, 80, 82, 236n37
Jordan, Winthrop, 12
Justice, Daniel Heath, 37–38, 63–64, 229n8, 230n20, 230n22

Kagi, J. H., 117
Kansas-Nebraska Act (1854), 107, 134
Karcher, Matt, 185
Kazanjian, David, 4, 222n7; *The Colonizing Trick*, 77–78, 235n27
Kennedy, Lionel H., 69
Kettner, James, 17–18, 19, 148
Key, Francis Scott, 235n19
Kiernan, James, 168
Killian, Bernard Doran, 152, 247n41
Knapp, Isaac, 27, 76–77
Know-Nothing Party, 145–146
Knox, Henry, 36, 229n11
Kong Chow (Gangzhou) Company, 194–195, 253n44
Konkle, Maureen, 42, 45, 61

"labor theory of nationality," 99–100, 239n89
LaFeber, Walter, 175
Lai, Him Mark, 255n72; *Becoming Chinese American*, 253n44
Lai Chun-chuen, 207–208
Lai Sai, 196, 254n48
Lambin, Chen, 200
Lapsansky, Philip, 83
Last Days of the Republic, The (Dooner), 191–192
Law of Nations, The (Vattel), 14, 41, 231n32
Leather-Stocking Tales (Cooper), 33, 229n7
Leavitt, Humphrey Howe, 147
"Lectures on the Philosophy and Practice of Slavery, as Exhibited in the Institution of Domestic Slavery in the United States, with the Duties of Masters to Slaves" (W. A. Smith), 112
Lee Kan, 196, 254n48
Leonard, Daniel, 20
"Letter of the Chinamen to His Excellency, Gov. Bigler" (Hab and Tong), 205–206
Letters from a Farmer in Pennsylvania, to the Inhabitants of the British Colonies (Dickinson), 18–19
Levine, Robert S.: on absence of unifying American ideology, 105; on African American nationalism, 71; on African American print media, 83; on *Blake*, 122; on Cooper's frontier novels, 229n7; on defining African American community, 79; on Delany, 126; on differences between Delany and Douglass, 121; *Dislocating Race and Nation*, 79; on Douglass as nationalist, 132; on Missouri statehood issues, 72–73; on national position of black citizenship, 73; on U.S. nationalism in 1790s, 32; on writings of David Walker, 95
Lévy, Pierre, 228n97
Lewis, E. J., 184–185
Liberia, 109, 126, 235n19
Liberia (Hale), 109–110

Liele, George, 80, 236n37
Linebaugh, Peter, 95
Ling, Huping, 253n41
Literary Magazine, 75
literature: African colonization, 109–110; black print media, 82, 83–84, 85–86; Chinese immigrant, 190–192; creation of national, 32–33; development of emphasis on territorial nationhood, 13; emphasis on ethnic nation, 13; federal system as qualified imperium in imperio, 24; Fenian attacks on Canada, 140, 163, 165–170, 179; Fenian fiction, 163, 165–169; Fenian link with American, 166–168; Fenian nation-building through, 162–163; Fenian publication of conventions' proceedings, 164–165, 249n84; identity and, 9–10, 32–33; Irish American newspapers, 249n81; racialization and frontier novels, 166; utopian, 216; Whitman's "Old Ireland," 249n81. *See also* black jeremiads
Loomis, A. W., 201
Looney, John, 66
Louverture, Toussaint, 74, 75
Love and Land (M. Scanlan), 163, 171
Low, F. F., 194
Lumpkin, Wilson, 44–45, 51
Lyman, Stanford, 199
Lynch, Timothy G., 247n38
Lytle, Clifford M., 5

MacDonald, John A., 163
Madison, James, 23–24; *The Federalist Papers* (with Hamilton), 21, 23
majority as societal model, 215
Making of Racial Sentiment, The (Tawil), 166
Manifest Destiny, 110, 156, 168
Manifesting America (Rifkin), 252n12
Marrant, John, 80, 236n37
Marshall, John, 56–57, 231n38
Mason, James Murray, 139
"Massachusetts" (Leonard), 20
Massachusetts General Colored Association, 82
Mathews, George, 43
Maxey, Samuel, 67
McCarroll, James, 140, 163, 165–167, 179
McClain, Charles J., 200, 201
McCoppin, Frank, 188
McCullough, Kate, 176
McDonald, Forrest, 2; *E Pluribus Unum*, 227n72
McDougal, John, 180
McGee, Michael, 236n32
McLoughlin, William, 39
McTyeire, Holland Nimmons, 112
"Meaning of July Fourth for the Negro, The" (Douglass), 132
"Memorial of the Chinamen to the President, A" (Chinese Six Companies), 200, 211

memorials and petitions, 203–204, 205–208, 209, 211
Mercer, Charles Fenton, 235n19
Mexico, 24
Miller, Perry, 90
Milwaukee Sentinel, 160
minority and creativity, 215
Missouri, statehood debates, 69, 72–73
Missouri Compromise (1820), 72, 107
Mitchel, John, 152, 249n81
mixed-bloods, 37–38, 230n20
mobility: black emigration and, 128; challenges presented by, 129–130; as characteristic of nationhood, 114, 170; numbers of black Americans and, 131–132; of slaves as property, 73–74, 122–123; as source of power, 122
"Modern Ireland" (Reilly), 246n28
monarchy, 6, 15, 19
Morrill, Justin, 73
Morrison, Toni, 78
Morse, Samuel F. B., 146
Morton, Oliver P., 186
Morton, Samuel, 11–12
Moses, Wilson: on black jeremiads, 90; on black nationalism, 92, 236n33; *Classical Black Nationalism*, 236n33; on Walker, David, 96, 97, 236n33, 238n81
multinationalism: of African Americans, 89, 123, 132–133; of America as continent of refuge, 126–127; of Cooper's frontier, 33; in Fenian 1863 Constitution, 153; nationhood and, 95; virtual nationhood and, 29–30; Walker and, 95, 238n78. *See also* sovereignty of God
Murray, Hugh, 182

Nagle, William J., 158
National Intelligencer, 50–52
nationalism: Cherokee, 37–38; in fiction, 166–169, 250n89, 250n95
National Negro Convention movement, 84–85; birthright citizenship, 88–89; dual affiliation to Africa and America, 87–88; political rights as more important territory, 79; as representative of free black people, 70; terminology used, 86; use of U.S. founding documents, 70, 86–88
—works of: "Declaration of Sentiment," 87–88; "To the American People," 88–89
nationhood: of American Indian peoples, 37, 39, 43; of Cherokee as new and illegal, 42, 45, 48–49; concept of U.S., in early years, 32; as cultural construction, 2–3; defining, 12–13, 57–58, 59; as divisible and multiple, 123; in early literature, 33; fused with religion (*see* sovereignty of God); genealogy and, 11; labor-based communal claims, 99–100, 239n89; Manifest Destiny and, 110, 156, 168; mobility as characteristic, 170; as model of majority, 216; multinationalism and, 95; not bound by time, 171, 244n2; political leverage, 103–104; politicization of sovereignty and, 128–129; population numbers and, 130–131; racialized, 2–3, 11–12, 78–79, 110–111, 216–218, 224n25; recognition of Haiti and Liberia, 109; versus state, 12; territorial borders as fluid, 126; as territorial in John Brown defense, 119–120; territory as important component, 34, 102, 151, 156, 173; territory as not important component, 34, 79, 80; of unassimilable peoples, 4. *See also* African American nationhood; civic-territorial nation; ethnic nations and ethnic nationalism; sovereignty of God
"Nation's Problem, The" (Douglass), 217
nation within a nation. *See* imperium in imperio
Native Americans. *See* American Indian peoples
nativism, 145–146, 245n22
natural history, 12
naturalized citizenship: European attitudes, 142; extraterritoriality and, 178; fear of Chinese with, 183, 187, 192; Fenian Brotherhood members as, 155, 175, 222n5, 247n53; inability of Chinese to qualify for, 176, 179, 222n5175; Irish Americans, 141–142; racialized, 143; rights and responsibilities, 158, 172; severance to country of birth, 146–147, 246n27; U.S. responsibilities, 147–148; volitional allegiance and, 142–143
Negotiations (Deleuze), 215
Negri, Antonio, 226n40
Neidhardt, Wilfried S., 157
Nelson, Joshua B., 37–38, 233n77; *Progressive Traditions*, 37, 230n20
New Bedford AME Zion Church, 82
New Haven Daily Palladium, 157
Newman, Richard, 82, 83
New York Daily Tribune, 156
New York Times, 160; "Exeunt the Fenians," 161; "The Fenian Explosion," 157
New-York Tribune, 184, 189, 253n30
"Nietzsche, Genealogy, and History" (Foucault), 8–9
Ning Yung (Ningyang) Company, 194–195
Norgren, Jill, 231n38
Normans and Saxons (Watson), 248n54
North American, 46
North Star, 121–122
Notes on the State of Virginia (Jefferson), 73
"Notice to the Public" (*Sacramento Daily Union*), 208–209
Novanglus (Adams), 20

Official Report of the Trials of Sundry Negroes, Charged with an Attempt to Raise an Insurrection in the State of South-Carolina, An, 69–70, 234n2
Oldest and Newest Empire, The (Speer), 209–210
"Old Ireland" (Whitman), 249n81
"Old Settlers," 65–66, 229n8, 230n20
O'Mahony, John, 149, 150, 152, 156, 162

"On Being Brought from Africa to America" (Wheatley), 81
O'Neill, John, 249n81
On Lingering and Being Last (Elmer), 7
Oson, Jacob, 81–82
O'Sullivan, D., 162
Otis, Harrison Gray, 141–142
Otis, James, Jr., 18
Oxford English Dictionary, 14, 224n25

Paine, Thomas, 25, 26
Paley, William, 25–26
Pamphlets of Protest, 83
pan-Africanism, 86, 92, 95, 122
Parker, Thomas, 69
Parliament (British), 17–20
Peace of Westphalia (1648), 14, 16
"people, the": defining, 227n80; as definition of nation, 13, 59, 64, 65; as sovereign, 15
People v. Hall (1854), 181–182, 185
Perdue, Theda, 37, 49, 50, 63–64, 233n92
petitions and memorials, 203–204, 205–208, 209, 211
Phan, Hoang Gia, 86
Philadelphia, Pa., 85, 151–152, 153, 247n38
Pixley, Frank, 186
"Political Destiny of the Colored Race" (Delany), 124–125, 127
Political Theology (Schmitt), 226n40
popular sovereignty: defining, 239–240nn4–5; definition of "the people" and, 227n80; development of concept, 14–15; as God-given, 128; importance of, in U.S. Constitution, 23, 227n73; legitimate resistance against government and, 118; as misunderstood in public discourse, 134; petitioning and, 204; political claims of African Americans and, 124–125; in Provisional Constitution, 117, 136
populism, 106
Prairie, The (Cooper), 33
"Present Condition and Future Prospects of the Negro People, The" (Douglass), 130, 131–132, 133–134
Prigg v. Pennsylvania (1842), 239n4
Progressive Traditions (Nelson), 37, 230n20
Protonationalists, 80, 236n33
Provisional Constitution (1858): as agreement of voluntary organization, 119–120; Cherokee Constitution as inspiration, 104, 115; citizenship, 117; Delany and, 121; Douglass and, 115–116, 121; ratification, 114; slavery as attribute of sovereignty, 29, 105; territoriality and, 120, 136; trial of John Brown and, 242n48; U.S. Constitution as model, 116
Prucha, Francis Paul, 45
public, the: appeals by Chinese immigrants to, 198, 206–207; in democracy, 7; foreign nationals and, 178; misleading discourse about popular sovereignty, 134; perception of Irish immigrants as unassimilable, 143–144; practice of petitioning, 204, 205; rhetoric in arguments for Indian Removal and, 55, 58; sovereignty and, 15; as substitute for courts, 209; U.S. protection of citizens abroad and, 178. *See also* "people, the"
Pu Chi, 209–210
Putnam's Magazine, 249n86

Qin, Yucheng, 193–202 passim

Raboteau, Albert, 92
race and genealogy, 11
racialization: of American Indian peoples, 36, 40, 42; blood quantum and, 38; of Chinese immigrants as "other," 182, 189, 204–205, 206–207; by Chinese immigrants of "inferior groups," 209–210; of citizenship, 78, 143, 222n5; Confederate States of America and, 137; development of, 11–12, 224n25; in early literature, 33; by free blacks, 85–86; frontier novels and, 166; of Irish immigrants, 144, 245n16; of nationhood, 2–3, 11–12, 78–79, 110–111, 216–218, 224n25; of nomads, 113; of political allegiance, 76; skin color as component, 12, 224n25; of sovereignty, 7, 78–79
Rael, Patrick, 83
Rafinesque, Constantine Samuel, 11
Ramón, Marta, 246n28
Raustiala, Kal, 228n94
Rediker, Marcus, 95
Reilly, Eileen, 246n28
religion: African American institutions, 82–83; African Americans and Israelites, 81–82; Chinese as "pagan horde," 188; regenerative power of God, 96; sovereignty in England and, 17; United States as Protestant nation, 145, 245n22. *See also* Catholics and Catholicism; sovereignty of God
Remarks of the Chinese Merchants of San Francisco on Governor Bigler's Message (Lai Chunchuen), 207–208
"Remonstrance from the Chinese in California to the Congress of the United States, A" (Pu Chi), 209–210
Report of the Niger Valley Exploring Party (Delany), 128
"Report of the Secretary of Civil Affairs" (O'Sullivan), 162
Reynolds, David S., 111, 115, 242n49, 242n52
Richmond Enquirer, 46
Ridge, John, 63, 64
Ridge, Major, 63
Ridgeway (McCarroll as Dubh), 140, 163, 165–167, 179
Rifkin, Mark, 36, 37; *Manifesting America*, 252n12
Rights of the British Colonies Asserted and Proved (J. Otis), 18

Robbins, Asher, 50
Robert Emmet Club (Cincinnati), 146–147
Roberts, William R., 151, 152–153, 156, 160, 163–164
Rogers, John, 66
Ross, John, 28–29, 38; Cherokee Nation as modern but not new, 61–62; Cherokee relationship to Georgia, 60–61; Cherokee relationship to United States, 59–60; as embodiment of binary of assimilationist-traditionalist, 233n77; reunification of Cherokee removed and "Old Settlers," 65–66; sovereignty of Cherokee as granted by God, 62; territory as central to nationhood, 63–64
Roughing It (Twain), 182–183
Russwurm, John, 82
Rutherford, John, 246n36
Ryan, Susan M., 109–110

Sacramento Daily Union, 208–209
Sadowski-Smith, Claudia, 198–199
Samito, Christian, 141, 157, 171–172, 178
Sampson, Calvin T., 184
Samuels, Shirley, 166
Sam Yup (Sanyi) Company, 194–195
Sang Yuen, 206–207, 255n72
Santo Domingo, 74–75
Saunders, Prince, 91–92; "An Address before the Pennsylvania Augustine Society," 101, 239n91
Savage, John, 162
Saxton, Alexander, 184, 252n20
Scanlan, John, 249n81
Scanlan, Michael, 163, 171
Schmitt, Carl, 226n40
Schoolman, Martha, 122
scientific racism, 12
Scott, Dred, 108
Seabury, Samuel, 20
Search for Truth, A (Oson), 81–82
Sergeant, John, 54–55
Seward, William, 152, 156, 247n41
Shaw, W. J., 194
Signatures of Citizenship (Zaeske), 203
Six Companies. *See* Chinese Six Companies
Slauter, Eric, 228n90
slaves and slavery: as act of war, 116, 118; Africanness of Israelites and Egyptians, 97; as appropriate government for African Americans, 104, 111–112; as attribute of sovereignty, 29, 105, 135; Chinese contract labor and, 183–184, 186; in Confederate Constitution, 137; convenantal role of African Americans and, 94, 96; in "Declaration of Sentiment," 87; free blacks and, 74, 130; fugitive slaves, 106, 239n4; as imperium in imperio, 104, 111–113, 133; increasing population as threat to United States, 74; as movables, 73–74, 122–123; severance of all relations between Africa and African Americans, 100–101; uprisings, 69–70, 73–74, 234n2, 234n11
Slidell, John, 139
Smith, Anthony, 13
Smith, Rogers, 72, 108; *Civic Ideals*, 252n20
Smith, Theophus, 92
Smith, William Andrew, 112
Snay, Mitchell, 155, 244n2; *Fenians*, 250n95
Society Must be Defended (Foucault), 219
Sociology for the South (Fitzhugh), 113
Southern Recorder, 46
South Side Democrat, 105
sovereignty: of American Indian peoples as strategic value for United States, 35, 36; in Articles of Confederation, 21; belligerent acts and, 156; in Cherokee Constitution, 39–40, 230n25; of Cherokee Nation, 44–45, 46–48, 49, 55; citizenship and, 205; in Confederate Constitution, 138; contests over jurisdiction on frontier, 33; defining, 14–16, 225n40, 231n32; defining tribal, 6, 223n15; in democracy, 6; development of link to territory, 14, 34, 173, 225n40; as divisible and limited, 107–108; as emerging from another nation, 168–169; in English political thought, 17–18; ethical, 114, 241n39, 241n42; exclusion of immigrants and, 213; extension of Chinese, in America, 175–176, 185–190, 191–192; external/extraterritorial (*see* extraterritoriality); in federal system, 3, 21–22, 107–108, 227n72; Fenians and, 153, 160, 167; in Georgia State Constitution, 39; images of, in art, 167–168; immigration control and, 205, 207, 208; increasing emphasis on territory, 34, 173; as indivisible, 24, 160; over internal versus external matters, 18–19; limits to divisibility, 46; locus of, in Constitutional ratification debates, 227n72; management of populations and, 219; more than one, in same territory, 167; movement of population and, 28, 30, 170; of Parliament, 17–20; politicization of, and nationhood, 128–129; in Provisional Constitution, 136; racialized, 7, 78–79; reciprocal relationship between community and sovereign, 93–94; sacralization of territory tied to, 76–77; as shared between government and nongovernmental organization, 197–200, 210–211, 212; slavery as attribute, 29, 105, 135; of Southern plantations, 112–113; threat of nomadic races and, 113; treaties and, 35, 36, 231n32, 251n12; in U.S. Constitution, 21–22, 227n72; virtual nations and, 159. *See also* allegiance and sovereignty; extraterritoriality; popular sovereignty; states' rights
sovereignty of God: America as continent of refuge, 126–127; Cherokee and, 62; convenantal role of African Americans, 91–92, 93–94; Declaration of Sentiment, 87, 88; equality of all

men, 101; Ethiopian prophecy, 92–96; national regeneration and, 88; nullification of slavery and, 87; political inclusion within United States simultaneously, 89; popular sovereignty, 128; Puritan/Calvinist roots, 80–81, 90, 236n40; resultant spiritual boundaries, 89
Speer, William, 196; *The Oldest and Newest Empire*, 209–210
spiritual geographies. *See* sovereignty of God
Sprague, Peleg, 50
Starr, M. B., 192
state: British empire as, 18, 226n48; defining, 225n31; versus nation, 12
State as a Work of Art, The (Slauter), 228n90
State racism, 219
states' rights: as basis of Confederacy, 155; enforcement of Fugitive Slave Act and, 239n4; immigration and citizenship and, 205, 213; as imperium in imperio, 52–53; relations with American Indian peoples and, 43; trial of John Brown and, 242n49
statistical citizenship, 125
Staudenraus, P. J., 75
Stauffer, John, 114
Stephens, Alexander, 137–138
Stephens, James, 149
Stewart, Maria W., 98–100, 236n33; "Address at the African Masonic Hall," 95–96, 99
Story, Joseph, 57–58, 233n75, 239n4
Stowe, Harriet Beecher, 103–104
Sui Sin Far, 176
Sumner, Charles, 183, 192
Supreme Court: *Cherokee Nation v. Georgia*, 54–58, 233n75; *Dred Scott v. Sandford*, 108; as enforcer of federal sovereignty, 107; federal system, 23; *Prigg v. Pennsylvania*, 239n4
Sweeny, Thomas, 152, 153, 160
Sze Yap (Siyi) Company, 194–195

Takaki, Ronald, 199
Taney, Roger, 108, 116–117
Tanner, Benjamin, 217, 255n4
Tawil, Ezra, 33; *The Making of Racial Sentiment*, 166
Taylor, John M., 43
territorialization, 10, 27–28, 71, 220, 228n95
territory: absence of African American collective claim, 29; black nationalism without, 80, 88; borders as fluid for nationhood, 120, 126; Brown's provisional government, 118–120; ceded by Cherokees, 38; Cherokee as historical presence in its, 45, 53; in Cherokee Constitution, 39–40, 230n25; of Cherokee granted by God, 62–63; of Cherokee Nation as not in that of Georgia, 55–56; citizenship and, 39, 40–41; as containment method, 71; contests over sovereignty on frontier and, 33; cultural manifestations and, 13, 27–28; definition of "Indian Country," 239n25; development of link to sovereignty, 14, 34, 173, 225n40; eminent domain and, 67, 68; in ethical sovereignty, 114; as facilitator of nationhood, 64–65; in Fenian constitutions, 153; Fenians and, 153, 160, 167; Georgia claims as predating Cherokee Nation claims, 45; in Georgia State Constitution, 39; Georgia Yazoo land scandal, 43–44, 231n38; labor-based communal claims, 99–100, 239n89; as less important than political rights for nationhood, 79; location and valuation issues, 51; newness of claims and, 42, 45, 48–49; primacy of peoplehood over, 65; in Provisional Constitution, 136; sacralization of, tied to sovereignty, 76–77; single sovereignty within same, 18, 46–48; slaves and, 73–74, 112–113. *See also* civic-territorial nation; virtual nationhood
Thomas, Jesse B., 72
Thompson, Smith, 57–58, 233n75
Times (London), 157
Tocqueville, Alexis de, 6, 7, 15, 24
Tong Achick, 205–206
tongs, 193, 253n41
"To the American People" (National Negro Convention movement), 88–89
To the Inhabitants of Great Britain (Iredell), 20
transatlanticism, 5–6
Transcendentalists, 242n52
Transformable Race (Chiles), 12
transnationalism: defined, 5; Ethiopianism and pan-Africanism, 86, 92, 95, 102, 122; in scholarship, 5–6, 223n10, 223n14
Traveler (Boston), 109
Treatise on the Intellectual Character and Civil and Political Condition of the Colored People of the United States, A (H. Easton), 100–101
treaty making: American Indian peoples and, 173; Chinese immigrants and, 178–179, 192, 211; extraterritoriality and, 177–179; as federal prerogative, 43; as recognition of sovereignty, 36, 61
Tredwell, Thomas, 22–23
Trent incident (1861), 139
Trodd, Zoe, 114
Troublous Times in Canada (MacDonald), 163
Troup, Alexander, 184
Tsai, Robert L.: *America's Forgotten Constitutions*, 8, 111, 228n92; on Brown, John, 114, 116, 241n39, 241n42, 242n48; on Calhoun, 111; concepts of written constitution and popular sovereignty united, 8, 228n92; on Confederate leaders, 137; on government formed at Chatham Convention, 117
Tsiyu Gansini (Dragging Canoe), 230n22
Turner, Nat, 73–74, 234n11
Twain, Mark, 182–183

Uncle Tom's Cabin (Stowe), 103–104
United Keetoowah Band of Cherokee Indians, 229n8
United States: as in common cause with Fenian Brotherhood against England, 166–168; as different than America, 126–127; Grant administration and Chinese immigrants, 186; Grant administration response to Fenians, 172–173; Jackson administration and Cherokee Removal, 48–49, 60–61; Johnson administration and Fenians, 156–157, 160, 172, 247n41; sovereignty of British Parliament and colonists, 17–20
United States Constitution: classes of people in United States, 133; commerce clause and American Indian peoples, 40, 42; as empowerment tool, 26–27, 228n92; foreign nationals and, 197; Fourteenth Amendment, 183; goal of drafters, 26; popular sovereignty, 23, 227n73; ratification debates, 22–23, 227n72; references to United States in, 32. *See also* federal system
—as inspiration: for Cherokee Constitution, 35; for Confederate Constitution, 137; for Fenian Brotherhood / Irish Republic, 151–152, 153; for founding documents of National Negro Convention, 70, 86–88; for Provisional Constitution, 116
United States v. Lumsden (1856), 147, 153
"usable past," 81, 237n41

Vattel, Emmerich de, 14, 41, 231n32
Vesey, Denmark, 69–70, 73–74, 234n11
"View of the Controversy between Great Britain and Her Colonies, A" (Seabury), 20
Vindication of the British Colonies, A (J. Otis), 18
"virtual," defining, 228n97
virtual nationhood: of all African Americans, 29–30, 80, 81, 101, 111, 135; antislavery, 104; Fenian Brotherhood, 159; of free black people, 71, 72, 75–76; of Irish Americans, 30; Irish Republic in America, 140; multinationalism and, 29

Wald, Priscilla, 34, 57, 108
Waldstreicher, David, 13
Walker, Cheryl, 41–42
Walker, David: African Americans as ethnic nation, 96–98, 238n81; *Appeal in Four Articles*, 83–84, 94–95, 96–98; call for national organization of African Americans, 83–84, 93; classical black nationalism and, 236n33, 238n81; Ethiopian prophecy and black nationalism, 94–95; on home of African Americans, 98–99; labor-based communal claims to territory, 99–100
Walker, Mabel, 247n41
Walled States, Waning Sovereignty (W. Brown), 16
Wanghia, Treaty of (1844), 178–179, 205
Warren, John, 158
Washington, Booker T., 218
Washington, Bushrod, 235n19
Washington, George, 62
Watson, Ritchie Devon, Jr., 248n54
Webster, Daniel, 106
"Western Cherokee," 229n8
Western Recorder, 46
Wharton, William, 213
Wheatley, Phillis, 80; "On Being Brought from Africa to America," 81
Wheaton, Henry, 246n27
Wheeler, Roxann, 12
White over Black (Jordan), 12
Whitman, Walt, 110–111; "Old Ireland," 249n81
Whitney, Atwell, 190–191
Wilkes, Charles, 139
Wilkins, David E., 36
"William Penn" essays, 50–52
Williams, George H., 183
Williams, Henry Llewellyn, 163
Wilson, James, 23, 227n73
"Winter Piece, A" (Hammon), 80–81
Wirt, William, 54, 55–56, 58
Wise, Henry, 242n49
Wood, Gordon S., 20, 26; *The Creation of the American Republic*, 19, 106

Yan Wo (Renhe) Company, 194–195
Yarbrough, Fay A., 36, 40
Yazoo land scandal (Ga.), 43–44, 231n38
Yeoung/Yeung Wo (Yanghe) Company, 194–195, 196–197, 199
Yin, Xiao-huang, 205, 206; *Chinese American Literature*, 180
Young, Robert Alexander, 236n33; *The Ethiopian Manifesto*, 92–94
Yung, Judy, 255n72

Zaeske, Susan, 204; *Signatures of Citizenship*, 203
Zarefsky, David, 107
Zolberg, Aristide, 142

www.ingramcontent.com/pod-product-compliance
Lightning Source LLC
Chambersburg PA
CBHW011749220426
43669CB00022B/2954